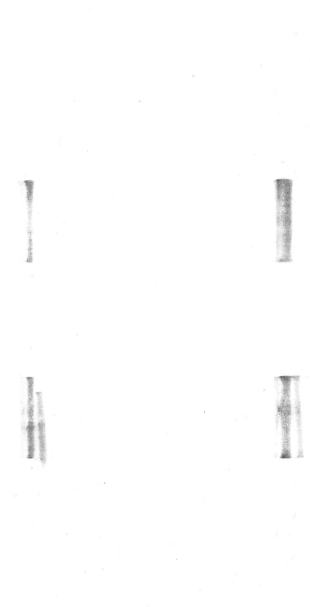

Hopkins the Jesuit

GERARD MANLEY HOPKINS
1880

Hopkins the Jesuit

THE YEARS OF TRAINING

Alfred Thomas, S.J.

LONDON
OXFORD UNIVERSITY PRESS
NEW YORK   TORONTO
1969

Oxford University Press, Ely House, London W. 1

GLASGOW NEW YORK TORONTO MELBOURNE WELLINGTON
CAPE TOWN SALISBURY IBADAN NAIROBI LUSAKA ADDIS ABABA
BOMBAY CALCUTTA MADRAS KARACHI LAHORE DACCA
KUALA LUMPUR SINGAPORE HONG KONG TOKYO

PRINTED IN GREAT BRITAIN

TO MY MOTHER

AND THE MEMORY OF

MY FATHER

CONTENTS

LIST OF ILLUSTRATIONS

PREFACE

GERARD MANLEY HOPKINS is one of those rare writers whose genius moves in a mysterious way so that it is impossible to forecast what may or may not be a clue to its understanding. It is for this reason that I have set down exactly and in detail what happened to him between the destruction of his early verses and his emergence as a major poet during the final years of his training as a Jesuit. There is, of course, no question of trying to say the last word—for this never is said—but the work will fulfil its purpose if it provides grist for other mills. Others may pluck the heart from his mystery: for me the enigma remains.

This book itself is a revised form of a doctoral thesis written for the University of London. In having as supervisor Professor Geoffrey Tillotson I am well aware how distinctly and singularly privileged I was. To his kindness and generosity, his sustained and unfailing encouragement, I must ever remain indebted. Additional incitement to add to my already considerable zest for Hopkins came in different ways. My appetite was whetted by coming across two items directly connected with him. The first of these was the manuscript of the Journal he kept as Porter in the noviceship and now published for the first time. The second was the discovery of the very copy of one of the books read in the refectory which had so startlingly and dramatically reduced him to tears. This set me on the road of tracking down many of the other books which may have influenced him and played their part in shaping his poetry. In this task I was helped by the happy circumstance of completing my own noviceship in the same house where he had lived for four years. This house, after serving as the novitiate of the English Province of the Society of Jesus for over a century, has now been disposed of and much of its contents scattered. Fortunately, while at Manresa House, I was able to search the libraries there thoroughly before these were dispersed. In the process of twice moving some books disappeared and to trace the rest might well now prove impossible.

If I required any further urging it was provided by the growing chorus of legitimate complaint that what Hopkins studies most badly wanted were the biographical facts for these crucial years of formation. It is with the hope of supplying this need that the present work is offered.

A. T.

Heythrop College, Oxon.
8 September 1968

ACKNOWLEDGEMENTS

MY greatest debt is to the Hopkins copyright holders for their generous permission to quote freely from the published *Poems*, *Letters, Journals and Papers, Sermons and Devotional Writings*, as well as from unpublished material. In particular I am indebted to the Very Rev. Fr. Provincial, S.J., the Master of Campion Hall, the Master of Novices, the Rectors of Heythrop, Stonyhurst, and St. Beuno's Colleges, and the Province Archivist, Fr. Francis Edwards, S.J., for allowing me to make use of the manuscript material in their care. At Heythrop I enjoyed the sustained interest and consistent encouragement of the then Director of Studies, Fr. Brinkman, S.J.; I am also grateful to the librarian at Heythrop, Fr. Francis Courtney, S.J., and Campion Hall's librarian, Fr. Basil Fitzgibbon, S.J., for their assistance and co-operation. My debt to my religious superiors and Jesuit colleagues in general is considerable. Among fellow Jesuits, Fr. Anthony Nye calls for particular mention for his constant and unstinted help, and I willingly acknowledge my gratitude for the stimulus of his criticism in discussion. Acknowledgement is also due to Fr. J. H. Crehan, S.J., Dom Edward Croft, O.S.B., and Mr. R. A. Miller for help on particular points, and to Mr. Graham Storey for permission to adapt his chronological table of Hopkins's life. I am glad, too, to express thanks to my examiner Dr. Ball of Royal Holloway College (University of London), for her kindly and painstaking examination and her detailed and helpful comments.

In the course of collecting material I have received kind and efficient assistance from the staffs of the British Museum both at Bloomsbury and Colindale, the Bodleian Library, Oxford, and the National Library of Wales.

For permission to quote from *Obedient Men* by G. Denis Meadows I am indebted to Appleton Century. As regards the many other shorter extracts from copyright prose and verse which I have ventured to quote for the purpose of illustration and comment, I trust that the authors (if alive) and publishers concerned will accept this general acknowledgement of my indebtedness.

ABBREVIATIONS

THE following are the chief abbreviations used in the Notes:

Boase	Frederick Boase, *Modern English Biography*, 6 vols., Truro, 1892–1921
Cath. Encycl.	*The Catholic Encyclopedia*
DNB	*The Dictionary of National Biography*
Foley	Henry Foley, *Records of the English Province of the Society of Jesus*, 7 vols., 1877–83
Gillow	Joseph Gillow, *Bibliographical Dictionary of the English Catholics*, 5 vols.
Jesuit Directory	*The Jesuit Directory and Calendar for 1921* [*etc.*], edited by David H. Thompson, 1921, etc.
LLNN	*Letters and Notices*, 1862–[1]
Sutcliffe	Edmund Felix Sutcliffe, *Bibliography of the English Province of the Society of Jesus 1773–1953*, Roehampton, 1957
JBJ	Juniors' Beadle's Journal
MMJ	Manresa Minister's Journal
NBJ	Novices' Beadle's Journal
PBJ	Philosophers' Beadle's Journal
TBJ	Theologians' Beadle's Journal

The abbreviations used for Hopkins's works together with a note on sources will be found at the beginning of the bibliography on p. 257.

[1] This is a private domestic publication of the English Province of the Society of Jesus.

CHRONOLOGICAL TABLE
OF HOPKINS'S LIFE

1844   Born at Stratford, Essex (28 July).
1852   Family moves to Oak Hill, Hampstead. At day school in Hampstead.
1854–63 Boarder at Highgate School.
1857   Tour through Belgium and the Rhineland with his father and
        brother.
1860   Wins school poetry prize with 'The Escorial' (Easter). Tour through
        South Germany with his father.
1863   'Winter with the Gulf Stream' published in *Once a Week*, 14 Feb-
        ruary. Wins a Classical Exhibition to Balliol College, Oxford.
1863–7 At Balliol College. Meets Robert Bridges, Alexander Baillie, William
        Addis. Writes most of his early poetry; sketches a good deal.
1864   Takes a First in 'Mods'.
1865   Meets Digby Mackworth Dolben (February). Has religious crisis and
        begins his daily spiritual notes (March).
1866   Decides to leave the Church of England (17 or 18 July). Received into
        the Roman Catholic Church by Newman (21 October).
1867   Takes a First in 'Greats' and graduates B.A. In Paris (July).
1867–8 Teaches at the Oratory School, Birmingham.
1868   First extant use of the words 'inscape' and 'instress' in his notes
        headed *Parmenides*. Decides to become a priest and a Jesuit. Burns
        his early poems (11 May). Walking tour in Switzerland with
        Edward Bond (July). Enters the Jesuit novitiate, Roehampton
        (7 September).
1870–3 Studies Philosophy at St. Mary's Hall, Stonyhurst.
1872   Discovers Scotus's *Opus Oxoniense* (August).
1873–4 Teaches 'Rhetoric' at the S.J. Juniorate, Roehampton, including a
        course on 'Poetry and verse'.
1874–7 Studies Theology at St. Beuno's College, St. Asaph.
1875–6 Writes 'The Wreck of the Deutschland' (December–January).
1877   Ordained priest (23 September).
1877–8 Sub-minister at Mount St. Mary's College, Chesterfield.
1878   Preaches at Farm Street Church, London (August). Correspondence
        with R. W. Dixon begins (June).
1878–9 Priest at St. Aloysius Church, Oxford.
1879   On temporary staff at St. Joseph's, (Bedford) Leigh, near Manchester
        (October–December).
1880–1 Priest at St. Francis Xavier's Church, Liverpool.
1881   On temporary staff at St. Joseph's Church, Glasgow (August–
        October).
1881–2 Tertianship at Roehampton.
1882–4 Teaches Classics at Stonyhurst College.

1883   Correspondence with Coventry Patmore begins (August). In Holland with his parents (August).

1884–9   Professor of Greek, University College, Dublin, and Fellow of the Royal University.

1889   Dies in Dublin of typhoid fever (8 June). Buried in Glasnevin cemetery, Dublin.

1893   Eleven of his poems (three of them extracts), published by Bridges in A. H. Miles's *Poets and Poetry of the [Nineteenth] Century.*

1916   Six of his poems (two of them extracts) published by Bridges in *The Spirit of Man.*

1918   *Poems of Gerard Manley Hopkins* published, edited by Robert Bridges.

'I am so happy, I am so happy.' (Hopkins's last words)

'. . . this life here though it is hard is God's will for me as I most intimately know, which is more than violets knee-deep.' (*Further Letters*, 2nd ed., p. 235)

'Over again I feel thy finger and find thee.' ('The Wreck of the Deutschland', stanza 1, line 8)

CHAPTER 1

The Road to Roehampton

Sept. 7. Dim, fine, and very hot.
Horace Dugmore called in the morning and said goodbye.—In the evening when I had said goodbye at home I found my train did not go for three quarters of an hour, so I walked to Victoria Road in the meantime and Aunt Annie came back with me to the train.—Then to the Novitiate, Roehampton.[1]

IT is in this unemphatic way that Gerard Manley Hopkins chose to record the day which set him on his career of a Jesuit priest. The casual reader could hardly be blamed if he interpreted the diarist's attitude as nonchalant. But he would not be quite right if he saw in it nothing more than its superficial matter-of-factness. Present-day depth-psychology might conceivably take such moderation of expression as indicating unexpressed emotional conflict contributing perhaps to his very action of entering the Society of Jesus, but it is better regarded as being founded on responsible self-determination. Hopkins's decision to join the Jesuits was one which was arrived at with no less thought and deliberation than that which made him transfer his allegiance from Church of England to Church of Rome. Both steps were taken after careful and mature consideration which once accepted had to be acted on. This quality of determination grounded on strength of character was not something that suddenly and unaccountably appeared. It was there in the schoolboy who stood up to his unjust headmaster,[2] in the bet binding him to abstain from all liquids for a week,[3] and in the self-imposed destruction of

---

[1] *The Journals and Papers of Gerard Manley Hopkins*, edited by Humphry House, completed by Graham Storey (1959), pp. 188–9; cited hereafter as *Journals and Papers*.

[2] *Further Letters of Gerard Manley Hopkins including his correspondence with Coventry Patmore*, edited by Claude Colleer Abbott, 2nd edition (1956), pp. 2, 395; cited hereafter as *Further Letters*.

[3] His brother, Cyril, says 'a week'; see G. F. Lahey, *Gerard Manley Hopkins* (1930), p. 6; cited hereafter as Lahey, *G. M. Hopkins*. Luxmoore says 'three weeks', *Further Letters*, p. 395.

his poems. It lay, too, at the base of his personal asceticism. The temper of this metal was sterling throughout.

This high quality of determination is further underlined for us by his friend of Highgate days, Luxmoore, who has provided several valuable clues to his character. Hopkins, as a schoolboy, risking the ridicule of his fellows, read his New Testament every night, as his early biographer notes, 'tenacious when duty was concerned',[1] in this, as elsewhere, 'his face always *set* to do what was right'.[2] In fact his resolution, backed by increasing intellectual maturity, far from diminishing, strengthened as manhood displaced adolescence. It showed itself most decisively when he joined the Roman Church in the teeth of opposition from those he loved best—his parents—and despite the utter disapproval of his dearest friends, and even against all that could be urged by counsellors so close and valued as Liddon and Pusey. But this is to anticipate.

Hopkins, as we know, went up to Oxford in 1863 from a moderate High Church family. Before he left in 1867, he had become a full-fledged Roman Catholic, passing in the interim through a Puseyite Gothic-Revivalist stage: he fasted, went fairly frequently to confession and Holy Communion, and even visited churches notorious for their Romish practices; and even if he did not join the Brotherhood of the Holy Trinity[3] as his friends Urquhart, Challis, Addis, and Bridges did, yet he did attend Liddon's soirées and partook of the 'tea-and-toast-and-testament'. He was writing religious poetry,[4] discussing doctrine in his letters, and arguing religion on his walks.

But his progress from Anglicanism to Roman Catholicism is best told in his own words.

In autumn 1865 he shows himself unsettled when he writes somewhat cryptically: 'Note that if ever I should leave the English Church the fact of Provost Fortescue . . . is to be got over.'[5] The

---

[1] *Further Letters*, p. 395.

[2] Ibid., p. 394.

[3] See *Journals and Papers*, pp. 305–6.

[4] See 'Early Poems (1860–75?)' in *The Poems of Gerard Manley Hopkins*, Fourth Edition based on the First Edition of 1918, edited with additional notes by W. H. Gardner and N. H. MacKenzie (1967); cited hereafter as *Poems*.

[5] *Journals and Papers*, p. 71. I have nothing new to add to the note in *Journals and Papers*, pp. 338–9. At present I accept W. H. Pearson's explanation, namely, that if

following June[1] on a walking tour through the Wye valley he visited Belmont Priory, Hereford, with Addis who significantly records of their conversation with the Benedictine, Canon Raynal:[2]

I think he made a great impression on both of us and I believe that from that time our faith in Anglicanism was really gone. He insisted that Anglican orders were at least of doubtful validity; that some grave and learned men questioned or denied their validity and that this being so, it was unlawful till the doubt was cleared by competent authority to accept Anglican orders or even to participate in the Anglican Communion. So far as I knew, Father Raynal was the first priest whom Hopkins had ever spoken to.[3]

Perhaps the importance of this encounter with Canon Raynal is reflected in his Journal entry for 17 July: 'It was this night I believe but possibly the next that I saw clearly the impossibility of staying in the Church of England, but resolved to say nothing to anyone till three months are over, that is the end of the Long, and then of course to take no step till after my Degree.'[4]

A week later, the strength of his new-found conviction was disclosed to Macfarlane[5] who jotted down in his diary: 'Walked out with Hopkins and he confided to me his fixed intention of going over to Rome. I did not attempt to argue with him as his grounds did not admit of argument.'[6] And six weeks later Hopkins wrote decisively to

---

Provost Fortescue with his well-known Romanizing tendencies could remain in the Church of England, Hopkins felt that he too could remain there.

[1] That is, June 1866, ibid., p. 141. Lahey, *G. M. Hopkins*, p. 21, makes Addis imply 'early summer 1865'. This was probably a slip on Addis's part writing after the lapse of years. Further information on the incident is given by Fr. J. H. Crehan in his article 'More Light on Gerard Hopkins', *The Month*, N.S. 10 (Oct. 1953), 205–14.

[2] Rt. Revd. Paul Wilfrid Raynal, O.S.B., Abbot (1830–1904; see *Journals and Papers*, p. 358, n. 141. 4). He taught church history and canon law at Belmont, and according to his obituary 'had the gift of bringing out the salient point and presenting it forcibly'. During this time he published a book on the Ordinal of Edward VI which was 'one of the earliest and most effective contributions to the question of Anglican Orders'.

[3] Lahey, *G. M. Hopkins*, pp. 21–2.

[4] *Journals and Papers*, p. 146. Elsewhere Hopkins suggests that his decision to become a Catholic was taken at Horsham; see *Further Letters*, p. 98, also p. 96.

[5] *Journals and Papers*, p. 147, entry for 24 July.

[6] *Further Letters*, Appendix II, p. 397. One wonders how Urquhart answered the argument advanced in the final paragraph of Hopkins's letter of 13 June 1868, ibid., pp. 51–2. Some reasons which may have influenced GMH are discussed by Fr. M. C. Carroll in his essay 'Gerard Manley Hopkins and the Society of Jesus', contributed to *Immortal Diamond*, ed. Norman Weyand (1949), pp. 8–11.

Newman: 'I am anxious to become a Catholic . . . I do not want to
be helped to any conclusions of belief, for I am thankful to say my
mind is made up . . . by God's mercy I am clear as to the sole
authority of the Church of Rome.'[1] A few weeks later (20 September),
he confides the news of his expected early reception to Urquhart.[2]

Newman, for his part, treated him gently and cautiously, and
Hopkins writing to Bridges told him that Newman 'thought there
appeared no reason, if it had not been for matters at home of course,
why I shd. not be received at once, but in no way did he urge me on,
rather the other way'.[3]

Newman had wisely questioned him to make sure that he was
acting deliberately, and was given as confident an assurance as that
confided to Urquhart:

. . . although my actual conversion was two months ago yet the silent
conviction that I was to become a Catholic has been present to me for a
year perhaps, as strongly, in spite of my resistance to it when it formed
itself into words, as if I had already determined it.[4]

Yet he was equally able to write ten days later, 'my conversion when
it came was all in a minute'.[5] For despite the fact that he had not
yet been received into his new church, his difficulties, unlike
Urquhart's, were resolved. Already, in retrospect, he sees his conversion as very simple, so that he can now write: 'I have even almost
ceased to feel anxiety . . . the happiness it has been the means of
bringing me I cd. not have conceived.'[6] And yet we might easily be
misled into thinking that Hopkins's decision had been reached more
easily than was the case, but part of a letter to his mother corrects
this misapprehension:

You seem to think that my doubts of the English Church occurred to
me on three occasions only after I had been told to resist them and on the
third of these I gave in. So far is this fr. the truth that the doubts or the

---

[1] *Further Letters*, pp. 21–2.   [2] Ibid., p. 23.
[3] *The Letters of Gerard Manley Hopkins to Robert Bridges*, edited by Claude Colleer
Abbott (1935), p. 5; cited hereafter as *Letters to Bridges*.
[4] *Further Letters*, p. 27.
[5] Ibid., and compare the view of the convert Jesuit, Fr. Edmund Lester: 'Many
people go to bed Protestants and wake up Catholics', *Conversions to the Catholic Church*,
ed. Maurice Leahy (1933), p. 81.
[6] *Letters to Bridges*, p. 6. See also the postscript to the letter to his father, *Further
Letters*, p. 95.

conviction which remained when the doubts were forcibly not listened to were for ever present, sometimes they kept occurring for days, and I left off struggling (omitting trifling occasions) three times, in two of which I looked forward and saw what was inevitable, the third time I considered the thing itself and was converted. The subject has had years to bring its point before me, in fact I had long had the premises and had at arm's length kept off the plain conclusion.[1]

But the painful duty still remained of breaking the news of his conversion and the reasons for it to his father and mother. Given Hopkins's extreme sensitivity and warm-heartedness this severing of himself from family and friends must have proved a severe trial. And yet, such was the strength of his religious conviction that it admitted of no delay. If it would be right for him to become a Catholic after his degree, then it must be right now, and as he now saw it, to endure the months which would intervene if he put his reception off, would be intolerable whatever the cost, since in the interim he must be deprived of the sacraments of the true Church. And so writing to Newman on 15 October, he indicates his parents' reaction:

. . . they urge me with the utmost entreaties to wait till I have taken my degree—more than half a year. Of course it is impossible, and since it is impossible to wait as long as they wish it seems to me useless to wait at all. . . . I did not know till last night the rule about *communicatio in sacris*[2] —at least as binding catechumens, but I now see the alternative thrown open, either to live without Church and sacraments or else, in order to avoid the Catholic Church, to have to attend constantly the services of that very Church. This brings the matter to an absurdity and makes me think that any delay, whatever relief it may be to my parents, is impossible. I am asking you then whether I shall at all costs be received at once.[3]

The following day he explained to his father:

You ask me to suspend my judgment for a long time, or at the very least more than half a year, in other words to stand still for a time. Now to stand still is not possible, thus: I must either obey the Church or disobey. If I disobey, I am not suspending judgment but deciding, namely to take backward steps fr. the grounds I have already come to. To stand still if it were possible might be justifiable, but to go back nothing can

[1] Ibid., pp. 98–9.
[2] He wrote to his father: 'The Church strictly forbids all communion in sacred things with non-Catholics.' Ibid., p. 91.
[3] Ibid., pp. 29–30.

justify. . . . If the question which is the Church of Christ? cd. only be
settled by laborious search, a year and ten years and a lifetime are too
little, when the vastness of the subject of theology is taken into account.
But God must have made his Church such as to attract and convince the
poor and unlearned as well as the learned. And surely it is true, though it
will sound pride to say it, that the judgment of one who has seen both
sides for a week is better than his who has seen only one for a lifetime.[1]

The impossibility of waiting longer was reiterated in his letter to
Liddon shortly after his reception by Newman on 21 October:[2] 'I
must have decided as I have done if I had waited till after my Degree
for a leisure time of thought . . .'[3]

Among the negative reasons for his conversion might be noticed
his rejection of any extraordinary personal illumination (evidently
in a Revivalist sense):

You think I lay claim to a personal illumination which dispenses with the
need of thought or knowledge on the points at issue. I have never been so
unwise as to think of such a claim. There is a distinction to be made: in
the sense that every case of taking truth instead of error is an illumination
of course I have been illuminated, but I have never said anything to the
effect that a wide subject involving history and theology or any turning-
point question in it has been thrown into light for me by a supernatural or
even unusual access of grace. If you will not think it an irreverent way of
speaking, I can hardly believe anyone ever became a Catholic because two
and two make four more fully than I have.[4]

He rebuts the suggestion that he had been subjected to Catholic
pressure particularly from Newman,[5] nor was he going over to
Rome for any aesthetic delights. 'I am surprised you shd. say fancy
and aesthetic tastes have led me to my present state of mind: these
wd. be better satisfied in the Church of England, for bad taste is

---

[1] *Further Letters*, pp. 91–3.
[2] Newman's diary records simply: 'Oct. 21. Mr. Hopkins came from Oxford and was
received.' Quoted in Lahey, *G. M. Hopkins*, p. 43.
[3] *Further Letters*, p. 33.
[4] Ibid., p. 31. With this it is interesting to compare the following passage which occurs
at the end of a sermon he preached in Oxford on 21 Sept. 1879: 'But all converts
agree in feeling that they are led by God's particular will. They are bound to go, it will
be sin to stay, God calls them, bids them etc: "I hear a voice you cannot hear" etc. We
who are converts have all heard that voice which others cannot or say they cannot hear,
have seen that beckoning finger which others etc', *The Sermons and Devotional Writings
of Gerard Manley Hopkins*, ed. Christopher Devlin, S.J. (1959), p. 25; cited hereafter
as *Sermons and Devotional Writings*.
[5] *Further Letters*, pp. 27–8.

always meeting one in the accessories of Catholicism.'[1] Neither
could ties of friendship keep him where he was: 'Dr. Pusey and Mr.
Liddon were the only two men in the world who cd. avail to detain
me: the fact that they were Anglicans kept me one, for arguments for
the Church of England I had long ago felt there were none that wd.
hold water, and when that influence gave way everything was gone.'[2]

Hopkins's more positive reasons for becoming a Roman Catholic
are contained in letters to his father, his mother, and to Liddon. The
most significant passages seem to me the following:

... the Tractarian ground I have seen broken to pieces under my feet.[3]

My conversion is due to the following reasons mainly (I have put them
down without order)—(i) simple and strictly drawn arguments partly my
own, partly others', (ii) common sense, (iii) reading the Bible, especially
the Holy Gospels, where texts like 'Thou art Peter' (the evasions proposed
for this alone are enough to make one a Catholic) and the manifest
position of St. Peter among the Apostles so pursued me that at one time I
thought it best to stop thinking of them, (iv) an increasing knowledge of
the Catholic system (at first under the form of Tractarianism, later in its
genuine place), which only wants to be known in order to be loved—its
consolations, its marvellous ideal of holiness, the faith and devotion of
its children, its multiplicity, its array of saints and martyrs, its consis-
tency and unity, its glowing prayers, the daring majesty of its claims,
etc etc.[4]

---

[1] Ibid., p. 93. See too his remarks on the Douay version of the Scriptures, ibid., p. 42.
Evelyn Waugh felt similarly: '. . . my readers outside England should understand that
the aesthetic appeal of the Church of England is unique and peculiar to those islands.
Elsewhere a first interest in the Catholic Church is often kindled in the convert's imagination by the splendours of her worship in contrast with the bleakness and meanness of the
Protestant sects. In England the pull is all the other way. The medieval cathedrals and
churches, the rich ceremonies that surround the monarchy, the historic titles of Canterbury and York, the social organization of the country parishes, the traditional culture of
Oxford and Cambridge, the liturgy composed in the heyday of English prose style—
all these are the property of the Church of England, while Catholics meet in modern
buildings, often of deplorable design, and are usually served by simple Irish missionaries.'
From 'Come Inside', contributed to *The Road to Damascus*, i, ed. John A. O'Brien
(1949), p. 13.
[2] *Further Letters*, p. 94. For further acknowledgements of the influence of Liddon and
Pusey see ibid., pp. 31, 98.
[3] Ibid., p. 92. This was written in Oct. 1866, but there had been several earlier signs
of his growing dissatisfaction. Two years before, for instance, he complained to Baillie
of the opinion of extremists to be found in the *Church Times*, 'its pettiness, irreverence,
vulgarity, injustice, ignorance, cant, may well make one suspect one's party', ibid., p. 220;
see also ibid., pp. 17, 18.
[4] Ibid., p. 93.

Your not being a Catholic is, I suppose, on conviction that the Church
of Rome is wrong; my conversion is on conviction that it is *right*.[1]

In addition, his letter to Liddon shows his complete acceptance of
the doctrine of papal infallibility and his rejection of the Branch
theory.[2]

Hopkins's letter to his father, explaining his conversion, concluded
with the postscript: 'I am most anxious that you shd. not think of
my future. It is likely that the positions you wd. like to see me in wd.
have no attraction for me, and surely the happiness of my prospects
depends on the happiness to me and not on intrinsic advantages.'[3]
Not surprisingly, this letter struck his father as hard and cold, and
because of the ensuing temporary estrangement from his family,
Newman kindly invited Gerard to spend Christmas at the Birmingham Oratory. At the same time Newman answered Gerard's inquiry
about his future vocation, and in his reply counselled patience and a
caution and trust which echo the sentiments of 'Lead Kindly Light':
'As to your retreat, I think we have misunderstood each other . . .
it does not seem to me that there is any hurry about it . . . it seems
to me a better thing not to hurry decision on your vocation. Suffer
yourself to be led on by the Grace of God step by step.'[4]

In the event, Newman's words turned out prophetic, and Hopkins's progress to his goal can be plotted step by step. Hopkins, in
fact, spent Christmas at home and during the vacation met Darnell
who was leaving his teaching post at the Oratory and now offered it
to him.[5] Hopkins accepted. He returned to Oxford and took his
degree in the spring of 1867, and spent Holy Week with the Benedictines, returning to Belmont Priory to do so, finding it 'a delightful
place in every way'.[6] His rather vague inquiry about 'monasteries'
contained in the same letter might, I suggest, either be interpreted
as mere general interest, or, more likely, that he was considering

[1] *Further Letters*, p. 99. Newman in a letter to T. W. Allies wrote: '. . . *the* reason *why*
I left the Anglican Church was that I thought salvation was not to be found in it'. *The
Letters and Diaries of John Henry Newman*, ed. Charles Stephen Dessain, xiii (1963), 59.
[2] *Further Letters*, pp. 31–4.   [3] Ibid., p. 95.
[4] Ibid., p. 405. There has been a slip here in the date. '1886' should read '1866'.
[5] Lahey, *G. M. Hopkins*, p. 46.
[6] *Further Letters*, p. 39. He mentions Holy Week with the Benedictines in his letter
to Macfarlane, ibid., p. 37.

becoming a Benedictine himself. In September he took up the teaching post at the Oratory School.

During his first term there, he must have raised the question of his vocation again, for Newman wrote on 30 December: 'It seems to me you had better go into retreat at Easter, & bring the matter before the Priest who gives it to our boys.'[1] Ten days later Hopkins wrote from Blunt House, Croydon, the home of his grandfather, to Bridges who was leaving soon to visit Egypt:

This note accordingly is to say goodbye. The year you will be away I have no doubt will make a great difference in my position though I cannot know exactly what. But the uncertainty I am in about the future is so very unpleasant and so breaks my power of applying to anything that I am resolved to end it, which I shall do by going into a retreat at Easter at the latest and deciding whether I have a vocation to the priesthood.[2]

A month later, having returned to the Oratory School for his second and last term there, he wrote to Baillie: 'I am expecting to take orders and soon, . . . I want to write still and as a priest I very likely can do that too . . .'[3]

The rest of the story is quickly told. He made a ten-day retreat at the Jesuit novitiate, Manresa House, Roehampton from 27 April until 7 May, and in the course of this his Journal records: 'May 5. . . . Resolved to be a religious.'[4] And on 7 May, 'Home, after having decided to be a priest and religious but still doubtful between St. Benedict and St. Ignatius.'[5] His doubt must have resolved itself speedily for within a week he has had time to write and tell Newman of his decision to apply for admission to the Society of Jesus, and receive in return Newman's congratulations: 'I am both surprised and glad at your news . . . Don't call "the Jesuit discipline hard", it will bring you to heaven.'[6]

On 19 May Hopkins saw Fr. Weld,[7] the Jesuit Provincial, and his

[1] Ibid., p. 408.　　　　　　　　　　　　　[2] *Letters to Bridges*, p. 22.

[3] *Further Letters*, p. 231. The reason for his rejecting painting as a career (ibid.) I have suggested elsewhere: 'Gerard Manley Hopkins "Doomed to succeed by failure" ', *Dublin Review*, ccxl (Summer 1966), 161–3.

[4] *Journals and Papers*, p. 165.　　　　　　　　　　　[5] Ibid.

[6] *Further Letters*, p. 408.

[7] Alfred Weld (1823–90; see Boase vi, Sutcliffe), Jesuit priest, fourth son of George Weld (1786–1866), and grandson of Thomas Weld who gave Stonyhurst to the English Province S.J., was born at Leagram Park, near Preston, on 5 Aug. 1823. Educated at Stonyhurst, and entered the S.J. novitiate at Hodder in Oct. 1842. Matric. London Univ.,

Journal for 30 May shows that his application for admission had been accepted.

His parents seem to have grown reconciled to his decision, for whereas in February he had told Baillie, '. . . if I am a priest it will cause my mother, or she says it will, great grief . . .',[1] he is able to write in June to Urquhart: 'I am quite surprised—not that on reflection it is surprising—at the kind and contented way my parents have come to take the prospect.'[2] But were his parents really so surprised? Perhaps not.

Why did Hopkins become a Jesuit? The question still remains unanswered, and in the matter of religious vocation[3] the ultimate reason may well defy statement. An element of mystery persists. It is easier to give the 'how' of his choice rather than the 'why'. The known facts will prove the safest guide. Broadly speaking, we can look for the external and internal factors which could and may have influenced him. Not that these can be neatly separated in any final analysis, but it will serve to break the ice to proceed as though they could.

In an unpublished essay entitled 'On cumulative and chain evidence' which Hopkins wrote during his first year at Oxford, the following passage occurs:

> . . . if so-and-so get a scholarship, he will probably be able to enter the University, and if he enter the University he will probably read, and if he read he will probably get a first class, and if he get a first class he will probably be encouraged to read for a fellowship, and if he read for a fellowship he will probably get it, and if he get it he will probably take orders, and if he take orders he will probably become a bishop.[4]

1845; B.A., 1847; F.R.A.S., 1849. Ordained priest, 1854. Novice master, 1860–4. Appointed Provincial at the early age of forty-one. As Provincial (1864–7) he was responsible for admitting GMH into the Society of Jesus as a novice. His Provincialate was marked by a considerable increase of literary activity and an extensive building programme. Rector at St. Beuno's, 1871–3. Assistant to the Jesuit General, Fr. Beckx, 1873–4. Later worked in connection with missions in Zambezi, Gibraltar, and India. Died at Grahamstown on 24 July 1890. (*Journals and Papers*, pp. 165, 166.)

¹ *Further Letters*, pp. 231–2. ² Ibid., p. 51.

³ The Church requires three conditions on the part of the candidate for a vocation to the priesthood: (i) a right intention; (ii) the qualities fitting him for the office; (iii) he must be freely called to ordination by a bishop. The aspirant may or may not feel some special interior intimation or illumination in his call to serve God. But this is in no way to be regarded as necessary.

⁴ Manuscript at Campion Hall, Oxford, Oxford Essays D. 1. The essay of approximately 525 words is initialled by Edward Cooper Woollcombe (1816–80) (see *Journals*

Undoubtedly the coincidence in this chain of reasoning with the actual course of events in Hopkins's own life is striking—a scholarship to Balliol, a double first in Greats, priesthood, and a professorship—yet seen in the context of the Oxford of the period it would seem unwarrantable to infer from this that Hopkins was envisaging for himself a career in the Church of England. To do so is to substitute hindsight for evidence. At most it might point to the drift of his thought.

The religious poems of his adolescence, however, would seem to provide a surer guide to his inclination.[1] For example, if the sixth stanza of 'The Habit of Perfection' is interpreted autobiographically,

> O feel-of-primrose hands, O feet
> That want the yield of plushy sward,
> But you shall walk the golden street
> And you unhouse and house the Lord.
> (*Poems*, No. 22)

then Hopkins was thinking of the priesthood in January 1866. Certainly his parents seemed to think he might enter the Church. 'We believed', his father wrote to Liddon in October 1866 a week before Gerard became a Catholic, that 'he had lately resolved on taking orders in the English Church'.[2] What Manley Hopkins seems not to have realized is that he himself by his glowing praise of the ideal of the Roman Catholic priesthood in his history of Hawaii[3] might well have been responsible, in part at least, for directing his son's attention to the vocation he was to follow. The appearance of the first edition in 1862 would have caught the eighteen-year-old Gerard at a highly impressionable stage when ideals are often everything. More definite proof of his emerging vocation appears in the letter from Newman in the December of 1866, and in fairly

---

and Papers, p. 295), and is in a notebook dating from Hopkins's first year at Oxford. I suppose there is a touch of irony in the circumstances that Hopkins's namesake in the Jesuit noviceship, Frederick Hopkins, did become a bishop.

[1] One critic has written: 'In that section of Gardner's edition entitled 'Early Poems' there is not a poem that does not reveal an ascetic attitude, and most are explicitly religious.' David A. Downes, 'The Hopkins Enigma', *Thought* (Fordham University Quarterly), xxxvi (New York, Winter 1961), 578-9.

[2] *Further Letters*, p. 434.

[3] See Appendix 1, 'Manley Hopkins and the Roman Catholic Priesthood'.

quick succession came the further references in his letters to Bridges and Baillie already quoted.

It should not, I think, be ruled out that at this stage Hopkins could have been thinking of becoming a secular or diocesan priest. Certainly he tells Baillie in February 1868, that he is expecting to take '[minor] orders and *soon*'[1] (my italics), and this would seem to suggest that Hopkins had not yet decided to enter a religious order, since unless he were ignorant on the point, which seems unlikely, he would have known that any religious order would require him to complete at least a year's novitiate, if not its course of philosophy, before presenting him for these orders.[2]

That he thought of the Oratorians is clear from Newman's letter: 'You are quite out, in thinking that when I offered you a "home" here, I dreamed of your having a vocation for us. This I clearly saw you had *not*, from the moment you came to us.'[3] The appeal of the Oratorian Congregation hardly needs stating—Newman as superior, a community of fellow-converts nearly all Oxford men, and probably the opportunity of writing, to name only the more obvious attractions.

But the contemplative and the musician[4] in Hopkins's make-up

---

[1] *Further Letters*, p. 231—'minor orders', p. 232.

[2] The flexibility with which minor orders and even the priesthood could be conferred at this time is well illustrated by the following account related by Fr. Edward Purbrick: 'On hearing from me . . . that I was determined to study for the Priesthood, he [Wiseman] sent me down within six weeks of my reception [1850] into the Church to St. Edmund's to receive the tonsure and four minor orders, exempted me from following any Seminary course, sanctioned my studying privately under the direction of Dr. Ward . . . and declared his intention of ordaining me Priest at the end of two years.' (Wilfrid Ward, *The Life and Times of Cardinal Wiseman*, ii, 2nd ed., 1897, p. 164.) Again, as is well known, the speed with which Manning was raised to the priesthood fluttered several Catholic dovecotes. But then his case was no ordinary one. For some account of ordination in the Church of England during this period, see Appendix B, 'Training for Holy Orders' in C. K. Francis Brown's *A History of the English Clergy 1800–1900* (1953), pp. 240–9.

[3] *Further Letters*, p. 408. A scrap of letter written from the Oratory, Edgbaston, provides further evidence that Hopkins considered joining the Oratorians: 'I do not expect to be long here: if I get a vocation to the priesthood I shd. go away (I shd. . . . to be an Orato[rian] . . . and if not I s[hould] . . . better myself. . . . I knew for cer[tain] . . . was not to be . . . .' *Journals and Papers*, p. 534, 4 (d).

[4] Hopkins's fondness for plain-chant is clear from the entry in his Journal for 17 June 1866: 'Saw St. Raphael's . . . and heard a delightful Gregorian there.' *Journals and Papers*, p. 140. And twenty years later he wrote: 'To me plain chant melody has an infinite expressiveness and dramatic richness.' *Letters to Bridges*, p. 214.

must have drawn him in the direction of the Benedictines. Further, if as Addis stated,[1] Canon Raynal of Belmont Priory was the first Catholic priest Hopkins spoke to, a religious who clearly impressed him—the significance of the meeting has already been indicated— it would not be surprising for him to have thought of becoming a monk. Belmont he had found 'a delightful place in every way',[2] and even up to four months of joining the Jesuits he is still doubtful between St. Benedict and St. Ignatius'.[3] But eventually he did decide.

How Hopkins first came to know of the Jesuits is not certain. He might have heard of them directly from his father or have read about them in his history of Hawaii.[4] Like many another, he could have encountered his first Jesuits in fiction, perhaps in Thackeray's *Esmond* (1852), or Kingsley's *Westward Ho!* (1855).[5] One feels though that it was a touch of amused irony that he noted in his Journal for 21 May 1868: 'Cardinal d'Andrea being dead the *Times* Italian correspondent hints he was poisoned by the Pope or Jesuits.'[6]

We know, too, that some of Hopkins's friends had had contacts with Jesuits, even if this went no further than unobtrusively slipping into their churches. Alexander Wood,[7] of Trinity, we know, had made 'a stealthy visit to the Jesuit church in Edinburgh'.[8] His school

---

[1] Lahey, *G. M. Hopkins*, pp. 21-2. [2] *Further Letters*, p. 39.

[3] *Journals and Papers*, p. 165, entry for 7 May. Dom Edward Cruise, O.S.B., has conscientiously recorded the following interesting though melancholy fact: '. . . it can hardly be said that the Benedictines were at first in a position to react vigorously to the stimulus offered by the Oxford Movement and the re-establishment of the Hierarchy. It is not without significance that in contrast to many of the other orders none of the distinguished converts found his vocation with the Benedictines.' 'Development of the Religious Orders', *The English Catholics 1850-1950*, edited by George Andrew Beck (1950), p. 444. The plight of the other religious at the time was even worse as Dom Edward shows, see pp. 444 ff.

[4] In this history Manley Hopkins quoted twice from Sir James Stephen's essay 'The Founders of Jesuitism' which appeared originally in the *Edinburgh Review*, and was later republished with additions in *Essays in Ecclesiastical Biography*, i (1849), 154-290.

[5] See also the article by K. M. Grey, 'The Jesuit of Modern Fiction', *Catholic Progress*, xiii (June 1884), 222-6. Jesuits are still useful stock-in-trade as several contemporary novelists have shown, for example Thomas Mann in *Der Zauberberg* (1924), Albert Camus in *La Peste* (1947), and Giuseppe di Lampedusa in *Il Gattopardo* (1958). The early Waugh Jesuit is to be specially cherished!

[6] *Journals and Papers*, p. 165. [7] Ibid., p. 321.

[8] J. H. Crehan, 'More Light on Gerard Manley Hopkins', *The Month*, N.S. 10 (Oct. 1953), 206.

friend of Highgate days, Ernest Hartley Coleridge,[1] had a cousin in the Society, Fr. H. J. Coleridge,[2] whom Hopkins probably met when he gave the boys a retreat at the Oratory School in April 1868.[3] Again, Digby Mackworth Dolben,[4] who had made such an impression on Hopkins,[5] had visited Beaumont, the Jesuit College, while he was at Eton.[6] Another friend, Henry Oxenham,[7] tried his own vocation in the Society.

A different link with the Society which Hopkins could have discovered for himself was provided in Oxford itself by the Roman Catholic chapel of St. Ignatius in a house in St. Clements, which the Jesuits had originally founded as a mission.[8] It was a chapel dear to the hearts of Tractarians and perhaps Puseyites, for it was there that Newman had heard his first Mass as a Roman Catholic, and where he heard his last Mass before leaving Oxford.[9] The Jesuits had given up the chapel in 1859 and handed it over to the Birmingham diocesan authorities, so that when Hopkins was at Oxford it was in the charge of a secular priest. Fr. Crehan has related the anecdote of Hopkins's visit there which made a 'recusant' of him:

It was to this chapel that Hopkins and Wood came for their Sunday Mass during their last year of preparation for Greats at the University.

[1] *Journals and Papers*, pp. 319–20.

[2] Henry James Coleridge (1822–93; see *DNB*, Boase iv, *Cath. Encycl.*, Sutcliffe), Jesuit priest, second son of Sir John Taylor Coleridge, and grandnephew of the poet, was born on 20 Sept. 1822. Educated at Eton and Trinity College, Oxford; B.A., 1845; M.A., 1847; Fellow of Oriel College, 1845–52. Took Anglican orders in Dec. 1848. Received into the R.C. Church, 1852; ordained priest, 1856. Entered S.J. novitiate, 7 Sept. 1857. Appears to have been the first Jesuit that GMH met (*Journals and Papers*, p. 163), and GMH referred to him as 'my oldest friend in the Society' (*Further Letters*, p. 138). Edited *The Month*, 1865–81. Died at Roehampton on 13 Apr. 1893. (*Further Letters*, pp. 139, n. 3, 161, n. 1; *Journals and Papers*, p. 259.)

[3] *Journals and Papers*, p. 163, entry for 5 Apr.

[4] Ibid., pp. 325–6.

[5] *Letters to Bridges*, pp. 16–17. Bridges was to write later: '[Dolben] must have been a good deal with him, for Gerard conceived a high admiration for him, and always spoke of him afterwards with great affection.' Memoir in *The Poems of Digby Mackworth Dolben* (Oxford, 1911), pp. lxviii f., quoted in *Journals and Papers*, p. 325.

[6] Robert Bridges notes Dolben's 'stolen visit' to what RB quaintly terms 'a Lodge of Jesuits at Old Windsor' (ibid., pp. xxviii f.).

[7] *Journals and Papers*, pp. 320–1.

[8] For an account of this mission at Oxford, see Henry Foley, *Records of the English Province of the Society of Jesus*, v (1879), 958–9; cited hereafter as Foley; B. Stapleton, *A History of the Post-Reformation Catholic Missions in Oxfordshire* (1906), pp. 226 ff.; *Sermons and Devotional Writings*, p. 275, n. 13. 1.

[9] Wilfrid Ward, *The Life of John Henry Cardinal Newman*, i (1912), 95, 116.

There was only one Mass, at half-past ten, and so it was an easy matter for the University authorities to ascertain whether any of those *in statu pupillari* were being beguiled by the Scarlet Woman. One morning when the two were leaving the chapel they were accosted by the 'bulldogs' and had their names taken, being given an appointment with the Junior Proctor for 9.15 the next morning. At this they were fined for their breach of University discipline in attending the chapel, and thus Hopkins joined so late in the day the band of Oxford Recusants which began with Cardinal Allen, Persons and Campion.[1]

But leaving this link with the past, it seems fitting to ask what sort of public image the Society of Jesus presented to the country in the sixties, or better, for the sake of perspective, to go back a decade to the restoration of the English Roman Catholic hierarchy. Of the religious orders in England 'only the Jesuits', writes Dom Edward Cruise, 'could be described as being in a strong and flourishing state. . . . For more than 200 years they had maintained an average of 20 novices a year.'[2] The Province continued to expand despite opposition both from without and within the Catholic body.[3] Indeed, this very opposition may have been a factor in its growth, as it certainly was a condition; it may have served even as an added attraction to some aspirants.

To a youth on fire with religious derring-do [writes David A. Downes],

[1] 'More Light on Gerard Hopkins', *The Month*, N.S. 10 (Oct. 1953), 210.

[2] 'Development of the Religious Orders', *The English Catholics 1850–1950*, ed. G. A. Beck (1950), p. 443. The actual figures for the restored Society in England until the end of the century are as follows:

1815: 73	1840: 132	1880: 457
1819: 89	1850: 194	1890: 578
1829: 109	1860: 262	1900: 673
1831: 110	1870: 347	

(Statistics from *Synopsis historiae Societatis Jesu*, ed. L. Schmitt, A. Kleiser, J. B. Goetstouwers, and C. Van de Vorst (Louvain, 1950), col. 494.) If Dom Edward Cruise is right in reckoning the number of priests belonging to religious orders or congregations at 275 (op. cit., p. 442) in 1850, then Jesuit priests would seem to account for a third of the total. The figures of 194 for the year 1850 given above is made up as follows: 90 priests, 78 scholastics, 26 lay-brothers. For a generous account of the work of the English Province of the Society of Jesus see the essay 'Religious Orders of Men' contributed by Abbot Cuthbert Butler to *Catholic Emancipation 1829 to 1929*, with an introduction by [Francis Alphonsus] Cardinal Bourne (1929), pp. 191–3.

[3] For some account see the following articles by J. H. Pollen: 'An Unobserved Centenary', *The Month*, cxv (May 1910), 449–61; 'The Restoration of the English Jesuits, 1803–1817', ibid., cxv (June 1910), 585–97; 'The Recognition of the Jesuits in England', ibid., cxvi (July 1910), 23–36.

the Jesuits are the kind of lure that the French Foreign Legion has for young military adventurers. This was especially true in England where the Jesuits were either famous or infamous from the days of Elizabeth I for their brilliance, dedication, and success. What outfit could be more appealing to a young, gifted, English rebel-convert?[1]

A trifle over-dramatic perhaps, but possibly true nonetheless. Hopkins himself, commenting on the expulsion of the Society from Spain in 1868, wrote: 'To be persecuted in a tolerant age is a high distinction.'[2]

The schools run by the Society—Stonyhurst, near Blackburn; Beaumont, Old Windsor; Mount St. Mary's, near Sheffield; and St. Francis Xavier's, Liverpool—were holding their own and Jesuit education was well thought of, but doubtless Manning, as yet two years from Westminster, overstated his case in his zeal to get his Catholic University hobby-horse home when he wrote: 'The Society of Jesus alone contains in itself men capable of holding professors' chairs in all the chief faculties of arts, literature, and science.'[3]

Much of the support for the English Jesuits came from the old Catholics,[4] and while this was obviously not a bad thing, it carried with it the germ of stagnation. To counteract this new blood was needed. 'From this sterility', wrote J. H. Pollen, 'the English Province . . . was saved by the considerable number of converts who joined its ranks in consequence of the Oxford Movement.'[5] Pollen then gives a list of the more important converts at Oxford who became Jesuits—Ignatius Grant (1821–1904), Albany James Christie (1817–91), Henry Coleridge (1822–93), Thomas Harper (1821–93), Frederick Hathaway (1814–91), George Kingdon (1821–93), Edward

---

[1] 'The Hopkins Enigma', *Thought* (Fordham University Quarterly), xxxvi (New York, Winter 1961), 581.

[2] *Further Letters*, p. 106.

[3] 'The Work and the Wants of the Catholic Church in England', *Dublin Review*, N.S. 1 (July 1863), 158, reprinted later in Henry Edward Manning, *Miscellanies*, i (1877), 25–71.

[4] 'Many prominent Catholics in these years of Cardinal Wiseman were closely attached to the Society of Jesus; they were the penitents of those old fathers who had taught at Stonyhurst before any one had thought about the Oxford Movement.' David Mathew, 'Old Catholics and Converts', *The English Catholics 1850–1950*, ed. G. A. Beck (1950), p. 231.

[5] 'The Centenary of the Restoration of the Society of Jesus,' *The Month*, cxxiii (Jan. 1914), 64.

Purbrick (1830–1914), George Tickell (1815–93), John Wynne (1819–93)—'and many others (over fifty before 1864)'.[1] It is clear there was precedent in plenty for Hopkins.

Fr. Pollen would date the growing strength of the new movement from Newman's 'Second Spring' sermon of 1852, but adds:

In the Society of Jesus, however, . . . the full effect of the movement would naturally take some years longer before reaching maturity. It is impossible, of course, to give a precise date for this, but it will be convenient for us to survey it at the year 1864, the fiftieth year of the restored Society, when the new force was certainly in full operation.[2]

This date coincides with the beginning of Hopkins's career at the University.

Living as Hopkins did in London, and given his interest, it would have been almost impossible for him not to have known of the principal Jesuit church in the country—Farm Street.[3] The part it played in the contemporary Catholic life of London is too well known to need retelling. The sermons,[4] services, and missions given both in Mayfair and in the provinces were a byword of the period as the newspapers and periodicals of the time show. As a result the parlours of Farm Street produced a steady stream of converts.[5]

---

[1] Ibid. Some interesting statistics of converts who became priests are given in W. Gordon Gorman's *Converts to Rome*, 4th ed. (1899), pp. xi–xiii. The figures related to the period 'since the Tractarian movement to May, 1899'. What follows is an extract: 'Converts who have become Priests:—
'Regular Clergy: Benedictines, 18; Carmelites, 2; Carthusians, 2; Institute of Charity, 9; Cistercians, 2; Dominicans, 23 ; Franciscans, 2; Jesuits, 78; Passionists, 10; Redemptorists, 9; Servites, 2; Trappist, 1.   [total] 158.
'Secular Clergy: including Oratorians, 26; Oblates of St. Charles, 18.   [total] 290.'
[2] 'The Centenary of the Restoration of the Society of Jesus', *The Month*, cxxiii (Jan. 1914), 64.
[3] See [George Charles Hungerford Pollen], *Guide to the Church of the Immaculate Conception, Farm St., Berkeley Square* (1912); Bernard Basset, *Farm Street* [1948].
[4] See *Sermons by Fathers of the Society of Jesus*, 3 vols. (1869–75); these include sermons by Fathers Coleridge, Hathaway, Parkinson, Gallwey, Harper, Weld, and Anderdon.
[5] Fr. Crehan states that the number of converts annually received at Farm Street Church 'dropped in 1864 below one hundred for the first time since 1849 and did not reach that figure again until 1915'. 'More Light on Gerard Hopkins,' *The Month*, N.S. 10 (Oct. 1953), 208. Among the more notable converts in the early days at Farm Street were Archdeacon Manning and Mr. Hope Scott of Abbotsford who were received there by Fr. James Brownbill on 6 Apr. 1851; see Edmund Sheridan Purcell, *Life of Cardinal Manning*, i (1895), 627–8. Purcell reminds us that Manning occupied a unique position there from 1852 until 1856: 'He was not attached to the Jesuits' Church at Farm Street; neither did he live with the community, nor was he a candidate for novitiate in the Society, but was received for a time by the Jesuit Fathers as a spiritual guest, saying mass

1864 also serves to mark an upsurge of literary activity in the Province. 'Before that year,' Pollen says,

the English Jesuits had written so little, that the early book catalogues of Messrs. Burns and Lambert, of Dolman and of Duffy, make no mention of any except Father William Waterworth and Father Corry. In that year, however, a printing press was opened at Roehampton, *The Month*[1] was begun, and a quarterly publication of papers for private circulation relating to the Order itself, entitled *Letters and Notices*, and there were numerous translations from Italian and French. The latter were, after a time, merged into *St. Joseph's Catholic Library*, and this was in its turn supplanted by the *Quarterly Series*, and others. In divinity, one might mention Father Harper's ample and erudite answer to Dr. Pusey's *Eirenicon*, his *Peace through the Truth*, and his profound philosophical work, *The Metaphysics of the School*.[2]

Besides its writers, the Farm Street community was also fortunate in possessing some outstanding preachers, notably the Rector, Fr. Gallwey,[3] and Fathers Hathaway[4] and Clare.[5] But perhaps the finest

every morning in the church, and having a confessional of his own. It was in one sense a position of special advantage, for it placed the newly-ordained convert at one of the greatest centres of Catholic life and activity in London', *Life of Cardinal Manning*, ii (1895), 50.

[1] *The Month* was founded in July 1864, edited by Miss Fanny Margaret Taylor with assistance from the Fathers at Farm Street, who next year took over its publication altogether. Three out of four of the editors spanning the years 1865–1901 were converts; these were: Henry J. Coleridge, editor 1865–81, Richard F. Clarke, editor 1882–94, and Sydney F. Smith, editor 1897–1901. Their photographs form the frontispiece to the Jan.–June volume of *The Month* for 1914. For a short account of *The Month*, see David H. Thompson, *The Jesuit Directory and Calendar . . . 1921* (1921), pp. 72–4; J. J. Dwyer, 'The Catholic Press 1850–1950', *The English Catholics 1850–1950*, ed. G. A. Beck (1950), pp. 495–502.

[2] J. H. Pollen, 'The Centenary of the Restoration of the Society of Jesus', *The Month*, cxxiii (Jan. 1914), 64–5.

[3] Peter Gallwey (1820–1906; see *DNB*, *Cath. Encycl.*, Sutcliffe), Jesuit priest, born at Killarney on 13 Nov. 1820. Educated at Stonyhurst College. Entered the S.J. novitiate at Hodder in Sept. 1836; ordained priest in 1852. Prefect of Studies at Stonyhurst, 1855–7. Rector of Farm St., London, 1857–69. 1869–73, Rector and novice master at Manresa, Roehampton, and so became GMH's first novice master. 1873–6, Provincial. Rector of St. Beuno's, and Professor of moral theology, 1876–7, GMH being among his pupils. Twice represented the Province as elector at the General Congregations S.J. of 1883 and 1892. Remained at Farm Street until his death on 23 Sept. 1906 (*Further Letters*, pp. 112, 150, 'the Provincial' 127; *Journals and Papers*, pp. 191, 227, 230, 232, 'Father Rector' 193, 'the Provincial' 236, 249).

[4] Frederick Hathaway (1814–91), see Gorman, *Converts to Rome* (1884), p. 39. His obituarist in *LLNN* speaks of him as 'the Demosthenes of the English Province'. He died in Jamaica.

[5] James Clare (1827–1902). Hopkins thought him 'a famous preacher', *The Correspondence of Gerard Manley Hopkins and Richard Watson Dixon*, edited by Claude Colleer

and most stimulating of human influences in the Province was its Provincial, Fr. Weld, described as

a true representative, both by birth and training, of the English Catholic families, and of the old colleges, to which he owed the whole of his education. To say nothing in detail about his courtly manners, his great and striking personal and priestly virtues, he was an enthusiastic astronomer, an historical writer, and a zealous and far-sighted patron of literature.[1]

It was Fr. Weld who accepted Hopkins as a novice into the Society of Jesus.

But having glanced at the image presented by the English Jesuits, what can be said of Hopkins's personal and more intimate reasons for joining them? At this point it might be easier to ask 'Who can read hearts?' and leave it at that. But this would be to burke the issue. What are offered are some suggestions only.

Hopkins, as we saw earlier, wrote to Baillie in February 1868, saying that he still wanted to write and that as a priest it was very likely that he could do so.[2] From what has been said already, I think it is clear that in joining the Society at this time Hopkins would be joining a body that was beginning to show its literary paces. Of another Oxford convert who joined the Jesuits earlier J. L. Patterson commented: '. . . the natural drawing towards literary work, had [its] weight in the bias which he felt towards the Society of Jesus.'[3] It is true that Hopkins seemed to have cut loose his literary moorings with the destruction of his poems before embarking on his new life, though as we know the 'slaughter of the innocents' recorded in his Journal for 11 May 1868 was not so wholesale as might at first sight appear. I am merely suggesting that it would be unwise to rule out subconscious motivation entirely.

Another factor which may have played its part in deciding Hopkins in his choice might have been the 'Englishness' of the English Province—and this despite the fact that it contained a fair sprinkling of Irish and Scots. This is a quality easier to state than

Abbott (1935), p. 62, cited hereafter as *Correspondence with Dixon*. See also the index to *Sermons and Devotional Writings*.

[1] J. H. Pollen, 'The Centenary of the Restoration of the Society of Jesus', *The Month*, cxxiii (Jan. 1914), 65.

[2] *Further Letters*, p. 231.

[3] Bishop of Emmaus [James Laird Patterson], 'Recollections of Henry James Coleridge', *The Month*, lxxviii (June 1893), 166.

define: like St. Augustine we know very well what time is—but do
not ask us to define it. But Dom Edward Cruise clearly had it in
mind when he described the atmosphere of Stonyhurst as 'inescap-
ably and almost aggressively English'.[1] It seems to me not very
different from what Manning called the 'English Catholicism, of
which Newman is the highest type'.[2] This Englishness of his new
church, and more specifically of the English Jesuits, quite likely
exerted its attraction on Hopkins the patriot.

Newman's share in helping Hopkins arrive at his goal is clearly
important. And it seems right that it should be so, for what could
be more natural than to discuss the question of your vocation with
the priest who received you into the Church. Newman, as stated
earlier, saw that Hopkins had not got an Oratorian vocation and later
told him so. But I think it can be pertinently asked to what extent did
he direct the young convert's attention towards the Jesuits. There
is no positive evidence to go on, but we have a close parallel. John
Walford,[3] another recent convert (1866), had taught at the Oratory
School, Edgbaston, at Newman's invitation, and he, too, feeling a
call to religious life, asked for advice. In his obituary we read:

> While happy in his work, he felt little, if any, inclination to join the
> Oratorian Congregation. It seemed to him that his own need was that he
> should be under vows of obedience, not only under a strict rule, from
> which he might free himself at any moment.[4] He talked over his future life
> with Cardinal Newman, who while expressing his entire satisfaction with

---

[1] 'Development of the Religious Orders', *The English Catholics 1850–1950* (1950),
p. 443.
[2] Quoted in Meriol Trevor's *Newman. Light in Winter* (1962), p. 376. Something of
what is intended by 'Englishness' in this context is to be found in the religious symposium edited by Maisie Ward, *The English Way. Studies in English Sanctity from St.
Bede to Newman* (1933). Among other names included are: St. Thomas of Canterbury,
Dame Juliana of Norwich, William Langland, St. John Fisher, St. Thomas More, and
Edmund Campion.
[3] John Thomas Walford (1834–94; see Boase iii, Sutcliffe), Jesuit priest, born at Hat-
field Peverell, nr. Chelmsford, Essex, on 27 Mar. 1834. Educated at Eton, and King's
College, Cambridge; Fellow, 1855–66; B.A., 1858; M.A., 1861. Assistant master at
Eton, 1861–5. Received into the R.C. Church, Mar. 1866. Entered the S.J. novitiate at
Roehampton in Sept. 1867; ordained priest in Apr. 1883. Taught for periods in Liverpool, Malta, Beaumont, Stonyhurst, and Preston. Died at Roehampton on 9 Jan. 1894.
(*Letters to Bridges*, pp. 5–6; *Further Letters*, pp. 43, 105, 106, 406.)
[4] After a two-year novitiate the Jesuit scholastic novice takes simple but perpetual
vows. The Oratorians are a Congregation of secular priests living under obedience with
an agreed rule of life but bound by no vows.

Walford's work at the Oratory, said: 'I think St. Ignatius wants you,' and those words decided his fate.[1]

Walford left the Oratory School to enter the Society when Hopkins arrived to take up his teaching post there. He had, of course, met Walford earlier,[2] and it seems to me reasonable to suggest that Walford's departure for Manresa also served to point the path for Hopkins.

Again, another Oxford convert, Richard Clarke,[3] sought Newman's advice at Edgbaston. He was sent to consult Fr. Henry Coleridge at Farm Street, and having been received into the Church, later joined the Society.[4]

But Newman's close and happy connection with the Jesuits, and with Fr. Coleridge in particular, has been noted more than once. It was Wilfrid Ward who pointed out that 'the English Jesuits, largely owing to the influence of Father Coleridge, were ever his good friends'.[5] More recently Meriol Trevor has told us: 'There was a wave of *Apologia* converts, some of whom Newman received himself. But he often sent those who lived in London to Father Henry Coleridge . . .'.[6]

It was Newman who advised Hopkins to discuss his vocation with the priest who came to give the Oratory boys their retreat in April 1868. This priest was Fr. Coleridge. The fact is, that in part at least, the Jesuits are indebted for Hopkins to Newman.

Replying to Hopkins's letter informing him of his decision to become a Jesuit, Newman, as we have seen, expressed himself surprised and glad: 'I think it is the very thing for you', he wrote. 'Don't call "the Jesuit discipline hard", it will bring you to heaven.'[7]

That Hopkins should have regarded the Jesuit discipline as hard seems a little strange when the distinctly ascetic strain in his nature is recalled. His fasting and practised self-control, the burning of his

[1] 'Father Walford', *LLNN*, xxii (July 1894), 508–9.
[2] *Letters to Bridges*, pp. 5–6.
[3] Richard Frederick Clarke (1839–1900). See *Journals and Papers*, pp. 421–2.
[4] Joseph Rickaby, 'In Memoriam, Richard Frederick Clarke', *The Month*, xcvi (Oct. 1900), 339.
[5] *The Life of John Henry Cardinal Newman*, ii (1912), 123.
[6] *Newman. Light in Winter* (1962), p. 347. Coleridge like Newman was a Fellow of Oriel.
[7] *Further Letters*, p. 408.

poems, and the resolution 'to give up all beauty until I had His leave for it',[1] leave little room for doubt as to the cast of his mind and the bent of his disposition. The loftiness of his ideals is obvious and increased as his priestly life progressed, so that he could write of himself later with a beautiful and revealing self-depreciation, 'I have never wavered in my vocation, but I have not lived up to it.'[2]

In the final analysis, only the individual himself can account for his vocation, and even he may not be able to render a full or adequate account. Hopkins, if taxed, might have said in reply what he wrote of his conversion '. . . it is God Who makes the decision and not I'.[3]

Perhaps the matter is best concluded with the reason offered by the man himself:

It is enough to say that the sanctity has not departed fr. the order to have a reason for joining it. Since I made up my mind to this I have enjoyed the first complete peace of mind I have ever had.[4]

---

[1] *Journals and Papers*, p. 71, entry for 6 Nov. 1865.
[2] *Correspondence with Dixon*, p. 88, in a letter dated 29 Oct.–2 Nov. 1881.
[3] *Further Letters*, p. 92.
[4] Ibid., p. 51.

CHAPTER 2

The Noviceship 1868-1870

WITH his vocation now decided and his entrance to the Society of
Jesus arranged, Hopkins had time to fill in until the date fixed for
entry to the novitiate. Like many another before entering religious
life, he used the opportunity for a final fling of travel abroad[1]—
in his case in Switzerland, and with an Oxford friend, Edward
Bond,[2] as companion. The expansive and closely observed impressions noted in his diary as he moved through the towns and villages
of the Alps stand in marked contrast to the balder entries which
precede and follow. The richness of his observation serves as an
index to his enjoyment as he notes the inscapes of people, trees,
and rocks.

A touch of that determination noticed earlier reveals itself in an
enigmatic incident when, unlike his companion, he refused to allow
the Swiss guide to carry his knapsack, provoking from the moun-
taineer the rebuke: 'Le bon Dieu n'est pas comme ça.'[3]

Hopkins, after his month abroad, returned to Hampstead at the
beginning of August and seems to have spent the remaining weeks
with his family and in leave-takings, until on Monday, 7 September
1868, he entered on his new life at Manresa House, Roehampton.[4]

How did he get there? In the afternoon or early evening of that
Monday he called on his grandmother to say goodbye, and his Aunt
Annie saw him to the station in Finchley Road where he caught a

---

[1] *Journals and Papers*, pp. 168-84.
[2] Ibid., pp. 302-3.
[3] Ibid., p. 177.
[4] See Herbert Thurston, 'The Romance of a Religious House', *The Month*, cxxviii
(Nov. 1916), 424-36; *The Jesuit Directory and Calendar . . . 1921*, ed. David H. Thompson (1921), pp. 100-1. The Jesuit novitiate moved from Roehampton in Sept. 1962 to
Harlaxton Manor, Grantham, Lincs., and in Sept. 1964 to Woodhall House, Juniper
Green, Edinburgh. Manresa House has now become Battersea Training College for
Teachers run by the London County Council. *Journals and Papers*, p. 401.

train to Richmond (Surrey).[1] Now if he had any luggage to speak of, and unless he was prepared to carry it for about two and a half miles, he probably took a cab through the park from Richmond to Roehampton. If we are prepared to accept an Edwardian instead of a Victorian picture, then the following account, *mutatis mutandis*, will help to recall the scene on arrival.

It was late afternoon on a mild, vaporous day in mid-November. A youth sat alone in a hansom cab that spanked along at ten mile an hour between rows of newish red-brick houses in suburban Barnes and out onto a road across the Common. Patches of faded heather and thickets of bramble stretched away on both sides. The hansom crossed the railway bridge, passed a pub where a red motorbus, with acetylene headlamps, stood with its engine running noisily, then turned to the left and sped up Roehampton Lane. . . . Although so near London, this was the country now. It had the opulent Edwardian look—dignified white houses with wrought-iron gates and spacious grounds beyond.[2]

But however he got there, we know he was amongst the last of the new novices to arrive.[3] Still the likelihood is that he was in for supper at 7.30, though it is possible that his first meal was breakfast as was the experience of one of his contemporaries, Henry Kerr.[4] Kerr had been a commander in the navy before he joined the Society a year ahead of Hopkins; his biographer has described his first breakfast:

Accordingly, at a quarter past eight on Sunday morning, Henry, with

---

[1] *Further Letters*, p. 104. Bradshaw lists the station as 'Finchley Road for St. John's'. In giving Bridges directions to reach Roehampton, Hopkins pointed out 'it is quite near, and easy of access by Putney or Barnes'. *Letters to Bridges*, p. 23.

[2] Denis Meadows, *Obedient Men* (New York, 1954), p. 3; cited hereafter as Meadows, *Obedient Men*.

[3] 'Whether I was last in that night I cannot quite make out', *Further Letters*, p. 104. The trains available on Monday afternoon 7 Sept. 1868 were:

> Finchley Road for St. John's   12.51   2.51   4.51   7.21
> Richmond arr.   1.34   3.37   5.34   8.6

[4] Henry Schomberg Kerr (1838–95; see Boase v, Sutcliffe), Jesuit priest, second son of Lord Henry Francis Charles Kerr (1800–82), rector of Dittisham, Devon, born on 15 Aug. 1838. Educated at Winchester and Glenalmond. Entered the Royal Navy; Commander, 16 Nov. 1866; retired Captain, Nov. 1881. Received into the R.C. Church, May 1855. Entered S.J. novitiate at Roehampton, 8 Sept. 1867, at the age of twenty-nine; ordained priest, Sept. 1875. Minister at Beaumont College, 1875–7. Attached to mission at Garnet Hill, Glasgow, 1877–8. Minister of Holy Name, Manchester, 1886–8; declined the Archbishopric of Bombay in 1886. Superior of the Zambezi mission from Mar. 1891 until his death at Grahamstown on 18 Aug. 1895. He had a brother a Jesuit, Fr. W. H. Kerr. (*Journals and Papers*, pp. 213, 257 (2), 262 (2).)

some thirty other novices, many of them 'new' like himself, sat down to breakfast. The 'new hands' were assigned a long table to themselves, at one end of which he had been placed, and he was glad to recognise at the other a friend whom he had met before in Nova Scotia. All the other faces were new to him; but they were most of them youthful enough, those of young men ranging from seventeen to twenty-one, and none of them whiskered, he was careful to notice, except his own. Meanwhile the older novices, for all their demureness, made as good use of their eyes as he did himself, since he remarks, 'I fancy all the greenhorns were pretty well measured up and down, and in and out, by the older ones,' who, no doubt, surveyed the new-comers with critical glances very much as drill-sergeants might a new batch of recruits.[1]

Supper finished, Hopkins would have made a short visit to the Blessed Sacrament and then have gone to his first community recreation in the novices' hall, or *aula*, described as having 'a fine ceiling, with baroque plaster work and a place where once a crystal chandelier had hung. The walls were covered with modern pine paneling, harmless but bleak.'[2] After recreation, Litanies would be recited in the chapel, and perhaps Fr. Fitzsimon, the Rector and novice master,[3] would have talked to his new charges and before they went to bed have given them points to meditate on the following morning.

Hopkins had a room of his own to begin with, but he knew from the outset that it was only a matter of time before he moved into a dormitory, or quarters,[4] which he would share with others, with only a cubicle to call his own. What were the cubicles like?

They were like stalls in a well-kept stable, except for the red curtains that could be drawn across the front. Our bags and suitcases had been put

[1] M. M. Maxwell Scott, *Henry Schomberg Kerr: Sailor and Jesuit* (1901), p. 92; cited hereafter as Scott, *H. S. Kerr*.

[2] Meadows, *Obedient Men*, p. 13.

[3] Christopher Fitzsimon (1815–81; see Foley vii, Sutcliffe), Jesuit priest, born at Broughal Castle, Offaly, Ireland, on 3 July 1815. Educated at Downside and Stony-hurst Colleges. Entered the S.J. novitiate at Hodder in Apr. 1834; ordained priest at Liège in Sept. 1843. Held various posts in the English Province—teaching at St. Mary's Hall, and Stonyhurst, 1844–7; 1851, Socius to the Provincial; 1862, Superior at St. Mary's Hall; 1863, Vice-rector at St. Beuno's. In 1864 appointed as Rector and novice master at Roehampton, retaining this position until Sept. 1869, and was thus GMH's first novice master. In later years he acted as Spiritual Father at Beaumont, Stonyhurst, Farm Street, and Manchester. In 1871 he was Superior at St. Mary's Hall when GMH was a second-year philosopher. Died at Stonyhurst on 24 June 1881. (*Further Letters*, p. 108; *Journals and Papers*, pp. 191, 227.)

[4] *Further Letters*, p. 105.

in the cubicles, where there was little room for anything more than a single iron bedstead, a washstand with a pitcher and basin, and a 'Charley,' or chamber pot, shoved modestly away underneath. An oblong piece of carpet of indeterminate color lay on the floor boards beside the bed.[1]

Twenty-five past five would have seen the novices up on this the first day, and after twenty-five minutes in which to wash, shave, and dress, they would go down to the chapel to make their morning offering of the day to God. They would then return to their quarters to make the morning meditation. After this to Mass. The day, 8 September, was a special one, the Nativity of the Virgin Mary, when those who had entered two years previously now pronounced their first vows. Today the ceremony is more spectacular than in Hopkins's time. For now those who have completed their novice-ship, new-rigged out from top to toe, and with a brand new gown— till now they have worn older Jesuits' cast-offs—take their vows during the community Mass. What happens is this. After the priest celebrating Mass has himself communicated, he turns round as usual holding the host over the ciborium and says the customary 'Behold the Lamb of God'. Then he turns back to the altar and each novice proceeding in alphabetical order repeats the vow formula. When all have pronounced their vows the priest turns round again and gives the Holy Eucharist to each. But in Hopkins's time it was different.

In a tiny chapel upstairs, lit by a skylight . . . Father Fitzsimon sat near a small table on which stood a crucifix, and we entered singly one after another, as though going to confession, and kneeling, took our vows in secret,—this as a precaution, because of the Penal Clause in the Eman-cipation Act forbidding the presence of Jesuits in England. The Master of Novices merely answered *Amen*, took the written formula of the vows, and the young Religious withdrew.[2]

I suppose it is an interesting fact that one of the first events a new novice witnesses is a passing-out parade. Hopkins, however, says nothing of this in his first letter home but tells his mother of the other new arrivals: 'There are five novices besides myself now entered and another is expected.'[3] He also mentions that he and the

---

[1] Meadows, *Obedient Men*, p. 14.
[2] 'Reminiscences of Novice-days 1865', *LLNN*, xxx (Apr. 1910), 387–8.
[3] *Further Letters*, p. 104.

other newcomers 'do not as yet mix with the other novices'.[1] The purpose of this segregation is explained by R. F. Clarke.

The new-comers are not at once admitted to the ranks of the noviceship; they spend their first week or ten days separate from the rest, and during that time the rules of the Society are put into their hands, and are explained to them; they are instructed as to the kind of life they will have to live, and the difficulties that they will have to encounter. They have to study the 'Summary of the constitutions,' in which is set forth the end and object of the Society, the spirit that must animate its members, the obedience they must be ready to practise, the sacrifice of their own will and judgment that they must be prepared to make; in fact, they have every possible opportunity given them of ascertaining what it is that they are undertaking when they declare their intention of serving God in the Society according to its laws and constitutions. Of course, there are but few who realise at first all that is involved in the sacrifice they are making; but this must be the case with all who are entering on a new and difficult career. After they have spent a few days in studying the obligation they are going to accept, they are put into retreat for a short time, during which they are kept in perfect silence, and have to spend their time in listening to a series of instructions on the fundamental truths of religion given by the master of novices, each instruction containing a number of suggestive thoughts, on which they have to meditate for an hour after the instruction is finished.

When this time of retirement is over, they are duly received as novices, and are clad in the Jesuit habit.[2]

During this probationary period Hopkins and the other new novices were shepherded by two second-year novices who acted as 'Angel Guardians'.[3] John Walford, Robert Bridges's friend, whom Hopkins had met at Birmingham,[4] was one of these; the other is

---

[1] Ibid., p. 105.

[2] 'The Training of a Jesuit', *The Nineteenth Century*, xl (Aug. 1896), 215, cited hereafter as Clarke, 'Training of a Jesuit'. Fr. R. F. Clarke has already been mentioned amongst the distinguished Oxford converts who joined the Society of Jesus. For an account of his life see *The Times* for 11 Sept. 1900; *The Month*, xcvi (Oct. 1900), 337–44; *Journals and Papers*, pp. 421–2. What makes Fr. Clarke's article particularly relevant to a study of Hopkins's training as a Jesuit is that he himself joined the Society only three years after Hopkins and so his account is virtually contemporary; he, too, had Fr. Gallwey as novice master.

[3] Hopkins in his turn was an 'Angel Guardian' to Walter Ratcliff (b. 16 May 1840), who came to the noviceship on 13 Apr. 1869; Ratcliff left the Society in 1873, see *Journals and Papers*, p. 239.

[4] *Letters to Bridges*, pp. 5–6.

not stated. During this time, too, Fr. Fitzsimon saw them frequently as these entries from the Porter's Journal[1] show:

Sept. 9th. [1868]

Fr. Rector again saw new Novices in Lay-brothers' Recreation room at 4.

Sept. 11th.

Fr. Rector saw the new novices in lay-brothers' recreation room at 9.45.

Sept. 13th.

Fr. Rector began to see the new novices singly at 9.

How long Hopkins's 'probation "week" ' lasted is not clear.

What would strike present-day Jesuits as very strange is that Hopkins and his fellow novices began the Long Retreat in less than a fortnight after entering the noviceship. This is to be plunged in at the deep end indeed.

It consists of thirty days occupied exclusively in prayer, meditation, and similar employments. Five times a day the master of novices gives points of meditation to the assembled novices, and they have subsequently to spend the following hour in a careful pondering over the points proposed to them, . . . A regular system is followed; during the first few days the subjects proposed are the end for which man is created, the means by which he is to attain that end, the evils of sin and its consequences, and the four last things, death, judgment, heaven, and hell. During the second portion of the retreat the Kingdom of Christ, His Incarnation, Nativity, and His life on earth occupy the thoughts of the novices for a space of ten or twelve days, with separate meditations on the two standards of Christ and Satan, under one of which every one is fighting, on the tactics of the evil one, the choice that has to be bravely made of a life of hardship under the standard of the Cross, and other subjects akin to these. During a third period of four or five days the Passion of Christ is dwelt upon in detail, and finally some two or three days of the joyful subjects of the Resurrection, the appearances of our Lord to his disciples, the Ascension, with one or two concluding meditations on the love of God and the means of attaining it, bring the retreat to an end. Three recreation days are interposed between the various portions of the retreat, which are spent in long walks, and in recovering from the fatigue which is caused by the constant mental strain involved in the long time of meditation and prayer. Except

---

[1] The Porter, or Beadle, is a second-year novice appointed by the novice master to help in the general ordering of the day-to-day duties of the noviceship; he passes on the Superior's instructions and does what he can to see that they are carried out. One of his duties is to keep a Journal.

during these three days there is no time of recreation, and silence has to be strictly kept throughout.[1]

It would seem that Hopkins was misinformed when he wrote, 'The retreat begins I believe on Monday',[2] for it actually began on Wednesday, 16 September, according to the Porter's Journal. The retreat itself was given by Fr. Fitzsimon, the novice master, and Hopkins mentions the repose days which in this retreat occurred on 24 September, and 5 and 13 October. The usual practice during the Long Retreat is that letters are neither written nor received, thereby enabling the retreatant to cut himself off as far as possible from all secular interests. This was the rule in Hopkins's time, despite his expectations to the contrary.[3]

Hopkins did not keep his diary during the retreat and only at the beginning did he permit himself to note, 'Chestnuts as bright as coals or spots of vermilion'[4] which gestated to emerge nine years later as 'Fresh-firecoals, chestnut-falls' in 'Pied Beauty'. His decision to 'keep no regular weather-journal but only notes'[5] may have formed part of the resolution which exercitants are encouraged to form during the retreat. Hopkins does not say when the Long Retreat ended but the Porter's Journal supplies the information:

Sunday, Oct. 18th.
Te Deum sung at Benediction in thanksgiving for all graces received during the Spiritual Exercises.

And with this exacting task completed the novice master went away for a short rest, while the novices, the new now merged with the old,

---

[1] Clarke, 'Training of a Jesuit', p. 218. The practice in recent years in the English Province has been for those who enter on 7 Sept. to begin the Long Retreat on 14 Oct., and finish on 13 Nov., the feast of St. Stanislaus, patron of novices. But other novice masters have favoured different arrangements. For example, when Fr. Gallwey became novice master the Long Retreat began on 25 Nov. and ended at Christmas, see *Journals and Papers*, p. 195. Apparently Fr. Fitzsimon made a practice of beginning the Long Retreat early, see Scott, *H. S. Kerr*, p. 94. Fr. Devlin has asserted, 'It seems certain that the First Week of his *noviceship* Long Retreat had contained the profound religious experience which was reproduced much later in the first part of *The Wreck of the Deutschland'. Sermons and Devotional Writings*, p. 12.

[2] *Further Letters*, p. 105. GMH gave the correct date in his diary, see *Journals and Papers*, p. 189, entry for 16 Sept.

[3] '. . . this may perhaps give me the chance of writing.' *Further Letters*, p. 105.

[4] *Journals and Papers*, p. 189, entry for 17 Sept.

[5] Ibid., entry for 18 Sept.

were given the brief respite of 'long sleeps', that is, of getting up in
the morning half an hour later. The Manresa Minister's Journal[1]
makes this clear:

Oct. 19th.
Long Retreat over. Rose at 5.30 b'fast at 8.30. Meat for breakfast—dinner
at 2.30. Fr. Fitzsimon went to Beaumont.

With the Long Retreat behind him, and the return to regular
daily recreations, Hopkins could now inquire about the community
he found himself in. What did he find? The Province catalogue for
that year shows that at Manresa there were in all forty-nine men
divided as follows: a Rector and novice master, a Minister, nine
Jesuit lay-brothers, thirty scholastic novices—including one former
secular priest—and eight lay-brother novices or postulants. These
groups constitute separate 'communities' which normally operate
independently, but which would mix occasionally, for example, on
certain important feast days. In Hopkins's first year at Manresa there
were no Juniors[2] there. For since 1867 the influx of novices had
made it necessary to send the Juniors to Stonyhurst, or Belgium, in
order to make room for the newcomers. However, additional accom-
modation was provided and the catalogue for 1869–70 shows that
the Juniors had returned to Manresa, thereby reintroducing an
additional 'community' and swelling the total to sixty-six. The
Juniors, too, had an ordo of their own.

During Hopkins's first week the purpose and general methods and
working of the noviceship would have been set out by Fr. Fitzsimon.
Hopkins would have learned that the aim of the Society was twofold
—personal sanctification and the sanctification of one's neighbour.
The noviceship would put his vocation to the test and this would be
achieved through a number of experiments which Fr. Pollen[3] has
summarized as follows:

---

[1] The Manresa Journal is a handwritten account of daily happenings and items of
interest written by the Fr. Minister at Manresa House. It is different from, and not to
be confused with, the Porter's Journal, nor yet with GMH's own private Journal.

[2] The Juniorate was the post-noviceship stage, usually of two years' duration, and was
a prelude to the philosophy course. It provided those who needed it with an opportunity
for further study of secular subjects. It will be referred to again later.

[3] John Hungerford Pollen (1858–1925). His account is valuable because he entered
the Society in 1877, and therefore the situation and conditions described approximate
fairly closely to those experienced by Hopkins. In GMH's time novices did not do the

Wherever it is possible some are submitted to certain tests of their vocation and usefulness: to teaching catechism in the village churches; to attendance on the sick in hospitals; to going about on a pilgrimage or missionary journey without money or other provision. As soon as possible all make the spiritual exercises for thirty days. This is really the chief test of a vocation, as it is also in epitome the main work of the two years of the novitiate and for that matter of the entire life of a Jesuit. On these exercises the Constitutions, the life, and activity of the Society are based, so that they are really the chief factor in forming the character of a Jesuit. In accordance with the ideals set forth in these exercises, of disinterested conformity with God's will, and of personal love of Jesus Christ, the novice is trained diligently in a meditative study of the truths of religion, in the habit of self-knowledge, in a constant scrutiny of his motives and of the actions inspired by them, in the correction of every form of self-deceit, illusion, plausible pretext, and in the education of his will, particularly in making choice of what seems best after careful deliberation and without self-seeking. Deeds, not words, are insisted upon as proof of genuine service, and a mechanical, emotional, or fanciful piety is not tolerated. As the novice gradually thus becomes master of his judgment and will, he grows more and more capable of offering to God the reasonable service enjoined by St. Paul, and seeks to follow the Divine will, as manifested by Jesus Christ, by His vicar on earth, by the bishops appointed to rule His Church, by his more immediate or religious superiors, and by the civil powers rightfully exercising authority. This is what is meant by Jesuit obedience, the characteristic virtue of the order, such a sincere respect for authority as to accept its decisions and comply with them, not merely by outward performance but in all sincerity with the conviction that compliance is best, and that the command expresses for the time the will of God, as nearly as it can be ascertained.[1]

Soon the novices were following the regular noviceship timetable, and since we are fortunate enough to possess the ordo followed by Fr. Gallwey, Hopkins's second novice master, I quote it directly.

They rise at 5.30, make a short visit to the chapel at 6, in order to make their morning oblation of the day to God, and from 6 to 7 make their meditation. . . . At 6.55 the bell rings for Holy Mass, and all the novices repair to the chapel. After Mass, which occupies half an hour, another quarter of an hour is assigned to a reconsideration of the meditation and

pilgrimage or hospital experiments, see Clarke, 'Training of a Jesuit', 217–18. For some account of Pollen see J. Keating, 'Father John Hungerford Pollen, S.J.', *The Month*, cxlv (May 1925), 446–8; an appreciation and obituary will be found in *The Tablet*, 2 May 1925, pp. 590, 604, which mistakenly gives 1876 for his entrance to the Society instead of 1877.

[1] 'Society of Jesus', *Cath. Encycl.* xiv. 83–4.

the care with which it was made, and to the writing down of any thoughts that may have suggested themselves in the course of it. Breakfast is at 7.45, and at 8.30 the novices have to be present, each at his little desk, for half an hour's reading of *Rodriguez on Christian Perfection.* At 9 an instruction on the rules is given by the master of novices, after which they have to make their beds and arrange their little cells, and, when this is done, to repair to some appointed place, where one of their number, appointed for the purpose, assigns to each a certain amount of manual labour—dusting, sweeping, washing up dishes and plates, laying the refectory for dinner, sometimes cleaning and scrubbing, and other menial offices of the humblest description. At 10.15 they have to learn by heart, for a quarter of an hour, some portion of the rules of the Society, or such prayers, psalms, or ecclesiastical hymns, the knowledge of which may be useful to the young ecclesiastic. After this they have some free time, during which they can walk in the grounds, pray in the chapel, or read some Life of the saints or other spiritual book. At 11.30 they assemble for 'out-door manual works,' which consist in chopping and sawing wood for fuel, sweeping up leaves, picking up leaves, weeding the flower beds, or some similar occupation allotted to them by one of the older novices, who is termed 'master of out-door works.' At 12.30 they return to the house, and at 12.40 the bell summons them to the chapel, where they spend fifteen minutes in prayer, and in examining their consciences as to how they have performed the various duties of the morning, whether they have kept silence (for during all this time no talking is allowed), obeyed promptly and exactly, kept up a remembrance of God in all that they have done, showed kindness and consideration for others, executed the work assigned to them in the best manner possible, &c.

The dinner-bell rings at 1, and all repair to the refectory. During dinner a portion of Holy Scripture is read aloud, and some useful and edifying book, the life of one of the saints, or the history of the Society. After dinner a short visit is made to the chapel, and an hour's recreation follows. The occupations of the afternoon are a repetition of those of the earlier portion of the day, save that on three days in the week a walk of about two hours has to be taken in companies of two or three. No one is allowed to choose his companions, but the master of novices arranges the various companies. Sometimes a game of cricket or football is substituted for the walk. At 6 a second hour [period?] of meditation of half an hour has to be made in the chapel, after which the recital of some vocal prayers, and some free time which they can dispose of for themselves, bring them on to supper at 7.30. After this they have an hour's recreation, during the first half-hour of which Latin has to be spoken. At 9, night prayers in the chapel; then fifteen minutes spent in the preparation of their meditation of the following morning, and after a final examination of conscience on their performance of the duties of the day all lights are put out by 10 p.m., and the novices sleep their well-earned sleep in their dormitories.[1]

Governed as he was by such a closely packed ordo, I think we can more readily understand why Hopkins told his mother, 'Just now I cannot write any more because of the post and disposition of our times.'[2] And again, when he apologized to Bridges, 'I have not till today had an opportunity of writing to you, as I wished to do.'[3] Perhaps the pressure on his time accounts for the relative paucity in his diary entries for this period. Certainly he has taken to writing up his diary after a considerable lapse.[4]

With the time-table established we can now attempt to fill out the skeleton. For the sake of convenience I have decided to treat the noviceship training under three broad headings: religious formation, recreation, and domestic and public events. Finally, this chapter concludes with some personal details concerning Hopkins, and the manuscript of the Journal kept by Hopkins when he was Porter. As might be expected, the section on religious formation is the lengthiest: I deal with it first.

Foremost amongst the factors which go to form the novice is the Church's liturgy and her liturgical year; and although it would be incorrect to regard the eighteen-sixties as viewing the liturgy with the renewed interest of our own times, it is still true to say that the life of the noviceship was closely geared to the liturgical year. In addition to the major divisions of that year—Advent, Christmas, Lent, Easter, and Pentecost—the great feast days were also solemnly celebrated, such as the Ascension, the Assumption, SS. Peter and Paul, and All Saints, not to mention the feasts proper to the Society of Jesus itself. As an Anglican Hopkins was highly conscious of liturgy as the entries in his diary and the dating of some of his

---

[1] Clarke, 'Training of a Jesuit', pp. 215–17.

[2] *Further Letters*, p. 105. Compare with this Hopkins's view of the tertianship expressed in a letter to Bridges, where he speaks of 'a day so sliced up into the duties of a noviceship as this life is', *Letters to Bridges*, p. 137.

[3] Ibid., p. 25. GMH was not alone in finding himself with little time to spare. Augustus Law commented, 'we never have an idle moment', Ellis Schreiber, *The Life of Augustus Henry Law* (1893), p. 88. And Denis Meadows speaks of 'the luxury of a few minutes of spare time', *Obedient Men*, p. 53.

[4] '(I was made porter on the 12th of the month, I think, . . .)', from his diary entry for 23 Dec. 1869, *Journals and Papers*, p. 193.

letters show.[1] Of his personal reaction to the liturgy and spiritual reading he gives us just a glimpse:

> One day in the Long Retreat (which ended on Xmas Day) they were reading in the refectory Sister Emmerich's account of the Agony in the Garden and I suddenly began to cry and sob and could not stop. I put it down for this reason, that if I had been asked a minute beforehand I should have said that nothing of the sort was going to happen and even when it did I stood in a manner wondering at myself not seeing in my reason the traces of an adequate cause for such strong emotion—the traces of it I say because of course the cause in itself is adequate for the sorrow of a lifetime. I remember much the same thing on Maundy Thursday when the presanctified Host was carried to the sacristy.[2]

The books selected for refectory reading[3] are often chosen deliberately because of the feast or season. So, too, there was special reading matter during the Long Retreat, the annual community retreat, and the tridua.[4] The value and formative influence of some of the spiritual classics which recur regularly it would be difficult to overestimate—the Scriptures go without saying—I am thinking, for instance, of *The Imitation of Christ*, Parson's *Christian Directory*, and Rodriguez, *Practice of Perfection*. The general pattern of reading would be as follows: at dinner a passage of Scripture from Old or New Testaments, then perhaps a devotional book, hagiography, history of the Church or the Society, or the bishop's 'Pastoral

[1] For example: 'Rogation day' 1866; 'The Assumption' 1867; 'Palm Sunday', 'Maundy Thursday' 1868, *Journals and Papers*, pp. 135, 151, and 163 respectively.

[2] Ibid., p. 195. The Long Retreat referred to was not that made by Hopkins but that given to the first-year novices when he was in his second year at the novitiate. That Anne Catherine Emmerich's book *The Dolorous Passion of Our Lord Jesus Christ* impressed GMH greatly is clear not only from this extract but from the fact that he is still referring to this work a decade later, see the index to *Sermons and Devotional Writings*. For a critical discussion of Sister Emmerich's 'visions' see the following articles by Fr. Herbert Thurston, S.J.: 'The Problem of Anne Catherine Emmerich, Pts. I–IV', *The Month*, cxxxviii (Sept.–Dec. 1921), 237–48, 344–56, 429–39, 519–30; 'The Stigmata of Sister Emmerich', ibid., cxl (Aug. 1922), 158–63; 'The Authenticity of the Emmerich Visions', ibid., cxliii (Jan. 1924), 42–52; 'Anne Catherine Emmerich', ibid., cxliii (Mar. 1924), 256–60; 'The Emmerich Problem yet again', ibid., cxlv (Apr. 1925), 355–8; see also *Dictionnaire de spiritualité*, tom. IV (Paris, 1960).

[3] See Appendix 2A. Refectory Reading in the Novitiate (Manresa House, Roehampton), 7 Sept. 1868–7 Sept. 1870.

[4] The dates were as follows: Long Retreat: 16 Sept.–18 Oct. 1868; 25 Nov.–25 Dec. 1869; Community retreat: 31 Aug.–7 Sept. 1869 and 1870; Tridua: 11–13 Jan.; 31 May–2 June 1869; 13–15 Jan. 1870.

Letter', finishing with the day's Roman Martyrology in Latin.[1] At supper the *Menology* was read in French, followed by the book being currently read. This pattern was not invariable but could be modified, or even omitted, for instance, when sermons were preached at meals, or when 'Deo gratias' was given and talking was allowed. The purpose of the reading at mealtimes—breakfast is taken in silence—is stated in the Rule: 'While by eating the body is refreshed let the soul also have her food.'[2] In addition to this public spiritual reading, each novice had a religious book to read in private for half an hour daily. A portion of *The Imitation* was read every day, and another thirty minutes, 8.30–9.00 a.m. as the ordo given by Fr. Clarke shows, was spent in reading Rodriguez, *Practice of Perfection and Christian Virtues*.[3]

The novices increased in awareness of the liturgy chiefly through attendance at daily Mass with its changing proper according to the feast or season.

Not all days were alike, for unlike present custom, the novices did not receive Holy Communion daily. Actually, we know what their precise practice was:

Communion Days for Ours & Benediction Days. (F. Fitzsimon).[4]

Besides all Sundays, Holydays of obligation, Feasts of Saints of the

---

[1] Secular books read will call for comment later.

[2] Pars Constitutionum III c. 1 n. 5. This and future references to matters concerning the Jesuit Constitutions can be found in *Institutum Societatis Iesu*, 3 vols. (Florence, 1892–3).

[3] Some old Customs' Books of the noviceship contain the rule: 'The Novices of the first year read Rodriguez in English, and those of the second year in French. A Kempis & Holy Scripture always in Latin.' Further, the Porter's Journal for 11 Sept. 1864 states: 'Crétineau's History [Crétineau-Joly, *Histoire religieuse, politique et littéraire de la Compagnie de Jésus*, 6 vols., Paris, 1844–56] given to Novices of 2nd year, also French ed. of Rodriguez.' The novitiate still contains copies of these books. It will have been noted above that the *Menology* was read in French at supper; it is entered in the Porter's Journal as 'Ménologe' as part of the entry for 31 Dec. 1868. One would like to know more about their knowledge of French. Andrew Steinmetz tells us that in his day (1838), 'All the novices had acquired the French language, and were well grounded in Latin', *The Novitiate* (1846), p. 103. And again, discussing a Christian doctrine course he writes, 'The book was in French, and each novice, when his turn came round, . . . translated it into English, as if he were reading an English book', ibid., p. 177. Doubtless GMH took it in his stride despite the modest disclaimer recorded in his Journal for 2 May 1866: 'Reading Maurice de Guérin's Remains, enjoying but without sufficient knowledge of French.' *Journals and Papers*, p. 133.

[4] This manuscript note and that immediately following on Benediction are taken

Society & such Feasts of our Lady & the Apostles as are Doubles of 1st or 2nd class, there are the following:

Mar. 12.	June 24.
Maundy Thursday.	Aug. 7.
May 3.	Sept. 14.
May 16.	Sept. 27.
Feast of the S. Heart.	Sept. 29.
	(at Manresa Dec. 28.)

First Fridays of the month for all, & all Fridays for lay-brothers (ad libitum).

Benediction.[1]

Besides the above mentioned days, all through the Octaves of Corpus Christi, & St. Ignatius, & (at least in the Colleges) each day of St. Francis Xavier's Novena in March, & immediately after Mass on Jan. 30 for health, and Oct. 2nd against fire, and on the re-opening of schools.

It will have been noticed that the note mentioned the devotion in honour of the Sacred Heart which was observed on the first Friday of each month. Another special devotion was that of choosing a novice to go to Communion on a Wednesday. The Porter's Journal records:

Wednesday, April 14th [1869]
Br. G. Hopkins went to Holy Communion in honour of St. Joseph.

Other devotions practised included the Ten Fridays in honour of St. Francis Xavier, and the Six Sundays in honour of St. Aloysius.

Mental prayer is of the utmost importance in the training of religious, and to this end the novices meditated twice a day, for an hour in the morning and half an hour in the evening followed in both cases by a short period of reflection. The foundations of meditation were laid down during the Long Retreat by the novice master, who also taught them different methods of prayer. Fr. Clarke has preserved for us an example of Fr. Gallwey's points for meditation.

Subject of the Meditation: 'Let us make haste to enter into our eternal rest' (Hebrews iv. 11).

from the inside back cover of the Manresa Journal, vol. 2 (1875–84). Some abbreviations have been expanded.
   [1] On nights when they did not have Benediction, Litanies were recited in common in chapel.

Point 1.—How are we to make haste towards eternal rest with God? It is certain that he who during the hours of the day most frequently does the very thing that his Father in Heaven wishes is he who during that day makes most progress. Penance will not advance us if we do it when our Father in Heaven wishes us not to do penance. Prayer will only retard us if prayer is not our Father's will at the moment. Resting when He wishes us to rest, labouring when He wishes us to labour, speaking and being silent just as He wishes—this is the short and direct road to our eternal repose.

Point 2.—This life is a time of traffic. 'Traffic till I come,' our Lord says. He who traffics most wisely is the one who is making most haste to enter into his eternal repose. St. Paul tells us how to carry on our spiritual business. 'Some,' he says, 'build with gold and precious stones and silver on the foundations of faith. Others with wood, stubble, and hay.' We build with gold and precious stones when our intention is very good; with hay and stubble when our intention is unworthy. Two men read the same book or work together; how different the value of their work according to their intention!

Point 3.—Of all the ways of making haste to heaven and to God, there is none so rapid as the way of charity and love. 'Many sins are forgiven, because she loved much.' How slow and how weary a task it is to conceal sins by any other process!

Beg very earnestly for an increase of Divine love, in order that you may run in the way of God's commandments.[1]

Points such as these would be given by the novice master or prepared by the novice himself during the quarter of an hour, 9.15–9.30 p.m., before going to bed. The following morning he ponders the points during the hour devoted to the morning meditation, that is, from six to seven o'clock, ending with some good resolution, and a short prayer that he may keep it during the ensuing day.

Hopkins noted in his Journal an occasion when Fr. Gallwey gave points on the Apostles[2] but tells us little about the actual subject discussed, or the way in which it was treated. More informative of Gallwey's method is the account given by Fr. Charles Blount:

The phrase, 'Points for Meditation,' had a special application to his method of preparing the subject for mental prayer. He *pointed out*, as with the finger, all sorts of unexpected aspects and illustrations of the

---

[1] Clarke, 'Training of a Jesuit', p. 216.
[2] *Journals and Papers*, p. 193. This entry of 23 Dec. is more intrinsically interesting for what it tells us of GMH's conscious awareness of dreaming.

matter in hand, and each of these seemed, almost at once, the moment it was presented, to incline the will to some devout desire or sentiment. Seldom was there suggested any formal process of reasoning, calculated to lead in a systematic way to a definite conclusion. The concrete example and illustration was the chief means for arousing the will. If, to take the first sentence of the Foundation Exercise of St. Ignatius, he was proposing for meditation the truth that man is created to praise God, he did not reason from the nature of man and of God, and the meaning of the word *praise*; but immediately the way in which a man praises a person or a thing was brought up before the mind, and it was felt that some similar conduct was the becoming one for a man towards his Maker. A Meditation on Death, as given by Father Gallwey, was more likely to be a contemplation of the administration and reception of the Sacrament of Extreme Unction, than any consideration of the shortness and uncertainty of life, or of the nature of death, followed by the conclusions which naturally flow from such considerations.[1]

Novices trained by Fr. Gallwey had much to be grateful for in his enlightened approach to their religious formation, and it was not for nothing that he was called 'an acknowledged master of the spiritual life'.[2] His biography states that when he was appointed novice master, 'He set himself at once to introduce what he believed to be the main principle of progress in the spiritual life, that of making experiments. You never know what you can do till you try.'[3] And a good example of one of his innovations is given.

Formerly the points of meditation were read out[4] by one of the novices for all from an appointed book; now when the Rector did not propose them, every one made them for himself out of a book, which he chose with the approval of his Superior, though it was considered better still if a novice could prepare his meditation directly from the Gospels, or even the Epistles of St. Paul.[5]

Other spiritual duties may be mentioned briefly. Twice during the day, before dinner and before going to bed, an examination of conscience was made, five decades of the rosary were fitted in as well as some vocal prayer, and short visits were made to the Blessed

[1] Michael Gavin, *Memoirs of Father P. Gallwey, S.J.* (1913), pp. 154–5; cited hereafter as Gavin, *Memoirs of Fr. Gallwey.*
[2] Ibid., p. 22.   [3] Ibid., p. 159.
[4] Cf. 'Then followed the reading of the "Points" of the meditation for the next morning . . .', Andrew Steinmetz, *The Novitiate* (1846), p. 115.
[5] Gavin, *Memoirs of Fr. Gallwey*, pp. 160–1.

Sacrament after dinner and supper. All in all, time spent in mental and vocal prayer, spiritual reading, and other pious practices accounted for four-and-a-half to five hours of the novice's day.

Hopkins, as we saw earlier, as an Anglican and with the fervour of adolescence in practising austerities had sometimes allowed zeal to outstrip prudence. But in the novitiate he would be allowed to practise only such penances as his Superior judged fit. This in itself was an act of obedience. In the matter of penance Fr. Gallwey, far from stifling spontaneity, upheld the view that it is what you do

of your own initiative, extra prayer or mortification or work of any kind which really counts. Sanctification is the business of the individual, and cannot be managed in companies under a drill-master, however useful and necessary drill may be in itself.[1]

However, for the six months' custody-of-the-eyes penance[2] lasting from January to July 1869, Hopkins would almost certainly have asked and obtained the novice master's permission. On the other hand, Fr. Fitzsimon showed the prudence we would expect in not allowing him to keep the somewhat rigorous fast of the times.[3]

[1] Ibid., p. 159.
[2] *Journals and Papers*, p. 190, entry for 24 Jan.
[3] '. . . I am not allowed to fast in Lent.' From a letter dated 7 Feb. 1869, *Further Letters*, p. 106.
The following regulations appear in *The Catholic Directory* for 1869, p. 5.

Fasting Days in England.
On which flesh-meat is forbidden, and only one meal, with a collation, allowed to those who are bound to fast.

The Forty Days of Lent; the Ember Days; the Vigils of Whitsunday, SS. Peter and Paul, the Assumption, All Saints, and Christmas; and the Wednesdays and Fridays in Advent.

Abstinence Days in England.
On which flesh-meat is forbidden.

The Sundays in Lent, unless leave be given to eat meat on them, and all Fridays, except the Friday on which Christmas Day may fall.

Manresa House, Roehampton, coming under the jurisdiction of the diocese of Southwark, the following modifications applied:

Lenten Dispensations
Granted with leave of His Holiness, 1869.

1. Flesh meat is allowed at the single meal of those who are bound to fast, and at the discretion of those who are not so bound, on all days except Wednesdays and Fridays, Ember Saturday, and the four last days in Holy Week. On Sundays even those who are bound to fast may eat flesh meat at their discretion.

2. Eggs are allowed at the single meal of those who are bound to fast, and at the

Other corporal mortifications in moderation were practised throughout the year but they all required the consent of the Superior. Here again the liturgy was underlined, and penances would not be undertaken at Christmas, Easter, and Whitsun, or on the more important feasts.

Penances could also play their part in inculcating humility, as Denis Meadows reminds us:

> Most of the novices wished to do extra penances . . . but the rector was sparing of permissions. The devout, however, might go in for spiritual mortification by penances in the refectory. They were not physically onerous. After grace and before the reading began, you 'told your fault' in the framework of a formula: 'Reverend Fathers and loving Brothers, by order of holy obedience I tell my fault [then you named it], for which fault holy obedience enjoins on me the penance of [whatever it was].' The faults were usually small violations of rule or carelessness about property of the house. We broke a good many plates and dishes in our two years, and that was a fault against religious poverty. The penances were minor humiliations, like kissing the feet of the novices at the nearest table, or taking your own meal on bended knees at the 'little table.' This last was rather trying, as you were immediately under the eye of your superior a few feet away.[1]

Another way the novice is taught humility is by having his external faults pointed out to him. With the novice master present, his fellow novices mention in a spirit of charity the defects they have noticed in him.[2] He is also expected to help in the correction of others. An extension of this attempt at self-conquest is the practice of private admonitions. Each novice has an admonitor appointed

discretion of those who are not so bound, on all days except Ash Wednesday and the three last days of Holy Week.

3. Cheese under the same restrictions, is allowed on all days except Ash Wednesday and Good Friday.

4. The use of dripping and lard is permitted at dinner and collation on all days, except Good Friday.

On those days, Sundays during Lent included, whereon by dispensation flesh meat is allowed, fish is not permitted at the same meal. This rule applies to all fasting days throughout the year.

[1] *Obedient Men*, p. 119.

[2] Even in the admittedly difficult business of trying to grow in virtue there always lurks the danger of exaggerated self-importance. As a corrective to this I like the story of the novice who once asked permission, as an exercise in humiliation, to make himself ridiculous in public. The Superior's reply must have been peculiarly soothing to his feelings, 'Don't strain, my dear brother, don't strain; it will come naturally.'

for a specified time to observe and correct him and in turn he performs the office for some one else.

Training in obedience is of no less importance than in humility. The special object of the young Jesuit's life in the noviceship, Fr. Clarke maintains

has been to train him up in that spirit of implicit and unquestioning obedience which is the aim of the Society of Jesus to cultivate more than any other virtue in her sons, simply because it is the virtue that underlies all the rest, and without which no other virtue can attain its full perfection in the soul of man. The routine of monotonous and often apparently useless employments has for its object to foster the habit of what is rightly called blind obedience. The novice is taught to obey his superior without ever questioning the wisdom of the order given; the perfection of Jesuit obedience includes not only the obedience of the will, so that he does what is commanded promptly, bravely, and thoroughly, but also an obedience of the judgment, so that he regards what is commanded as the best thing possible for him. Here it is that Jesuit obedience differs from the obedience practised generally by a good subordinate in the world. In the army or in a house of business, blind obedience is necessary to efficient action. No well-ordered system could be carried on successfully without it; if the subordinate obeyed only where he approved of the wisdom of the command given the results would be fatal to any well-organised community. It is the habit, the difficult habit of abstaining from any mental criticism of the order given that is the distinctive feature of the obedience of the Society of Jesus.[1]

But in addition to being practised in humility and obedience the novices had also to learn the theory. If they were to understand all that the vows they were preparing to take comprised, they must be instructed not only in what the vow itself entails but also in the perfection of the virtue. The instruction would also have included a systematic study of the rules.

Hopkins during the two years he spent at Manresa listened to

[1] 'Training of a Jesuit', p. 219. Fr. Clarke continues with an anecdote of a military officer who found the army discipline easier to bear than that of the novitiate—'in the army you can swear to relieve your feelings'. On the other hand, Fr. Law thought the obedience demanded in the navy 'blinder' than that asked of Jesuits, see Ellis Schreiber's *Life of Augustus Henry Law* (1893), p. 116. For a different view from Fr. Clarke's on obedience see Gavin, *Memoirs of Fr. Gallwey*, pp. 11–13, where the author draws the reader's attention to what he considers to be the implications of St. Ignatius's famous Letter on Obedience. The text of this letter will be found in *Institutum Societatis Iesu*, iii. 27–33.

exhortations five days a week from his two novice masters, Fr. Fitzsimon and Fr. Gallwey. Of the former's approach we have little record. 'He was', we are told, 'greatly revered by his novices as a man of God, brimful of fervour, and as possessing in a remarkable degree that twofold spirit of prayer and self-denial, which was the ever recurring refrain of his exhortations.'[1] In the case of Fr. Gallwey we are somewhat better off, for although we have no complete summary of his subject matter, we have an account which reveals something of the man's personality and methods. We have the word of one who was a novice under him for it, that it was in his exhortations that his gifts were seen at their best.

In these Exhortations the spiritual life, and in particular, the life of the perfect Jesuit, was presented in the most vivid and winning manner, so that one who was no mean judge said of them, that they were the best examples of true rhetoric that he had ever heard. Not that they were delivered in any lofty style or in flowing periods; on the contrary, they consisted rather of jerky, and even of seemingly disconnected remarks, shot out in all directions and with every variety of aim and character, the most ludicrous and humorous mingled with the most serious. All sorts of witty sayings and stories entered into these Exhortations, and they were looked forward to with great eagerness and listened to with ever renewed delight. The dangers and deficiencies to be met with in the Jesuit's life were all there, together with its glorious realities and possibilities. The great motives of *The Spiritual Exercises*, such as the unlimited rights of the Creator, the awful evil of sin, the invitation and example of our Saviour, entered in everywhere; Holy Scripture furnished innumerable illustrations; experience gained in college and residence gave point and reality to every warning or advice; spiritual books were often quoted and even followed sometimes at considerable length, as in a series of exhortations on St. Bernard's twelve degrees of Pride; but at the same time, everything had passed through his own shrewd and original mind, his deeply spiritual heart, his versatile and humorous imagination.[2]

This gives us an inkling of the impact Fr. Gallwey made on those he trained. A comment of Fr. Clarke helps us to understand one

---

[1] 'Manresa House, Roehampton', *LLNN*, xxx (July 1910), 468. In this series of reminiscences of noviceship days, GMH's name occurs twice in lists of some of the more distinguished novices of the late eighteen-sixties—'Father *Gerard Hopkins*, styled by Dr. Pusey "the Star of Balliol" ', ibid. (Apr. 1910), 391; and again '. . . G. Hopkins (1868). Many of these have risen to distinction as Prelates, Rectors, Writers, &c.', ibid. (July 1910), 468.

[2] Gavin, *Memoirs of Fr. Gallwey*, pp. 156-7.

aspect at least of the attractiveness in Gallwey's presentation of what would otherwise be unredeemably dull. He happened to hear his exhortations on the Rules for a second time, and 'was specially impressed by the fact that the treatment was quite different, and seemed to show that Father Gallwey made little or no use of any previous notes, but prepared his instruction afresh, and presented the subject in quite a fresh light'.[1]

The novices not only had instruction on the Rules but on Christian doctrine also. In this instance, however, it was given by the novices themselves on Thursday afternoons, the novice who was to give the instruction having been warned in advance so that he could prepare his matter. The Fr. Minister presided at these sessions[2] and doubtless expunged the unintentional heresies propounded. The Porter's Journal records two occasions when Hopkins gave the catechism.

Dec. 31st. [1868]
Catechism 2.45 by Br. Gerard Hopkins.

Oct. 7th. [1869]
3.15 p.m. Catechism by Br. G. Hopkins on the Sacraments in general.

But the novices' catechetical powers were tested more strenuously when, in fulfilment of one of the 'experiments' mentioned earlier, they went to various neighbouring parishes to instruct the local children. The novices seem to have catechized on Sundays, Tuesdays, and Fridays though the Porter's Journal is not clear on the point.

I think the fact that he would be out taking a catechism class explains why Hopkins warns Bridges in October 1869,

I am afraid that if you come on Sunday I shall be able to be but a short time with you, for I am away till a quarter past five.[3]

---

[1] Ibid., p. 158.
[2] The entry for 15 Oct. 1869 in the Manresa Journal reads: 'No Catechism for the Novices, Minister too much engaged.' Fr. Vincent Bond (1828-92) was Minister when GMH joined the novitiate, but was later moved to Lulworth. Generally, in a Jesuit house, the Fr. Minister has charge of all day to day practical affairs—catering, upkeep and repairs, and the health of the community. At this time he seems also to have filled the role of Socius, or assistant to the novice master. The first holder as such of the office of Socius to the master of novices appears to have been Fr. John Morris who was appointed to help Fr. Gallwey in Oct. 1869. He was also Minister, see *LLNN*, xxx (July 1910), 471.
[3] *Letters to Bridges*, p. 26.

And again in May 1870 when he tells Baillie,

> I shall be delighted to see you. Any day will do for me excepting as a general rule Tuesday and Friday mornings and Sundays but this does not apply to next Sunday. But a letter of warning is best.[1]

Hopkins's career as a novice-catechist can be reconstructed from these entries in the Porter's Journal.

Friday, April 30th. [1869]

Br. G. Hopkins goes to Isleworth in Br. Walford's place.

Sunday, July 18th.

Usual number of catechists to Homer Row & Isleworth. Br. G. Hopkins went for the day in place of Br. H. Kerr.

Sunday, October 3rd. Rosary Sunday.

BB. G. Hopkins & Simmons[2] went to Brentford[3] to open a Sunday catechism [centre] there, but through some misunderstanding, they not having been expected were unable to do anything this Sunday.

Tuesday, Dec. 21[4]

. . . the catechists were—for Isleworth Br. G. Hopkins, Br. Southern,[5] Br. Wilcock,[6] . . .

Friday, Christmas Eve

Catechism at Isleworth—Br. G. Hopkins and Br. Wilcock.

---

[1] *Further Letters*, p. 233.

[2] Gilbert Simmons, born in Lancashire on 13 Nov. 1846. Read theology intending to take Anglican orders. Received into the R.C. Church at the Oratory. Entered the S.J. novitiate at Roehampton in Sept. 1869. Left in Aug. 1871 before taking first vows.

[3] Cf. 'On March 27 I asked the Brentford boys about a ghost story they had told me before that', *Journals and Papers*, p. 197.

[4] This and the following two entries are from GMH's manuscript. The complete manuscript is given later.

[5] Joseph Southern (1850–78; see Foley vii), born at Ness, nr. Chester on 30 June 1850. Educated at Mount St. Mary's, and Stonyhurst Colleges. Matric. London Univ. Entered the S.J. novitiate at Roehampton on 8 Sept. 1868, the day after GMH arrived. In Sept. 1876 sent to teach at St. Francis Xavier's College, Liverpool, and died there aged twenty-eight on 12 Oct. 1878. Buried at Gillmoss, Liverpool.

[6] Charles Barrow Wilcock (1845–1927), secular priest, born at St. Helens, Lancs. on 11 Oct. 1845. Educated at a technical school near Liverpool and Mount St. Mary's College. Entered the S.J. novitiate at Roehampton in Sept. 1868, on the same day as GMH. Left the Society of Jesus in 1882. Ordained for the Liverpool diocese in May 1885. 1886–98, parish work at Bootle, Manchester, and Blackburn. 1899–1917, St. Tudwal's, Barmouth. He began this mission in a little tin chapel near the beach and later built the fine church and presbytery at great personal sacrifice. He died at Southport on 25 Dec. 1927, and was buried at Old Windleshaw, St. Helens.

Tuesday, Jan 25 [1870]

Br. G. Hopkins appointed catechist at Fulham in Fr. Wright's[1] place and Br. Gillet[2] in his place at Isleworth: Br. Southern head of that mission.

Sunday, June 12th.

Br. G. Hopkins has been appointed first Catechist at Homer Row & Br. Colley[3] to take his place at Brentford.

So far as I know Hopkins himself makes no reference to his catechizing activities. There is, however, a relevant contemporary account preserved in Mrs. Maxwell Scott's biography of Henry Schomberg Kerr. As the last entry from the Porter's Journal shows Hopkins succeeded to the centre which had been in the charge of Kerr.

Brother Henry, after some experience in less difficult circumstances, was named as one of the catechists who went from Manresa every Sunday afternoon to the Catholic school at Homer Row. They had an early dinner, and then started to walk to Hammersmith, a distance of some four miles, taking tickets thence to Edgeware Road, which is within a few minutes' walk of the Homer Row Church. On the arrival of the catechists the doors of the school were thrown open, and there flocked in up the stairs into a large room on the first floor a crowd of children, boys and girls, whom piety or curiosity had attracted from the neighbourhood. These children

[1] Patrick Augustine Wright (1835–89), secular priest, born at Sutton St. Mary's, Lincolnshire on 17 Mar. 1835. Educated privately. Received into the R.C. Church by Newman at the Oratory in Oct. 1860. Ordained priest at Nottingham on 24 Aug. 1867, and subsequently worked in Nottingham diocese. Entered the S.J. novitiate at Roehampton in Jan. 1869, but left in Sept. 1871 before taking first vows. In 1872 worked in Glasgow archdiocese at Maryhill, and Old Cumnock, and later at Newton Stewart, and Girvan. Last years spent in the south of England. Died on 30 Nov. 1889 at Burgess Hill, Sussex. (*Further Letters*, p. 106.)

[2] Anselm Gillet (1848–84), Jesuit priest, was the second of four brothers all of whom became Jesuits and died on the missions; the other three were Henry (1842–1911), Cassian (1850–1904), and Silvin (1856–1910). Educated at Stonyhurst College. Entered S.J. novitiate at Roehampton 7 Sept. 1868, the same day as GMH. Within a year he was obliged to leave Manresa on account of ill health; readmitted on 23 June 1870; ordained priest, July 1881. After only two months' tertianship at Roehampton, he left for Honduras in Dec. 1882. Died of fever there two years later on 28 Dec. 1884. (*Journals and Papers*, pp. 191, 235.)

[3] Reginald Edward Wellesley Colley (1848–1904; see Boase iv, Sutcliffe), Jesuit priest, born at Gipsy Hill, Norwood, London on 26 May 1848. Educated at Stonyhurst; B.A. London Univ. Entered the S.J. novitiate at Roehampton in Apr. 1870; ordained priest in 1883. Rector of Stonyhurst, 1885–91. 1888, Province Consultor. Vice-Rector and Prefect of Studies at St. Aidan's, Grahamstown, 1891–3. 1893, Prefect of Studies at Stonyhurst. Became Provincial in 1901, a position which he kept until his death on 12 Feb. 1904. (*Journals and Papers*, p. 234.)

had first to be sorted into their respective classes in two large rooms, then new-comers, of whom there were often many, were examined by the head catechist and assigned to what seemed their proper division, and the work of teaching began. The attendance of the children was voluntary, and none of their ordinary superiors were present, so that all the firmness and ingenuity of each catechist were needed to control and to interest his youthful audience. When the classes had been taught separately for a certain time they were all gathered together in one room to listen to an address from the chief catechist, and were then conducted, after some hymns had been sung, into the galleries of Homer Row Church to be present at Benediction.[1]

But when it came to teaching children Christian doctrine, the novices were after all novices, and so too apparently thought Fr. Gallwey, for the Porter's Journal for 31 October 1869 reads: 'Fr. Rector saw the novices in the Hall to give some instructions upon catechising.' The journeying backwards and forwards from Manresa which catechizing necessitated brought with it its own share of penance and one wonders if the instructors were not relieved when bad weather occasionally intervened, as, for example, when the Porter recorded:

Sunday, March 13th. [1870]
No Catechisms on account of the heavy fall of snow.

Catechizing is not the only means used in the noviceship to prepare future Jesuits for their apostolate. They preach as well. They deliver their sermons, or 'tones',[2] not outside to strangers, but generally in the community refectory. Hopkins's first sermon, however, was given in the chapel, and the occasion was an important one—the special feast of the house. The entry reads:

Saturday, November 13th. [1869] Feast of St. Stanislaus.
The hymn to St. Stanislaus was first sung and then the panegyric delivered by Br. G. Hopkins. Benediction followed. All was over a few minutes after 3 and the dinner bell was rung immediately.

The impression he created survived, for in his obituary written twenty years later we read: '. . . his fellow-novices well remember

---

[1] Scott, *H. S. Kerr*, pp. 100–1. Apparently catechizing was much the same in Denis Meadow's time. See his lively account in *Obedient Men*, pp. 168–9.
[2] See A. Thomas, 'G. M. Hopkins and "Tones"', *Notes and Queries*, xii, no. 11 (Nov. 1965), 429–30.

his panegyric of St. Stanislaus, which was as brilliant and beautiful as it was out of the usual routine of pulpit deliveries'.[1]

This is the only record of Hopkins's preaching in the noviceship, yet there must have been other occasions, since it was the practice of the novices to preach on the Blessed Virgin during the month of May. They were given a month in which to prepare a sermon as the Porter's Journal explains:

April 1st. [1869]
The texts for the May Discourse were given up by last Monday evening and after being arranged and settled by Fr. Minister, the order was drawn out and today was posted in the Recreation Hall.

From this review of the chief items in the novices' spiritual formation we can go on to their other occupations. This is not to suggest that any dichotomy exists in the training, far from it, for the novice realizes from the outset that everything he does, can be done 'Ad majorem Dei gloriam', appreciating that all things can be turned to good. But it is convenient to deal with the more mundane side of life separately.

So that a clearer picture may emerge it will be useful at this point to glance back and recall the novices' morning. They got up at half past five, washed, meditated for an hour, heard Mass, reflected on their meditation, ate breakfast, and read Rodriguez, *Practice of Perfection*, for half an hour. At nine an instruction on the rules was given by the novice master and, when asked, a novice was expected to be able to repeat the substance of the exhortation. After this each novice went to make his bed, and dusted and arranged his cubicle. One of the first points of the noviceship which struck Hopkins was the neatness expected. In his first letter home he writes, 'we have to keep our rooms tidy to an extraordinary degree'.[2]

The next duty, as Fr. Clarke has stated, was housework—'dusting, sweeping, washing up dishes and plates, laying the refectory for dinner, sometimes cleaning and scrubbing, and other menial offices

---

[1] 'Father Gerard Hopkins', *LLNN*, xx (Mar. 1890), 174.
[2] *Further Letters*, p. 105. One feels that GMH must have found the noviceship difficult, certainly in the beginning. Still, he must have learned to count his socks without the aid of nurse! See the postscript on p. 105 of *Further Letters*.

of the humblest description'.[1] Mrs. Maxwell Scott's practical and feminine standpoint confers an unusual insight on the jobs they did, and in addition she helps us to see with the eyes of the time.

The menial offices which exercise the humility of the scholastic novices are the work which would be done by domestic servants in a private family, for there are no servants in a Jesuit novitiate; lay brothers attend to the cooking and the employments for which trained skill is required, but with these exceptions, the whole work of the house, or those portions of it which are inhabited by novices, is managed by the novices themselves. It will easily be understood that for young people any sensitiveness as to the supposed degradation of such work does not last very long, and they quickly become merry and willing, and sweep, and dust, and 'tidy up' generally with more zeal perhaps than knowledge.[2]

But even when carrying out one of the less pleasant chores—cleaning the water-closets[3]—the poet in Hopkins was alive to beauty: 'The slate slabs of the urinals even', he noted in his diary, 'are frosted in graceful sprays.'[4]

[1] Joseph Thorp, himself an ex-Jesuit novice, described the menial exercises of the noviceship as 'the work of housemaid, parlourmaid, under-gardener, boots, probationer nurse, charwoman, scullion'. 'T' [of *Punch*], *Friends and Adventures* (1931), p. 25.

[2] Scott, *H. S. Kerr*, p. 98. Perhaps at this time, certainly a few years later, Manresa had a laundress. We learn this from a facetious letter written by Henry Patmore who made a retreat there with his father Coventry Patmore in 1876. Henry Patmore, not quite sixteen years old, is writing to his stepmother: 'The butter is very good, praps they make it themselves. We had sardines at tea last night, cold beef this morn^g highish. . . . All the novices are very gloomy. They're not allowed to read novels, and all the pictures of female saints in the house have beards added to them to make them less attractive. The elder Jesuits have to keep patrolling up and down all day to prevent the novices from escaping. Only one woman ever comes within the walls,—the laundress, *aetat* 64. Every Saturday, when she brings the linen, she receives, on an average, 5 proposals, besides innumerable billets, all expressive of enthusiastic devotion on the part of the writers. All of the novices think her a perfect and blooming beauty, except such as, judging from the bearded female saints above mentioned, maintain that miss (outside called Mrs.) Juggins can't yet have reached maturity, since she lacks a beard.' Basil Champneys, *Memoirs and Correspondence of Coventry Patmore*, i (1900), 306–7.

[3] Cf. 'being that week "A Secretis" ', *Journals and Papers*, p. 194, and see the note on p. 406.

[4] Ibid., p. 196 entry for 12 Feb. Geoffrey Grigson has admirably pointed out how free Hopkins was from 'our common associative poetic preferences'. GMH, he claims, was as 'concerned with the beauties and severities of the winter and neutrally alive to things as much in one place as another, . . . with letter-leaves, ant's egg clouds, roping ooze and frost-sprayed urinals, we are divorced from the averagely fine poetic detection of the nineteenth century. Here—and almost everywhere in Hopkins—we knock our sensibilities against exactitudes and starknesses which may still repel or dismay either those who live aesthetically in older, gentler modes or those who do not require to live outwardly at all.' *Gerard Manley Hopkins* (1955), pp. 7–8.

At 10.15 there was a quarter of an hour's learning by heart to be done, when the novices would memorize some portion of the rules of the Society, prayers, hymns, or psalms, which they would be asked to repeat later. One entry in the Porter's Journal shows that they also grew familiar with those Papal Bulls which specially concerned the Society.

Jan. 11th. [1869]

Brs. H. Kerr, and F. Hopkins[1] read 'Bullae' with Brs. G. Hopkins and Walford respectively.

'By heart' would be learnt in Latin, and, in fact, the novice was taught to regard Latin as his second mother tongue. The novices kept silence throughout most of the day and if it was necessary to say anything, did so briefly and in Latin. Hopkins does not say what he thought of the Latin-speaking in the novitiate. He might well have been pained, that is, unless he was amused. The anonymous contributor of 'Reminiscences of Novice-days, 1864, 1865' gives us some idea of the standard.

Latin Conversation.—'Some few there were who talked barbarous Latin, but on the whole pains were taken to speak correctly. (a) Sent to help another in the garden I said to him: Frater, venio te adjuvare'. He admonished me of a grammatical error: 'Frater, post verbum motionis ponitur Supinum: non debes dicere *te adjuvare*, sed *te adjuvatum.*' To

---

[1] Frederick Charles Hopkins (1844–1923), titular Bishop of Athribis, and Vicar Apostolic of British Honduras, third son of Mr. William Hopkins, manufacturer, born at Birmingham on 25 Mar. 1844. Educated at Ratcliffe College, Leicester, and Oscott College. Studied medicine at Birmingham Medical School, qualified as M.R.C.S., London, and practised at Aston. Entered the S.J. novitiate at Roehampton on 7 Sept. 1868 on the same day as GMH; ordained priest with GMH on 23 Sept. 1877. 1888–96, Minister of S.J. Residence, Belize, British Honduras, and editor of *The Angelus.* 1896, appointed as Vicar General. Succeeded Bishop Salvador di Pietro, and was consecrated on 5 Nov. 1899. Revisited England in 1901, 1909, and 1920. Drowned in the sinking of a motor-boat *E.M.L.* on his way for a yearly pastoral visitation of Corozal on 10 Apr. 1923. Buried in the Holy Redeemer Cathedral, Belize. Among the appreciations which followed his obituary in *LLNN* occurs the following anonymous contribution: 'We were ordained together, nineteen priests in all, thirteen of the English Province, of whom I am the last survivor, September 23rd, 1877. Among us was the poet, Gerard Hopkins —"the gentle Hop." we called him in contra-distinction to "the genteel Hop.," for Frederick never lost his "bedside manner" . . .' The pun, it seems to me, adds point to the following sentence from GMH's own obituary notice in *LLNN*: 'What struck me most of all in him was his child-like guilelessness and simplicity, his gentleness, tender-heartedness, and his loving compassion for the young, the weak, the poor, and all who were in any trouble or distress.' (*Further Letters*, pp. 104-5, 'one of [the novices] is called Hopkins'.)

which I promptly retorted: 'Frater, pace tua non dixerim *te adjuvatum*, sed *te adjutum*'. I remember how he blushed at my correction. (b) A novice seeing his companions sweeping leaves without any order, requested them to follow each other in a line, 'Fratres, melius foret procedere agmine facto'. An ablative absolute was so unusual that it was greeted with laughter. (c) Returning once from some ceremony at Farm Street, and arriving at Fulham Bridge, a novice wishing to descend from the top of the bus, the vehicle having begun to move on, amazed the conductor by crying out, 'Siste paulisper, velim descendere'. (d) Two young novices out for a walk near Richmond passed a wild-beast show. The vans containing the animals were arranged in a circle, the interstices being protected with canvas. Prying through an opening in the canvas they had a cheap view of the interior, till one of the menagerie men catching sight of them, used language too awful to transmit to paper, and sent the two innocents flying. Relating their experience afterwards, one said: 'O, qualem elephantem! et quam ingentem habuit truncum', the other replying: 'Frater precor, ne dixeris *truncum*, sed *proboscidem*.'[1]

But the novices needed encouragement and this was supplied by Fr. Gallwey:

Feb. 25th. [1870]

Fr. Rector announced to the brothers that in future a quarter of an hour of every walk, going to Catechism or elsewhere, was to be employed in speaking Latin: and that all should endeavour to say something, on account of the great utility of being able to speak Latin in future years.[2] [Novices' Beadle's Journal]

But on occasion the rule of speaking Latin was relaxed:

Dec. 24th. [1868]

Working at decorations in the morning, English allowed. [NBJ]

When the novices had learned their 'by heart' for the day, they had roughly half-an-hour's free time, referred to as *ad lib.*, and during this they could walk in the grounds, pray in the chapel, read a saint's life, or some other spiritual book. At 11.30 they reported for outdoor manual works, and could then be assigned to chopping and

---

[1] *LLNN*, xxx (Jan. 1910), 318–19. Fr. Henry Kerr, who was twenty-nine when he joined the Society, clearly had difficulty with his Latin speaking, particularly when he found himself groping for the equivalent of 'to cut one's cable', 'get things ship-shape'. See Scott, *H. S. Kerr*, pp. 104–5.

[2] Fr. Gallwey's words probably carried more weight because he was able to practise what he preached. For example, his biography states that when he attended the Provincial Congregation he spoke Latin 'easily and correctly', Gavin, *Memoirs of Fr. Gallwey*, p. 246.

sawing wood for fuel, sweeping and gathering leaves, digging, weeding the flower-beds, cutting grass, picking fruit[1] and so on. During Hopkins's first year as a novice Henry Kerr was master of outdoor works. Kerr's naval service seems to have stood him in good stead, and as his biographer relates

He communicated his keenness to others, and it was a matter of common remark that never before had the novices worked so heartily or to such purpose as under his command. His characteristic dislike of listlessness or slipshod work showed itself in his impatience, compounded perhaps more of pity than of anger, when the task he set was not completed within the given time. The official Latin was not always equal to expressing his feelings on such occasions, and 'all hands' were made aware in their mother-tongue that they had not done their duty. His idea of what could be done and well done by novices in the forty minutes allotted to 'outdoor works' seemed at first ridiculously large, but by degrees his subordinates saw that he was in earnest, and soon did all or more than he asked of them.[2]

One wonders if the 'trees . . . pulled down to the ground with ropes by an enthusiastic force of novices swaying all together at the master's word of command'[3] provided the painful occasion wringing from Hopkins the protest 'a grievous gap has come . . . with falling and felling'.[4]

When gardening had finished, the novices washed, made their examination of conscience and went to dinner in the refectory at one o'clock. Dinner began with the long Latin grace, and afterwards, while they ate, they listened to the reading. The refectory reading has already been mentioned; it is only necessary to add that besides saints' lives and ascetical works, works of history or apologetics were sometimes read and from time to time articles from *The Tablet*, the *Dublin Review*, and *The Month*. It is probably no more than coincidence, but at the time when Hopkins was noting in his Journal certain north-country expressions, for example, *whisket, lead, geet*,[5] *The Month* was publishing a series of articles entitled 'Loomland Papers' which, as their title suggests, discussed Lancashire ways and

---

[1] 'We were gathering mulberries . . .', *Journals and Papers*, p. 192.
[2] Scott, *H. S. Kerr*, pp. 99–100.
[3] Ibid., p. 99.
[4] *Journals and Papers*, p. 189, entry for 6 Dec. 1868.
[5] Ibid., pp. 190–1.

dialect.[1] While the noting of these particular words is of no more
than minor importance, the real significance of the practice is somewhat greater, marking as it does Hopkins's continued interest in
recording highly individualized expressions of the sort that he was
later to introduce into his poetry. It is just such an interest which
was to produce, say, the sprinkling of dialect at the end of the
following line from 'The Leaden Echo and the Golden Echo':

> O then, weary then whý should we tread? O why are we so
> haggard at the heart, so care-coiled, care-killed, so fagged, so
> fashed, so cogged, so cumbered.

Perhaps the force of this suggestion is best seen by quoting
the explanation offered by Hopkins himself of another phrase in the
same poem: 'the seed that we so carelessly and freely flung into the
dull furrow, and then forgot it, will have come to ear meantime'.[2]
These, or similar 'seeds' of dialect, were stored now for use later.

Mispronunciations in public reading were corrected by the Rector,
who in addition to insisting on clear diction and correct phrasing
curbed any tendency to dramatize. To read well was an act of charity
to the community, and if you were corrected, whether rightly or
wrongly, so much the better for your humility. Hopkins himself, as
the Province *Catalogue* for 1873 shows, when in his third year of
philosophy at St. Mary's Hall, Stonyhurst, was in charge of the
reading at table.

While it would be accurate to say that an attempt was made to
teach the novices to read aloud correctly, of studies in general there
is no mention. Apparently there was no great need:

> Nearly all the novices having matriculated before entering the Society,
> the only study allowed to us was the reading of the history of the Society
> in the works of Orlandini, Sacchini, Cordara, &c.[3]

'Studies' on the time-table could also mean the writing up of the
exhortations given by the novice master. But presumably if your

---

[1] *The Month*, x (Feb.–June 1869), pp. 97–111, 323–38, 532–47; 'geet' p. 103, 'whisket'
p. 324. The author of these articles was Joseph Walton (1845–1910).

[2] *Letters to Bridges*, p. 159.

[3] 'Some Reminiscences of Novice-Days, 1864, 1865', *LLNN*, xxx (Jan. 1910), 320.
The works of the three writers can be found in Carlos Sommervogel's *Bibliothèque de la
Compagnie de Jésus* (Brussels, Paris, Louvain, 1890–1960).

Latin was as rusty or non-existent as, say, Henry Kerr's, you were helped to improve it.

Recreation played too important a part in formation to be left to chance. After dinner a visit to the Blessed Sacrament was made, and then the novices went to the first recreation of the day. It was taken inside or outside according to the weather and season, and lasted an hour. You recreated with the first brother encountered. During the first half-hour of the evening recreation after supper, Latin had to be spoken.[1] Denis Meadows remembered evening recreation in this way.

When we went up to the novices' hall after the visit to the chapel, we found the chairs arranged in a large circle in the middle of the room. As you came in, you took the first vacant chair. I don't know how we managed to make conversation. Sometimes it was very hard to keep it up.

Toward the end of the recreation the porter looked at his watch, clapped his hands for silence, and then announced, 'Brother So-and-So will give us a *pia fabula.*' Someone had been deputed to prepare a short, edifying story, an incident in the life of a saint or something similar, to deliver to the assembled novices before we went down to the chapel for Litanies or a benediction service. Most of these pious anecdotes were rather emotional, often incredible, but not consciously humorous or witty. Satire was frowned on in the noviceship.[2]

When the bell rang recreation ended instantly.

The voice of the bell was the voice of our superiors, and that for us was the voice of God. One of St. Ignatius' own rulings was that an obedient subject would, at the sound of the bell, immediately leave what he was doing, and if writing or studying would leave even a letter unfinished.

The practice sounds a bit disconcerting, but we soon grew used to it, and would break off in the middle of a sentence, smile at our companions, and walk off in silence.[3]

What of the rest of the day? Fr. Clarke tells us that

the occupations of the afternoon are a repetition of those of the earlier portion of the day, save that on three days in the week a walk of about two hours has to be taken in companies of two or three. No one is allowed

[1] Clarke, 'Training of a Jesuit', p. 217.
[2] *Obedient Men*, pp. 55-6. Compare also the account in Andrew Steinmetz, *The Novitiate* (1846), p. 30.
[3] *Obedient Men*, p. 51.

to choose his companions, but the master of novices arranges the various companies. Sometimes a game of cricket or football is substituted for the walk.[1]

Whether Hopkins joined in the games or not we cannot be certain. His brother Cyril states that 'of games he took no heed . . . football and cricket were nothing to him'.[2] Yet he had played football with the boys at the Oratory School.[3] Perhaps he skated with his fellow novices on the Pen Ponds in Richmond Park, or on those on Wimbledon Common. His Journal for the early part of 1870 records, 'There were three spells of frost with skating, the third beginning on Feb. 9.'[4]

The regular weekly recreation day in the noviceship was Wednesday[5] and the novices set off in threes for Richmond, Barnes, and Putney, or perhaps Caesar's Camp.[6] On certain days they went for long walks taking sandwiches with them. Hopkins has several references to these walks. Once he went no further than Kew. On that occasion he noted having seen 'the Egyptian sacred bean, the leaves dimpled in the middle and beautifully wimpled at the edge, the flower a water lily with the petals flagging and falling apart'.[7]

Two walks which were special occasions in the year were those on the Feast of the Holy Innocents (28 December), and one to Bushy (or Bushey) Park. The first of these was eagerly awaited because it was the one walk in the year for which money was provided. Each novice was given a shilling. On Holy Innocents' Day 1870, Hopkins now in the second year of his novitiate visited Hampton Court and later told his mother that he had seen 'a duck trying to walk on ice,

---

[1] 'Training of a Jesuit', p. 217. Some have found these compulsory walks their *bête noire*: 'Long years after, when one drove Fr. Steuart past Manresa . . . he used to recall the difficulties of those days, and it was possible to glimpse a little of what the strain had been on a thoroughbred, high-mettled, brilliant, and fastidious young man. "To have to go out for long walks two and two, and find yourself landed with a person with whom you had absolutely nothing in common, no mutual interests; whose whole background and trend of thought were on utterly different lines; that"—he used to burst out with deep feeling fifty years later—"that—yes, I think it was almost the worst of all." ' Katharine Kendall, *Father Steuart* (1950), p. 36.
[2] Lahey, *G. M. Hopkins*, p. 8.
[3] *Further Letters*, p. 45.
[4] *Journals and Papers*, p. 195.
[5] *Further Letters*, p. 233.
[6] *Journals and Papers*, p. 195.
[7] Ibid., p. 192. Was this entry the inchoate 'wimpled-water-dimpled, not-by-morning-matchèd face' of 'The Leaden Echo and the Golden Echo'? *Poems*, no. 59.

which he could not manage at all: some children threw bun-crumb to him and every time gobbling at it he fell over upon his chest'.[1]

The Bushy Park walk was generally timed to ensure that the splendid masses of chestnuts were seen at their best. In 1869 the day chosen was 13 May and the holiday was given in honour of the Provincial.

Thursday, May 13th.
Provincial's Day. Long Walks. All to be home by 3.45. This is the only opportunity the Brothers would have of seeing the chestnuts in Bushy Park. 4: dinner. [NBJ]

On this occasion Hopkins missed the treat since he was in London visiting the dentist.

'Churches Walks' were another activity of the noviceship. On these you were instructed to walk to certain churches and to make a short visit. Hopkins was probably on such a walk when he visited 'Fr. Rawes' church'.[2]

National pride seems to have contributed something to the Rector's choice of certain days for special walks as these entries from the Porter's Journal make clear:

Wednesday, Oct. 13th. [1869]. Feast of St. Edward.
Recreation Day. Four novices started at 9 for our church at Westminster,[3] to serve on the altar during High Mass which began at 11. They dined with our Fathers & returned at about 5.30 p.m. Three also went to visit Westminster Abbey on occasion of the day's feast but were not able to gain admission to the Saint's Chapel.

Saturday, April 23rd. [1870].
This afternoon Father Rector sent all out to take a walk in honour of St. George.

Hopkins would have enjoyed keeping English feasts in this way.

---

[1] *Further Letters*, p. 109, and see the following: 'And on one red-letter day in the year, Holy Innocents, you actually had a shilling to spend—I wonder if it is one and ninepence now to meet the increased cost of living—so that you might mount a bus and ride into the very heart of wicked London and see some church or, if inclined to be worldly, a museum or even, I think, the Zoo. We certainly were innocents if not yet conspicuously holy.' 'T.' [of *Punch*], *Friends and Adventures* (1931), p. 27.

[2] *Journals and Papers*, pp. 194–5.

[3] See Bernard W. Kelly, *Historical Notes on English Catholic Missions* (1907), p. 426. The Society of Jesus had charge of the mission at Horseferry Road, Westminster, London, until Mar. 1901.

Of entertainments such as plays or concerts there was very little. On the whole they would be regarded as unsuitable. Yet in 1870 when the Juniors were again living at Manresa they put on some shows. Fr. Gallwey, we read, 'greatly appreciated any effort made to interest and amuse the Community . . . and did a great deal to encourage literary or musical talent among younger men. *Séances*, as he called them . . . seemed to give him great pleasure, and he was really an audience in himself as he listened in his intense way, or with that whimsical and genial smile of his, to the serious or witty compositions of the young students or novices.'[1]

Wednesday, June 29th. [1870]. Feast of SS. Peter and Paul.[2]

At 5 there was a 'Séance' given by the Juniors under the cedar tree, to which the novices were invited. [NBJ]

Wednesday, July 20th [1870]

At 11 the Community was assembled to be entertained by the Juniors by a 'Séance' in honour of the definition of the Infallibility.[3] [NBJ]

On one occasion Fr. Gallwey himself contributed to the entertainment, as Hopkins tells us:

Tuesday, Dec. 28 [1870]—Holy Innocents

Rodriguez 8.55 but the reading was broken off. ~~in order to practise the old glee of 'Who's the fool now?' with new words by Fr. Rector which was sung in alternate [verses] by Juniors and Novices after dinner.~~[4]

---

[1] Gavin, *Memoirs of Fr. Gallwey*, p. 153. In this same paragraph Fr. Blount mentions a séance given by the Italian scholastics who had been driven from Rome in 1870, and who found a temporary home with the English Jesuits at Manresa. This séance was an entertainment 'consisting of songs and addresses in Latin prose and verse'. The photograph frontispiece to Gavin's *Memoirs* hints at Fr. Gallwey's smile.

[2] This day was chosen because it was 'the feast of the Rector's patron, St. Peter', and apparently 'the Juniors caused considerable merriment by their witty verses and other compositions in praise of the novices'. 'Manresa House, Roehampton', *LLNN*, xxx (July 1910), 471.

[3] See under the entry for 15 July 1870 in *Journals and Papers*, p. 202.

[4] This is from the Journal kept by GMH when he was Porter in the noviceship. The extract quoted is cancelled thus in the manuscript the whole of which is given later. See also *Further Letters*, p. 109, where Hopkins writes, 'we had a very stirring old glee sung called "Who's the fool now?" It is in Chappel and is worth learning'. As Professor Abbott states in his footnote the glee occurs on pp. 76 and 768 of W. Chappell's *The Ballad Literature and Popular Music of the Olden Time . . .*, 2 vols. [1855–9]. I could not find these volumes in the noviceship library, but there is a copy of the work in Heythrop Library, the Theologate and Philosophate of the English Province, and this copy may have been transferred there at some time in the past. The only stamp it bears is that of

But the recreation the novices looked forward to most eagerly was probably the 'hay-season'. The novices did not go away for a holiday, and to these growing young men brimful of energy, the prospect of spending hours out of doors haymaking was a welcome change and relief. Denis Meadows's description retains something of the mixture of charm and excitement which the work had for the novices.

The hay season was the nearest thing to a summer vacation for us. Even after supper, when the twilight was fading, we went to have a last look before going upstairs for recreation and the *pia fabula*.

Then, one morning, when the sunlight was streaming over the red curtains of our cubicles, and the birds began singing before the caller's '*Deo gratias*,' we heard the whirr of a mowing machine and the voice of the man in charge of it calling to his horses. The hay season had started.

When we went down to the chapel for morning oblation, even the recollectedness of the greater silence could not prevent some of us peeping through the glazed door of the Long Gallery to look at the tiny swaths of new-cut hay waiting for our rakes and pitchforks.

Daily until the hay was all dried and carted we turned out in our oldest clothes after dinner to work in the field. Toward teatime we assembled at what in America would be called a picnic spot. There were benches under the trees, and a big garden table. We called the place the Temple, because it was near Lord Bessborough's classical summerhouse. Tired and hot, with our shoes and trouser legs yellow with buttercup pollen, we sat and listened to a novice reading a religious book. This took the place of our private spiritual reading.[1]

For the years 1869 and 1870 the facts are these:

Saturday, June 5th. [1869]
Hay-making began. Novices turned out at 10.15: remained out until 1.

The Porter's Journal shows that they were still haymaking on 21 June. The following year they began on 8 June: 'Hay-making commenced today. There was talking during the morning but in the afternoon talking and silence alternately.'

Anyone ignorant of the ways of a religious novitiate would probably be struck by the triviality of many of the daily items recorded. And rightly so. For a humdrum monotony, intended or not, plays

Heythrop Library. There is, however, a pencilled shelf-mark on the inside front cover which indicates that it was previously part of some other library. The volumes contain no notes or marginalia. I have not been able to trace the version written by Fr. Gallwey.
[1] *Obedient Men.*, p. 94.

its own part in the training. Whether this ought to be so or not, this is no place to debate. I merely state the fact.[1] Hopkins underlined the comparative uneventfulness of the life when he wrote to Bridges, 'I wd. make this letter longer if I had more to say.'[2]

Among the domestic trivialities which the records have preserved for us are the purchase of a new cow,[3] the dispatch of the big clock for repair, the putting up of Christmas decorations, and the following annoying feature of the pre-refrigeration era:

August 8th. [1869]
On account of its scarcity, which will probably continue during the rest of the month, all were cautioned to be more sparing in the use of milk. Those who usually take milk alone for breakfast will cease to do so for the present, and, instead of the usual proportions, 2/3 coffee will be taken with 1/3 milk by all. [NBJ]

Several times exceptional weather calls for comment:

Sept. 13th. [1869]
There was to have been a walk but the weather would not permit this. A heavy gale blew all day through, doing great damage to trees, etc. The mulberry tree near the farmyard was snapped across close to the trunk.[4] [NBJ]

---

[1] According to Fr. Clarke, 'The routine of monotonous and often apparently useless employments has for its object to foster the habit of what is rightly called blind obedience.' 'Training of a Jesuit', p. 219.

[2] *Letters to Bridges*, p. 25. Perhaps in fairness to the noviceship it should be added that GMH's plea of 'having nothing to say' was not peculiar only to that time. The following extracts prove this:

To E. H. Coleridge, 2 Mar. 1863: 'I will reserve all news (which is none) . . .', *Further Letters*, p. 15.

To his mother, 2 Mar. 1871: 'I can think of nothing at all to tell you, for everything here is "as dank as ditchwater" ', ibid., p. 113.

To Baillie, 10 Apr. 1871: 'I can seldom write and when I do I have nothing to say', ibid., p. 234.

To Bridges, 25 Feb. 1878: 'Write me an interesting letter. I cannot do so. Life here is as dank as ditch-water', *Letters to Bridges*, p. 47.

Hopkins was not alone in finding religious life uneventful. Fr. Gallwey himself when living at St. Beuno's reminded his former pupil, '. . . you do not remember that I am living in a sort of monastery, where from one end of the week till another not a bit of news happens: you are living in Dublin, and travel three or four times a year to London.' Percy Fitzgerald, *Father Gallwey: a sketch*. With some early letters (1906), p. 27.

[3] Manresa at this time had its own farm.

[4] See also *Journals and Papers*, p. 192, top of page.

Arrivals and departures in the noviceship were carefully noted and doubtless proved a fecund topic for conversation. Actually, comparatively few left the noviceship in Hopkins's time though some were to leave the Society later. Official records state that in 1868 sixteen novices were admitted and three left, and in 1869 twenty-one came and three went. Hopkins himself, as Porter, in his entry for 28 January 1870 recorded the departure of Brother Ingledew.[1] In his own diary he notes in early July 1869: 'Br. Shoolbred[2] and Br. Anselm Gillet had left the noviceship from ill health.'[3] His letters to his mother tell of the new arrival at Manresa of the secular priest, Fr. Wright, and also of the 'very clever and really . . . most charming'[4] young Canadian novice, Br. Monk.[5] But the most momentous change which took place was the departure of Hopkins's first novice master, Fr. Christopher Fitzsimon,[6] on 12 September 1869, and the arrival of his successor, Fr. Peter Gallwey, the next day.[7] I have suggested elsewhere[8] the good effect of Gallwey's influence on Hopkins; it is sufficient here to underline the importance of the change by repeating the opinion of one of Gallwey's own most gifted novices, Fr. Charles Blount, who asserted that, 'it is not an exaggeration to say that he did inaugurate a new era in the training

[1] George Aloysius Ingledew, born in Newark on 27 July 1848. Educated at Wesley College, Sheffield (now King Edward VII School). Entered the S.J. novitiate at Roehampton in Oct. 1869. Last appears in S.J. catalogue in 1870.

[2] Jocelyn Laurence Shoolbred, born in London on 17 Nov. 1847. Received into the R.C. Church as a child. Educated at Mount St. Mary's and Stonyhurst Colleges, followed by a year in Glasgow studying engineering. Entered the S.J. novitiate at Roehampton in Sept. 1867. Left the noviceship in Aug. 1869 before taking first vows. (*Journals and Papers*, p. 191.)

[3] Ibid., p. 191.

[4] *Further Letters*, p. 111.

[5] Lewis Wentworth Monk (1847–1909), son of the Hon. Cornwallis Monk, Justice of Appeal for Lower Canada, born on 31 Jan. 1847. Educated at Collège Sainte Marie, Montreal. Entered the S.J. novitiate at Roehampton in Sept. 1869, for the New York–Canada S.J. mission. Year's Juniorate also at Roehampton. 1873–6, teaching at St. John's College, Fordham, and at St. Mary's College, Montreal. Last reference in S.J. catalogue for 1876. (*Further Letters*, p. 111—'a young Canadian . . . half French and very clever and really a most charming man and it is greater pleasure to hear him talk than anyone I ever listened to', and see also p. 108. The identification of the 'young Canadian' as Lewis Wentworth Monk is established from Province catalogues and confirmed by Manresa Minister's Journal.)

[6] *Journals and Papers*, p. 191: *Further Letters*, p. 108.

[7] *Journals and Papers*, p. 191.

[8] A. Thomas, 'A Note on Gerard Manley Hopkins and his Superiors 1868–77', *Irish Ecclesiastical Record*, civ (Oct.–Nov. 1965), 287–8.

of the novices of the Society'.[1] And within a month Gallwey had at his disposal the first-rate abilities of Fr. John Morris[2] who was appointed his Socius, or Assistant.

We saw earlier that the monotony of the novices' week was regularly punctuated by their catechetical excursions, but, in addition, there were exceptional occasions which took them to London, for example, to take part in a dirge:

Monday, Dec. 7th [1868]

Scholastic Novices went to Farm St. to sing the Office for the Dead for the Hon. Charles Langdale, S.J.[3] Went by train from Barnes at 8.45. & 8.50., & from Putney at 8.49. & 9.54. and by bus. Returned by 2.15 train from Waterloo Station. [NBJ]

Farm Street provided an oasis more than once:

Tuesday, March 2nd. [1869]

Half of the Scholastics, 15 in number, went to Exposition[4] at Farm Street. [NBJ]

Friday, March 26th. [1869] Good Friday.

Six went to London to sing the Passion. They had their breakfast at 7.15.

---

[1] Gavin, *Memoirs of Fr. Gallwey*, p. 158. One of the changes introduced, as we have seen, was in the preparation of points for meditation.

[2] John Morris (1826–93; see *DNB*, Gillow, Boase ii, *Cath. Encycl.*, Sutcliffe), Jesuit priest, born at Ootacamund, Southern India, on 4 July 1826. Educated at Temple Grove, East Sheen, and Harrow; Admitted pensioner of Trinity College, Cambridge, Oct. 1845. Received into the R.C. Church on 20 May 1846. Studied at the English College, Rome, 1846–9; ordained priest in Sept. 1849. Missioner at Northampton, then at Great Marlow. Appointed Canon of Northampton in 1852. Vice-rector of English College, Rome, 1852–5. Private secretary to Cardinal Wiseman and afterwards to Cardinal Manning. Canon Penitentiary of Westminster, 1861. Entered the S.J. novitiate in Feb. 1867. Successively Minister at Manresa, Socius to the Provincial, Fr. Whitty, and first Superior of the Oxford Mission. Professor of Church History and Canon Law at St. Beuno's, GMH being among his pupils. Fr. Morris preached the sermon at St. Beuno's on the occasion of the episcopal silver jubilee of the Bp. of Shrewsbury in July 1876; GMH's poem 'Silver Jubilee' was published with this sermon. First rector of St. Ignatius's College, Malta, 1877–8. Vice-rector Roehampton in 1879, and Rector, 1880–6. F.S.A., 10 Jan. 1889. Died at Wimbledon on 22 Oct. 1893. (*Letters to Bridges*, p. 65; *Correspondence with Dixon*, p. 76; *Further Letters*, pp. 140, 141, 161; *Journals and Papers*, pp. 191, 258.)

[3] Charles Langdale (1787–1868). See *DNB*; *The Tablet*, 5, 12, 19 Dec. 1868, pp. 147, 183, 201, 238; Peter Gallwey, *Salvage from the Wreck* [1889], pp. 19–61 with photograph; Henry James Coleridge, 'A Father of the Poor', *The Month*, x (Feb. 1869), 175–82; and the indexes to Wilfrid Ward's *The Life and Times of Cardinal Wiseman*, 2 vols. (1897), and Bernard Ward's *The Sequel to Catholic Emancipation*, 2 vols. (1915), water-colour sketch, i. 197.

[4] *Journals and Papers*, p. 379.

and their train started from Putney at 8.28. Tickets taken as usual to Waterloo tho' they were to get out at Vauxhall and take cabs from there to Mount Street and return with the rest after *Tenebrae* . . . The brothers who did not go to Farm Street worked in the chapel, dusting and putting back the carpet. [NBJ]

July 31st, the feast of St. Ignatius Loyola, the founder of the Jesuit Order, fell on a Saturday in 1869, and the novices were allowed to go to London:

All the Novices went to Farm St. for High Mass beginning at 11. A panegyric of our Holy Father was preached by Very Revd. Monsignor Capel.[1] [NBJ]

But the following year, the feast falling on a Sunday, the entry read: 'We were not allowed to visit Farm St. because of the crowd.'

In 1870, on 19 March, the feast of St. Joseph, a small iron church[2] was opened:

Father Rector gave the novices permission either to go to Farm Street, or to the Church where Exposition was going [on],[3] or to remain at home & chance to get to High Mass at the New Church (St. Joseph's) which was opened today. The greater number remained. There was grand High Mass at 11 celebrated by Dr. Morris[4] & sermon by Fr. Rector.[5] [NBJ]

Dr. Morris, Bishop of Troy, lived in Roehampton Lane, not far from Manresa House. He was on the friendliest of terms with the

---

[1] Thomas John Capel (1836-1911). See *DNB*, 2nd Supp.

[2] *Journals and Papers*, p. 196, entry for 19 Mar., and *Further Letters*, bottom of p. 110. Elsewhere we learn: 'It . . . was removed in 1872, being found too cold in winter and too hot in summer.' *LLNN*, xxx (July 1910), 470.

[3] The devotion of Quarante 'Ore, or 'Forty Hours', was being held at St. Mary's, Hampstead, and had begun on 17 Mar., see *The Tablet*, 12 Mar. 1870, p. 336. A note on the Quarante 'Ore is given in *Journals and Papers*, p. 379.

[4] William Placid Morris (1794-1872; Gillow, Boase ii), Bishop of Troy, born in London on 29 Sept. 1794. Professed at the Benedictine College at Acton Burnell, Shropshire; ordained priest in 1818. 1819, was appointed one of the chaplains to the Portuguese Embassy, South St., London. 1832, appointed Vicar-Apostolic of Mauritius, and was consecrated Bishop of Troy, i.p.i., on 5 Feb., at St. Edmund's College, Ware. Resigned his charge nine years later and returned to England. For the remaining thirty years acted as chaplain to the Sisters of the Sacred Heart, Roehampton, living at Subiaco Lodge. Died on 18 Feb. 1872 at Roehampton.

[5] Peter Gallwey, *St. Joseph and the Vatican Council. The Substance of a Sermon preached at the Opening of St. Joseph's Chapel, Roehampton, March 19, 1870* (1870).

Fathers there,[1] and was a not infrequent visitor. I include the report of two occasions only:

Wednesday, July 7th. [1869]

All went to the chapel at 10 to be present at the confirmation by his Lordship Dr. Morris of a recent convert, an exercitant here. The 'Veni Creator' was sung before and the 'Te Deum' after the ceremony, which was finished by his Lordship giving his blessing to all. [NBJ]

Thursday, 28 October 1869, must have been long remembered as a red-letter day by the novices, since they entertained at Manresa, not one, but three bishops at the same time. I quote the entry in its entirety:

Feast of the Holy Apostles Simon and Jude.

Holy Communion. Double-table[2] day on occasion of the visit of Dr. Etheridge[3] & Dr. Meurin.[4] Dr. Morris also was present at dinner. There were long walks in the morning. 3. Dinner. After dinner the 3 Bishops conversed for some time with the novices in the Hall. [NBJ]

The presence of the two Jesuit Bishops, Drs. Etheridge and Meurin, is simply explained; they were both on their way to attend the opening

[1] 'And the members of our Society have lost in him a valuable friend—a friend ever willing not only to confer the sacred Orders on its approved members at any time, and at much personal inconvenience to himself, but likewise, in the unavoidable absence of the Ordinary, to add a lustre by his presence to the more solemn services of our churches.' From an obituary in *LLNN*, viii (Mar. 1872), 70.

[2] 'Double-table' is a term still in use in the English Province and indicates that the dinner will be grander than usual. In some houses, for example, the novitiate, the refectory tables are joined together in much the same way as is done, say, for wedding receptions. The same term occurs later in the Porter's Journal as kept by Hopkins, but he sometimes uses 'long-tables' instead of 'double-table'.

[3] James Etheridge (1808–78; see Foley vii, Gillow, Boase i), Bishop of Torona and Vicar Apostolic of British Guiana, born at Redmarley, Worcs., on 19 Oct. 1808. Educated at Sedgley Park and Stonyhurst Colleges. Entered the S.J. novitiate at Hodder in Sept. 1827; ordained priest in Sept. 1836. Parish work at Pontefract and Norwich. 1851, Rector of St. Beuno's College. 1857, Superior of mission in British Guiana. 1858, consecrated by Cardinal Wiseman as Bishop of Torona and Vicar Apostolic of Brit. Guiana. After a useful episcopate of nineteen years he died on 1 Jan. 1878 on the mail-steamer *Eider*, travelling from Barbados to Georgetown, and was buried at sea.

[4] Johann Gabriel Leo Meurin (1825–95; see Buckland, *Dict. of Indian Biography*, *Lexikon für Theologie und Kirche*, Sommervogel), Vicar Apostolic of Bombay, born in Berlin on 23 June 1825. Educated in Cologne. Ordained priest in 1848. Entered the Society of Jesus in Apr. 1853. Arrived in India in Oct. 1858. Military chaplain at Poona; parish work in Candolim and Bombay Cathedral. 1860, Superior of the diocesan seminary. 1867, nominated as Bishop of Ascalon, i.p.i., and Vicar Apostolic over the Vicariate of Bombay and Western India; consecrated as Bishop on 2 Feb. 1868. Attended Vatican Council I, 1869–70. 1876–7, acted as Visitor Apostolic to the community of the Syrian rite. Recalled to Rome, July 1886, and made Archbishop of Mauritius. Died June 1895.

of the First Vatican Council. The novices were comparatively well-informed about the Council as the refectory reading list shows.[1] Further, because of the important issues involved they were urged to pray for the Council's success:

June, 29. [1869]
It was suggested that today all the Priests, shd. offer up Mass, and all non-priests their Communion and other prayers for the Holy See and the General Council. [NBJ]

Again in 1870 the novices had their attention directed to world affairs, this time on the occasion of the threat of war between France and Prussia:[2]

July 15th.
Fr. Rector asked the Community to pray that the horror of a war which was imminent might be averted & gave permission to those who wished to go to Holy Communion for that intention. [NBJ]

Two different incidents can conclude this brief list of happenings. The first was religious—the celebration of the tercentenary of the Jesuit, St. Stanislaus Kostka.[3]

Friday, Nov. 13th [1868]
Tercentenary of St. Stanislaus—Right Rev. Dr. Grant[4] said Mass for us and gave Holy Communion. Walk 10. Right Rev. Drs Grant & Morris present at dinner. Recreation in the refectory after dinner to which the two bishops came. [NBJ]

The other event concerned the Spanish Revolution of 1868 which had as one of its results the expulsion of the Jesuits:

[1] The Supplements to *The Tablet* on 'The Nineteenth General Council; or, The First Council of the Vatican' were read in the refectory throughout 1869 on the following dates: 24 Jan., 6 Feb., 29 Mar., 26 Apr., 8 May, 14 May, 17 May, 11 Sept.

[2] See Hopkins's entry for 15 July 1870 in *Journals and Papers*, p. 202.

[3] *LLNN*, vi (Mar. 1869), 3–6, gives an account of the celebrations at St. Andrea del Quirinale on the occasion of St. Stanislaus's being proclaimed Patron of all Jesuit novitiates.

[4] Thomas Grant (1816–70; see *DNB*, Gillow, Boase i, *Cath. Encycl.*). First Bishop of Southwark, born in Ligny-les-Aires, France, on 25 Nov. 1816. Educated at Chester, Ushaw College, and the English College, Rome. 1844, Rector of the English College, Rome. Secretary to Cardinal Acton, and agent at Rome for the English Vicars Apostolic. Nominated by Pope Pius IX to be Bishop of the new R.C. see of Southwark; consecrated on 6 July 1851. He died at Rome on 1 June 1870. (*Journals and Papers*, p. 202.)

Nov. 15th. [1868]

Fr Forn, exiled from Spain by the Revolution came here today.[1]
[NBJ]

Two months later we read:

Jan. 25th. [1869]

After supper a letter from the exiled Spanish Novices residing at Angers
was translated from the Latin for us.[2]

On the next occasion that Hopkins wrote to his mother he told her
of the plight of his fellow Jesuits:

Some had to escape in disguise. At Cadiz the Admiral though belonging
to the revolution stood their friend and marched them through the town
to the fleet. They all had the power of going to their homes but most chose
exile and those who did go back seem to have done so against their will and
by the advice of their superiors. A boy of 14 who was to be sent home
begged with tears to go with the rest into exile and at last his wish was
granted. The Spanish provinces are dispersed abroad but chiefly through
France and our correspondents write from Angers. To be persecuted in a
tolerant age is a high distinction.[3]

And some while later the Porter entered in his Journal:

Sunday, March 28th.

A letter that was being sent to the Spanish Novices read by Br. G.
Hopkins.

Friday, April 2nd.

Those who were at home signed their names to a letter sent by us to the
Spanish novices residing at Angers . . . The rest signed their names . . .
after dinner.

Did Hopkins write the Latin letter? It could well have been so.

There are few additional details to relate which concern Hopkins

[1] Contemporary accounts of the Revolution which began in Sept. 1868 are to be found
in *The Times*, *The Tablet*, and the *Annual Register*, and see also Lesmes Frias, *La
Provincia de Castilla de la Compañía de Jésus 1863–1914* (Bilbao-Deusto, 1915), pp. 25–6,
33. Apparently there is no copy of Frias's history in the B.M., Bodleian, or libraries working in conjunction with N.C.L. The copy consulted has been deposited in the library of
Heythrop College. Fr. Joachim Forn, S.J. (1818–70), belonged to the Province of
Aragon.

[2] Extracts of a letter dated 21 Feb. 1869 from Spanish novices at Angers to the
English novices were published in *LLNN*, vi (Mar. 1869), 41–6. The Admiral, the
disguise of secular attire, and the incident of the fourteen-year-old boy of Hopkins's
letter are all to be found there.

[3] *Further Letters*, p. 106.

personally, but when these are set down every occasion in the noviceship on which his name occurs will have been recorded. Proportionately, his name crops up most often in matters concerning his health. But first the following note clarifies the general health background:

We had no games of any kind: the only exercise we took was walking: yet we kept healthy enough, and there was no work for a Brother Infirmarian: the office in fact did not exist.[1]

Games, as we have seen, were being played in Hopkins's time, but the Catalogues for 1868-70 still show no Infirmarian. Perhaps Fr. Gallwey himself supplied the deficiency, for as his biographer relates, 'There was something very tender in his kindness and care of the novices. In all that concerned their food, exercise and sleep he was most vigilant.'[2] Two entries bear on this:

April 12th [1870]
N.B. By Order—'No one is to take a bath within three hours after dinner.'

August 16th [1870]
½hr. long[er] sleep which is to be the order for a few days as many are suffering from fatigue. [NBJ]

Visits to the doctor and dentist are methodically noted in the novitiate, and the records show that Hopkins went to see Dr. Fincham[3] twice, on 25 November 1868 and on 22 July 1870. He visited Mr. Sass,[4] the dentist, nine times. His series of regular

---

[1] 'Some Reminiscences of Novice Day, 1864, 1865', *LLNN*, xxx (Jan. 1910), 318.

[2] Gavin, *Memoirs of Fr. Gallwey*, p. 164. For Fr. Gallwey's later personal care for GMH, see these entries: 27 Oct. 1872 and 21 Jan. 1873 in *Journals and Papers*, pp. 227 and 230 respectively. Fr. Fitzsimon, it will be recalled, would not allow him to fast during Lent (*Further Letters*, p. 106).

[3] George Tupman Fincham (1818-90; see Boase v), consulting physician to Westminster Hospital, first son of George Fincham, was born in London on 28 Jan. 1818. Educated at Westminster School, King's College, London, and St. John's College, Oxford; B.A., 1839; M.B., 1843; M.D., 1847. Studied at St. George's Hospital, London, also Paris and Dublin: M.R.C.P.L., 1844; Fellow, 1855. Assistant physician Westminster, 1853, physician, 1855, senior physician, 1877-83. Examiner in medicine, 1881-3; senior censor, 1883; Vice-President, 1885. Consulting physician from 1883 to his death. In 1855 he had joined the R.C. Church. Died on 26 May 1890.(*Journals and Papers*, p. 230.)

[4] Sass—probably Frederick Archibald Sass, M.R.C.S. (d. 1879), dentist, of 83 Gloucester Place, Portman Square, London. According to Dentists' Register for 1878: '. . . said to have practised dentistry since 1851.' His son, Joseph Sass, of the same address, and also of 1 King Street, Twickenham, registered as a dentist in 1879. No record of death, but in 1883 he went to South Africa and ceased to be registered in 1890.

dental appointments in 1869 spread out from March until May.[1]
And he paid a last visit on 27 June 1870.

Little else is related of him. Three of his friends, Bond, Baillie,
and Bridges visited him at Manresa,[2] but apparently none of his
family.

There are two more isolated entries concerning Hopkins, but what
they tell us is negligible:

Tuesday, Oct. 27th. [1868]

Brs. W. Kerr[3] & G. Hopkins went to London.

Saturday, July 10th. [1869]

Br Gartlan[4] & G. Hopkins went out to walk at 10, returning at 1.

During his noviceship, Hopkins, as we have seen, was a catechist
and also acted as 'Angel-Guardian' to a new novice. In addition he
was Porter, or chief novice, from 11 December 1869 until 19 February 1870.[5] During this time he wrote up the Journal which goes
with that office. I record it in full because I think that the very
baldness and even, on occasion, poverty of the entries convey more
strikingly than screeds of explanation what life in the noviceship
was like.

---

[1] The dates of his visits were 18 Mar., 1, 15, 22, 29 Apr., 6, 13, and 31 May.

[2] *Further Letters*, p. 107. Bond and Baillie together; Bridges apparently alone. For
the visit paid by two more friends of Oxford days, Richard Lewis Nettleship (*Journals
and Papers*, p. 351) and Henry Scott Holland, see *Henry Scott Holland*, ed. Stephen
Paget (1921), pp. 29–30.

[3] William Hobart Kerr (1836–1913), Jesuit priest, eldest son of Lord Henry Kerr, son
of the 6th Marquis of Lothian, was born at Dittisham Rectory, Devonshire, on 25 July
1836. His younger brother, Henry Schomberg, was also a Jesuit. Educated at Harrow,
Stonyhurst and Haileybury Colleges. Received into the R.C. Church in 1852. Madras
Civil Service, 1856–66. Entered the S.J. novitiate at Roehampton Nov. 1867, his brother
having arrived in September; he and his brother were ordained together at St. Beuno's
in Sept. 1875. Socius to the master of novices 1879, with charge of the newly founded
mission at Wimbledon. Built the Sacred Heart church, Wimbledon, St. Winefride's,
and the parish schools. Died on 24 Mar. 1913. (*Further Letters*, p. 410; *Journals and
Papers*, pp. 190, 257.)

[4] Ignatius Gartlan (1848–1926), Jesuit priest, born at Monalty, Northern Ireland, on
8 Dec. 1848. Educated at Mount St. Mary's and Stonyhurst Colleges. Entered the S.J.
novitiate at Roehampton in Sept. 1867; ordained priest, Sept. 1883. 1899–1904, Rector
of St. Aloysius's, Glasgow. Prefect Apostolic and Superior of the Zambezi Mission,
1904–11. Instructor of Tertians at St. Stanislaus's College, Tullabeg, Ireland, 1911.
Last years spent at Osterley, acting as spiritual director and retreat giver. Died on 12 Dec.
1926. (*Journals and Papers*, pp. 191, 243.)

[5] Ibid., pp. 193, 196, entries for 23 Dec. 1869 and 19 Feb. 1870.

The Manuscript of the Journal kept by Hopkins as Porter[1]

Saturday—December 11th [1869]

Bidellus—Br Gerard Hopkins. Other[2] offices changed. See next Saturday.

Reading: Tobias ii—St. Bonaventure's Life of our Lord[3] continued[4]

Sunday, Dec. 12

Non-exercitants[5] catechised at Homer Row excepting Br. Macmullin.[6]— Benediction—The Rector came to recreation: the Pope[7] had sent his blessing to the novices at Dr. Grant's request.

[1] The Porter's Journal in which GMH when holding that office wrote his account is a small brown or buff unlined notebook measuring 105×160 mm. containing 158 unnumbered leaves. Hopkins has written on 24 pages; in the case of the first two leaves he wrote on the verso and recto pages, thereafter recto pages only. The whole notebook covers the period 9 Dec. 1869 to 26 Oct. 1871. Hopkins began keeping the Journal on 11 Dec. 1869 and finished on 19 Feb. 1870.

(i) Abbreviations—these are retained as in the manuscript. Where necessary they are expanded, but this is indicated either by square brackets [ ] or by annotation. If they are clear from the context they are allowed to stand.

(ii) Corrections and cancellations in the manuscript are not normally noted, but any important adjustments are retained or mentioned in the notes.

(iii) Punctuation and spelling are given as in the original; any special points of interest are matter for footnotes.

(iv) In some instances it is doubtful whether GMH intended a capital or a small letter, but as his practice was not consistent each doubtful letter has been judged on its merit (e.g. 'high mass' and 'High Mass').

(v) Square brackets denote editorial addition.

For the sake of completion I have included the daily refectory reading, but this has been also included in Appendix 2A and details of the editions used are reserved for that Appendix. Further, items previously annotated are here passed over in silence.

[2] Hopkins's handwriting begins with 'Other offices changed'.

[3] He sometimes fails to underline a book-title as here.

[4] Full-stop omitted after 'continued' as also at the end of several entries, but GMH's practice is not consistent, nor is it always clear whether he intends a full-stop or not. The editors of *Journals and Papers* state that after Apr. 1870 it was 'Hopkins's normal rule to put no stop at the end of a paragraph' (p. 408, n. 199. 2). The Porter's Journal shows that this idiosyncrasy had begun in Dec. 1869.

[5] Non-exercitants, that is, those like Hopkins who were not making the Long Retreat which had begun this year on 25 Nov. Fr. Gallwey had become novice master only on 13 Sept. He therefore deferred the L.R. until he had settled in. GMH's L.R., it will be remembered, had started on 16 Sept.

[6] Thomas McMullin (1851–1928), Jesuit priest, born at Weedon, Monmouthshire, on 31 Jan. 1851. Educated at St. Francis Xavier's, Liverpool, and Stonyhurst Colleges. Entered the S.J. novitiate at Roehampton on the same day as GMH, 7 Sept. 1868; ordained priest in 1884. Taught at Beaumont, Stonyhurst, Mount St. Mary's, and Wimbledon Colleges. Parish work at Blackpool and Wigan. Retired to Petworth in 1918, and died there on 3 Mar. 1928. Hopkins consistently writes 'Macmullin' for 'McMullin' throughout the manuscript.

[7] Pius IX (Giovanni Maria Mastai-Ferretti, 1792–1878); Pope 1846–78.

Reading: Matt. v.—*Summary* 1–12—John ii, Matt. vi, vii, Mark ii, iii 1–19

Monday, Dec. 13

Day of repose for the exercitants and recreation for all. Holy Communion for exercitants, also allowed to the rest[1] to be offered up for the retreat. Walk at 9.25 or 9.30, the last half-hour (from 12.30) if spent indoors to be public recreation; again at 3.15: no Latin. Public recreation at 5. spiritual reading (Rodriguez for non-exercitants) 5.30. A Kempis 6 (?). Points for meditation (all present) 6.15, meditation (made in chapel by all) 6.30, Benediction 7. Beads were said out walking in the afternoon. The Rector came to night recreation.

Reading: John vi 1–15—*The Bd. Sacrament* by Fr. Faber, III §7

Tuesday, Dec. 14

Brs. F. Hopkins and Southern went into retreat, two non-exercitants appointed servers at first table for the rest of the week in their place. Br. Wilcock no longer in retreat and catechised at Isleworth. Non-ex. swept house in afternoon. After Consideration[2] order of evening for non-exercitants: beads and free time till 5.15 spiritual reading, points for med[itation].[3] (non-ex. present) 5.45, med. 6, visit,[4] 6.30, A Kempis 6.45, free 6.55

Reading: John ix—Fr. Faber continued—Sister Emmerich's *Dolorous Passion of our Lord*

Wednesday, Dec. 15—fast[5]

Recreation for non-exercitants. Walk by 10, first half hour Latin. Free time 12.30. Walk 3. Consideration 4.15. Public rec[reation]. 5.15. Points for med. 5.45. Med. 6. Visit 6.30. A Kempis 6.45. Beads and free time 6.55

Reading: *Summary* (13–24)—*Passion of our Lord* (Sister Emmerich), med. ii–vi about.

Thursday, Dec. 16

Beads 3, indoor works for all but a few 3.15, Consideration 4.15,

---

[1] A reminder of the era before Pope St. Pius X, whose decree of 1905 encouraged daily communion. For the practice in the noviceship see pp. 35–6.

[2] Consideration, i.e. the name given to the afternoon religious discourse.

[3] The less obvious abbreviations used by GMH in this manuscript are: B.S.: Blessed Sacrament; man.: manual; med.: meditation; non-ex.: non-exercitants; public rec.: public recreation; spir.: spiritual.

[4] Visit to the Blessed Sacrament.

[5] This week being an Ember week, Wednesday, Friday, and Saturday were days of fasting. See the entries for 17 and 18 Dec.

spir[itual] reading 5.5, A Kempis 5.35, points for med. 5.45, med. 6, visit to B[lessed] S[acrament]. 6.30, free 6.45.—Admonitions[1]

Reading: *Summary* 24–36—Sister Emmerich continued

Friday, Dec. 17—fast

Catechisms as on Tuesday. Lesson by heart after Consideration, otherwise order of evening as yesterday

Reading: *Summary* 36–44—Sister Emmerich (*The Passion* ch. i forward)

Saturday, Dec. 18—fast (ember)

Rodriguez 9.10, reflection 9.40, man[ual] works out of doors 10.30, studies 11.30, lesson by heart 12.30. The same was also the order last Saturday. Afternoon as Thursday. Offices[2] not changed.

Reading. *Summary* 45 to end—Sister Emmerich continued

Sunday, Dec. 19

Br. Considine[3] went into retreat. The four non-exercitants catechised at Homer Row and two of the Juniors, Br. Bacon[4] and Br. Henry Kerr.

Reading: Common Rules 1–10—Sister Emmerich, chapter xxxviii and then xliv

Monday, Dec. 20

Communion, to be offered up for those in retreat. Repose and recreation day. Ad lib. recreation 12, public 12.30. Afternoon as last Monday, with Benediction

[1] Each novice has a fellow-novice as his admonitor to point out to him privately any exterior faults in his keeping of the rules or customs.

[2] Offices in this context means the weekly job assigned to a novice, e.g. waiting in the refectory, reader, washing-up, and so on. The offices were not changed since replacements were probably impossible because so many novices were making the Long Retreat and would be exempt from office as far as possible.

[3] Daniel Heffernan Considine (1849–1922), Jesuit priest, born at Derk House, Old Pallas, Limerick, on 1 Jan. 1849. Educated at Stonyhurst College and Lincoln College, Oxford, but left without taking a degree. Entered the S.J. novitiate at Roehampton on 14 Feb. 1868; ordained priest at St. Beuno's on 25 Sept. 1881. Prefect of Studies at Beaumont, 1887–94. Master of novices and Rector of Manresa, 1894–1908; Rector of Wimbledon College, 1908–13. Consultor of the Province, 1901–11. As novice master for fourteen years he was responsible for the initial training and formation of over two hundred Jesuits. Died at Manresa, Roehampton, on 10 Jan. 1922. (*Further Letters,* p. 56; *Journals and Papers,* pp. 199, 236, 250, 251, 256.)

[4] Francis Edward Bacon (1839–1922; see Sutcliffe), Jesuit priest, born at Hackney, London, on 1 Mar. 1839. Joined the R.C. Church at the age of twenty-seven; entered the S.J. novitiate at Roehampton in Oct. 1867; ordained priest, Sept. 1875. Taught at St. Aloysius's College, Glasgow, for most of his life. The text of some of GMH's poems survive only in copies which he made; one of the few of GMH's contemporaries who showed any appreciation of his poetry. Died in Glasgow on 11 Dec. 1922. (*Letters to Bridges,* p. 196; *Journals and Papers,* pp. 208, 213, 257 (2), 258.)

Reading: Common Rules 11–22—Sister Emmerich, chapter L forward to p. 304

Tuesday, Dec. 21

St. Thomas's day—Holy Communion and Benediction. Afternoon as Friday last but after med. free fr. 6.30 to Benediction.—Br. F. Hopkins and Br. Southern being no longer in retreat the catechists were—for Isleworth Br. G. Hopkins, Br. Southern, Br. Wilcock, for Fulham Br. Sidgreaves,[1] Br. F. Hopkins, Br. Macmullin

Reading: Common Rules 23–32—Fr. Faber's *Creator and Creature*, in bk. III, chapter iv (*our own God*) at page 412

Wednesday, Dec. 22—fast[2]

As last Wednesday except that beads were to be said out walking in the afternoon and attendance at Consideration was free

Reading: Common Rules 33–43—Fr. Faber continued

Thursday, Dec. 23

Washing basons[3] for those not in retreat 12.30. Admonitions

Reading: St. Austin's Confessions ix §17—St. John xiv 1–20

Friday, Christmas Eve

Washing basons for exercitants 8.40. Catechism at Isleworth—Br. G. Hopkins and Br. Wilcock. None at Fulham. For the other non-exercitants the time was free after Rodriguez till 10.30, then manual works, and again from 11.30 till 12.30 (study time) was free, but this hour and all the time till washing they spent in dressing the chapel.

---

[1] Edward Sidgreaves (1840–1930), Jesuit priest, born at Fernyhalgh, near Preston, on 18 May 1840. Educated at Stonyhurst College. Entered the S.J. novitiate at Roehampton in June 1868; ordained priest in Sept. 1879. Parish work at Denbigh and St. Helens. Worked on the mission in British Guiana until 1909. Retired to Bournemouth where he died on 24 Sept. 1930. (*Journals and Papers*, pp. 191, 235.)

[2] The Wednesdays and Fridays of Advent were days of fasting.

[3] 'basons' and similarly spelled at the entries for 24, 31 Dec., and 8 Jan. His unfinished poem 'Pilate' (dating from June 1864) contains the couplet: 'Some ice that locks the glacier to the rocks / And in a bason brings the blocks.' (*Poems*, p. 118.) In his diary, however, he uses the spelling 'basin':

    (i) 'the current is strong and if the basin into which it runs' (entry for 1863 in *Journals and Papers*, p. 8)

    (ii) 'Ice on my tadpole basin' (entry for 28 Mar. 1868, ibid., p. 163)

    (iii) 'Ice on basin again.' (entry for 10 and 11 Apr. 1868, ibid., p. 164)

    (iv) 'a basin of hills' (entry for 6 Sept. 1874, ibid., p. 258).

GMH's use of the variant 'bason' as late as Jan. 1870 would seem to postdate any example recorded in *OED*.

Reading: Apocalypse xxi, omitting 12–20—Charlevoix' Hist[ory] of Japan: life of Fr. Francis Mastrilli begun

Litanies 3. Manual works 3.15. Beads, and confessions for exercitants 4.15. Spiritual reading 5. Points of meditation 5.30 Med. 5.45. Visit for non-exercitants 6.15. Confessions for the same 6.30. Supper (no scholastic novices serving at second table) 7. Examen[1] 7.30. Going to bed 7.45. Rising 10.55. Points of meditation (in chapel) 11.15. Meditation 11.30.

Saturday, Christmas Day
End of the Long Retreat

Adeste fideles 12, followed by midnight mass (by special leave[2] from the Holy Father got for the community by Dr. Grant) with communion, and then the *Te Deum*. Meal in the refectory at 1,[3] and to bed. Rising 6.30. Second and third masses of Xmas at 7 and 7.30. Breakfast 8. Beds 8.45. Rodriguez 8.55. Dressing for walk about 9.20. Walk to follow as fast as possible. Leave for hearing high mass was given at the pro cathedral,[4] Moorfields,[5] Hammersmith,[6] Clapham,[7] Fr. Rawes' church,[8] Fulham,[9]

[1] The examination of conscience was earlier than usual because of Christmas Eve.

[2] The Manresa Journal is more explicit: 'Midnight Mass and Holy Communion in virtue of a Rescript granted ad Triennium.' The entry in the Porter's Journal for 25 Dec. 1868 shows that they did not have Mass at midnight that year: 'First Mass said at 6 & during the 2nd [Mass] half of the hour's Meditation was made. Holy Communion given at the 2nd Mass during which there was singing.' At this time, of course, Midnight Mass was normally only allowed in parish churches; the privilege was extended to all religious houses having a chapel in which the Blessed Sacrament was reserved only in 1907 by a decree of the Holy Office, Canon 821, *Codex Iuris Canonici*. For a description of Midnight Mass at Manresa see Meadows, *Obedient Men*, pp. 76–7.

[3] 'Meal in the refectory at 1', that is, after the Midnight Mass. Less sumptuous than it sounds: 'Soup and cocoa were provided in the Refectory', Manresa Journal entry for Xmas Eve 1869. This 'meal' is referred to generally as 'haustus'. See also Meadows, *Obedient Men*, p. 77.

[4] Pro-Cathedral—Our Lady of Victories, Kensington, W. 8. This church was opened as the new Pro-Cathedral on 2 July 1869, St. Mary's, Moorfields, having previously served. For the opening see *The Tablet*, 10 July 1869, p. 185.

Photographs and brief histories of almost all the churches mentioned here will be found in the following two books: Bernard W. Kelly, *Historical Notes on English Catholic Missions* (1907); Alexander Rottman, *London Catholic Churches* (1926). In listing the churches in Hopkins's entry I have given the present address which in some cases differs from the one formerly given in the *Catholic Directory* of the time. The *Catholic Directory* shows that all the churches named here had Mass at 11 a.m., in the majority of cases High Mass, and in a few instances accompanied by a sermon. Denis Meadows states that he and his fellow-novices were 'connoisseurs of sermons', *Obedient Men*, p. 182.

[5] St. Mary's, Eldon Street, Moorfields, E.C. 2.

[6] The Holy Trinity, Brook Green, Hammersmith, W. 6.

[7] Our Immaculate Lady of Victories, Clapham Park Road, S.W. 4.

[8] Fr. Rawes' Church—St. Francis of Assisi, Pottery Lane, Notting Hill, W. 11. See also *Journals and Papers*, pp. 195, 406.

[9] St. Thomas of Canterbury, Rylston Road, Fulham, S.W. 6.

Surbiton,[1] St. George's,[2] the Carmelite church[3] and Haverstock Hill.[4] Examen and beads out. Litanies 2.45. Then beds taken to the same places as before the retreat.[5] Dinner with a sermon by Br. Bacon 4. Wine after dinner. Recreation 5.30. A Kempis 6. Points for med. 6.15. Med. 6.30. Benediction 7. Supper 7.45. Then recreation. At 9* points for meditation shd. have been read from the book[6] but by the porter's mistake the novices went to chapel and waited till examen-time 9.15. Going to bed 9.30.

Br. Campbell,[7] who a day or two before had ended a retreat in the house under Fr. Minister,[8] came as a novice on Xmas Eve and spent Xmas Day in recreation with the Community.

*Read after examen in Hall

Sunday, Dec. 26—St. Stephen's day

Communion. Rodriguez 9, man. works 9.30, office 10, and all as usual. Ad lib. 5, Public recreation 5.30, beads 6, etc.

Catechisms at Homer Row, Brentford, and Westminster, with a few changes in the catechists.

---

[1] St. Raphael, Portsmouth Road, Surbiton, Surrey. The contemporary *Catholic Directory* reads 'Kingston-on-Thames' in place of 'Surbiton'.

[2] St. George's Cathedral, Lambeth Road, Southwark, S.E. 1. This was blitzed in Apr. 1941, but has now been rebuilt.

[3] Our Lady of Mount Carmel and St. Simon Stock, Kensington Church Street, W. 8.

[4] St. Dominic's Priory, Southampton Road, Haverstock Hill, N.W. 5. The more distant of the churches mentioned are seven or eight miles and more from Manresa. Whether the novices could have reached them on foot in an hour and a half is more than doubtful.

[5] For general convenience those making the Long Retreat had been grouped together in the same Quarters. Now that it had finished the retreatants were no longer segregated but rejoined the rest of the community.

[6] It is not possible to say with certainty what this book was, nor is it clear whether it was in manuscript or printed. The Porter's Journal shows that the *Meditations* of Fr. Louis de Ponte, S.J., were in use at the period. A six-volume English translation of this work was published by Richardson & Son, 1852–4. But other meditation collections were available, for example, Cardinal Wiseman's.

[7] Donald Charles Vores Campbell (1849–1922), secular priest, son of James Archibald Campbell, J.P., of Inverane, born in Edinburgh on 13 Jan. 1849. Educated at Rugby and Edinburgh Univ. Entered the S.J. novitiate at Roehampton on 24 Dec. 1869; ordained priest, 28 Apr. 1882. Served St. Asaph mission, 1884–6, followed by work in Edinburgh and Glasgow. Left the Society of Jesus in July 1887. Remaining years spent as a secular priest in London. Died at Kensington on 23 Apr. 1922. This is the 'Br. Campbell', at the time a Junior at Manresa, who visited GMH at Hampstead, as shown in the entry for 30 Dec. 1872 in GMH's diary (*Journals and Papers*, p. 229). The editors have mistakenly taken the entry to refer to Archibald Campbell, S.J., but he was in the S.J. novitiate in Belgium at this time.

[8] John Morris (1826–93). See p. 60 n. 2.

Monday, Dec. 27—St. John

Holy Communion.—Close day:[1] Rodriguez 9, works 9.30, exhortation
10 (in the regular course,[2] on rule 29 of the Summary), etc. Tone[3] 3.15
(Br. Considine). Confessions *ad libitum* 5.30. Benediction.

During evening recreation Fr. Rector and Fr. Minister came in and
lots were drawn for Innocent Porter.[4] Br. Fred. Hopkins was drawn.

Tuesday, Dec. 28—Holy Innocents

Holy Communion.—The time for making beds was not kept to. Rodriguez
8.55 but the reading was broken off.[5] Walk,[6] with leave for visiting
Catholic churches: examen and beads and lunch out[7]—all to be out by
9.45. Dinner 4—Dr. Morris and several Fathers of ours and seculars
present.[8]—long tables.[9] Then recreation. Br. Campbell spent the day

[1] 'Close day', or 'close ordo', as opposed to 'open ordo'. On a 'close ordo' day the
novices did more work, or, in other words, had less recreation.

[2] The novice master gives regular exhortations on the rules of the Summary of the
Constitutions and also on the Common Rules. Fr. Gallwey, according to Fr. Charles
Blount, gave in addition 'a series of exhortations on St. Bernard's twelve degrees of
Pride'. Gavin, *Memoirs of Fr. Gallwey*, p. 157.

[3] One or two of the novices preached a 'tone' every week, cf. Reg. 76. Mag. Nov.
Institutum Societatis Iesu, iii. 129, and see above p. 46.

[4] Some details of the practice of choosing the 'Innocent Porter' are made clear by the
following:

'On great festivals, such as Christmas, Easter, the feast of Sts. Ignatius, Xavier,
Aloysius, and Holy Innocents, we always made merry. On the eve of the last-named
festival, the Superior would come to the recreation-room, with a number of small slips
of paper in his hand, each having a sentence from A' Kempis, or some other ascetic,
inscribed on it: except one, on which was written, I think, "Ego sum innocens"—"I am
the innocent". We each drew a slip, and the novice who drew the one in question was to
be *Porter* for the next day.... Of course the office of porter, thus assumed by *chance*, was
like many similar chance-appointments in the world, very clumsily discharged. But the
fun of the thing did good to the mind, and we were always permitted to laugh when we
could not help it.' Andrew Steinmetz, *The Novitiate*, pp. 233-4. See also James George
Frazer, *The Golden Bough*, Part VI. *The Scapegoat*, 3rd ed. (1933), 336-7.
The entry in the Manresa Journal for the feast of the Holy Innocents reads: 'Meat
breakfast, long walk, dinner at 4...' What they had for dinner this year we are not told,
but the previous year's entry reads: 'Meat for b'fast—dinner at 3.30. 2 Turkeys,—
2 Geese, 4 Partridge, Hare Soup—Plum Pudding—Mince Pies—Cheese Cake, &c.'

[5] Following '... broken off' GMH, using a thick-nibbed pen, has heavily scored out
'in order to practise the old glee of "Who's the fool now?" with new words by Fr. Rector
which was sung in alternate [verses] by Juniors and Novices after dinner'. Hopkins
mentions this glee in his letter to his mother, see *Further Letters*, p. 109.

[6] On this occasion Hopkins went to Hampton Court, cf. ibid.

[7] Sandwiches prepared by the novices themselves is the current practice.

[8] Usually only members of the Society eat in a Jesuit refectory; guests are entertained
elsewhere. But there are exceptions to this rule as here.

[9] 'long tables' or more usually 'double table(s)', see p. 62 n. 2.

with the novices. A Kempis 7.20. Meditation 7.30. Visit 8. Supper without public grace[1] 8.15. Then recreation. Litanies 9 etc.

Wednesday, Dec. 29[2]

Rising 5.55 and all duties half an hour later till breakfast, which immediately followed mass, 8.15. Rodriguez 9, broken off at 9.15 for Repetition in Quarters (wh. shd. always be at 9 and public Repetition at 9.15). Public Rep. 9.30, after which a quarter of an hour's Rodriguez. Beds 10.25. Works 10.35. Studies 11 etc. Catechism 3.15—Fr. Rector came in to speak about the prizes to be given at the Sunday catechisms and afterwards Fr. Minister explained the system[3] on which catechisms wd. be given in Hall for the future: no instruction in the Catechism itself was given today.

Thursday, Dec. 30

Recreation day. Latin spoken for the first half hour in the morning and last quarter in the afternoon: it shd. have been for the first half hour of both (reckoning fr. setting out) as is the rule for the future.

Friday, Dec. 31

Washing basons 9.10, works 9.20, and the order of a close day. Studies interrupted to practise the *Te Deum* with the Juniors: it was sung at Benediction in thanksgiving for all the graces of the outgoing year. In the afternoon studies 3.15, works 3.45 etc. Confessions heard late. Br. Campbell put on his gown.[4]

---

[1] Instead of the customary formal Latin grace each would say grace privately.

[2] Followed in the manuscript by 'St. T' cancelled.

[3] I have discovered no record about the systems, old or new, by which catechism was imparted. See below also the entry for 8 Jan. 1870. Copies of different catechisms to be found in the libraries of the Province are far too numerous to be listed in detail. I give merely a selection of those published in the nineteenth century. Besides the well-known catechisms of Lingard, Hornihold, and Ullathorne, there were compendious works in French, e.g., those of Jean Couturier (Dijon, 1830), L'Abbé du Clot (Lyons, 1843), V. Bluteau (Paris, 1860), and catechisms in German, Italian, and Spanish. Among popular catechisms in English were: Stephen Keenan, *Catechism of the Christian Religion*, 2 vols. (Glasgow, 1851); Patrick Power, *Catechism: Doctrinal, Moral, Historical, and Liturgical* (1859); James Doyle, *An Abridgment of the Christian Doctrine* (Dublin, 1860); *The Catechism of the Council of Trent*, trans. J. Donovan (Dublin, 1867).

[4] Donald Campbell had entered the noviceship on Christmas Eve, and as Fr. Clarke reminds us newcomers 'spend their first week or ten days separate from the rest, . . . When this time of retirement is over, they are duly received as novices, and are clad in the Jesuit habit'. 'Training of a Jesuit', p. 215. J. P. Thorp described the Jesuit gown as 'a simple *surtout* of relatively imperishable material (which "colours" with age to an engaging moss-green) with armholes, and wings which are, I suppose, rudimentary sleeves'. *Friends and Adventures*, p. 28.

Saturday, New Year's Day 1870

Holy Communion. Recreation day: no Latin was spoken. Sermon at dinner by Br. Kane[1] a Junior. Benediction.

Sunday, Jan. 2

No catechism at Westminster.

Monday, Jan. 3

Exhortation. After the Tone out of door manual works, the indoor for the last 20 minutes instead of the first, which is the order now to be observed for the dark weather.

Tuesday, Jan. 4

Repetition of two Exhortations. The catechists whose missions had been in the hands of the Juniors during the Long Retreat went to find out when the holidays ended. The rest swept the rooms and chapel and at 11.30 went to the wood-shed, speaking Latin for the first quarter of an hour instead of the last.

Wednesday, Jan. 5

Dressing for walk at 10 but it being wet Fr. Rector met the novices in Hall at 10.15 to speak about the prizes for catechism to be given at the various missions. Walk a few minutes past 11—till washing. For those who stayed at home recreation—public till 11.45, optional[2] till 12.30, public again till washing. In the afternoon a catechism. Confessions. Benediction. Walk granted today at request of Bishop.[3]

Thursday, Epiphany

Holy Communion. After Rodriguez walk, with leave for High Mass: examen outside. Benediction.

Friday, Jan. 7

Holy Communion in honour of the Sacred Heart.[4] Rodriguez 9. Exhortation 9.15. After repetition Rodriguez (10.5) finished; then manual works and catechisms. Walk 11.40.

[1] Robert Kane (1848–1929), Jesuit priest—'the blind orator'—son of W. J. Kane of Dublin, and nephew of Sir Robert Kane, F.R.S., born in Dublin on 29 Mar. 1848. Educated at Clongowes Wood and Ushaw Colleges. Entered the S.J. novitiate at Milltown Park, Dublin, in Nov. 1866. Juniorate at Roehampton and St. Acheul. Tertianship at Roehampton, 1886–7. Achieved a considerable reputation as a preacher and lecturer, and published several volumes of sermons. Died at Milltown Park on 21 Nov. 1929.

[2] 'ad libitum' is cancelled in the manuscript before 'optional'.

[3] This sentence 'Walk . . . Bishop.' seems to be in a different hand.

[4] 7 Jan. was the First Friday in the month. The novices practised the devotion of the Nine First Fridays in honour of the Sacred Heart. See also the entry below for 4 Feb. 1870, and Sermons and Devotional Writings, pp. 251–2.

Saturday, Jan. 8

Washing basons, Reflection, and confessions as usual. Instead of reading lesson, which is discontinued, a catechism on the new system.

Sunday, Jan. 9

Domestic Exhortation[1] 10; then office; studies 11.30; free 12. Catechisms at Homer Row, Westminster, and Brentford. That at Sunbury shd. have begun today but the catechists cd. not start through the porter's mistake.

Monday, Jan. 10

Exhortation, tone, etc as usual

Tuesday Jan. 11

Two Exhortations repeated. Catechisms.

Wednesday, Jan. 12

Recreation.

Thursday, Jan. 13

The Triduum of Recollection[2] began (in preparation for which the points for meditation have been given in chapel since the Eve of Epiphany). Order—9 consideration and preparation for confession; 9.30 beds; 9.40 manual works and free time; 10.30 studies; 11.30 free; 12 works; after dinner free time; 3 litanies; 3.15 works; 4.15 conference in Hall; 4.45 beads and free time; 5.30 spiritual reading; 6 *Imitation*; 6.10 points (in chapel), after which exposition of the B.S.; 6.30 meditation; 7.30 reflection; 7.40 supper and free time; 8.45 examen; 9 Benediction; 9.15 points and going to bed. The Rector spoke a few words to the scholastic novices and juniors in Hall at 9

The *Examen Generale* and Bulls[3] are read in English at 8 and 5.30 for half an hour to the laybrothers and some of the scholastic novices, the first from a M.S. and the Bulls read off from the book.

Friday, Jan. 14

Times appointed for confessions—4 o'clock and again after the Conference till meditation. No abstinence of the Society.[4]

---

[1] It is one of the Rector's duties to see that exhortations on religious life are given regularly to the whole community committed to his care.

[2] The Triduum of Recollection is a three-day period of prayer prior to renewal of vows and takes place twice a year. The novices also took part in the Triduum, for, although they had not yet taken vows, it would serve as a time of renovation of spirit and religious fervour. The Triduum at roughly the same period in the previous year (11–13 Jan. 1869) is referred to by Hopkins in a letter, see *Letters to Bridges*, p. 25.

[3] See p. 245 at the end of Appendix 2E.

[4] Reg. 5. Regulae Communes, *Institutum Societatis Iesu*, iii. 10. This special practice of the Society would have been postponed until the following day, that is, the final day of the Triduum.

Saturday, Jan. 15
Conference and 'Spiritual Alms'[1] asked at 9: no Conference in the evening—the time free. Times appointed for confessions 9.30 to 11.30, 3.15 to 4, and 5 to 6, and some were heard later. No admonitions were given today or on Thursday.

Sunday, Jan 16
Walk for High Mass after Rodriguez except for catechists. They followed the usual order till 11.32, when washing; examen 11.45; dinner 12. After dinner wine till they set out. There was wine after First Table also and no Second Table. *Angelus* at 7.40 instead of 7.45, and in future no difference is to be made for Benediction. Catechism opened at Sunbury. Prizes given at Homer Row, Westminster, and Brentford.

Monday, Jan. 17
Manifestations[2] heard from after Exhortation till 11.30

Tuesday, Jan. 18
Manual works at 11.30 for those who did not catechise. Prizes given at Isleworth and Putney and to the girls at Fulham.

Wednesday, Jan. 19
Recreation.—Four who are in weak health were moved into St. Joseph's.[3]

Thursday, Jan. 20
The order of the morning for these is rising and meditation half an hour later, the 7.30 mass, and reflection after mass: Rodriguez read during studies.
   A quarter of an hour's repetition in companies is to follow the Thursday catechism, which was begun today.

Friday, Jan. 21
Prizes given at Wandsworth and to the boys at Fulham. At Mortlake no prizes are given and at Richmond the catechists found the schools shut up. —Walk for non-catechists at 11.30.

Saturday, Jan. 22
Confessions.

Sunday, Jan. 23 (Espousals of our Lady and St. Joseph)
Exhortation at 10—Dr Fincham saw a number of the sick.

[1] See Gavin, *Memoirs of Fr. Gallwey*, pp. 109, 182.
[2] Examen Generale, c. 4. n. 36–40, *Institutum Societatis Ieus*, ii. 14–15.
[3] St. Joseph's Quarters was on the first floor of Manresa House.

Monday, Jan. 24

Tuesday, Jan. 25

Br. G. Hopkins appointed catechist at Fulham in Fr. Wright's[1] place and Br. Gillet in his place at Isleworth: Br. Southern head of that mission.

Wednesday, Jan. 26

Recreation.

Thursday, Jan. 27

The last manifestations heard.

Friday, Jan. 28

Prizes given at Richmond. Br. Ingledew left the noviceship.

Saturday, Jan. 29

Confessions.—Br. Currie[2] and Br. Ratcliff went to town in the morning.

Sunday, Jan. 30 (St. Martina)

Mass as usual offered for health of the community.[3]—Br. Simmons went to town in the morning and did not catechise.

Monday, Jan. 31

The chapel swept between 12 and 1. This is to be done in future at indoor manual works on Monday and Thursday mornings.

---

[1] According to the Manresa Journal Fr. Wright ceased to be a member of the Society on 28 Jan. 1870.

[2] John Bernard Currie (1849–1925), born in Glasgow on 4 Aug. 1849. Educated at Mount St. Mary's and Stonyhurst Colleges. Entered the S.J. novitiate at Roehampton, Sept. 1869; last appears in S.J. catalogue in 1875. 1876–83 taught English in Halifax, Nova Scotia. Conducted a private school for several years. From 1898 until his death was Secretary to Provincial Department of Marriage Licences; acted also as examiner in English literature to local High Schools. Died 12 Jan. 1925.

[3] It is a tradition of the English Province to have Mass on this day for the health of the community. The following note gives some account of the origin of this custom: 'It dates back to St. Omers days. During a severe visitation of the plague the relics of the Saint were carried in procession through the house and supplication made to her to ward off the sickness. St. Martina did not fail her clients and the College was preserved immune from sickness. The date of the first occurrence is unrecorded, but whenever the plague visited the town, as it did fairly often, the relics were venerated as before, and St. Martina became the patroness of health in the College. In one of the migrations the relics were lost, but St. Martina's feast has ever since been an occasion of special prayers for health.' *Stonyhurst Magazine*, xxiv (Feb. 1938), 302–3. See also George Gruggen and Joseph Keating, *Stonyhurst* (1901), p. 63, and for St. Martina see *The Lives of the Saints* compiled by Alban Butler, revised by Herbert Thurston, i (1926), 383–4.

Tuesday, Feb. 1
Br. Campbell catechist at Fulham in Br. Ingledew's place.—Confessions.

Wednesday, Feb. 2 (Candlemas)[1]
Candles blessed before mass at 7.2. Rodriguez 9, after which walk as soon as the rain allowed. Those who returned early took public recreation till examen and after that the time was free till dinner (double[2] tables) at 4. Beads to be said before dinner. After dinner recreation till A Kempis, 6.15. Benediction.

Thursday, Feb. 3
All duties half an hour later till breakfast. Rodriguez 9.—Confessions *ad libitum*. Asking for little things.[3]

Friday, Feb. 4
Communion in honour of the Sacred Heart.—Custom book read.[4]

Saturday, Feb. 5 (Japanese Martyrs)[5]
Holy Communion. Confessions free.[6]

Sunday, Feb. 6
Domestic exhortation at 10.—The Brentford catechists to dine henceforth at the catechists' dinner: they did so today. A seventh catechist appointed at Homer Row, Br. Campbell, but Br. Barker[7] took his place

---

[1] For an explanation of the feast of Candlemas see *Cath. Encycl.* iii. 245-6; *A Catholic Dictionary of Theology*, i (1962), 317-21.

[2] 'double' written above 'long' cancelled.

[3] Novices had to ask permission from the novice master to be allowed to retain the use of certain personal belongings such as a watch, razor, a pocket-knife, or scissors. 'Little leaves', as the practice is called, were renewable monthly. Soap, shoelaces, combs, etc., were obtained from the pro-porter on personal application. The purpose of 'little leaves', was to prepare the novices in a practical way for the vows of poverty and obedience they were soon to take by letting them experience dependence at first hand.

[4] The custom book was read out periodically to enable the novices to grow familiar with noviceship ways and practices. An entry from the Porter's Journal for 21 Mar. 1870 shows that the custom book at Manresa had been recently rewritten. Many of the old custom books are still preserved even from the eighteen-forties when the novitiate was at Hodder, Stonyhurst, but since the year is often omitted it is not easy to date them with accuracy.

[5] This feast and those on 11 and 15 Feb. are special to the Society of Jesus. The date of celebration of some of these feasts has been altered.

[6] 'free', that is, at a time of the novice's own choice, cf. the entry for Feb. 3: 'Confessions *ad libitum*.'

[7] Thomas Aloysius Barker (1845-1905), Jesuit priest, born at Kipling Cotes, Yorks., on 2 Sept. 1845. Joined the R.C. Church at the age of seventeen. Entered the S.J. novitiate at Roehampton in Sept. 1869; ordained priest, June 1881. Parish work at St. Helens, Lancs., and Preston; mission work in Brit. Guiana. On parish staff of St. John's, Wigan, until his death there on 24 Nov. 1905.

today. Br. Considine and Br. Strappini[1] went into[2] retreat in the evening.

Monday, Feb. 7

Chapel swept: this was not done last Thursday.

Tuesday, Feb. 8

No repetition: time free till 9.45; then beds. Custom-book read.

Wednesday Feb. 9

Recreation.—Br. Macmullin and Br. Tempest[3] went to the dentist.

Fr. Baron[4] was brought to the house to be nursed, with his thigh broken by a fall fr. a railway carriage.

Thursday, Feb. 10

Scholastic novices are sent to sit with Fr. Baron fr. 7.45 to breakfast time (Br. Ratcliff), fr. 12 to washing (Nov[ice] from the kitchen), from 4.30 to 5, from 5.30 to meditation, and (Br. Hopkins,[5] who sleeps there) from 9 for the rest of the night. At other times Juniors, laybrothers, etc.

[1] Walter Diver Strappini (1849–1927), Jesuit priest, born in Guernsey on 16 Jan. 1849. Received into the R.C. Church in Dec. 1861. Educated at Mount St. Mary's College. Entered the S.J. novitiate at Roehampton in Feb. 1868; ordained priest in Sept. 1882. Successively Superior of Bury St. Edmunds, and Oxford, missioner at St. Wilfrid's, Preston, and Superior of St. John's, Wigan. 1898–1903, Superior at St. Aloysius's, Oxford. 1903–21, parish work at Bournemouth. 1922, retired to Wimbledon. Died at Roehampton on 31 May 1927. (*Further Letters*, p. 66; *Journals and Papers*, p. 231.)

[2] The manuscript has two interesting cancellations by GMH. Here he had originally written 'entered', but crossed it out and inserted 'went into' above. Again in the entry for 13 Feb. he first wrote 'attend', but cancelled it in favour of 'wait on'. This preference of Hopkins for a simpler verb plus preposition is one which can be readily paralleled from his letters and diaries. In its own way it provides interesting evidence of contemporary fondness for 'the cult of the Saxon'. Hopkins, Bridges, and William Barnes, to name but three writers of this period, each indulged and exploited the current fashion for his own purpose.

[3] Tempest, Aelred (1850–1920), Jesuit priest, sixth son of Joseph Francis Tempest of Wootton, Warwickshire, born at Ackworth Grange, Yorkshire, on 21 Sept. 1850. Educated at Mount St. Mary's and Stonyhurst Colleges. Entered the S.J. novitiate at Roehampton in Oct. 1868, a few weeks after GMH arrived there ('. . . another [novice] is expected', *Further Letters*, p. 104). After ordination in 1881, he taught for twenty-five years at Glasgow, Stonyhurst, Roehampton, St. Mary's Hall, and Mount St. Mary's. 1904–7, Minister at St. Beuno's, later spending four years as sub-Minister at Osterley. Died at St. Mary's Hall, Stonyhurst, on 21 May 1920.

[4] John Baron (1807–78; see Foley vii), Jesuit priest, born at Blackburn, Lancs., on 2 Sept. 1807. Educated at Stonyhurst College. Entered the S.J. novitiate at Hodder in Sept. 1827; ordained priest, Sept. 1841. Varied offices—Superior at St. Mary's Hall, assistant to novice master, Rector of Mount St. Mary's College, missioner and prison chaplain at Wakefield. Died at Holywell on 11 July 1878. (*Further Letters*, p. 110.)

[5] This might refer either to Gerard or Frederick.

MANRESA HOUSE, 1862
(The Novitiate and Tertianship House)

Friday, Christmas Eve.
Washing basons for exercitants
8.40. Catechism at Isleworth — Br.
G. Hopkins and Br. Wilcock. None
at Fulham. For the other non-exer
citants the time was free after Ro?
ranks) till 10.30 then manual
works, and again from 11.30 till
12.30 (study time) was free. (but
this hour and all the time till
washing they spent in dressing
the chapel.

Reading: Apocalypse XXI, omitting 12—20 — Challoner' Hist.
of Japan : Life of Fr. Francis Mas-
Grilli begun

Litanies 3. Manual works 3.15.
Beads and confessions for exercitants 4.15. Spiritual reading 5.
Points of meditation 5.30
Med. 5.45. Visit for non-exercitants 6.15. Confessions for the same
6.30 Supper (no scholastic novices serving at second table)

7. Examen 7.30. Going to bed 7.45
Rising 10.55. Points of meditation
(in chapel) 11.15. Meditation 11.
30.

Saturday, Christmas Day
End of the long Retreat
Adeste fideles 12. (followed by
midnight mass (by special leave
from the Holy Father got for the
community by Dr Grant) with
communion, and then the Te
Deum. Meal in the refectory at
1 Med on the quarterdeck, and to
bed. Rising 6.30. The second
and third masses of Xmas at 7
and 7.30. Breakfast 8. Beds 8
45. Rodriguez 8.55. Dressing for
walk about 9.20. Walk to
follow as fast as possible. Learnt
for Mary's high mass cards given
at the procathedral, Moorfields,
Hammersmith, Clapham, Fr. Rivers'
church, Fulham, Surbiton, Mortlake, St. Georges, the Carmelite.

Facsimile of two pages from the Journal kept by G. M. Hopkins as Porter in the noviceship

Friday, Feb. 11 (Blessed John de Britto)

Holy Communion.—Two Exhortations repeated; then manual works and catechisms.—Br. Barker appointed catechist at Richmond in Br. Considine's place.—Rodriguez. 3.

Saturday, Feb. 12

Confessions free.

Sunday, Feb. 13 (Septuagesima)

Beds after Rodriguez.

Br. Clarke,[1] Br. A. Marchant,[2] and Br. Monk are appointed to wait on Fr. Baron in turn each for a day and other scholastic novices not employed, except Br. Ratcliff (as above) to read Rodriguez: those who are off duty as far as possible fill the offices which may be held by those who are on.

Br. Campbell catechised at Homer Row: there are to be six catechists there (as today), not seven.

Monday, Feb. 14

Confessions free.

Tuesday, Feb. 15 (Blessed John Baptist Machado and his companions)

Holy Communion.

Br. Considine and Br. Strappini took their vows.[3]

Wednesday, Feb. 16

Br. Macmullin went to town with Fr. Harper[4] and Br. Considine, to see the dentist. Fr. Wright, Br. Southern, and Br. Simmons also went to town together to the optician's.

[1] Charles Cowley Clarke (1851–1916), secular priest, born at Bath on 6 June 1851. Educated at Downside, Oscott, and Stonyhurst Colleges. Entered the S.J. novitiate at Roehampton in Oct. 1869; ordained priest, Sept. 1881. Left the Society in Feb. 1885, and went to Clifton. For the next twenty years he served St. Mary Magdalene's, Brighton, retiring in 1906 for tutorial work, study, and writing. He died at Bath on 4 Jan. 1916.

[2] Austin Marchant (1843–1916), secular priest, born in London on 28 May 1843. Educated at Dr. Kenny's School, Richmond, Surrey, and at the English College, Douai. Entered the S.J. novitiate in Sept. 1869; ordained priest in Sept. 1876. Parish work at Galashiels and Great Yarmouth. Left the Society of Jesus from his tertianship at Roehampton in Aug. 1881. The remainder of his life seems to have been spent in Folkestone as chaplain to a convent, and in assisting the local clergy. He died on 27 Dec. 1916.

[3] Both had entered the noviceship on 14 Feb. 1868.

[4] Thomas Norton Harper (1821–93; see Boase v, *Cath. Encycl.*, Sutcliffe), Jesuit priest, born in London on 26 Sept. 1821. Educated at St. Paul's School, London, and Queen's College, Oxford; B.A. 1844. Took Orders in the Anglican church, working for five years as curate, his first mission being at Barnstaple, Devonshire; curate at Christ Church, Broadway, Westminster, 1849–50; incumbent of St. Peter's Chapel, Charlotte St., Pimlico, London, 1850–1. Received into the R.C. Church and entered the Society of Jesus in Oct. 1852; ordained priest in 1859. Taught theology and philosophy. He died at Virginia Water, Surrey, on 29 Aug. 1893. (*Further Letters*, p. 409.)

Thursday, Feb. 17

Friday, Feb. 18

Rising half an hour later. Rodriguez at 3.
    Fr. Wright and Br. Macmullin went to town to Dr. Fincham's.
    Prizes given at Mortlake.

Saturday, Feb. 19[1]
Br. Macmullin appointed Porter.

With the appointment of Br. McMullin as Porter, Hopkins slipped back into the ranks. He had still more than six months of his noviceship to complete. Fortunately, the monotony would be relieved by the Brothers' experiment. As Fr. Clarke explains this consists in

a month spent in the kitchen, during which the novice has to wash up the plates and dishes, to pare potatoes, to grind the coffee, and to perform any other menial tasks assigned to the novice by the cook, whom the novice has to obey implicitly, as for the time being his superior. He has also to take his recreation during this month with the lay brothers, and to make himself one with them in their ordinary life and conversation.[2]

Whether Hopkins spent his month as is customary at one stretch is not clear, since the reference in his Journal could suggest that he did the experiment piecemeal: 'I was with the laybrothers that week.'[3] However, the experiment over, Hopkins rejoined his own community. Did he relish the experience? He does not say, but assuming as in the Anglo-Saxon Chronicle that the length of the entries reflects the measure of success, then Hopkins enjoyed his time with the lay brothers. His Journal expands as he jots down the folklore tales and turns of phrase told him by some of the Irish members of the community.[4] But in the light of his subsequent poetry much more important than the anecdotes of phantom plough-

---

[1] See the entry for the same date in *Journals and Papers*, p. 196.

[2] 'Training of a Jesuit', p. 218. Herbert Thurston (1856–1939), who did the Brothers' experiment a few years after GMH, wrote to his mother: 'A line is all it can be for I was moved down to the kitchen this morning, and have not time to write; even now I fear that I am late.' After a week or two he can report some progress: 'I am rather slow at the work as yet, but I think I am improving. To-day, for instance, with a little help I washed up the dinner things, i.e. about four hundred plates, dishes, etc., in an hour and a half.' Joseph Crehan, *Father Thurston* (1952), p. 14.

[3] *Journals and Papers*, p. 197.   [4] Ibid., pp. 197 f.

men and horses, or the frolics of Irish fairies, were the descriptions of natural objects and phenomena which found their way into his diary. As with Wordsworth present spots of time were hoarded for future years and an entry in his Journal written soon after he entered the novitiate states significantly: 'Remember the solar halo as an illustration.'[1]

During these two years of noviceship sunsets and trees seem especially to have fascinated him:

Jan. 4, '69. The other evening after a very bright day, the air rinsed quite clear, there was a slash of glowing yolk-coloured sunset.[2]

The sunset June 20 was wine-coloured, with pencillings of purple, and next day there was rain.[3]

Crossing the Common Oct. 13 a fine sunset—great gold field; along the earth-line a train of dark clouds of knopped or clustery make pitching over at the top the way they were going; higher a slanting race of tapered or else coiling fish-like flakes such as are often seen; the gold etched with brighter gold and shaped in sandy pieces and looped and waved all in waterings.[4]

The trees at Manresa caught Hopkins's attention almost as soon as he arrived:

The cedars at the bottom have their flakes so modulated from the horizontal and so taking one another up all along the row that they look like the swaling or *give* of water in a river when you look across it and moonlight, say, picks out the different faces with light and dark.[5]

His first winter at Manresa was very mild and was followed by an early spring, so that at the opening of February he could write:

Daffodils have been in bloom for some days. A weeping-willow here is all green. The elms have long been in red bloom and yesterday (the 11th) I saw small leaves on the brushwood at their roots. Some primroses out.[6]

But it was in the early summer that trees revealed themselves to greatest advantage:

May 14 The chestnuts down by St. Joseph's were a beautiful sight: each spike had its own pitch, yet each followed in its place in the sweep with a deeper and deeper stoop. When the wind tossed them they plunged and crossed one another without losing their inscape. (Observe that motion multiplies inscape only when inscape is discovered, otherwise it disfigures)[7]

[1] Ibid., p. 189, entry for 15 Sept.   [2] Ibid.   [3] Ibid., p. 191.
[4] Ibid., p. 193.   [5] Ibid., p. 189, entry for 15 Sept.   [6] Ibid., p. 190.
[7] Ibid., p. 199, entry for 14 May.

The inscape of massed trees, however, had been noted earlier and with singular precision:

Oct. 21. From a height in Richmond Park saw trees in the river flat below inscaped in distinctly projected, crisp, and almost hard, rows of loaves, their edges, especially at the top, being a little fixed and shaped with shadow.[1]

In the autumn of the following year he noted:

My eye was suddenly caught by the scaping of the leaves that grow in allies and avenues: I noticed it first in an elm and then in limes. They fall from the two sides of the branch or spray in two marked planes which meet at a right angle or more. This comes from the endeavour to catch the light on either side, which falls left and right but not all round. Thus each branch is thatched with a double blade or eave of leaves which run up to a coping like the roofcrest all along its stem, and seen from some places these lie across one another all in chequers and X's.[2]

A winter walk on Wimbledon Common led him to extend his feel for inscape to the snow encrusted grass. His diary entry is of particular interest because it shows him straining to find words to express the uniqueness of his perception:

As we went down a field near Caesar's Camp I noticed it before me *squalentem*, coat below coat, sketched in intersecting edges bearing 'idiom', all down the slope:—I have no other word yet for that which takes the eye or mind in a bold hand or effective sketching or in marked features or again in graphic writing, which not being beauty nor true inscape yet gives interest and makes ugliness even better than meaninglessness.—On the Common the snow was channelled all in parallels by the sharp driving wind and upon the tufts of grass (where by the dark colour shewing through it looked greyish) it came to turret-like clusters or like broken shafts of basalt.—In the Park in the afternoon the wind was driving little clouds of snow-dust which caught the sun as they rose and delightfully took the eyes: flying up the slopes they looked like breaks of sunlight fallen through ravelled cloud upon the hills and again like deep flossy velvet blown to the root by breath which passed all along. Nearer at hand along the road it was gliding over the ground in white wisps that between trailing and flying shifted and wimpled like so many silvery worms to and from one another.[3]

The precision and exactness of Hopkins's detailed descriptions

[1] *Journals and Papers*, p. 189.   [2] Ibid., p. 192.
[3] Ibid., pp. 195–6.

probably owes something to his interest in science. He was sufficiently interested to record his observation that, 'some brownish paste in the library formed in big crystals',[1] or again he carefully notes:

In taking off my jersey of knitted wool in the dark with an accidental stroke of my finger down the stuff I drew a flash of electric light. This explains the crackling I had often heard.[2]

Beneath all these peculiarities Hopkins perceived an unmistakable regularity, and this notion combined with his religious outlook to produce in him a sacramental view of nature. The famous passage which illustrates this point is too long and too well known to be quoted in full, but a few lines will make the matter clear:

One day when the bluebells were in bloom I wrote the following. I do not think I have ever seen anything more beautiful than the bluebell I have been looking at. I know the beauty of our Lord by it.[3]

What had happened to his self-imposed custody-of-the-eyes penance mentioned earlier? Clearly he had made up for lost time.

Of the six months of noviceship which still remained when he ceased to be Porter, Hopkins said little. In the letter he wrote his mother for her birthday in which he enclosed a present of a duck's feather with his love, he explained:

I practise at present the evangelical poverty which I soon hope to vow, but no one is ever so poor that he is not (without prejudice to all the rest of the world) owner of the skies and stars and everything wild that is to be found on the earth, and out of this immense stock I make over to you my right to one particular.[4]

In addition to spending a month working with the lay brothers he continued his catechizing at Fulham and Brentford, and on 12 June, as we saw earlier, he was appointed head catechist at Homer Row. With June also came the respite of the hay season.

Finally, on the last day of August the eight-day Vow retreat began under Fr. Gallwey's direction. And with its conclusion the momentous day had come at last:

Thursday, Sept. 8th. [1870]
Close of Retreat. Nativity of Bl. V. Mary. BB. Fred. & Gerard Hopkins, McMullin & Wilcock took their vows. There was wine after dinner. Brs.

---

[1] Ibid., p. 189, entry for 4 Nov.   [2] Ibid., p. 196, entry for 4 Apr.
[3] Ibid., p. 199.   [4] *Further Letters*, p. 111.

F. Hopkins, Gerard Hopkins, McMullin & Wilcock took leave of the novices in the evening & joined the Scholasticate. [NBJ]

The account of Vow-taking although already quoted in part will bear repetition.

Vow Day.—September 8th was the happy day long looked forward to through twenty-four months of probation, but the ceremony of the vows had none of the solemnity that accompanies it at present. In a tiny chapel upstairs,[1] lit by a skylight still seen in the novice lay-Brothers' quarters (the diamond-paned skylight), Father Fitzsimon sat near a small table on which stood a crucifix, and we entered singly one after another, as though going to confession, and kneeling, took our vows in secret,—this as a precaution, because of the Penal Clause in the Emancipation Act forbidding the presence of Jesuits in England. The Master of Novices merely answered *Amen*, took the written formula of the vows, and the young Religious withdrew. We received no Crucifix, no Thesaurus, no Rule book, nothing but a blessing.[2] The Renovation of Vows took place secretly in the same way. I believe it was in Father Morris' time [Novice master 1880–7] that this secrecy was done away with.[3] Novices blossoming into juniors found themselves rigged out in a new gown, a biretta, Roman collar, and other accessories necessary to make them feel new men, and so they took leave, often with sadness, of the happy life of the noviceship, which would be remembered in all after-life as a sort of incipient beatitude on earth.[4]

On 9 September the four new Jesuit scholastics who had joined the novitiate two years before now split up. McMullin and Wilcock remained at Manresa passing into the Juniorate, Frederick Hopkins went to Mount St Mary's, Chesterfield, to teach, while Gerard himself records for us, 'To Stonyhurst to the seminary'.[5]

---

[1] Shown on the second floor plan of Manresa House in *LLNN*, i (1863), inserted between pp. 6 and 7.

[2] GMH writes of 'the crucifix and things' given him by Fr. Gallwey, see *Further Letters*, p. 112.

[3] With this compare the following: 'Jan. 15th [1871]. The renovation of vows was made publicly in the chapel for the first time.' *LLNN*, xxx (July 1910), 473. Fr. Gallwey was the novice master in 1871.

[4] 'Reminiscences of Novice-days, 1865', *LLNN*, xxx (Apr. 1910), 387–8. I am aware that the picture of the noviceship conveyed in these pages must often seem at times a grim one, so to redress the balance I add the following quotation: 'I suppose it all sounds a dreadful life to the "worldling"! I can testify that it was a very happy one.' Thorp, *Friends and Adventures*, p. 27. Hopkins, too, enjoyed his noviceship, at least in retrospect: '. . . we used to roar with laughter if anything happened', *Further Letters*, p. 161. For vow-taking see also Meadows, *Obedient Men*, pp. 125–6.

[5] *Journals and Papers*, p. 200, entry for 9 Sept.

CHAPTER 3

The Philosophate 1870–1873

THE cross-country journey from Roehampton to Stonyhurst was broken at Manchester, and Hopkins and his fellow scholastics had dinner there at the recently founded Jesuit house, and took the opportunity of seeing the new church which was then being built. Hopkins described it to his mother as 'so big as to be a sort of cathedral', adding, 'but I did not think very highly of it'.[1] Afterwards they resumed their journey and reached Whalley, 'a little place in a valley of the moors with an abbey ruin and otherwise worth seeing and we were driven four miles over the Hodder and Calder rivers ("yon brig's over the Cauder" a little native told me) up and down hill to this house'.[2] Hopkins was to give a fuller and more animated picture of the college and its setting in a letter to Bridges which he wrote enthusiastically when he returned there twelve years later to teach Latin and Greek.

I wish I could show you this place. It is upon my word worth seeing. The new college, though there is no real beauty in the design, is nevertheless imposing and the furniture and fittings are a joy to see. There is always a stirring scene, contractors, builders, masons, bricklayers, carpenters, stonecutters and carvers, all on the spot; a traction engine twice a day fetches stone from a quarry on the fells; engines of all sorts send their gross and foulsmelling smoke all over us; cranes keep swinging; and so on. There are acres of flat roof which, when the air is not thick, as unhappily

---

[1] *Further Letters*, p. 112. The Mission began in 1868 with a temporary church in Ackers Street. For its history see Alan Robinson, *Church of the Holy Name, Manchester* [Manchester, 1950].

[2] *Further Letters*, p. 112. For the history and photographs of the College at Stonyhurst see [Percy Fitzgerald], *Schooldays at Saxonhurst*, by 'One of the Boys' (Edinburgh, 1867); A. Hewitson, *Stonyhurst College, Present and Past*, 2nd ed. (Preston, 1878); John Gerard, *Centenary Record, Stonyhurst College* (Belfast, 1894); Percy Fitzgerald, *Stonyhurst Memories; or, Six Years at School* (1895); George Gruggen and Joseph Keating, *Stonyhurst* (1901); Joseph Keating, *Stonyhurst* (Letchworth, 1909); Michael Trappes-Lomax, 'Stonyhurst College, I and II', *Country Life*, 16 and 23 July 1938, pp. 60–5, 84–9; Hubert Chadwick, *St. Omers to Stonyhurst* (1962).

it mostly is, commands a noble view of this Lancashire landscape, Pendle Hill, Ribblesdale, the fells, and all round, bleakish but solemn and beautiful. There is a garden with a bowling green, walled in by massive yew hedges, a bowered yew-walk, two real Queen Ann summerhouses, observatories under government, orchards, vineries, greenhouses, workshops, a plungebath, fivescourts, a mill, a farm, a fine cricketfield besides a huge playground; then the old mansion, ponds, towers, quadrangles, fine cielings, chapels, a church, a fine library, museums, MSS illuminated and otherwise, coins, works of art; then two other dependent establishment[s], one a furlong, the other ¾ a mile off; the river Hodder with lovely fairyland views, especially at the bathingplace, the Ribble too, the Calder, Whalley with an abbey, Clitheroe with a castle, Ribchester with a strange old chapel and Roman remains; schoolboys and animation, philosophers and foppery (not to be taken too seriously) a jackdaw, a rookery, goldfish, a clough with waterfalls, fishing, grouse, an anemometer, a sunshine guage, a sundial, an icosihedron, statuary, magnetic instruments, a laboratory, gymnasium, ambulacrum, studio, fine engravings, Arundel chromos, Lancashire talked with *naïveté* on the premises (Hoo said this and hoo did that) . . .[1]

In one of the 'dependent establishments' mentioned in his letter, the Seminary, St. Mary's Hall,[2] Hopkins was to live for the next three years. It was less attractive than the College:

About 300 yards behind the College, westward, there is the Seminary. It is a plain, substantial building—a rather serious, studious-looking building—surrounded by trees, and quite out of the reach of the 'vulgar gaze'.[3]

---

[1] *Letters to Bridges*, pp. 151–2.

[2] Photograph of the Seminary and Pendle Hill in John Gerard, *Centenary Record, Stonyhurst College* (Belfast, 1894), p. 223, and text pp. 142–3; Photographs of St. Mary's Hall and its chapel will be found in Joseph Keating's *Stonyhurst* (Letchworth, 1909), pp. 60–1; a sketch of St. Mary's Hall in Maude Petre's *Autobiography and Life of George Tyrrell*, ii (1912), 43. These illustrations show St. Mary's Hall with the extensions which were added after GMH's time; the wings flanking each side of what is now the centre block were added 1880–2. For the history of the Seminary see the anonymous article 'St. Mary's Hall, 1828–1926', *Stonyhurst Magazine*, xviii (June–July 1926), 469–71.

[3] A. Hewitson, *Stonyhurst College* (Preston, 1870), p. 119. This author's description of St. Mary's Hall is of more than usual interest since the date it appeared coincided with the commencement of Hopkins's three years of philosophy. Hewitson continues: 'The Seminary is in connection with the College, and is occupied by those in the advanced classes who intend joining the priesthood. Here they study the more serious and recondite subjects of their curriculum, and, considering the quietude and sequestration of the position, they could not well have more appropriate quarters. As a rule there are from 20 to 30 students in the Seminary. There is nothing specially attractive to visitors in the place; all being set apart strictly for close, earnest study. Near the main building—at the back of it—there is a small covered recreation ground, with a high end wall for hand ball

Arrival preliminaries over, Hopkins would have been shown to his room. Denis Meadows related his arrival in this way:

The lay brother helped me to carry my baggage to my room. . . . To say that my room was simply furnished is an understatement. It had two doors, an inner and an outer. There was a window overlooking the terrace and garden in front of the building. In the window embrasure was a wooden seat with a hinged top. This was a coal scuttle as well as a seat. You needed to keep it well filled in the winter. The Lancashire winter is raw, cold, and wet—and we had no central heating in our rooms.

In an alcove was a small iron bedstead, and by the bed a piece of carpet —a drugget, the lay brother called it—that may once have been of a definite color, but now was merged into the prevailing greyness. There was a fireplace in the middle of one wall, a table with two bookshelves on it, a plain wooden chair at the table, and by the fireplace a Windsor chair. A deal chest of drawers with a small mirror over it stood cattycorner to the right of the window. Against the wall opposite the fireplace was a deal washstand with the usual crockery. Near the foot of the bed there was a prie-dieu, and by it a kneeling stool. There were a few clothes hooks on the back of the door.

'Holy poverty,' I remarked to the lay brother.

'Perhaps you'll brighten it up a bit,' he suggested. 'A few holy pictures or a map or something. Some of the philosophers manage to make their rooms look quite cozy, especially the Australians.'

I don't know why the Australians were thus successful in softening the austerity. Perhaps Lancashire fog, mist, and rain are more trying to people used to the sunshine and clear air of Australia.[1]

But what caught Hopkins's eye was the view from his room rather than its contents: 'The window of the room I am in commands a beautiful range of moors dappled with light and shade.'[2] He was pleased too with his reception: 'there was moonlight,[3] supper, and a pleasant sociable bustle which made a welcome'.[4] And what follows reveals that he had already grown roots in the Society, and felt the wrench at being disturbed: 'By daylight I feel the strangeness

playing. The Seminary was established in 1835; and it is one of the indispensable auxiliaries of the College.' Percy Fitzgerald's description in his *Stonyhurst Memories* (1895) has a touch of *couleur de rose*: 'A massive, square-built house, built of yellow sandstone of the country, with sloping, lofty roof. Large and imposing as it then appeared, . . .' (p. 365). Denis Meadows's impression is more grimly realistic: 'There wasn't much to learn about the house of studies. It was just a big rectangular barrack of three floors and the attic. The rooms were all alike . . .', *Obedient Men*, p. 138.

[1] Ibid., pp. 129-30.   [2] *Further Letters*, p. 112.
[3] Full moon occurred this night at 10.11 p.m.   [4] *Further Letters*, p. 112.

of the place and the noviceship after two years seems like a second home: it made me sad to look at the crucifix and things Fr. Gallwey gave me when I was going. He was very very kind.'[1] The three[2] scholastics who went with him from the noviceship must have helped him to settle in and there were others[3] there he knew already. He assures his mother confidently 'the brotherly charity of everyone here can be felt at once: indeed it is always what you take for granted'.[4]

Hopkins would have quickly discovered that he was still one of a large community, numbering in fact eighty-five, made up of nineteen priests, fifty-four scholastics, and twelve lay brothers, all of whom came under the general jurisdiction of the Rector[5] of Stonyhurst. But in practice the Seminary, St. Mary's Hall, formed a separate entity with a Superior of its own and a fair measure of autonomy. Here the community amounted to forty, made up as follows: three priests, thirty-five scholastics, and two lay brothers. The scholastics were divided into three years—sixteen scholastics in their first year, nine in the second, and nine in the third; and one scholastic was preparing for the London B.A.

The earliest complete timetable[6] I have been able to find is dated 1882. It will give some guide to the order that Hopkins and his contemporaries would have followed:

[1] *Further Letters*, pp. 112–13.

[2] Ignatius Gartlan, Henry Kerr, and Sydney Morgan. The latter was born in 1848 and entered the Society in 1867, but left in 1876.

[3] William Hobart Kerr (1836–1913), and Herman Walmesley (1850–1927).

[4] *Further Letters*, p. 113.

[5] Edward Ignatius Purbrick (1830–1914; see Sutcliffe), Jesuit priest, born in Birmingham on 22 June 1830. Educated at King Edward VI's Grammar School, Birmingham, and Christ Church, Oxford. Friend of Edward Benson, Archbishop of Canterbury, and Lightfoot, the N.T. scholar, who later became Bishop of Durham. Received into the R.C. Church in 1850 by Canon Oakeley. On becoming a Catholic he was compelled to resign his studentship. Entered the S.J. novitiate at Hodder in 1851; ordained priest in 1864. Additional studies at Rome. Superior at St. Mary's Hall 1867–9, where he also taught logic. 1869, Rector of Stonyhurst, where he projected a considerable building programme. 1879, sent as Visitor to the Canadian mission. 1880–8, Provincial of the English Province S.J., visiting Malta in 1882. 1888–9, Instructor of Tertians at Roehampton. 1895–7, Superior of the new college at Wimbledon. In March 1897 appointed Provincial of the New York and Maryland Province. Returned to England because of ill health. 1903, Spiritual Father at Clongowes, and at Liverpool in 1904. 1906, Instructor of Tertians in New York. 1907–14, Spiritual Father at Manchester where he died. (*Journals and Papers*, p. 225, 'Fr. Rector'.)

[6] I have expanded the abbreviations used.

Rise	5.30	End of recreation	2.30
Angelus & Meditation	6.0	Circle	3.15
Community Mass	7.0	Recreation	4.15
Breakfast	7.30	Studies	5.0
Lecture	10.0	Angelus. Supper	8.10
,,	11.15	Litanies	9.30
Washing	12.30	Points	9.45
Examen	12.45	Examen	10.0
Angelus. Dinner	1.0	Bed	10.15
		Gas out	10.30

Sunday, Tuesday, Thursday—p.m. Recreation till 5.30

But for the present Hopkins did not need to pay too much attention to timetables since 'schools' had not opened and he had three weeks to get acquainted with his new surroundings.[1]

Two important changes took place in these three weeks. First a new spiritual director was appointed for the Seminarians.

13 Sept. [1870]

F. Gosford[2]—our Spiritual Father for the coming year—entered upon his new duties by hearing confessions at 7. [Philosophers' Beadle's Journal]

The other was the arrival a week later of a new Superior:

21 Sept.

Father A. Weld[3] arrived at Stonyhurst in the evening and was shortly after inducted into the office of Superior of the Seminary by Fr. Rector. Postea.[4] Recreation until supper.

[1] His sojourn in the Lancashire uplands gave GMH his first opportunity of seeing the Northern Lights amongst other things. See entry for 24 Sept. in *Journals and Papers*, p. 200.

[2] John Gosford (1818–1904), Jesuit priest, born near York on 21 Feb. 1818. Educated at Stonyhurst College. Entered the S.J. novitiate at Hodder in 1836; ordained priest in Sept. 1843. Parish work at St. Wilfrid's, Preston, until 1860, followed by two years at Skipton. 1862, became Spiritual Father at Mount St. Mary's College, and was associated with the College until 1890. Transferred from Mount St. Mary's to Stonyhurst, 1869–72, where he also acted as Spiritual Father at the Seminary, St. Mary's Hall, GMH being under his care for a time. Retired to St. Beuno's in 1890 where he celebrated the Golden Jubilee of his priesthood in 1893. Died there on 26 July 1904.

[3] Fr. Weld replaced as Superior Fr. Alexander Charnley (1834–1922). GMH now had as his Superior the priest who as Provincial had received him into the Society of Jesus two years earlier. See entries for 19 and 30 May 1868 in *Journals and Papers*. Fr. Weld taught the first-year philosophers mathematics, and in December he gave both first and second years a special course in spherical geometry lasting a week.

[4] Wine given to the community for some celebration.

Other changes followed. New catechists[1] were assigned to their centres by Fr. Weld on 25 September, and the next day Mr. Walmesley[2] was appointed Beadle of Philosophers. At the end of the week 'schools' were officially begun.

Saturday, 1 October. Opening Day.[3]

Rising 5.30. Mass of the Holy Ghost 7 by Fr. Rector. Singing. A harmonium had been brought from the College two or three days before for this occasion for which the choir had been diligently preparing. The 'Veni Creator' was sung before Mass, F. Rector kneeling at the altar, and intoning the versicle and prayer. F. Weld who had said Mass in the Sacristy at 6.30 attended our Mass. At 8 opening address by F. Bochum[4] . . . Breakfast immediately after, about 8.30. [PBJ]

Next day being a Sunday provided a further respite and so the lectures began on the third of October and not the second as Hopkins had thought.[5]

The entry for that Monday reads:

Rising 5.30. 'Breves lectiones'[6] F. Capaldi[7] 2nd & 3rd years 8.30. F. Bochum, 1st year 9.30. F. Weld Mathematics of 1st year 11.30. [PBJ]

---

[1] GMH's name never appears in the catalogue as a catechist during his time at the Seminary. The catechists' centres were the church at Stonyhurst, Billington, Clitheroe, Dutton Lea, Higher Bridge, and Hurst Green.

[2] Herman Walmesley (1850–1927), Jesuit priest, born at Gillow, Lancs., on 9 Feb. 1850. Educated at Stonyhurst College. Entered the S.J. novitiate at Roehampton in Dec. 1867; ordained priest in Sept. 1882. Prefect General at St. Aloysius's, Glasgow, 1883–4. At Stonyhurst 1884–98, being Rector from 1891–8. Rector of St. Aidan's College, Grahamstown, 1898. 1908–23, English Assistant to Fr. General in Rome. Died in Rome on 22 Jan. 1927.

[3] 1 Oct., the feast of St. Remigius, was the official date for the opening of 'schools', but earlier entries show that the Philosophers were back to their studies by the second or third week of September:
'17 Sept. Black Monday—reopening of schools.
18 Sept. Mr Hunter broke the ice this morning at 8 a.m. by giving a Mathematical Lecture to those of the 3rd and 2nd year. Mr Sidgreaves at 11 a.m. followed this example by conferring a similar benefit on the Logicians [first-year Philosophers].' [From PBJ for 1866.] The opening day was marked by a short dissertation (15–20 minutes?), later to become known from its traditional opening word as the 'Quamquam', though I have not seen the title used for it before 1911. Cf. *Obedient Men*, pp. 134, 140–1.

[4] Heinrich Bochum (1841–1902), Jesuit priest, born near Cologne on 29 Mar. 1841. Entered the S.J. novitiate in Oct. 1856; philosophy at Aachen, theology at Maria Laach. Lectured in logic and general metaphysics at St. Mary's Hall 1870–2, and would therefore have had GMH among his students. Died 23 July 1902 at St. Francis Xavier's College, Bombay.

[5] '. . . the scholastics are still in their holidays till the 2nd of October.' *Further Letters*, p. 112.

[6] Short introductory lectures.

[7] Nunciatus Capaldi, priest, born in Lazio, Italy, on 26 Feb. 1834. Entered the

Fr. R. F. Clarke, who began his philosophy course the year Hopkins finished his, is a reliable guide to the courses taught at St. Mary's Hall. He writes:

During the first year he [the Jesuit scholastic] goes through a course of logic, pure and applied, and continues his mathematics.[1] The second and third years are devoted to psychology, ethics, metaphysics, general and special, cosmology and natural theology. He has about two lectures a day in these subjects from Jesuit professors, who are always priests, and are selected on account of their special knowledge, and their gift of a clear power of exposition.[2]

In his first year Hopkins would have attended lectures in logic and mathematics every morning except on Thursdays and Sundays. On Mondays, Wednesdays, and Fridays there were also logic lectures in the evening, and on Monday and Wednesday afternoons at half-past three there were 'circles', about which a word will be said later. The Beadle's Journal shows that the first-year Philosophers were referred to generally as Logicians. But the name could mislead. What they called logic we would now call minor logic and epistemology. The Logicians were probably introduced to general metaphysics also, since, Fr. Bochum, Professor to the first year, appears in the catalogue as lecturer in logic and general metaphysics. As to what precisely was being taught it is difficult to say, and it is therefore with some hesitancy and diffidence that I make the attempt.

We have Fr. Copleston's authority for it that

In the seventeenth, eighteenth and early part of the nineteenth centuries philosophy in ecclesiastical seminaries and teaching institutions generally tended to take the form of an uninspired Scholastic Aristotelianism amalgamated with ideas taken from other currents of thought, notably Cartesianism and, later, the philosophy of Wolff.[3]

S.J. novitiate in Oct. 1854; ordained priest at Vals, France, in 1864. 1870–2, taught ethics and special metaphysics at St. Mary's Hall, Stonyhurst, GMH being among his students. Afterwards taught Church history at St. Beuno's College. 1875–82, teaching and parish work in Italy chiefly in the diocese of Lorana. Last appears in the S.J. catalogue in 1882.

[1] GMH tells Bridges: 'I am now at Stonyhurst reading philosophy and mathematics.' *Letters to Bridges*, p. 26.

[2] 'Training of a Jesuit', p. 221.

[3] Frederick Copleston, *A History of Philosophy*, vii (1963), 387–8. Elsewhere he states: 'Wolff's division of philosophy had a considerable influence on subsequent Scholastic manuals and text-books', ibid. vi (1960), 109 n. 1, and cf. ibid. iii (1953), 356.

A further testimony to this eclecticism is provided by Newman's well-known letter written from Rome in 1846:

Hope told me we should find very little theology here, and a talk we had yesterday with one of the Jesuit fathers here shows we shall find little philosophy. It arose from our talking of the Greek studies of the Propaganda and asking whether the youths learned Aristotle. 'O no—he said—Aristotle is in no favor here—no, not in Rome:—not St Thomas. I have read Aristotle and St Thos, and owe a great deal to them, but they are out of favor here and throughout Italy. St Thomas is a great saint—people don't dare to speak against him—they profess to reverence him, but put him aside.' I asked what philosophy they *did* adopt. He said *none*. 'Odds and ends—whatever seems to them best—like St Clement's Stromata. They have no philosophy. *Facts* are the great things, and nothing else. Exegesis, but not doctrine.' He went on to say that many privately were sorry for this, many Jesuits, he said; but no one dared oppose the fashion.[1]

The rise and development of neo-Thomism has been thoroughly discussed in recent years,[2] and with certain reservations it would be safe to conclude with Fr. Glenn that, '. . . by 1870 there was almost unanimous agreement among philosophers of the Catholic Faith in the acceptance of Scholasticism'.[3] This is not to say that complete agreement prevailed on all issues, for as Glenn continues, 'there was much controversy . . . as to the manner of conciliating Scholastic Psychology and Cosmology with the data of modern science'.[4]

If we turn now to the situation existing in the English Province

---

[1] *The Letters and Diaries of John Henry Newman*, ed. Charles Stephen Dessain, xi (1961), 279. And compare the following: 'Father Curci, who entered the Jesuit Order in 1826, described the situation which then prevailed at the Collegio Romano in this way: "I deplored the Babylon which the Collegio Romano seemed to me to have become in this respect. In fact, with regard to philosophy, everyone could teach what he wanted to, so long as he despised and scorned all peripatetics, though no one had yet said what Aristotelianism was or what it taught." ' Georges Van Riet, *Thomistic Epistemology*, Eng. trans. from 3rd revised and augmented edition, *L'Épistémologie thomiste*, by Gabriel Franks, i (St. Louis and London, 1963), 31 n. 5.

[2] Joseph L. Perrier, *The Revival of Scholastic Philosophy in the Nineteenth Century* (New York, 1909); A. Pelzer, 'Les initiateurs italiens du néo-thomisme contemporain', *Revue néo-scolastique de philosophie*, 18 (1911), 230–54; Paolo Dezza, *Alle origini del neotomismo* (Milan, 1940); Georges Van Riet, *L'Épistémologie thomiste* (Louvain, 1946), English translation as above; Edgar Hocedez, *Histoire de la théologie au XIXe siècle* (Brussels and Paris, 1948–52), i. 51, 58–60, ii. 323–8, 350–3, iii. 45–52; Ueberweg–Heinze, *Grundriß der Geschichte der Philosophie*, v (Basel, 1953). The last three works provide comprehensive bibliographies.

[3] Paul J. Glenn, *The History of Philosophy* (St. Louis and London, 1929), p. 358.

[4] Ibid.

and at St. Mary's Hall in 1870 it is not completely clear what was being taught since no records apparently survive. However, there are a few pointers:

1. The teaching of St. Thomas had been frequently recommended in the Constitutions of the Society.[1]

2. This recommendation is repeated in the letter to the Provinces sent in 1858 by the General of the Society, Fr. Peter Beckx:

. . . it is our considered opinion that our lecturers and writers as the Institute lays down in more than one place should follow (especially in those philosophical questions which have a connection with theological points) the footsteps of St Thomas the Angelic Doctor; in this being led by the example of those Jesuits who have shown the greatest excellence in these studies throughout the history of the Society.[2]

As a result of this directive the course in philosophy was extended from two years to three, the change-over being shown in the Province catalogue for 1861.

3. There is a good representative selection of scholastic manuals[3] surviving from the St. Mary's Hall period which suggest that neo-Thomistic manuals were abundantly provided.

4. The Professors teaching the courses were German or Italian,

[1] See the index, under 'S. Thomas', to vol. iii, *Institutum Societatis Iesu* (Florence, 1893). Fr. Georges Van Riet suggests that at the beginning of the nineteenth century it was a Suarezian Thomism which was being taught: 'La philosophie de saint Thomas n'a jamais été totalement délaissée, mais il y eut des périodes où elle ne compta plus que des défenseurs malhabiles et peu nombreux: ainsi en était-il, dans le Nord de l'Italie, au début du XIXᵉ siècle. L'enseignement des sciences sacrées était alors aux mains des jésuites, ou des ex-jésuites, comme on les appelait depuis la suppression de la Compagnie (1773). Ils professaient un thomisme retouché par Suarez.' *L'Épistémologie thomiste* (Louvain, 1946), pp. 32–3.

[2] '. . . expresse declaramus . . . id nobis necessarium visum esse, ut in iis praesertim quaestionibus philosophicis, quae cum theologicis connexae sunt, Lectores et Scriptores nostri, quoad Institutum non uno in loco praecipit, vestigia Angelici Doctoris S. Thomae, exemplo et ductu eorum, qui omni tempore his studiis in Societate maxime floruerunt, consectentur.' 'Ordinatio pro Triennali Philosophiae Studio', in G. M. Pachtler, *Ratio Studiorum et Institutiones Scholasticae Societatis Jesu*, iv (Berlin, 1894), 573–4; this is vol. xvi of *Monumenta Germaniae Paedagogica*, edited by Karl Kehrbach.

[3] Notably the works of Liberatore, Kleutgen, Tongiorgi, and also Sanseverino. I quote only those prior to GMH's period in philosophy, 1870–3. There are many others, of course, for example—Lepidi, Zigliara, Palmieri, etc. It is somewhat surprising that so many copies survived, since fashion is as rife in Scholastic manuals as elsewhere, and the new can easily oust the old. It seems to me that the course of Liberatore is the one most likely to have been used. His course had been rewritten and adapted to meet the new three-year requirement and carried the General's recommendation.

and this was so because the English Province was probably not yet equipped to provide its own men. Perhaps this was no bad thing since it at least connected the English Province with philosophical developments in Europe, and thus in some measure broke down the insularity so largely characteristic of nineteenth-century England. Unfortunately, those who taught Hopkins have published nothing, so we have no means of judging their precise standpoint in the current philosophical maelstrom.[1] Further, this was still the pre-specialization era and a Professor could teach not only all branches of philosophy but even theology.[2]

In passing it seems worth pointing out that at least Hopkins and his fellow scholastics had the opportunity of giving their full attention to philosophy, unlike their North-American counterparts as the following extract shows:

The greatest evil which the plan of a common house of studies sought to remedy was the practice of having the scholastics act as instructors in the colleges and at the same time get up the studies preparatory to ordination.[3]

[1] George Tyrrell (1861–1909)—*DNB*, 2nd Supp. iii—the Modernist, who read philosophy at St. Mary's Hall 1882–5, has left an account of the situation there at that time. 'The encyclical "Aeterni Patris" (on the study of St. Thomas) was just out [1879], and Father M. . . . was preaching "Aquinas his own interpreter," as opposed to Aquinas filtered through the brain of Suarez. . . . the Liberatore school was whispered against as disloyal to our traditions. . . . In strong opposition to Father M. and his neo-Thomism was Father H., the professor of the second year course . . . Naturally Father H. was severely tried by those who passed into his hands, in their second year, having received their first bias from Father M. . . . Hence the house was in philosophical factions, . . . Father T., the prefect and controller of studies, not only tolerated but rather enjoyed all this ferment, which, as contrasted with the sleepy lethargy of former years, seemed a symptom of waking mental activity.' Maude Petre, *Autobiography and Life of George Tyrrell*, i (1912), 242–6.

[2] For example, Fr. Capaldi, who taught Hopkins at St. Mary's Hall, appears at different times as lecturer in logic, general and special metaphysics, and ethics, and later as lecturer in Church History in the Theologate. Again, there was the old Polish Jesuit who impressed Newman—Norbert Korsack (1773–1846) born at Polotsk in White Russia, became a Jesuit in 1787, and after teaching theology at Polotsk came to Stonyhurst in 1807. 'Here he spent the rest of his life as Professor of either philosophy or Theology . . .' (Foley, vii (1882), pt. 1, 427, and quoted as a footnote in *The Letters and Diaries of John Henry Newman*, ed. C. S. Dessain, xi (1961), 104). Fr. David Milburn records: 'When, therefore, the bishops in the 1890s, . . . reviewed the situation of higher studies in the college, they were dismayed to find only one professor of philosophy, no provision made for a professor of either scripture or church history.' *A History of Ushaw College* (Durham, 1964), pp. 305–6.

[3] Gilbert J. Garraghan, 'The project of a common scholasticate for the Society of Jesus in North America', *Archivum Historicum Societatis Iesu*, ii (Rome, 1933), 3.

ST. MARY'S HALL, STONYHURST

(The Philosophate)

ST. BEUNO'S COLLEGE, ST. ASAPH

(The Theologate)

What then can be concluded of what Hopkins was taught in philosophy? Very little with certainty. Probably Thomism in the broad sense of the term, but more than likely St. Thomas as interpreted by Suarez.[1] But on the method used in teaching we are on surer ground. Fr. Clarke states:

Besides the lectures, which are given in Latin, the students are summoned three times a week to take part in an academical exercise which is one of the most valuable elements in the philosophical and theological training of the Society. It lasts an hour, during the first quarter of which one of the students has to give a synopsis of the last two lectures of the professor. After this, two other students, previously appointed for the purpose, have to bring against the doctrine laid down any possible objection that they can find in books or invent for themselves. Modern books are ransacked for these objections, and the 'objicients' do their best to hunt out difficulties which may puzzle the exponent of the truth, who is called the 'defendent.' Locke, Hegel, Descartes, Malebranche, John Stuart Mill, Mansel, Sir William Hamilton, and other modern writers, are valuable contributors for those who have to attack the Catholic doctrine. Everything has to be brought forward in syllogistic form, and to be answered in the same way. The professor, who of course presides at these contests, at once checks any one who departs from this necessary form and wanders off into mere desultory talk. This system of testing the soundness of the doctrine taught, continued as it is throughout the theological studies which come at a later period of the young Jesuit's career, provides those who pass through it with a complete defence against difficulties which otherwise are likely to puzzle the Catholic controversialist. It is a splendid means of sifting out truth from falsehood. Many of those who take part in it are men of ability and experience, and who have made a special study of the subjects discussed, and are well versed in the objections that can be urged against the Catholic teaching. Such men conduct their attack not as a mere matter of form, but with the vigour and ingenuity of practised disputants, and do their best to puzzle the unfortunate defendent with difficulties, the answer to which is by no means simple or obvious at first sight. Sometimes he is put completely 'in the sack,' and the professor has to intervene to explain where he has failed, and how the objection has really to be met. . . .

When the two objicients have finished their attack, there still remains a quarter of an hour before the circle is over. This time is devoted to objections and difficulties proposed by the students. Every one present has full

[1] Articles and bibliographies on Suarez and Suarezianism can be found in *New Cath. Encycl.*, vol. 13.

freedom to ask of the professor any question he pleases on the matter in hand, and may require of him an explanation of any point on which he is not satisfied. It is needless to say that full advantage is taken of this privilege, and the poor professor has often to submit to a very lively and searching interrogatory. If any question is proposed that is foolish, or beside the subject, the questioner is soon silenced by the open marks of disapprobation on the part of the rest of the class, and a good objection is sometimes received with quiet applause. Any fallacy or imperfect knowledge on the part of the professor is very speedily brought to light by the raking fire he has to undergo, and while all respect is shown him in the process, he must be well armed if he is to win the confidence of the class by his answers.[1]

The Beadle's Journal shows that circles began on 17 October, but Hopkins's class, the Logicians, only had questioning on this occasion. The Philosophers' reaction to this exercise can be partially gauged by this entry:

Wednesday, 9. Nov. 1870.
The community asked to be freed from circle, but there not being a ratio sufficiens, the request was not granted; especially as the recreation day came the following day.

And they repeated their request the following Monday '. . . on account of the feast of the previous day [St. Stanislaus]; the weather being very bad, and as the feast of St. Stanislaus is not kept in any peculiar manner at the Seminary, the request was not granted. Circles as usual.'

But occasionally they were freed. Hopkins, we can be sure, would have acted as 'defendent' or 'objicient' several times during his three years' stay at St. Mary's Hall.

Hopkins's reactions to the philosophical course are not made explicit. He informs Bridges non-committally in April 1871 that he is 'now at Stonyhurst reading philosophy and mathematics',[2] but tells Baillie a week later that he is 'going through a hard course of scholastic logic . . . which takes all the fair part of the day and leaves one fagged at the end for what remains. This makes the life painful to nature.'[3] In the last reference he makes to the course he sounds as

---

[1] 'Training of a Jesuit', pp. 221-3.
[2] *Letters to Bridges*, p. 26.
[3] *Further Letters*, p. 234. In fairness it should be added that he appears to acknowledge the course's beneficial effect on him since he adds: 'I find now too late *how* to read—

though he were anything but enjoying it: 'I am here for another year and now they are having at me with ethics and mechanics. Today is a whole holiday: I spent a miserable morning over formulas for the lever . . .'[1] Some months before writing this, that is at the end of his second year in philosophy, Hopkins discovered for himself the philosophic soulmate he had hungered for since he joined his new Church. This kindred spirit was Duns Scotus:

At this time I had first begun to get hold of the copy of Scotus on the Sentences in the Baddely library and was flush with a new stroke of enthusiasm.[2]

In making this discovery of Scotus he appears to anticipate a freshly reviving interest soon to show itself elsewhere. Fr. Edgar Hocedez states:

Le retour à la scolastique et le mouvement historique ne profitèrent pas au seul thomisme; les autres docteurs du moyen âge et spécialement Duns Scot en bénéficièrent: on peut même parler d'une véritable renaissance du scotisme. K. Werner publia *Die Scholastik des spätern Mittelalters, J. D. Scotus*, 1881; J. Müller, *Biographisches über D. Scotus*, 1881; Pluzanski, *Essai sur la philosophie de Duns Scot*, 1887, etc.[3]

So it would seem that here as in other respects Hopkins was running ahead of his time. The effect of his discovery was of prime importance. Whereas before entering religious life he had told Baillie, 'I find myself in an even prostrate admiration of Aristotle and am of the way of thinking, so far as I know him or know about him, that he is

at least some books, e.g. the classics: now I see things, now what I read tells, but I am obliged to read by snatches.'

[1] Ibid., p. 238.

[2] *Journals and Papers*, p. 221. Contributions on GMH and Scotus include the following: Christopher Devlin, 'Hopkins and Duns Scotus', *New Verse*, no. 14 (Apr. 1935), 12–17; W. H. Gardner, 'A Note on Hopkins and Duns Scotus', *Scrutiny*, v (June 1936), 61–70; Christopher Devlin, 'An Essay on Scotus', *The Month*, clxxxii (Nov.–Dec. 1946), 456–66; C. Devlin, 'Time's Eunuch', ibid., n.s. 1 (May 1949), 303–12; C. Devlin, 'The Image and the Word—I and II', ibid., n.s. 3 (Feb. and Mar. 1950), 114–27, 191–202; David A. Downes, 'Hopkins and Thomism', *Victorian Poetry*, iii (Autumn 1965), 270–2; see also the indexes to the following: John Pick, *Gerard Manley Hopkins* (1942); W. H. Gardner, *Gerard Manley Hopkins (1844–1889)* (1944–9); W. A. M. Peters, *Gerard Manley Hopkins* (1948). In a paper read at the Second International Scholastic Congress on Duns Scotus held at Oxford and Edinburgh, 11–17 Sept. 1966, the present writer attempted to answer the question 'Was Hopkins a Scotist before he read Scotus?', *Studia Scholastico-Scotistica 4. De doctrina Ioannis Duns Scoti*, vol. iv. *Scotismus decursu saeculorum* (Romae, 1968), 617–29.

[3] *Histoire de la théologie au XIXe siècle*, iii (Brussels and Paris, 1947), 50, and see pp. 361–3.

the end-all and be-all of philosophy.'[1] Yet writing in later years to
Bridges he reveals his change of preference: 'I can, at all events a
little, read Duns Scotus and I care for him more even than Aristotle
and more *pace tua* than a dozen Hegels.'[2] And the eulogy is repeated in 'Duns Scotus's Oxford':

> these walls are what
> He haunted who of all men most sways my spirits to peace;
> Of realty the rarest-veinèd unraveller; a not
> Rivalled insight, be rival Italy or Greece . . .

Hopkins's Scotism will recur in later chapters.

But studies were not the only concern for Hopkins and his contemporaries, for besides domestic changes there were upheavals
abroad. In Italy, for instance, the houses of the Society had been
seized and one of the results was that thirty-eight Italian theologian
scholastics with four of their professors from the Roman College
came to England and were accommodated at Manresa House, Roehampton. Manresa in turn was under pressure and appealed to
Stonyhurst to help out:

5 October 1870.

F. Rector asked today how much room we could find in the Seminary, in
case the second Rhetoricians [Juniors] were to be sent here to give their
places at Manresa to the Italian theologians, leaving Italy on account of
the late occupation of Rome by the Italians.[3] [PBJ]

And a few days later the log reads:

8 October. Saturday.

House very busy; five new beds being prepared for some Philosophers

[1] *Further Letters*, p. 231.

[2] *Letters to Bridges*, p. 31. Nevertheless, in 1879 GMH still identifies himself with
'Aristotelian Catholics', ibid., p. 95. Hopkins's last explicit reference to Scotus occurs in
a letter to Coventry Patmore written in Jan. 1884. Having observed of some of Patmore's
poems that they are 'almost . . . too full of meaning', he continues, 'And so I used to
feel of Duns Scotus when I used to read him with delight: he saw too far, he knew too
much; his subtlety overshot his interests; a kind of feud arose between genius and talent,
and the ruck of talent in the Schools finding itself, as his age passed by, less and less
able to understand him, voted that there was nothing important to understand and so
first misquoted and then refuted him.' *Further Letters*, p. 349. Christopher Devlin sees in
this extract 'a lament for the past, with a note of finality and a strong autobiographical
ring'. from 'Time's Eunuch', *The Month*, N.S. 1 (May 1949), 304. James Collins in his
article 'Philosophical Themes in G. M. Hopkins', *Thought*, xxii (Mar. 1947), 67–106,
shows on a wider scale the part philosophy played in GMH's work.

[3] Cf. *Journals and Papers*, top of p. 201, and the entry for 20 Sept., ibid., p. 203.

from the Irish Prov. who had been in Rome and leaving on account of the disturbances there. The workshop was cleaned out for a bedroom. The reference library was fitted up for two beds, also No 12: the parlour had one bed put in it; fires lighted in workshop, parlour, Ref. Library. Bedsteads, mattresses etc. sent from the College.

The reading in the refectory kept the scholastics informed of the Italian situation as they listened to Manning's sermon on the occupation of Rome by Victor Emmanuel and his army, as well as articles from *The Month* and the *Freeman's Journal*.[1] They prayed about the disaster sustained particularly by the Italian Jesuits, and had Exposition of the Blessed Sacrament on Friday evenings at the request of the General, Fr. Peter Beckx.[2]

28 Oct. 1870. Sts Simon and Jude.
Exposition of the B. Sacrament here from 5.15 to 9.30 for F. General's Intention, there being no inconvenience whatever in our having it. Watching before the B. Sacrament for a quarter of an hour each; two at a time in surplices. Benediction 9.20 Supper being at 8. At 5.15 the 'O Salutaris' was sung; at 9.20 the Litany of the B. Virgin was sung, followed by the Litany of the S. [Sacred] Heart wh: was said with the Act of Reparation. [PBJ]

But there were less serious events to provide a respite from the daily hurly-burly, and on 6 October St. Mary's Hall (the Seminarians) played the Stonyhurst lay-Philosophers[3] at cricket for the last time that season. The result was the Seminary 97 for three wickets, while the lay-Philosophers were 82 all out, and the Beadle records

---

[1] See Appendix 2B, 'Refectory Reading in the Philosophate' under the dates 12 Oct., 5 Dec., and 7–8 Dec. 1870.
[2] 'Letter of Our Very Rev. Fr. General to the Society', dated 28 Aug. 1870, in *LLNN*, vii (Sept. 1870), 121–3.
[3] For details of the Stonyhurst lay-Philosophers see chap. 16, 'The Epicureans' in *School Days at Saxonhurst*, by 'One of the Boys' [Percy Fitzgerald] (Edinburgh, 1867). Fitzgerald who had himself been a lay-Philosopher described their life as 'like living in a country house', ibid., p. 255; A. Hewitson, *Stonyhurst College: its Past and Present* (Preston, 1870), pp. 36, 84. See also the index to the 2nd edition (Preston, 1878); Joseph Walton, 'Stonyhurst Life', *The Month*, N.S. 1 (Mar. 1874), 325–36; 'An Evening with the Stonyhurst Philosophers', *The Tablet*, 8 Dec. 1888, p. 894; chap. xix, 'The Philosophical Year', in Percy Fitzgerald's *Stonyhurst Memories* (1895); George Gruggen and Joseph Keating, *Stonyhurst: its Past History and Life in the Present* (1901), passim; Michael Maher and Joseph Bolland, 'Stonyhurst College', *The Teacher's Encyclopaedia*, edited by A. P. Laurie, v (1912), 179; [Geoffrey Holt], 'The Phils', *Stonyhurst Magazine*, xxxiii (Oct. 1960), 508–13.

'A glorious victory'. A week later saw the first game of bandy[1] being played, and on the evening of the same day (13 October) the first meeting of the English Academy took place. The English Academy generally met on Tuesdays at 7.05 p.m. unless displaced by something more important; later it came to be called the Phil. and Lit. Society. Between October and May twenty-three papers were read:

18 Oct. 1870	Selection of a metre for the translation of Homer
25 Oct.	Positivists
1 Nov.	Thoughts occasioned by a letter of Mgr. Dupanloup on the disasters in France
8 Nov.	Prussian Army
15 Nov.	Causality (Part I)
22 Nov.	Causality (Part II)
29 Nov.	The Historical Plays of Shakespeare
6 Dec.	The Principles of the art of painting
20 Dec.	The Mission of Epaminondas
10 Jan. 1871	The Holy Grail
17 Jan.	Lisbon and its monuments (with illustrations)
24 Jan.	The Life of Sir Thomas More
31 Jan.	A sketch of the Plague in London
7 Feb.	Some thoughts on higher education
28 Feb.	Dynastic characteristics
7 Mar.	The spectroscope
14 Mar.	Photography
21 Mar.	The right of possessing
28 Mar.	Spain
18 Apr.	Ontologism and necessary truth
25 Apr.	Historical sketch of Grecian Sophists
2 May	The value of the syllogism
9 May	The Idealism of Berkeley (last meeting)

[1] Bandy: 'Generally known as Hockey, which name is at Stonyhurst confined to the game played on the ice.' John Gerard, *Centenary Record, Stonyhurst College* (Belfast, 1894), p. 191 n. The latest instance of 'bandy' recorded in *OED* is 1860, George Eliot, *Mill on the Floss*, i. 77: 'She's only a girl—she can't play at bandy.' See also: Anon, 'Stonyhurst Bandy', *Stonyhurst Magazine*, ii (Dec. 1884), 48; Charles Ryan, 'Rules for Bandy', ibid. iv (Aug. 1890), 557–8. In Mar. 1871 Hopkins tells his mother: 'We enliven some of our evenings with playing hockey.' *Further Letters*, p. 113.

At the inaugural meeting the Rector, who frequently attended, had suggested that occasionally there ought to be debates, but that these were in no way to interfere with the work of the Academy. Accordingly there were four debates that year:

3 Dec. 1870   Whether a representative were the best form of government.

25 Mar. 1871   Secular education is no education at all (in the system of Sec. Education) and cannot therefore offer any remedy for our social and political evils.

18 May   Secular education is no education at all etc. (adjourned from March 25th).

4 Dec.   [No subject stated]

Whether Hopkins spoke in the debates is not known, but he did not read a paper during this session of the English Academy. Both the papers read and the subjects debated reveal some topicality of choice. For example, the Forster Education Act was a major news item, and as in the case of the Revolution in Italy, it, too, cropped up in the refectory reading.

The manner of reading aloud to others in the refectory—a perennial problem—must have called for attention at this time, for the Beadle notes on 17 October: 'Fr. Harper came over to read for us at supper, to give us an idea as to how he would have us read.' Fr. Harper, like so many of the cloth, had a dramatic flare and gave readings at the college from *Hamlet*,[1] *The Merchant of Venice*, a farce, and moved the motion in the debate 'Secular education is no education at all'. It was also his job to supervise the scholastics' 'tones', or practice sermons, and the day after you had preached you went to him for a criticism. But when Hopkins preached on 18 December Fr. Harper was absent.

Possibly the day Hopkins enjoyed best in this his first semester was the Blandyke, or free day, in October, held on the 20th of the month. His diary records:

Laus Deo—the river today and yesterday. Yesterday it was a sallow glassy

[1] '10 Nov. Fr. Harper read passages from "Hamlet" to the boys at 5.45. As both F. Weld and F. Rector were away, we presumed leave to attend.' [PBJ]

gold at Hodder Roughs and by watching hard the banks began to sail up-stream, the scaping unfolded, the river was all in tumult but not running, only the lateral motions were perceived, and the curls of froth where the waves overlap shaped and turned easily and idly.—I meant to have written more.—Today the river was wild, very full, glossy brown with mud, furrowed in permanent billows through which from head to head the water swung with a great down and up again. These heads were scalped with rags of jumping foam. But at the Roughs the sight was the burly water-backs which heave after heave kept tumbling up from the broken foam and their plump heap turning open in ropes of velvet[1]

An innovation introduced at the beginning of December was an optional class in German by Fr. Bochum on Thursday mornings from 8.30 to 9.15. Did Hopkins attend? We are not told, but he wrote to Bridges years later, 'I know almost no German',[2] so perhaps he did not go, or if he did, did not take it very seriously.

Little else of note took place before Christmas. Umbrellas were given to those without them and they were marked not with your name but with the number of your room. On 23 December there was a Menstruum, or philosophical scholastic disputation, held at 9 a.m. in the presence of the Rector and several Fathers from the College; it passed without comment.

But already the onset of Christmas excitement is clear from the Beadle's record:

24 December. Saturday.—Christmas Eve—
Fast day. Rise 5.30. Hard frost during the night; ice quite strong—Recreation, outside and in from 9 to 11. Confessions 11.15 in No 15. On account of the Chapel being decorated with festoons, etc., the B. Sacrament was removed into the Sacristy about 8.30 a.m. and not carried back to the chapel till after 6 p.m. Decorations in chapel on an extensive scale; crib not under the altar, but high up between the pillars on the Gospel side, where the statue of our Lady generally stands. Festoons made in the Philosophy school room; a few had been made the previous evening. . . . No Martyrologium at dinner. . . . Coffee 4.30. Benediction at the College 5. End of Recreation 6. Night Litanies 7.15 said by the Bedel, as all the Fathers were away. 7.30 Martyrologium, sung by Mr Remedios, the community standing as at grace. Before night litanies the singer of the

---

[1] *Journals and Papers*, p. 200. The Beadle's Journal records: 'Sunday, 23 Oct. The Billington Catechists had to return, not being able to cross the river on account of the flood.'
[2] *Letters to Bridges*, pp. 30-1.

martyrologium got a glass of negus. . . . A few tingles given to the bell at 12. . . . A harmonium had been brought over from the college the previous day. Singing during Mass; an English hymn at the end. Negus for choir only 11.45 p.m.

Somewhat surprisingly the scholastics did not go to Communion at Midnight Mass but went at the seven o'clock mass on Christmas Day, having risen at 6 a.m. After High Mass at ten with a sermon, there was skating with the thermometer in the region of 25 °F. There was a 'double-table' dinner, Vespers and Benediction at four, and a concert at the College at six. Permission was also given to attend the other Christmas entertainments in the Academy Room. The day finished with a talking supper at 8.20, Litanies at 9.30, followed by the usual spiritual duties.

The Christmas entertainments began on Boxing Day. The lay-Philosophers put on Sheridan's *The Critic*, on the 27th and 28th the College staged *The Tempest*, on the 29th two farces, J. B. Buckstone's *The Irish Lion*, and J. M. Morton's *Box and Cox*, and on the 30th *King John*. On New Year's Day there was a concert, probably given by the Seminary choir and deferred from 29 December, and Fr. Harper read Fielding's farce *The Mock Doctor*. Next evening, *Box and Cox* was repeated together with M. W. B. Jerrold's *Cool as a Cucumber* presented by the lay-Philosophers.

In the long hard winter noted by Hopkins,[1] the skaters came into their own[2] and there was skating continuously from Christmas till Candlemas and beyond. Perhaps the highlight of this vacation was the evening of 29 December:

After supper F. Rector gave leave for the Seminarians to go on the Infirmary Pond in front of the College, which had been illuminated by Tar Barrels and Chinese Lanterns, at the expense of the Philosophers. There were there the Higher Line [i.e. Sixth Formers], the College Community, the Seminarians, and many strangers. Fireworks were displayed by the Philosophers. We left the pond about a quarter to ten.[3] [PBJ]

[1] *Journals and Papers*, p. 201.

[2] 'Stonyhurst records can show few skating winters equal to that of 1870–1.' Charles V. Hickie, 'In the Early Seventies', *Stonyhurst Magazine*, xviii (Feb. 1926), 317.

[3] The following seemed too good to miss: 'January 1st, 1871.—Torchlight skating on the Mill Pond, 8.0 p.m. to 10.30 p.m.—band, cigars, Mr. Jackson, cornet solo, "Rule Britannia"—glorious! glorious!!' And there was an equally 'glorious' encore on Saturday, the 21st, followed by a whole week's skating. Ibid.

The vacation finished on 2 January and the following day the scholastics were back to their lectures and books. The rest of this academic year is singularly uneventful. The tailor came to measure the community for new clothes in early January. On Sunday the 8th of the month Julius Maclaurin a scholastic died:[1]

About 9, by some mismanagement, the news not having been brought over before, we heard of the death of Br Julius McLaurin; he died very peacefully this morning at 2.30, in presence of F. Rector, F. Minister & Br Barraud. The usual suffrages, three Masses or three pairs of beads, announced at dinner. [PBJ]

Monday 9 Jan.
Officium Defunctorum for Mr McLaurin 8.30. It finished about 9.35. [PBJ]

Tuesday 10 Jan.
Requiem High Mass 6.40, sung by F. Weld, after which Mr McLaurin was buried. We got back for breakfast just at 8. F. Capaldi's class 8.40. After dinner we tried to clear the snow off the pond, as the snow was three or four inches deep. [PBJ]

The community was further depleted two months later when another scholastic, George Boeufvé,[2] died on 3 March:

Br Boeufvé died very quietly this morning between one and five, so quietly that Br. Starkie did not know precisely at wh. hour. His body was laid out in No. 3, and laid in the coffin in the evening. The lid was not screwed down till next day in the evening. Everything as usual. Rules begun at dinner. [PBJ]

'Everything as usual' epitomizes and must epitomize the community's reaction to the loss of one of its members.

Before the onset of Lent, Stonyhurst and St. Mary's Hall were entertained by a Liverpool musical group with an operetta, *The*

---

[1] Julius Maclaurin (1844–71; see Foley vii), Jesuit scholastic, born at Elgin, Scotland, on 5 Apr. 1844. Educated at Mount St. Mary's and Stonyhurst Colleges. Entered the S.J. novitiate at Roehampton in May 1862. After reading philosophy at St. Mary's Hall, he taught chemistry at Stonyhurst, and died there of tuberculosis on 8 Jan. 1871. (*Journals and Papers*, p. 203, 'Maclauren'.)

[2] George Louis Boeufvé (1850–71; see Foley vii), Jesuit scholastic, born in Holland on 6 Apr. 1850. Educated at St. Francis Xavier's College, Liverpool, and at Turnhout, Belgium. Entered the S.J. novitiate on 14 Sept. 1866 with the intention of working with Fr. de Smet, S.J., in North America on the Rocky Mountain mission. Died of tuberculosis at Stonyhurst College during his philosophy course on 3 Mar. 1871. (*Journals and Papers*, p. 203, 'Boeuvé'.)

Musical Box, on 9 February, and a week later by more Liverpool actors with a miscellaneous concert and two farces—*Taming a Tiger* (an anonymous translation from the French), and J. M. Morton's *Sent to the Tower*. The 19th was a Villa day, dinner was at three, and at six o'clock the scholastics went across to the College where the Grammarians presented *Apartments—Visitors to the Exhibition may be accommodated* by William Brough, and *The Steeple Chase* by J. M. Morton.

The ensuing months were punctuated with Villa days and Blandykes; the Easter vacation lasted from 9 to 16 April. The Seminarians played the lay-Philosophers at Stonyhurst cricket.[1] The Provincial's visitation this year began early in May, and later that month bathing began. Hopkins writes to his mother:

We bathe every day if we like now at a beautiful spot in the Hodder all between waterfalls and beneath a green meadow and down by the greenwood side O. If you stop swimming to look round you see fairyland pictures up and down the stream.[2]

On 21 June, the feast of St. Aloysius, Hopkins preached at dinner.

Rector's Day was given on 13 July, and the St. Mary's Hall community had all their meals at the College and mixed freely with the priests and scholastics there. Except on the rare occasion of 'fusion' such as this the separation of communities seems to have been rigidly kept.

The final examination for the first and second year Philosophers began on 24 July, the third-year's examination 'de universa philosophia' having already been completed. Each member of the first and second year was examined orally for half an hour by a Board of which the Rector was president. All the philosophy examinations were finished by 26 July; and two days later the first year were examined in mathematics. The feast of St. Ignatius Loyola was also marked by 'fusion' with the College, but the Seminarians dined at home because the College was busily preparing for its prize-day,

---

[1] See the article by 'E.M.' 'Stonyhurst Cricket' in *Stonyhurst Magazine*, ii (May 1885), 83–6, 133; and John Gerard, *Centenary Record, Stonyhurst College* (Belfast, 1894), pp. 180–2; photographs on pp. 138, 178, and 180.
[2] *Further Letters*, p. 117.

or Academy, on the following day. Permission was not given to St. Mary's Hall to attend that year because of the large number of visitors expected.

On 3 August the Seminarians went to live in the College to leave St. Mary's Hall free for the Salford diocesan clergy retreat. They occupied the quarters of the lay-Philosophers. They seem to have enjoyed the change:

Thursday, 3 August.
We had the Community Ref. [refectory], Phil Recn. [recreation] room,[1] Billiard Ta. in long room Front of College, and Garden for recn; boats and cricket field out of time of ordinary recn. Salmon fishing. Most of Seminarians went.[2] Dinner 4. Supper 8. Two lay brothers served for us today; on other days we supply our own servers and readers.[3] Ben. [Benediction] 9. Our choir, thurifer and two acolythes [sic] from ours. [PBJ]

Certainly the abandon of billiards, boating, and salmon fishing must have served to whet their appetites for their Villa, or annual holiday, which was taken that year at Innellan, Argyllshire.[4] Earlier in the year they had been asked to check to see if they needed new shoes for Villa; alpaca coats had been given out, and the entries for 14 and 15 August read: 'Collars and felt hats distributed. Turndown

---

[1] Photograph in G. Gruggen and J. Keating, *Stonyhurst* (1901), p. 112.

[2] In view of Hopkins's laconic remark to Baillie one wonders if he went with the others: 'There is good fishing for those who do not see that after bad fishing the next worst thing is good fishing.' *Further Letters*, p. 235.

[3] *The Battle of Dorking* was read at this time, beginning on 6 Aug. GMH notes: 'The Battle of Dorking and the fear of the Revolution make me sad now.' *Journals and Papers*, p. 213.

[4] The house which was rented, 'Broom Lodge', still stands, today converted into flats. It faces over to Wemyss Bay and commands a good view of the Firth of Clyde. I am indebted to Mr. R. A. Miller of Dundee whose family took over the house in 1913 for the following details. 'Broom Lodge' as originally constructed had three separate houses in its three separate storeys. In the latter part of the nineteenth century, dating from the time that regular steamer services to Innellan and the Argyllshire coast came into operation, the village became a fashionable summer resort for Glasgow families. Larger houses were built and many of the existing houses converted from two or three flats to single mansions. 'Broom Lodge' was one of these converted. The garden was beautifully laid out, the main features being the number of flowering shrubs and decorative trees. A magnolia tree which still stands was probably the most unusual for Scotland. The fruit garden, too, was lavishly planned. There were Victoria plums, blue plums, greengages, a pear tree, four types of gooseberry, two types of raspberry, black and red currants. Some account of the scholastics' journey to Innellan that year will be found in Scott's *H. S. Kerr*, pp. 117-19.

or Roman Collars may be worn. Only a few did wear Romans[1]
. . . taking top hats is *ad lib.*' [PBJ] And a post-Villa entry for
9 September states; 'Villa books and neckties to be put in the
beadle's room.' [PBJ] To supplement Hopkins's own account[2] of
the Innellan Villa I give a few quotations from the Beadle's Journal:

Wednesday, 16 August.

Rose 5. Mass 5.45. Breakfast 6.15. Started about 7 to catch 8.13 train from
Whalley. F. Weld, F. Bochum & two scholastics drove. A thro' carriage
to Liverpool had been secured. . . . We arrived in Liverpool about 9.30.
The Mr Kerrs were put in charge of the luggage. Walked to Clarence
Dock, and embarked on the 'Bison'; left Liverpool 11.30 and after a calm
voyage got into Greenock about 5.15 a.m. The 'Bison' is to be much
recommended. Heard Mass at S. Mary's, Patrick Street, F. Bochum and
F. Weld saying Mass at the High Altar. Breakfasted sumptuously at the
Tontine and started for Inellan [*sic*] at 9.30 reaching that place at 10.30.
. . . Found our three adjacent houses at Broom Lodge very convenient:
we had to fit them up ourselves as we found them in a very unprepared
state. Two portmanteaus being lost, Mr W. Kerr had to return to
Greenock[;] we got them on the morrow.

Friday, 18 August.

Rose 6.30. F. Bochum said Mass 7.30 in our ordinary Recn Room which
was used as a chapel for Mass, the B. Sacrament being brought down
each morning for an hour from a little room upstairs.

Wednesday, 23 August.

Villa Day (par excellence) Seven went to Inverary to see the reception of
the Marquis of Lorne & gathering of the Highland Clans. Six went out for
a sail (duce Mr H Kerr). Four went to Rothesay. Dinner 3. . . . N.B.
Rowing boats were taken only about six times during this villa sailing or
fishing once or twice, all on account of the wet & bad weather.

Thursday, 24 August. S. Bartholemew.

Holy Communion. Mass 5.45. Breakfast 6.15. Three started for Inverary,
but were too late. 15 started for Edinburgh at 8.15 by Wemyss Bay (third
class) getting there at 12[.] Lunch at station provided by Lord H Kerr.

---

[1] See the following: 'The [Jesuit] community, it might be supposed, dressed in the
same fashion then and now, but it was not so. Until the Christmas of 1853 the Roman
collar was unknown amongst them and they wore stand-up collars ("gills" they were called)
and black ties, with an open white shirt front. Great was the excitement when on
Christmas Eve, of the year named above, Fr. Fitzsimon appeared in a Roman collar to
give Benediction.' ' '56', 'Stonyhurst in the Fifties', *Stonyhurst Magazine*, iii (Dec.
1887), 78.

[2] *Journals and Papers*, pp. 213–14.

Saw Holyrood, the town[,] the Castle, our church etc. Left at 4 arriving at Broom Lodge about 8. Supper with meat, mutton chops etc. Punch.

Saturday, 26 August.

Six went to Loch Lomond (just 5s a head) going by steamer to Arrochar, steamer Tarbet to Balloch & from Helensburg to Dunoon.

Tuesday, 29 August.

After rather rough voyage got to Liverpool 4.30. Train to Preston 5.30. Drove from Pres. to Stonyhurst; got in 8.45. Supper cold meat and Punch.

The following night the Philosophers began their annual retreat,[1] and on the day it finished Gerard's brother Cyril arrived and stayed at Stonyhurst for three days. They both left on 11 September travelling together as far as Blackburn where Cyril left him to go to Liverpool, while Gerard went on to Hampstead. His father and his sister were at home, and he took the opportunity of going to see his grandmother and Aunt Anne. Then on the thirteenth he joined his mother and the rest at Bursledon in Hampshire.[2] As usual with Hopkins, holiday periods cause his notes to expand. This week in Hampshire fills two pages of his Journal, the three months which followed occupy half a page.

In glancing back through Hopkins's first year, among the impressions which emerge perhaps the strongest is the increase and deepening in his grasp of 'inscape'; this is clear from the greater variety of items which fall under his surveillance. His most startling single sentence of this year's Journal occurs in March: 'What you look hard at seems to look hard at you, hence the true and the false instress of nature.'[3] The following extracts are intended to illustrate the range and diversity of his observation.

End of March and beginning of April—This is the time to study inscape in the spraying of trees, for the swelling buds carry them to a pitch which the eye could not else gather—for out of much much more, out of little not much, out of nothing nothing: in these sprays at all events there is a new world of inscape. The male ashes are very boldly jotted with the heads of the bloom which tuft the outer ends of the branches. The staff

---

[1] *Journals and Papers*, p. 214, entry for 30 Aug.
[2] Ibid., pp. 214–17; *Letters to Bridges*, p. 28; he called on Baillie at his chambers in London, but he was out of town. Cf. *Further Letters*, pp. 235–6.
[3] *Journals and Papers*, p. 204.

of each of these branches is closely knotted with the places where buds are or have been, so that it is something like a finger which has been tied up with string and keeps the marks. They are in knops of a pair, one in each side, and the knops are set alternately, at crosses with the knops above and the knops below, the bud of course is a short smoke-black pointed nail-head or beak pieced out of four lids or nippers. Below it, like the hollow below the eye or the piece between the knuckle and the root of the nail, is a half-mooned-shaped sill as if once chipped from the wood and this gives the twig its quaining in the outline. When the bud breaks at first it shews a heap of fruity purplish anthers looking something like unripe elder-berries but these push open into richly-branched tree-pieces coloured buff and brown, shaking out loads of pollen, and drawing the tuft as a whole into peaked quains—mainly four, I think, two bigger and two smaller[1]

Flowers, too, come in for the same searching scrutiny:

The white violets are broader and smell; the blue, scentless and finer made, have a sharper whelking and a more winged recoil in the leaves

Take a *few* primroses in a glass and the instress of—brilliancy, sort of starriness: I have not the right word—so simple a flower gives is remark-able. It is, I think, due to the strong swell given by the deeper yellow middle[2]

This day and May 11 the bluebells in the little wood between the College and the highroad and in one of the Hurst Green cloughs. In the little wood/ opposite the light/ they stood in blackish spreads or sheddings like the spots on a snake. The heads are then like thongs and solemn in grain and grape-colour. But in the clough/ through the light/ they came in falls of sky-colour washing the brows and slacks of the ground with vein-blue, thickening at the double, vertical themselves and the young grass and brake fern combed vertical, but the brake struck the upright of all this with light winged transomes. It was a lovely sight.—The bluebells in your hand baffle you with their inscape, made to every sense: if you draw your fingers through them they are lodged and struggle/ with a shock of wet heads; the long stalks rub and click and flatten to a fan on one another like your fingers themselves would when you passed the palms hard across one another, making a brittle rub and jostle like the noise of a hurdle strained by leaning against; then there is the faint honey smell and in the mouth the sweet gum when you bite them. But this is easy, it is the eye they baffle. They give one a fancy of panpipes and of some wind instrument with stops—a trombone perhaps. The overhung necks—for growing they are little more than a staff with a simple crook but in water, where they stiffen, they take stronger turns, in the head like sheephooks

---

[1] Ibid., pp. 205-6.   [2] Ibid.

or, when more waved throughout, like the waves riding through a whip that is being smacked—what with these overhung necks and what with the crisped ruffled bells dropping mostly on one side and the gloss these have at their footstalks they have an air of the knights at chess. Then the knot or 'knoop' of buds some shut, some just gaping, which makes the pencil of the whole spike, should be noticed: the inscape of the flower most finely carried out in the siding of the axes, each striking a greater and greater slant, is finished in these clustered buds, which for the most part are not straightened but rise to the end like a tongue and this and their tapering and a little flattening they have make them look like the heads of snakes[1]

Hopkins's description of the peacock and its train makes us see the bird with new eyes, perhaps even for the first time:

It has a very regular warp, like a shell, in which the bird embays himself, the bulge being inwards below but the hollow inwards above, cooping him in and only opening towards the brim, where the feathers are beginning to rive apart. The eyes, which lie alternately when the train is shut, like scales or gadroons, fall into irregular rows when it is opened, and then it thins and darkens against the light, it loses the moistness and satin it has when in the pack but takes another/ grave and expressive splendour, and the outermost eyes, detached and singled, give with their corner fringes the suggestion of that inscape of the flowing cusped trefoil which is often effective in art. He shivers it when he first rears it and then again at intervals and when this happens the rest blurs and the eyes start forward.— I have thought it looks like a tray or green basket or fresh-cut willow hurdle set all over with Paradise fruits cut through—first through a beard of golden fibre and then through wet flesh greener than greengages or purpler than grapes—or say that the knife had caught a tatter or flag of the skin and laid it flat across the flesh—and then within all a sluggish corner drop of black or purple oil[2]

He delights himself and his readers with his pictures of the antics of lambs:

They toss and toss: it is as if it were the earth that flung them, not themselves. It is the pitch of graceful agility when we think that.—April 16— Sometimes they rest a little space on the hind legs and the forefeet drop curling in on the breast, not so liquidly as we see it in the limbs of foals though[3]

---

[1] *Journals and Papers*, pp. 208-9, and see also the last paragraph on p. 199, and entry for 11 May on p. 231.
[2] Ibid., pp. 209-10.
[3] Ibid., p. 206, and see GMH's letter to his sister Kate, in *Further Letters*, p. 115.

But inscape is to be found not only in nature, but also, for example, in drinking chocolate.[1] And if we may look ahead, he records towards the end of his second year:

Stepped into a barn of ours, a great shadowy barn, where the hay had been stacked on either side, and looking at the great rudely arched timber-frames—principals(?) and tie-beams, which make them look like bold big *A*s with the cross-bar high up—I thought how sadly beauty of inscape was unknown and buried away from simple people and yet how near at hand it was if they had eyes to see it and it could be called out everywhere again[2]

In short, he says, 'All the world is full of inscape . . .'[3]

But besides using his eyes, Hopkins used his ears to savour what was special and peculiar in the local dialect. He tells his mother:

It is so funny to hear the people of this country saying Ay. Our two gardeners for instance are often talking over their work. They are shy of being overheard but they cannot conceal their agreements. What the one says the other assents to by the roots and upwards from the level of the sea. He makes a kind of Etna of assent, without effort but with a long fervent breathing out of all the breath there is in him. The word runs through the whole scale of the vowels beginning broad in the barrel of the waist and ending fine in the drop of the lip. For this reason I believe it is a natural sign of agreement and not conventional. . . . It is equal to about four semibreves and morsels itself into vibrations like echos under a bridge and dying off like tufts of smoke against a ribbed vaulting.[4]

We get something of his own special and keen delight as he jots down in his diary the words and expressions of the country folk about him.

Lancashire—'of all the wind instruments big drŏŏm fots me best'.[5]

July 24—Robert says the first grass from the scythe is the *swathe*, then comes the *strow* (tedding), then *rowing*, then the footcocks, then *breaking*, then the *hubrows*, which are gathered into *hubs*, then sometimes another break and *turning*, then *rickles*, the biggest of all the cocks, which are run together into *placks*, the shapeless heaps from which the hay is carted[6]

His other literary interests seem to have been restricted, since he tells Baillie:

My time is short both for writing and reading, so that I can seldom

---

[1] *Journals and Papers*, p. 203.   [2] Ibid., p. 221.
[3] Ibid., p. 230, in the entry for 24 Feb.   [4] *Further Letters*, pp. 113–14.
[5] *Journals and Papers*, p. 211.   [6] Ibid., pp. 212–13.

write and when I do I have nothing to say. Don't you know, it is mainly about books and so on that I shd. be writing and I read so few.[1]

And later in the same letter he says, 'I am glad to hear literary etc news as I am here removed from it and get much behind.'[2]

From his letters we know that at this time he saw the *Illustrated London News*, *Punch*, and possibly *The Spectator*.[3]

We can turn now to Hopkins's second year at St. Mary's Hall. On 18 September[4] he returned from the week's holiday spent with his family.[5] A week later a new Beadle was appointed and the Philosophers changed their rooms. Denis Meadows has described the room change as follows:

The rooms were all alike and were distributed impartially among students and professors. The only distinction was that the latter were left peacefully in possession unless they asked for a change, while we were shifted about periodically. It didn't make any difference to us. We had very little property to move, and a second-floor front and a third-floor back were equally adapted to concentration on such things as the real distinction between essence and existence, or the subjectivism of Kant's categories.[6]

Lectures began again on 2 October, fires had reappeared in the recreation room, and the house was back on five-thirty rise. About the philosophical studies during the second and third years of the course little need be said. The subjects studied, as we have already seen, were psychology, ethics, special metaphysics, cosmology, and natural theology. Since both second and third year Philosophers were taken together by one professor it follows that a two-year cycle must have been followed. Hopkins is silent on the studies of these years.

In mid-October the newly built Jesuit church of the Holy Name was opened:

Sunday, Oct. 15. Opening of Gesu Manchester.

Rising 5.0. Mass 5.30. Breakfast 6.15. Train from Whalley 7.54: nine

[1] *Further Letters*, p. 234.   [2] Ibid., p. 235.
[3] Ibid., pp. 119, 120, 58.   [4] *Journals and Papers*, p. 217.
[5] He wrote to A. W. Garrett, 'I went to see my people for a week last autumn . . .',
Further Letters, p. 56.
[6] *Obedient Men*, p. 138.

stopped at home not including F. Bochum: we all had to take with us a gown, a biretta, & a pair of light shoes. Pontifical High Mass 11. Lunch (tickets 3s..6d) 2 p.m. Return Train 6.15, not arriving at Whalley till 9. F. Weld did not return with us. Wet walk from Whalley. Supper with Punch. Examen bell rung 11. [PBJ]

Two days later the English Academy recommenced and at this meeting a paper was read on 'The Use and Abuse of Genius'.[1]

Two domestic changes occurred about this time. Fr. Fitzsimon, Hopkins's first novice master, came from Beaumont College to be Superior at St. Mary's Hall. Ten days later Fr. Parkinson[2] took over as Spiritual Father to the Seminarians. Nothing especially exciting happened before Christmas. Hockey began again and rackets was inaugurated. Skates were sent to be sharpened at the beginning of December and six new pairs were bought at wholesale prices varying from 7s. to 9s. 6d. a pair.

On Sunday 17 December Hopkins preached a sermon. This night he found something unusual to record:

Dec. 17–18 at night—Rescued a little kitten that was perched in the sill of the round window at the sink over the gasjet and dared not jump down. I heard her mew a piteous long time till I could bear it no longer; but I make a note of it because of her gratitude after I had taken her down, which made her follow me about and at each turn of the stairs as I went

---

[1] Although twenty papers were read between October and May, the Beadle's Journal records the titles of only five in addition to the one quoted above:

1 Nov. 1871	The Arabs as they were found and left by Mahomet
7 Nov.	Humorous writing
14 Nov.	Whately the rhetorician a disciple of Aristotle
21 Nov.	Julian the Apostate
28 Nov.	The origin of Freemasonry.

[2] Thomas Brown Parkinson (1819–1904), Jesuit priest, born at Chester-le-Street, Durham, on 10 Nov. 1819. Educated at Houghton-le-Spring Grammar School, and at St. Catherine's Hall, Cambridge; migrated to Queens' College, 1840; B.A., 1842; M.A., 1846. Took Anglican orders in Ripon; incumbent of St. Mary's, Wakefield. After reception into the R.C. Church, entered the S.J. novitiate at Roehampton in 1851, aged thirty-two; ordained priest in 1857. Teaching and parish work in Glasgow. 1865–7, Superior at St. Mary's Hall, Stonyhurst. 1868–71, Superior at Glasgow, then Spiritual Father at St. Mary's Hall, at Liverpool, and Farm Street. 1875–87, Superior at St. Aloysius', Oxford, during which time GMH served under him. It was at St. Aloysius in Feb. 1878 that Newman preached his first sermon in Oxford since he vacated the pulpit at St. Mary's. After twelve years at Oxford, Fr. Parkinson worked on the parish at Bury St. Edmunds from 1887 to 1894. During his remaining years he acted as Spiritual Father at St. Beuno's, and at St. Mary's Hall until his death on 24 July 1904. (*Letters to Bridges*, pp. 68, 75, 81, 86, 97; *Correspondence with Dixon*, p. 27; *Further Letters*, p. 411; *Sermons and Devotional Writings*, p. 4.)

down leading her to the kitchen run back a few steps and try to get up to lick me through the banisters from the flight above[1]

With the end of the first semester in sight the Philosophers looked for some relaxation in the academic curriculum:

Friday, Dec. 22. Fast.

It being the day before the Menstruum we asked to be exempted from circle: both the Professors said that such was the custom in their respective provinces, sc. Neapolitan & German; but we were refused on the grounds that it was not the custom here. [PBJ]

The Christmas entertainment[2] followed a pattern similar to the previous year. Hopkins was not able to go to all the plays, and what he did see produced mixed feelings in him. He confides to Baillie:

The boys at the College have been giving concerts and plays every night but I have mostly had to stay away and husband precious time. I went however to Macbeth, not to see (for the swan of Avon is very very short of Castalia-water on this stage and would painfully recognise his shadow, especially as women's parts are not given and Lady Macbeth becomes an Uncle Donald—I am bound to say, incredible as it may seem, that whether the imagination helps them and one makes a mental correction or whatever it is the effect is not so disastrous as you might think it must be: but let us round the more and more beetling Cape-Horn headlands of this parenthesis) not to see, but to hear Lock's beautiful music.[3]

[1] *Journals and Papers*, p. 217.
[2] 27 Dec. 1871   C. Reade, *The Courier of Lyons*
    29 & 30 Dec.   Shakespeare, *Macbeth*
    31 Dec.   Concert
    1 Jan. 1872   G. Colman, *The Review*, & R. B. Peake, *The Master's Rival*
    6 Jan.   *The Master's Rival* repeated

For the sake of completion the plays for the following Christmas are given here.

    2 Jan. 1873   J. M. Morton, *Grimshaw, Bagshaw, and Bradshaw*
                   R. Butler, *The Irish Tutor*
    6 Jan.   R. B. Peake, *In the Wrong Box*
    9 Jan. Messrs Campbell and Co. came from Liverpool and played G. A. A'Beckett's *The Siamese Twins*, and A. Snodgrass's *The Tailor of Tamworth*. [Information derived from Stonyhurst Minister's Journal.] GMH would not have seen this last group of farces since he was away from 23 Dec. 1872 until 4 Feb. 1873.
    [3] *Further Letters*, p. 237. Cf. the following: 'As it was not allowed to impersonate female characters, these had to be eliminated, and hence resulted a terrible mangling of the original plays.' 'J.W.', 'Stonyhurst Life', *The Month*, N.S. 1 (Mar. 1874), 333; 'B. Marshall, who filled the part of Donald [Macbeth's son], the Stonyhurst substitute for Lady Macbeth, had several difficulties to overcome . . . the character of Donald was one of the hardest, if not the hardest, in the whole play, mainly owing to the change of sex rendered necessary by the requirements of the Stonyhurst stage', extracted from 'The Shrovetide Plays', *Stonyhurst Magazine*, vi (Apr. 1896), 155–8.

On New Year's Eve after a concert 'Farewell to the Old Year' at six in the evening, the Seminarians had their annual Oyster Supper. Presumably they had oysters this year. But the following year the Beadle notes plaintively: 'We had the so-called Oyster Supper which this year on acc/. of price of Oysters consisted of Lobsters, etc.'.

Lectures were resumed on 3 January, and a week later the first Triduum of the year took place finishing with the renewal of vows. Twice in February they debated the Topic 'Higher Education in England'.[1] Shrovetide saw the customary farces.[2] On 12 May Hopkins preached a tone at which the Provincial, Fr. Robert Whitty,[3] was present since he was making his annual visitation at the time. The usual holiday in honour of the Provincial was taken on 14 May, and on the previous day the Seminarians were given leave to watch the lay-Philosophers' Donkey Race in the lower park. On Whit Monday a contingent from St. Mary's Hall went to Preston to see the town's Roman Catholic procession through its streets. Hopkins, who had been there the previous year had written in his diary: 'Though not very splendid it moved me.'[4] Those who did not go on this treat, for it was a treat and included dinner at the 'Red

[1] At the end of 1872 (1 and 27 Dec.) they took a double session to debate 'Whether the pagan classics do not occupy too large a portion of our modern education'.

[2] W. T. Concrieff, *The Spectre Bridegroom*, and I. Pocock, *The Omnibus*. Earlier, on 8 Feb., the community had been entertained by 'Amateur Christy's Minstrels' from Preston. At Shrovetide 1873, 'Grammar' at Stonyhurst staged T. Taylor's *A Blighted Being*, and J. Courtney's *The Two Polts* [Stonyhurst Minister's Journal]. J. Gerard, in *Stonyhurst College*, p. 307, gives in addition [W. Brough], *Number One round the Corner*.

[3] Robert Whitty (1817–95; see Boase vi, *Cath. Encycl.*), Jesuit priest, born at Pouldarrig, Oylgate, nr. Wexford on 7 Jan. 1817. Educated at Maynooth College. Sent to work in England and was ordained in Sept. 1840 at St. Edmund's, Ware, where he also taught for a time. Friend of Newman, Oakeley, and W. G. Ward. He simultaneously filled the three important offices of Rector of the mission and pro-Cathedral at Moorfields, to which he was appointed in 1852, Provost of the Metropolitan Chapter when it was erected in June of the same year, and Vicar General of the diocese of Westminster from the end of the year 1850; held these posts until he was received into the Society of Jesus. As Vicar General he was responsible for the publication of Wiseman's famous pastoral 'From the Flaminian Gate'. Entered the S.J. novitiate at Verona; noviceship there and in Florence. On return taught Canon Law at St. Beuno's College. Socius to the Provincial. Provincial, 1870–3. Rector of St. Wilfrid's, Preston. Subsequent appointments were at Bournemouth, Spiritual Father at Beaumont, and Instructor of Tertians at Roehampton from 1881 to 1886; GMH completed his tertianship under Fr. Whitty, 1881–2. Later was appointed English Assistant to the General, Fr. Anderledy. Spiritual Father at St. Beuno's, 1893–5. Died on 1 Sept. 1895. (*Sermons and Devotional Writings*, pp. 176, 205, 208, 214, 220, 253, 299–300, 310, 311–12, 316.)

[4] *Journals and Papers*, p. 210, last paragraph.

Lion', stayed at home and played cricket for the first time that season on the new cricket ground. Next day bathing began. And at the beginning of June we read:

4. Tuesday.
We brought over to our Pond the old boat from the College Pond which the Minister of the College gave to us. [PBJ]

The pond as Hopkins must have known it is no more, but we can imagine what it was like:

The almost circular sheet of water that washed the bank close under the broad red-gravel avenue on the south side of the seminary wood!—so close, indeed, that many of the trees and hedges overhung the water.[1]

A month before the exams began, the June Triduum was held, the renovation of vows being made on the feast of St. Aloysius. A panegyric in Latin was preached on the saint in the College domestic chapel.

Villa was taken from 3 to 20 August at Douglas in the Isle of Man. It was at this time that Hopkins discovered Duns Scotus for himself.[2] His holiday journal abounds in the novelty and richness of his discoveries. 'Just then,' he writes, 'when I took in any inscape of the sky or sea I thought of Scotus'.[3] His mind is constantly on the alert for the counter, the original, the spare and the strange. The diary swells not only with inscapes of sea and sky but with interests as

---

[1] 'St. Mary's Pond', *Stonyhurst Magazine*, ii (Apr. 1887), 407. 'Since the work of enlarging the pond and of making it safe for skating purposes has been in progress, it has been rechristened—its new name being St. Mary's Pond. It now belongs exclusively to St. Mary's Hall in return for the old seminary pond which used to lie on the west flank of the Seminary . . . This pond was drained in 1877 while the East wing of the new College Buildings was being begun, for it was feared that the presence of a large sheet of water might weaken and undermine the foundations.' Ibid. The path from the Seminary to the College, now of black tarmac, was formerly red gravel, and calls to mind one of the better-known anecdotes concerning GMH at Stonyhurst. As given by Denis Meadows it runs: 'There was an old, old lay brother, . . . who had known the poet when he was a seminarian. . . . His memories were getting vague and a bit confused, but he told me one delightful anecdote of Father Hopkins. . . . One of Hopkins' special delights was our path to the college. After a shower and when the sun came out again, the crushed quartz glittered and sparkled like millions of diamonds. Hopkins would leave his books, run to the path, and then crouch down to gaze along the path of crystal. "Ay, a strange yoong man," said the old brother, "crouching down that gate to stare at some wet sand. A fair natural 'e seemed to us, that Mr. 'opkins." ' *Obedient Men*, pp. 142–3. For André Bremond's version see *Études*, 221, 5 Oct. 1934, p. 27.

[2] *Journals and Papers*, p. 221.

[3] Ibid.

diverse as overheard scraps of Manx, rock-pool paddling, the runes on Danish crosses, or his attempt to capture the flight of a heron with a squiggle. One quotation must try to convey the zest:

Peel castle is a ruin. . . . what pleased me most were the great seas under a rather heavy swell breaking under the strong rocks below the outer side of the castle—glass-green, as loose as a great windy sheet, blown up and plunging down and bursting upwards from the rocks in spews of foam . . .[1]

But at the end of the holiday Hopkins returned not unwillingly to Stonyhurst:

From Blackburn I walked and I never saw Lancashire or Ree Deep look so beautiful and the grass so fresh a green. The inland breeze after Douglas felt warm and velvety. Fr. Rector came over to wait on us at supper, which touched me[2]

But the holiday had repercussions as the Beadle's note shows:

Aug. 22. Rising 6. . . . The Community are suffering from languor which is attributed to the change from the bracing sea air.

The more important events at the opening of his third year in the philosophate are recounted by Hopkins in his diary—the annual retreat, the arrival of the new professor, Fr. Thiemann,[3] and of yet another new Superior for St. Mary's Hall, Fr. McCann,[4] who replaced Fr. Fitzsimon. Changes followed:

Monday, 14 October, 1872.

F. McCann ordered that the coal should be carried up in future by the Scholastics. Twelve were appointed under the direction of a thirteenth. It took them 3/4 hour. [PBJ]

[1] Ibid., p. 224. [2] Ibid., p. 225.
[3] Heinrich Thiemann (1829–89), Jesuit priest, born on 30 July 1829. Entered the Society of Jesus in Oct. 1852. Philosophy at Paderborn and Bonn. Theology at Paderborn, 1861–4; ordained priest in 1864. Taught philosophy and dogmatic theology at Maria Laach. 1873–9, taught special metaphysics and ethics at St. Mary's Hall, Stonyhurst with GMH as one of his students. Afterwards taught in various S.J. colleges. Died on 16 July 1889. (*Journals and Papers*, p. 227.)
[4] Henry McCann (1801–88), Jesuit priest, born at Drogheda, Co. Louth, Eire, on 15 June 1801. Educated at Stonyhurst College. Entered the S.J. novitiate at Rome in Oct. 1823; ordained priest in 1836. Studied mathematics in Paris. 1844, Vice-rector at Calcutta, afterwards to Rome as Procurator. 1855–8, Rector at Malta. Returned to England to become Province Procurator. Remaining years spent at Beaumont, St. Mary's Hall, and Mount St. Mary's. Died at Beaumont College on 18 May 1888. He was Superior at St. Mary's Hall during GMH's last year in philosophy. (Ibid., p. 227, 'Maccann'.)

Hereafter, coaling was a regular Friday duty.

Thursday, 1 May, 1873.

Baths will not be given on a fixed day as hitherto but each one may take one when he wants not oftener however than once a month. [PBJ]

Other domestic details occasionally creep into the Beadle's Journal and we know for instance when the window sash-cords were replaced, when the plumbing called for attention, and when new pictures arrived for the recreation room. Did Hopkins notice any of these things? Who knows? Certainly the pictures in St. Mary's Hall impressed themselves sufficiently on him to be recalled later, for he wrote from St. Beuno's to his mother:

I know many of those Arundels[1] you went to see. They are a very great gain to people who cannot go to see the originals, in fact to everybody. We used to have many of them hanging on the walls at the seminary.[2]

One of the great events of this year at Stonyhurst was the visit by an old alumnus, Herbert Vaughan, the newly consecrated Bishop of Salford.

Sunday, 17 November 1872.

Pontifical High Mass at 10. . . . Recreation after Mass till 12.30. Wine in honour of the Bishop. Pontifical Vespers & Benediction 5.30 after wh: presentation of addresses to Dr. Vaughan in the Academy-room, by the seminarians, the scholars & masters of the College. We contributed 7 pieces, 2 Latin, 2 English, & 1 Greek Verse, & 2 pieces of poetry 1 in French the other in Italian. [PBJ][3]

The request for presentation verse had the effect according to Hopkins of 'raising a blister' in his Greek, and of making him read *Iphigenia among the Tauri*.[4] But apart from these twenty-four iambics

---

[1] For details of the Arundel prints and a bibliography see Howard C. Levis, *A Descriptive Bibliography of the most important books in the English language relating to the art and history of engraving and the collecting of prints*, ii (1912), 537–8. There are still many of these prints at Heythrop College. They were probably removed from St. Mary's Hall to Heythrop in 1926.

[2] *Further Letters*, p. 130; see also *Letters to Bridges*, p. 151.

[3] The presentation of verses on special occasions was a common practice of the time. Fr. Gallwey, for example, wrote to a former pupil: 'I have indeed once or twice on compulsion tortured my brain for rhymes—to greet a new Provincial or for some other similar reason.' Percy Fitzgerald, *Father Gallwey* (1906), p. 43. For GMH's reference to Bishop Vaughan's visit see *Journals and Papers*, p. 227, entry for 17 Nov.

[4] *Further Letters*, pp. 238–9.

shed for the Bishop, he wrote no other poems at this time except
'Rosa Mystica' and possibly 'Ad Mariam'.[1]

The year which followed at St. Mary's Hall differed but slightly
from the two foregoing years. It will be sufficient to notice those
things which particularly concern Hopkins himself. He preached on
1 December, and on the 23rd of that month he went to stay with his
family at Hampstead. While there, as we know from his Journal, he
had an operation for piles, and during the fortnight he had to spend
in bed he was visited by friends and fellow-Jesuits from Manresa.[2]
During the subsequent period of convalescence he went across to
visit his old novice master, the solicitous[3] Fr. Gallwey, and was sent
by him to see Dr. Fincham.[4]

Hopkins seized the opportunity offered by his temporary residence
in London to attend the Old Masters' Exhibition at Burlington
House.

He returned to Stonyhurst on 4 February and began privately on
the 9th the Triduum which the other scholastics at St. Mary's Hall
had completed in early January. On 16 March he preached for the
last time as a philosopher. And on April Fool's Day he delivered
himself of the only paper he is known to have read at the English
Academy,[5] 'Thoughts on Mobs.' Perhaps the day decided the subject.

[1] *Poems*, nos. 27 and 26 respectively. Some years later discussing this period of his
life, he wrote to Canon Dixon, 'for seven years I wrote nothing but two or three little
presentation pieces which occasion called for'. *Correspondence with Dixon*, p. 14.

[2] *Journals and Papers*, p. 229.

[3] Ibid., p. 227, entry for 27 Oct.

[4] Ibid., p. 230, entry for 21 Jan. Records at Roehampton at the time yield the following: '31 Jan. 1873. Br Hopkins came and slept here.' [Manresa Minister's Journal]
'31 Jan. 1873, Br G. Hopkins arrived here on his way to Stonyhurst. 1. Feb. Br Gordon
went to London with Br Hopkins. 4 Feb. Br G. Hopkins left for Stonyhurst.' [JBJ]

[5] There were twenty-four papers read on Tuesday evenings for the English Academy
between Oct. 1872 and May 1873;

15 Oct. 1872	Essay in review of Schiller's Thirty Years' War.
22 Oct.	A review of Gibbon on the persecution under the Emperors.
29 Oct.	The causes of the massacre of St Bartholomew.
5 Nov.	The spirit of St Bernard.
12 Nov.	Dean Stanley's Life and Correspondence of Dr Arnold
26 Nov.	Milton's Paradise Lost considered as a work of great labour.
10 Dec.	A comparison between the styles of Macaulay and Carlyle.
17 Dec.	Review of Mr Galton's hereditary genius.
14 Jan. 1873	Review of Nassau W. Senior's Ireland
21 Jan.	Macaulay's Baconian & the previous philosophies reviewed
28 Jan.	,, ,, ,, ,, ,, ,, ,,

[*Footnote continued overleaf.*

Half-way through May the list of theses[1] which Hopkins and the other members of the third year would be called upon to defend was distributed. After almost six weeks' revision Hopkins, on 23 June, was orally examined in Latin for an hour 'de universa philosophia'.[2] I have been unable to discover any record of the result he obtained, but he must have passed, since there is nothing to suggest that he was referred or asked to repeat the examination. One reason for Hopkins's being examined early[3] was to enable him to replace the master at Stonyhurst who had to accompany several matriculators

4 Feb.	The Spanish Inquisition.
11 Feb.	The French Revolution (Carlyle Part I. The Bastille.)
18 Feb.	Review of Fr Pontlevoy's Life of Fr Ravignan.
4 March	India—her people—the Madura mission.
11 March	[No title given]
18 March	Comment on an Essay on Architecture.
25 March	Huxleys x?
1 April	Thoughts on Mobs.
22 April	The application of divine exemplarism.
29 April	„ „ „ „
6 May	Roscoe's Life of Leo X.
13 May	On L. Bacon, the Chancellor and the man.
27 May	The characteristics of Longfellow's poetry.

Following the last entry it reads: 'F. Rector unavoidably absent but sent word that he was thoroughly satisfied with the year's work of the Academy.' [PBJ]

[1] I have been unable to trace the theses which GMH was asked to defend in 1873. However, the following six theses will give some idea of what he could well have been questioned upon:

1. The existence is asserted not only of common terms but also of universal natures denoted by those terms; given always that these natures have no existence apart from singulars. (*Dantur non solum voces communes sed etiam naturae universales per illas voces significatae; quamvis extra singularia non existant.*)
2. The objective reference of ideas is an underived and non-demonstrable truth. (*Realitas objectiva idearum est veritas primitiva et indemonstrabilis.*)
3. Considered in its origin the world is not eternal; its final cause is the manifestation of the divine glory. (*Mundus non est aeternus a parte ante; et ejus causa finalis est manifestatio divinae gloriae.*)
4. The soul is immortal both intrinsically and extrinsically. (*Anima est immortalis ab intrinseco et ab extrinseco.*)
5. God is a provident God and orders and governs all things by his wisdom. (*Deus est providus et sua sapientia res omnes administrat ac regit.*)
6. This [natural] law is immutable, universal, eternal and the basis of positive law. (*Haec lex [naturalis] est immutabilis, universalis, aeterna et legis positivae fundamentum.*)

[2] *Journals and Papers*, p. 232. It may be of some comfort to the sceptical to know that another thesis to be defended ran 'A philosopher neither should nor can demonstrate or define everything' (*Philosophus neque tenetur neque potest omnia demonstrare vel definire*).

[3] The examination for the other members of the third year began on 15 July.

to Manchester. Hopkins taught the class of Rhetoric at the College for six days,[1] 30 June–5 July, though he continued to sleep at the Seminary. The College watchman had to let him out to return to St. Mary's Hall, and Hopkins records his dialect expression: 'I'll put on my shoon and let thee out'.[2]

Early in July Fr. Gallwey was appointed Provincial. At the end of that month Hopkins's brother Arthur, recently married, came with his wife on a visit.[3] Their stay was necessarily short for on 1 August Gerard was off to spend Villa, as last year, in Douglas. And now that the exam. was over he was able to indulge his personal reading preferences. His letter to Edward Bond shows that he is reading Arnold's 'Empedocles volume', Newman's *Grammar of Assent*, and De Morgan's *Budget of Paradoxes*.[4]

Before concluding this phase in Hopkins's training as a Jesuit there remain some issues which have so far during the scholasticate period scarcely been mentioned. These now call for a word.

Of the religious life and training in the Philosophate there is little to say. Of its very nature it is so personal that generalities are unavoidable. Basically the training begun in the noviceship continues though necessarily modified since studies now constitute the *opus Dei* for scholastics. For example, the evening meditation of the novitiate is omitted, and the time for spiritual reading is reduced. High Mass remained a comparative rarity. They had less than twenty a year including special occasions and Solemn Requiems. The major liturgical ceremonies are noted in the records, and Vespers or Compline were sung regularly. Devotions practised included those for the First Fridays, May and October devotions, Bona Mors (devotions for a Happy Death), and the novenas to St. Joseph, St. Francis Xavier, and St. Aloysius took place at the appropriate times. In their own place the annual retreats, tridua, and renovation of vows have already been mentioned. The scholastics practised preaching indoors, and catechized in the neighbourhood. Domestic exhortations were frequently given.

[1] *Journals and Papers*, p. 232.
[2] Ibid., entry for 2 July.
[3] Ibid., p. 234, entries for 28 and 30 July. Early in this academic year (14–16 Sept.) GMH's brother, Cyril, and his uncle John had been to see him. Cf. ibid., p. 226.
[4] *Further Letters*, pp. 58–9.

The religious event which roused most local interest was the annual Corpus Christi procession. The Seminary, too, was agog:

Wednesday, 7 June.

All to be in the College sacristy for a rehearsal of the Procession at 12. . . . Two large festoons made in the handball: flowers arranged in jam pots. We borrowed the bakers cart, and the flowers, and carpet were taken over tonight, and the paintings. Two side arches put up. F. Newsham lent us his donkey cart . . . ferns from Hodder Wood. Some boxes of flowers were taken from our garden. Nothing was done at the altar besides putting up the side arches, but we ought to have had more foresight as we were kept working hard up to the time of the procession on Corpus Christi.

Thursday, 8 June. Corpus Christi.

Holy Communion. The state of the weather doubtful during the first part of the morning. We set to work immediately after breakfast. The two joiners were helping us most of the morning. Candles, vases, steps, etc. taken over in the cart; F. Weld worked very hard. Everything was done except the arranging of the altar before dinner; antipendium [*sic*] taken over aft. dinner. Wine was dispatched as soon as possible. All the Seminarians except two (who were unwell) assisted in copes and dalmatics. The evening was beautifully fine. Procession began punctually at 3.30 and was not over till nearly 6. Everything went off beautifully. Supper as usual 8.10. No sermon in the Bowling Green. We cleared off everything this evening. [PBJ]

In later years the procession attracted such crowds of mere sightseers that it had to be stopped.

This chapter can be conveniently concluded by noticing three related points, each of considerable personal concern to Hopkins—the landscape, the weather, and his state of health. First the Lancashire scenery. Two days after arriving at Stonyhurst he tells his mother, 'it is certain that it is an excellent country for walks, beauty, and general interest'.[1] To Baillie he writes:

The country is also very bare and bleak—what its enemies say of Scotland, . . . nevertheless it is fine scenery, great hills and 'fells' with noble outline often, subject to charming effects of light (though I am bound to say that total obscuration is the commonest effect of all),[2] and three

---

[1] *Further Letters*, p. 112.
[2] As a local weather saw has it: 'If you can see Pendle it's going to rain; if you can't see Pendle, it's raining.'

beautiful rivers. The clouds in particular are more interesting than in any other place I have seen.[1]

A short residence at Stonyhurst would have been sufficient for Hopkins readily to have understood the wry entry in the Beadle's Journal, 'Plenty of weather.' Hopkins writes in March, 'Though we have had some fine days this country is far from looking like spring: I habitually think of it as dead winter.'[2] He writes in April:

Perpetual winter smiles. In the first place we have the highest rain-guage in England,[3] I believe: this our observatory shews and a local rhyme[4] expresses as much. Early in the year they told me there wd. be no spring such as we understood it in the south. When I asked about May they told me they had hail in May.[5] Of June they told me it had one year been so cold that the procession could not be held on Corpus Christi.[6]

[1] *Further Letters*, pp. 234–5, and cf. *Letters to Bridges*, p. 26. His diary for 28 Apr. 1871 states: 'I have never taken notice and I believe that I have never seen such size and such a noble bulk of member in the clouds as here and this day.' *Journals and Papers*, p. 207.

[2] *Further Letters*, p. 113. Hopkins was not alone in his opinion as the following verses show:

SPRING AT STONYHURST.

At Stonyhurst the months of Spring
With strange perverseness Winter bring,
    For when the gardens should look gay
    With all the flowering life of May;
When lark and linnet on the wing
Should make the woodland echoes ring,
One feels instead the East wind's sting,
    The trees are bare, the heavens grey
        At Stonyhurst.

Of the season mild that poets sing
The natives hear with wondering,
    And fancy poets have a way
    Of never meaning half they say—
For Spring is quite another thing
        At Stonyhurst.
                                    HYM.

Stonyhurst Magazine, v (Apr. 1894), 264.

[3] GMH incorrect. For more accurate information see S. J. Perry, 'Stonyhurst Climate', *Stonyhurst Magazine*, iii (July 1888), 192–4. According to Perry the annual rainfall at Stonyhurst was 47.84 inches compared with 139 inches at Seathwaite in Cumberland, and 22 inches at Shoeburyness in Essex.

[4]   'The Hodder, the Calder, the Ribble, and rain,
                All meet together in Mitton domain.'

These are the 'three beautiful rivers' of *Further Letters*, p. 234.

[5] 'At this time weather very cold, on May 18 snow and on Pendle lying'. *Journals and Papers*, p. 231.

[6] *Further Letters*, p. 234.

Even in mid-June he writes: 'The weather here is on the average fine but not hot or summery: I do not think we have had one hot day.'[1] One wonders how closely the weather is to be connected with the third point, Hopkins's health. In April 1871 the vaccination he received formed the subject of one of his most engagingly humorous letters, and reveals, incidentally, his delightful relationship with his younger sister, Kate. Still, not surprisingly he is forced to confess that he is 'in a miserable way just now'.[2] In a month, however, he tells his mother, 'My health is in the main robustious, more so than it has some time been.'[3]

But by the end of October 1872 the euphoria is less in evidence:

Oct. 27—Fr. Gallwey came up. Before night litanies he came to my room as I lay on my bed making my examen, for I had some fever, and sitting by the bedside took my hand within his and said some affectionate and most encouraging words

That fever came from a chill I caught one Blandyke and the chill from weakness brought about by my old complaint [piles], which before and much more after the fever was worse than usual. Indeed then I lost so much blood that I hardly saw how I was to recover. Nevertheless it stopped suddenly, almost at the worst. This was why I came up to town at Christmas[4]

His operation for piles has already been mentioned and it is clear that his religious Superiors were aware of the state of his health and dealt with him prudently, for he tells his mother, 'Lent has begun but I am not to fast at all, the Rector has forbidden it. My work has also been lightened.'[5]

His diary, too, shows that his spirits could sink quite low. His return from the 1873 holiday in the Isle of Man illustrates this. In company with some fellow scholastics he had walked the dozen miles from Blackburn station and later wrote:

We hurried too fast and it knocked me up. We went to the College, the

---

[1] *Further Letters*, p. 117.
[2] Ibid., p. 115. The Beadle's Journal states the 'medicine' mentioned by Hopkins in this letter: 'April 24, 1871. Rest of the Community (8 in num) and 3 kitchen boys vaccinated. Those who had been remanded from Friday took their "Senna Tea" this morning, and had to take the consequences. Beeftea and Rice Pudding for dinner, no meat for supper. Circles as usual.'
[3] Ibid., p. 117.   [4] *Journals and Papers*, p. 227.
[5] *Further Letters*, p. 121.

seminary being wanted for the secular priests' retreat: almost no gas, for the retorts are being mended; therefore candles in bottles, things not ready, darkness and despair. In fact being unwell I was quite downcast: nature in all her parcels and faculties gaped and fell apart, *fatiscebat*, like a clod cleaving and holding only by strings of root. But this must often be[1]

Two earlier instances in his Journal have already revealed his abnormal sensitivity:

March 13, 1872.—After a time of trial and especially a morning in which I did not know which way to turn as the account of De Rancé's final conversion was being read at dinner the verse *Qui confidunt in Domino sicut mons Sion* which satisfied him and resolved him to enter his abbey of La Trappe by the mercy of God came strongly home to me too, so that I was choked for a little while and could not keep in my tears[2]

April 8, 1873.—The ashtree growing in the corner of the garden was felled. It was lopped first: I heard the sound and looking out and seeing it maimed there came at that moment a great pang and I wished to die and not to see the inscapes of the world destroyed any more[3]

These are but isolated instances of 'the melancholy I have all my life been subject to',[4] which Hopkins looked back on in later years.

And yet despite the acute depression noticed above which he experienced on returning from Villa in mid-August, we read in the Beadle's Journal a few days later:

August 21, 1873.

As usual, except that the Seminarians gave an entertainment after supper in return for the two lately given by the Germans.[5] It consisted of music, comic and half comic pieces &c. It was mainly got up by Mr G. Hopkins,[6] and was a decided success

Hopkins's time at St. Mary's Hall was almost ended, but he did not know for certain as yet what work he would be doing in the

---

[1] *Journals and Papers*, p. 236.
[2] Ibid., p. 218.
[3] Ibid., p. 230.
[4] *Further Letters*, p. 256.
[5] *Journals and Papers*, p. 236, entry for 17 Aug.
[6] Hopkins was described by a fellow Jesuit as 'a delightful companion, full of high spirits and innocent fun'. The writer gives an instance of his wit: 'Once, while in Ireland, he called on a certain parish priest, the Rev. Father Wade, and was hospitably pressed to stay for dinner. Father Hopkins, an exact observer of discipline, replied that he had no leave to dine out. 'Is that all?' said Father Wade. 'Well now, I'll take the whole responsibility upon myself.' 'Ah, yes,' said Father Hopkins, 'you may be Wade; but *I* shall be found wanting.' 'C.B.' [Fr. Clement Barraud, S.J., 1843–1926], 'Reminiscences of Father Gerard Hopkins', *The Month*, cxxxiv (Aug. 1919), 158.

coming year. At the beginning of August he tells his mother: 'Next year, I mean from September, I am to teach one of the higher classes in one of our schools, I do not know which: perhaps it will be Stony-hurst.'[1]

It seems to me that Hopkins interpreted the Provincial's mind correctly when he added by way of explanation, 'The year's teaching was given as a rest', concluding, 'I think this is as good an arrange-ment as could have been made.'[2] Further, Fr. Gallwey had decided that the year's rest should be taken in the gentler climate of the south of England. Hopkins received his orders to go to Roehampton on 28 August. He took his leave of Lancashire in a way that in his case seems both fitting and characteristic: 'I walked with Herbert Lucas by the river and talked Scotism with him for the last time.'[3]

Despite the obvious trials encountered during these three not wholly congenial years, there is no reason to doubt that Hopkins would have endorsed his earlier opinion, 'this life here though it is hard is God's will for me as I most intimately know, which is more than violets knee-deep'.[4]

[1] *Further Letters*, p. 122.
[2] Ibid., pp. 122–3.
[3] *Journals and Papers*, p. 236.
[4] *Further Letters*, p. 235.

CHAPTER 4

Teacher of Rhetoric, Roehampton
1873–1874

ON the same night that he received his orders to teach rhetoric to
the Juniors, Hopkins packed his belongings. Early next morning, in
company with two fellow scholastics bound for Beaumont, he set off
for Roehampton travelling via Preston. At Manchester he saw the
Provincial, Fr. Gallwey, 'who spoke', wrote Hopkins, 'most kindly
and encouragingly'.[1] The following day, 30 August, having reached
Manresa, he began his annual eight-day retreat under the direction
of his new Rector and Superior, Fr. Porter.[2] His Journal states that
he made notes on this retreat in his meditation papers and that he
believed he had received 'a great mercy about Dolben'.[3] Two days
before the retreat finished he probably noticed at supper the faces
of the nine newly-arrived novices. On the Nativity of the Virgin
Mary, the close of the retreat, fourteen novices took their first vows,
and at Benediction that night the *Te Deum* was sung. But Hopkins
passes over this event and jots down instead what he learned from
one of the lay brothers who was ploughing—'the names of the
cross, side-plate, muzzle, regulator, and short chain. He talked of

---

[1] *Journals and Papers*, p. 236, entry for 27 Aug.
[2] George Porter (1825–89; see Gillow, Boase vi, *Cath. Encycl.*, Buckland, *Dict. of
Indian Biography*, Sutcliffe), first Archbishop of Bombay, born in Exeter on 27 Aug. 1825.
Educated at Stonyhurst College. Entered the S.J. novitiate at Hodder in 1841; ordained
priest in 1856. Professor of dogmatic theology at St. Beuno's until 1863, followed by a
period of teaching at St. Mary's Hall and Rectorship of St. Francis Xavier's, Liverpool.
In 1873 appointed as Rector and novice master at Roehampton; GMH teaching in the
Juniorate at this time. 1880, represented the English Province in Rome. Appointed
Superior at Farm Street, but was soon transferred to Fiesole as English Assistant to the
General, Fr. Beckx. Returned to Farm Street in 1883. Appointed Archbishop of Bombay
in Jan. 1887, and was consecrated at Allahabad. Died at Bombay on 28 Sept. 1889. For
an indication of his spiritual approach see George Porter, *Spiritual Retreats* (Roehampton, 1887). (*Journals and Papers*, pp. 236, 241, 244, 247, 'Fr. Rector'.)
[3] *Journals and Papers*, p. 236, last line.

something *spraying* out, meaning splaying out and of *combing* the ground'.[1]

The next day Hopkins set to work to find out what his charges knew:

Sept. 9. A trial examen in Greek & Latin. Geor.: II & Aeschines v Ctesiphon, c 122–123.[2] [JBJ]

But this trial-run apart, the Juniors were still on vacation, and Hopkins had time to look about him:

Sept. 14—There are really toadstool rings in the big pasture before the house, some very big, but whether fairy rings have been or will be there I cannot tell. They are not so complete nor so symmetrical as fairy rings but a little indented into loops. The grass inside them is, I think, dark and rank but outside for a few inches colourless and dead, white or grey as if dusty, not healthily tanned like hay but as if fagged, drained, and baked[3]

On the 18th of the month the Juniors had their Blandyke,[4] and Hopkins took the opportunity to visit the Victoria and Albert Museum, and his diary grows fat with his notes on the work of Della Robbia, Michelangelo, and Raphael, while in a painting of Watts he sees 'instress of expression in the faces, as in other characteristic English work, Burne-Jones', Mason's, Walker's etc'.[5] Dinner that day was at four, and there followed 'at 6 a reading'.[6] The reading was probably from Shakespeare or a novelist, perhaps Dickens, and given by Fr. Harper who was now stationed at Roehampton and had among his jobs the task of teaching elocution and of correcting the reading at table. But the Blandyke concluded for Hopkins with a terrible and terrifying nightmare as his diary shows.[7]

On 22 September schools partially began, and a week later an

---

[1] *Journals and Papers*, p. 237, entry for 8 Sept.

[2] For Hopkins's references to the *Georgics* see *Further Letters*, pp. 200, 359, and *Journals and Papers*, pp. 9, 280; for Aeschines see *Further Letters*, pp. 69, 73.

[3] *Journals and Papers*, p. 237.

[4] The Blandykes, or monthly holidays, fell during Hopkins's time at Roehampton, 1873–4, on the following dates (information from Juniors' Beadle's Journal except otherwise indicated); 16 Oct., 20 Nov., 18 Dec., 29 Jan., 19 Feb., 12 Mar. (MMJ), 16 Apr., 7 May, 18 June, 9 July.

[5] *Journals and Papers*, p. 237.

[6] From Juniors' Beadle's Journal. Other readings were given on 20 Nov., 19 Feb., 5 Mar., 7 and 16 Apr.; these dates it will be seen sometimes coincide with Blandykes. The Blandyke generally finished with a reading, seance (i.e. concert), or debate.

[7] *Journals and Papers*, p. 238.

experienced Father arrived to help with the work for the time being. But the official opening of schools, as in the Seminary, took place on 1 October, the 'Veni Creator' preceding the Community Mass that day. One domestic note, at the end of the month Fr. Goldie[1] was named as Minister for the house.

Before glancing at the work of the Juniorate it is perhaps worth stating that the job itself was probably regarded as something of a 'cushy berth' in the Province, as compared with the more hectic rough and tumble of teaching in one of the large schools. Jesuit Juniors are not notably intractable. Further, the fact that Hopkins was assigned the task of 'scriptor domus', that is house-historian, also indicates that he was not considered over-burdened. In another respect, too, he got off rather lightly, namely, in the length of time he was asked to teach. He taught for only a year before proceeding to theology. A comparison with his contemporaries is revealing. Of those who entered the noviceship with him in 1868, before reaching ordination they had taught as follows: Gillet for seven years, McMullin for eight, Southern for three before he died in 1878, Tempest for five, and Wilcock had taught for six years before he left the Society. True these men were younger than Hopkins when they joined, and in fairness it must be stated that his namesake, Frederick Hopkins, who joined at the age of twenty-four also only taught for a year. But all in all he can be said to have got off lightly. During his year of teaching his Superiors saw to it that he had a day off now and then by way of a break.[2]

Also, it is perhaps worth calling to mind what Hopkins brought to the task to which he had been assigned. At the head of the list would appear his first in Greats, then his essays written as an undergraduate revealing his grasp of critical principles both in literature and philosophy, and now available to us in his *Journals*

[1] Francis Goldie (1836–1912; see Sutcliffe), Jesuit priest, born at Shrewsbury on 20 Oct. 1836. Educated at Ampleforth and Ushaw Colleges. Theology at the English College, Rome; ordained priest in 1859. Served the Harrogate mission, 1861-8. Entered the S.J. novitiate at Roehampton in July 1868. Parish work at Farm Street, London, Manchester, Preston, Wakefield, Boscombe, and Stonyhurst. 1886-7, acted as Socius to the novice master at Manresa. In later years worked for the religious welfare of Catholic seamen. Died in London on 6 Dec. 1912. (*Journals and Papers*, pp. 191, 241.)

[2] For example, 'Fr. Johnson ... kindly sent me to town with Br. Bampton for change.' *Journals and Papers*, p. 244, para. 3.

and Papers. But in regard to his literary criticism I find myself agreeing in the main with the opinion expressed by Miss Anne Treneer in her article 'The Criticism of Gerard Manley Hopkins'. There she states:

> It is significant that his best criticism is not in his lecture notes or his vast projects for learned works, but in his private letters when he was freely following his natural bent. . . .
> In his letters Hopkins' ardent, relishing nature is seen working in conjunction with an analytical mind and rapid powers of generalization. He was naturally and by training argumentative; like lightning in defence. Of his correspondents Bridges, in particular, is to be blessed for not often agreeing with his friend; Hopkins leapt to confute him and in this outgoing of his disposition is much of his best writing. None of his set prose, either in printed sermon, Notebook, or proposed treatise is as good as the prose of the letters. He needed a correspondent to waken and resist him. It is significant that one of his attempts at sustained prose is cast in the form of the Socratic Dialogue. His best critical letters are thrusts in debate.[1]

Even though Hopkins's searching and detailed criticism of his poetic contemporaries, Bridges, Dixon, and Patmore, had not as yet been written—on which the last-named poet was to comment, 'Your careful and subtle fault-finding is the greatest praise my poetry has ever received'[2]—there is still sufficient for us to begin to judge the calibre of Hopkins's critical insight. Not yet twenty he had written:

> A perfect critic is very rare, I know. Ruskin often goes astray; Servius, the commentator on Virgil, whom I admire, is often too observant and subtle for his author, but nevertheless their excellences utterly outweigh their defects. The most inveterate fault of critics is the tendency to cramp and hedge in by rules the free movements of genius, so that I should say, according to the Demosthenic and Catonic expression, the first requisite for a critic is liberality, and the second liberality, and the third, liberality. . . . I agree with you [Baillie], you know, about general rules, but you are not nearly the first to object to them. You are only uttering your version of the often repeated warning against the dangers of generalizations.[3]

---

[1] *Penguin New Writing*, ed. John Lehmann (Harmondsworth, Middlesex, 1950), pp. 102–3.
[2] *Further Letters*, p. 324.   [3] Ibid., p. 204.

And for judgements on two of the more important figures in nineteenth-century letters this passage can still prove provocative:

> I have brought Mat Arnold's poems, the Empedocles volume, down here with me and read them with more interest than rapture, as you will easily understand, for they seem to have all the ingredients of poetry without quite being it—no ease or something or other, like the plum pudding of the English ambassador's, but still they do not leave off being, as the French say, very beautiful. Besides he seems a very earnest man and distinctly seeing the difference between jest and earnest and a master in both, and this praise will also apply to you, I hope. But then very unhappily he jokes at the wrong things, as I see by a very profane passage quoted from his new book: however that passage though profane is not blasphemous, for we are obliged to think of God by human thoughts and his account of them is substantially true. . . . This reminds me that I have been reading the *Grammar of Assent*: have you? It is perhaps heavy reading. The justice and candour and gravity and rightness of mind is what is so beautiful in all he writes but what dissatisfies me (in point of style) is a narrow circle of instance and quotation—in a man too of great learning and of general reading—quite like the papers in the *Spectator* and a want, I think a real want, of brilliancy (which foolish people think every scribbler possesses, but it is no such thing). But he remains nevertheless our greatest living master of style . . . and widest mind.[1]

But at this stage perhaps his nearest approach to a *locus classicus*, and one which is of at least as great importance for the light it throws on his own poetry, as for the view he took of the work of others, is contained in his perceptive and instructive letter to Baillie in September 1864.[2] The letter is too lengthy for quotation here but contains Hopkins's valuable distinction of the language used for verse into three kinds, the language of inspiration or 'poetry proper', Parnassian, and Delphic. This tendency to classify shown here had by 1873, with three years' training in scholastic philosophy behind him, been developed further. One critic states:

> In later years his Stonyhurst training provided Hopkins with ready tools for literary criticism. . . . What sets him off most strikingly from his many cloudy-minded literary contemporaries is precisely this disciplined

---

[1] Ibid., p. 58. Hopkins's later view of Newman must also be set down. In 1887 he tells Patmore that neither he nor the Cardinal 'know what *writing prose* is. At bottom what you do and what Cardinal Newman does is to think aloud, to think with pen to paper'. For Hopkins their writing lacks 'the belonging technic, the belonging rhetoric, the own proper eloquence of written prose'. Ibid., p. 380.

[2] Ibid., pp. 216–20.

incisiveness which could not tolerate shoddy reasoning or vague cosmic notions or a great flow of words masquerading as deep thought.[1]

Hopkins also shows he can ask the pertinent and stimulating question: 'The other arts seem to depend on truth (no: Truth) as well as Beauty. What then answers to, I mean what is, Truth in music?'[2]

His opinion of the Augustan poets marks him off from the generally prevailing viewpoint of the time: 'When one reads Pope's Homer with a critical eye one sees, artificial as it is, in every couplet that he was a great man.'[3]

Clearly, the Jesuit Juniors were to be taught by a man of no ordinary talent. But the work of teaching, too, struck sparks from Hopkins. In assigning the composition of 'Lecture Notes: Rhetoric'[4] to the period September 1873 to July 1874 I find no reason for differing from the opinion expressed by the editors of *Journals and Papers*.[5] In particular his notes on 'Poetry and Verse'[6] seem to me

---

[1] James Collins, 'Philosophical Themes in Gerard Manley Hopkins', *Thought* (Fordham University Quarterly), xxii (New York, Mar. 1947), 73.

[2] *Further Letters*, p. 224.

[3] Ibid., p. 222. His remarkable dictum on Dryden came later. He wrote rebukingly to Bridges: 'I can scarcely think of you not admiring Dryden without, I may say, exasperation. And my style tends always more towards Dryden. What is there in Dryden? Much, but above all this: he is the most masculine of our poets; his style and his rhythms lay the strongest stress of all our literature on the naked thew and sinew of the English language, the praise that with certain qualifications one would give in Greek to Demosthenes, to be the greatest master of bare Greek.' *Letters to Bridges*, pp. 267-8. This appreciation of Dryden and Pope rings markedly different from Arnold's dismissal of them as 'the classics of our prose'.

[4] *Journals and Papers*, pp. 267-90.

[5] Ibid., pp. xxvi f.

[6] Ibid., pp. 289-90. As the editors of the *Journals and Papers* have shown (p. 450, 287. 1) Hopkins drew for some of his illustrations on *Lectures on the English Language* by G. P. Marsh. There are also two other books in the noviceship house which indicate the approach to teaching 'rhetoric', though it is not claimed that Hopkins knew or used them:

1. J. Kleutgen, *Ars Dicendi*, editio quarta (Hertogenbosch, 1865). A summary of its index will indicate the book's content: 4 parts—I. 'de stilo in universum'; II. 'de nonnullis orationis solutae generibus'; III. 'de poesi'—(i) 'de poesi in universum', (ii) 'de variis poematis singillatim'; IV. 'de eloquentia'—(i) 'de inventione', (ii) 'de dispositione', (iii) 'de elocutione', (iv) 'de eloquentia sacra', (v) 'de eloquentia civili'. Appendix: Exhibens nonnullarum orationum synopses—Demosthenes, Cicero, Bossuet, Bourdaloue, Segneri.

2. A manuscript notebook with the caption 'In usum Prof. Rhet. Manresa 1876.' Here, too, the approach is largely deductive, and page after page is devoted to such

to be amongst the pithiest and most apposite, certainly in English literary criticism. As to what his pupils made of them one hardly dares to think. One hopes that they occasionally saw a text as well. But now for the Juniorate itself.

The Province catalogue shows that there were twenty-three Juniors, or Rhetoricians, at Manresa in 1873, twenty in their first year, and three in their second. On 6 October, five novices[1] were sent to follow the studies of the Juniors. The work of the Juniorate and the stage it represents in Jesuit training is made clear by Fr. Clarke:[2]

As soon as the young Jesuit has taken his vows, he enters on quite a different life. His religious exercises are now confined to a comparatively small portion of the day. The main part of his time is now devoted to study. He still makes his morning meditation, hears Mass, examines his conscience twice a day, and spends a short time each day in spiritual reading and in prayer before the Blessed Sacrament; but the chief portion of the next five years is given up to intellectual cultivation. During the first two years he has to apply himself to classical studies and to a course of rhetoric. This part of his career I can pass over without further notice, because there is in it nothing specially distinctive of the Society. His classical work, which consists in reading the best Latin and Greek authors, and translating from English into Latin and Greek, with a certain amount of English literature, and essay writing, is much the same as that of the higher forms of our public schools, and of those who take a classical degree at the Universities. A certain amount of mathematics has also to be learned, and the practice as well as the theory of rhetoric forms part of the course.[3]

I have discovered no daily time-table nor actual syllabus followed by the Juniors, but their day would be fully occupied and the curriculum could presume a good grounding in the classics in the case of most of them. However, the high-sounding office of Professor of

topics as Principles of Literature, Qualities of Thoughts, Kinds of Literary Composition, and The Different Parts of Rhetoric.

[1] Hopkins noting the death of Br. Alexander Byrne wrote: 'He was a novice but had been one of my pupils'. *Journals and Papers*, p. 243, entry for 25 April.

[2] Fr. R. F. Clarke's exposition is useful for the reasons set out earlier, but especially relevant in connection with the work of the Juniorate since he himself was Hopkins's immediate successor in the office of Professor of Rhetoric.

[3] 'Training of a Jesuit', pp. 220-1. See also: J. H. Pollen, 'Society of Jesus', *Cath. Encycl.* xiv. 84; 'T' [of *Punch*], *Friends and Adventures* (1931), p. 29. The Juniorate is temporarily suspended in the English Province.

Rhetoric was in reality an omnibus expression covering the teaching of Latin and Greek, English, and possibly French, though the latter was taught at this time by a French Jesuit scholastic who was staying in the house. One of the Juniors themselves, Brother O'Neill,[1] taught the others mathematics.

Towards the end of October, Fr. MacLeod,[2] the Prefect of studies for the Juniors, arrived. In addition to this office he was in charge of the parish of St. Joseph, Roehampton. One suspects that much of the duty of day-to-day teaching fell on Hopkins, but certainly in English he did not have the field to himself as these entries make clear:

17 April. 4.30 Lecture on Style by Fr McLeod.

5 June. Lecture on English by Fr McLeod 4.30 [JBJ]

Fr. Harper's name also appears as lecturing, probably in English. Lectures were given in the morning as early in some instances as 8.30, and in the evening. Hopkins in a letter to Bond says, 'Sundays and Thursdays are my free days, the afternoons best. Tuesday afternoon is also free.'[3] This arrangement would refer to a normal week, but when a feast occurred changes resulted. For example, the feast of St. Francis Xavier in 1873 fell on a Wednesday, so, to allow for the celebration, Tuesday was treated as a 'long school day'. Long school days were not infrequent.

By the time schools had got going properly autumn was under way and Hopkins lyrically records the season:

[1] Richard O'Neill (1851–74), Jesuit scholastic, born in London on 1 Aug. 1851. Educated at Mount St. Mary's and Stonyhurst Colleges. Entered the S.J. novitiate at Roehampton in Sept. 1871. Philosophy at St. Mary's Hall, Stonyhurst. Died of typhoid there on 19 Sept. 1874. (*Further Letters*, p. 128; *Journals and Papers*, p. 260.)

[2] John George MacLeod (1826–1914; see Sutcliffe), Jesuit priest, born in London on 27 July 1826 of a Morayshire family. Early years spent in Aberdeen. Higher education at King's College, London, and Exeter College, Oxford; B.A., 1847; M.A., 1851. Took Anglican orders and served for five years at Stoke Newington and elsewhere. Received into the R.C. Church in 1854, and spent a year in Rome at the Collegio Pio. Entered the S.J. novitiate at Beaumont Lodge in Sept. 1855; ordained priest in 1861. Afterwards, until 1866, missioner at Galashiels, Dalkeith, Edinburgh, and Glasgow. Prefect of studies to the Juniorate at Roehampton. Subsequent appointments at Farm Street, London, Bristol, Worcester, and Wigan. As editor (1894–1907) of *LLNN*, the domestic quarterly of the English S.J. Province, he was responsible for publishing extracts from GMH's journals under the title 'The diary of a devoted student of nature'. Died on 21 July 1914. (*Journals and Papers*, p. 240, 'MacCleod'.)

[3] *Further Letters*, p. 60.

A doe comes to our sunken fence to be fed: she eats acorns and chestnuts and stands on the bank, a pretty triped, forefeet together and hind set apart. The bucks grunt all night at this season and fight often: it is their season
At the end of the month hard frosts. Wonderful downpour of leaf: when the morning sun began to melt the frost they fell at one touch and in a few minutes a whole tree was flung of them; they lay masking and papering the ground at the foot. Then the tree seems to be looking down on its cast self as blue sky on snow after a long fall, its losing, its doing[1]

All Saints, and the feast of the house, St. Stanislaus, were duly kept and a concert[2] was given by the Juniors on the second of these feasts. Hopkins found time to turn from his books:

Fine sunset Nov. 3—Balks of grey cloud searched with long crimsonings running along their hanging folds—this from the lecture room window.[3]

Half-way through November tones were resumed and the preaching of dominicals began again at supper. These could occasionally embarrass, as for instance when we read that one Junior's 'Memory failed him after the exord: he read instead.'[4] And on the twenty-fifth of the month the most important event of the year in Manresa began—the novices' Long Retreat: its silence almost tangible, and the edification palpable.

December began with the first Menstruum[5] on a Monday. This was an oral examination similar to that commonly held in Jesuit and other Public Schools at the time, and sharing features with the University *viva*. A passage was chosen from a Latin or Greek author

---

[1] *Journals and Papers*, p. 239, entry for 17 Oct.

[2] Other concerts (or seances) were given on 29 Dec., 6 Jan. in the refectory, Provincial's Day 12 Feb., 23 Apr., 26 May in the refectory, Rector's Day 21 July under the cedar, 31 July.

[3] *Journals and Papers*, p. 240.

[4] Entry for 24 June 1874 in the Juniors' Beadle's Journal. For the Refectory Reading at this time see Appendix 2C.

[5] *Journals and Papers*, p. 240, entry for 1 Dec. Menstruums (Juniors' Beadle's Journal where not otherwise stated) were held on 14 Jan., 14 Feb. (MMJ), 3 Mar. (MMJ), 5 May, 2 June, and 7 July. This shows that they were monthly events. There is no record of a menstruum in April, but this is understandable because of the time needed for the Passiontide liturgy and the Easter vacation. The note on 'menstruum' in *Journals and Papers*, p. 426, 240. 1, interprets the term with the meaning applied to it in the Philosophate and Theologate. At the menstruum held once a term in St. Mary's Hall, philosophical theses were expounded, attacked, and defended (in Latin) in much the same way as practised in the Medieval Disputations with which the B.B.C. familiarized listeners some years ago.

specially studied, the examinee read it, construed and answered context questions put to him. The following day was a 'long school day' and extra work was done so that Wednesday, the feast of St. Francis Xavier, could be free. The Juniors recreated on the feast and the novices had their first repose day. On the 8th, the feast of the Immaculate Conception, some of the Juniors went to Farm Street to supply the altar staff, and afterwards remained to dinner. For the rest who remained at home there was a debate[1] in the evening at six o'clock.

A week before Christmas Hopkins went across to Old Windsor to the Academy at Beaumont College,[2] while the Juniors took their Blandyke. His diary repeats at this time his *cri de cœur* of April: 'Felling of trees going on sadly at Roehampton'.[3] On Christmas Eve the excitement in the house rose, for the 25th marked not only the feast but also the end of the Long Retreat:

Dec. 24.
Novices out of Retreat engaged in decorating the Corridor & Chapel. Litanies 2.30. At 6.15 Community assembled in Chapel, the Martyrologium was sung by Br Blount; thence they proceeded to the crib constructed by Br Masseurs in a room on the corridor, & it was opened by the hymn 'See amidst the winter's snow'. This was followed by supper. At 7.15 Points [of meditation] were given to the Community by Fr Rector & they then retired to rest; rising at 11. At 11.15 Medit. 11.45 'Adeste Fideles'.

Dec. 25. Xmas Day. Midnight Mass & Communion after which Cocoa and Soup in the Refectory & Bed. The BB's [Brothers] were called at 6, the rest at 6.30. Mass at 7.0. Breakfast at 8. High Mass at St Joseph's at 10. Mr G. Hopkins went away to spend the Xmas at Hampstead. Wine handed round once at dinner; dessert put on table immediately after Martyr: & wine. [MMJ]

While Hopkins spent his week at Hampstead, the rest of the community at Manresa entertained themselves with choosing the Innocent Porter, with a concert, and a debate. Hopkins returned to sad news: 'Br. Scanlan, who was a pupil of mine that six days I was

---

[1] Debates were also held on 18 Dec., 1 Jan. 1874, 29 Jan. (Provincial present), Shrovetide 16 and 17 Feb., 9 Apr., 14 and 28 May. In no instance is the subject debated stated.
[2] *Journals and Papers*, p. 240, entry for 18 Dec.   [3] Ibid.

at the College at Stonyhurst, died lately at Brighton. He insisted on wearing his gown to the last'.[1]

Schools reopened on 2 January and the Juniors were probably hard at work in preparation for the menstruum held on the 14th of the month at which the Provincial was present. The same night saw the beginning of the Triduum with its usual conclusion at the Rector's mass:

Sunday [18 Jan.]
Mass 13 mins to 7. Renewal of vows. Breakfast at 8. 9 Reading lesson. English Comp: as usual. 12.55. Dinner talking for desert [sic]. Wet evening. No tone. [JBJ]

A few days later Hopkins broke the silence which had prevailed for two and a half years between himself and Bridges. Was Bridges so annoyed by Hopkins's 'red' letter so as to be rendered speechless? This is how it appears to have struck Hopkins because he begins his letter with the bone of contention:

My last letter to you was from Stonyhurst. It was not answered, so that perhaps it did not reach you. If it did I supposed then and do not know what else to suppose now that you were disgusted with the *red* opinions it expressed, being a conservative. I have little reason to be red: it was the red Commune that murdered five of our Fathers lately—whether before or after I wrote I do not remember.[2] So far as I know I said nothing that might not fairly be said. If this was your reason for not answering it seems to shew a greater keeness about politics than is common.[3]

And at the close of the second paragraph he says more plainly: 'I think, my dear Bridges, to be so much offended about that red letter was excessive.' At the end of this letter he gives the piece of personal

---

[1] Ibid., p. 241. James Scanlan (1854-74). '31 Dec. R.I.P. Brother Scanlan died suddenly at Brighton whither he had gone to stay for a short time—being in consumption. Jan. 3. Fr Rector went to Brighton for Br Scanlan's funeral.' [MMJ]. He entered the Society of Jesus on 7 Sept. 1873.

[2] Hopkins's last letter to Bridges was dated 2 Aug. 1871. For accounts of the shooting of the priests see *The Times* for 29, 30, and 31 May 1871, and *The Tablet*, 3 June 1871, p. 669. Reports of the Requiem Masses offered in the Jesuit and Dominican churches in London for the victims of the Commune appeared in *The Tablet* for 10 and 24 June, pp. 720 and 785. An extract from the Archbishop of Westminster's pastoral letter (Trinity Sunday, 4 June 1871) on the revolution in Paris was given in *The Tablet* for 10 June 1871, pp. 719-20. *The Tablet* carried a series of articles on Communism in England from July to Aug. 1871. An account of the murder of the five Jesuits had been read in the refectory at St. Mary's Hall, see Appendix 2B, under 22 Nov. 1871.

[3] *Letters to Bridges*, pp. 28-9.

information that he is attempting to teach himself to play the piano
'not for execution's sake but to be independent of others and learn
something about music'.[1]

The month ended with the Provincial's visitation. Before the
Provincial's Day was celebrated on 12 February, Hopkins had again
visited Beaumont on the feast of Candlemas: 'Feb. 2. Fr. McLeod
& Mr. Hopkins to Beaumont' [MMJ]. Lent was now approaching
and the Juniors having got the Menstruum over on the 14th of the
month began a short Shrovetide vacation. Hopkins took the opportunity of seeing the collection of precious stones in Sir John Soane's
Museum with Fr. Goldie, and of visiting the National Gallery. On
Ash Wednesday,[2] he was present at part of the summing-up in the
notorious Tichborne case.[3] Next day was the Blandyke: 'Breakfast
as usual. Fasters were allowed their collation at B'fast. 4 Dinner.
Evening at 6 Reading' [JBJ]. Hopkins is again forbidden to fast and
tells his mother on the occasion of his birthday letter to her:

> You remember how you would have it I should take wine. Well so I do.
> 'The Lenten Festivities', as someone among us said, have begun for me,
> but in general, besides me, those who teach do not fast, as is but reasonable.
> (This is obscure and might mean the opposite of what it does. I mean that
> I in particular do not fast and that those who teach in general do not.)[4]

March was unusual for the visitors it brought Hopkins. Alexander
Wood came to see him on the first of the month,[5] and the entry for
24 March in the Minister's Journal reads: 'Messrs Challis[6] and
Bellasis[7] called on Mr. Hopkins.' Hopkins makes no reference to
this visit from friends of the past either in his diary or letters. One
wonders what the two barristers discussed with the Jesuit. Did

[1] *Letters to Bridges*, p. 130. A letter written to Baillie a year earlier (*Further Letters*,
p. 238) shows that GMH had begun to teach himself the piano at St. Mary's Hall.
[2] 18 Feb. GMH's entry 'One day later . . .', *Journals and Papers*, p. 241 in its
context, would suggest 17 Feb. Manresa Minister's Journal reads: '18 Feb. Messrs
Hopkins and Bampton to town to hear Chief Justice summing up the 2nd Tichborne
Trial.'
[3] *Further Letters* pp. 60, 123.   [4] Ibid., p. 123.
[5] Ibid., and *Journals and Papers*, p. 241.
[6] *Journals and Papers*, p. 378. Two years earlier Hopkins had noted in his diary:
'March 5—A letter from Challis saying he had left the Church', ibid., p. 218. See also
Newman's letter to GMH of 23 Feb. 187[4] in *Further Letters*, p. 409.
[7] *Journals and Papers*, pp. 377–8. Fifteen months earlier GMH had written to Baillie:
'Remember me very kindly to Bellasis when next you see him and don't forget.' *Further
Letters*, p. 239.

Challis say why he had left the Roman Church, and did Bellasis hint at his future Oratorian vocation? A few days after the meeting Bellasis returned to make a retreat from 29 March until 3 April, and he called again on 11 April.

Passiontide had begun before March was ended and schools continued until 1 April, the Wednesday in Holy Week. Tenebrae was sung before supper on the Wednesday, Thursday, and Friday. On Maundy Thursday the usual stripping of the altars took place and the Blessed Sacrament was removed to the altar of Repose, or Sepulchre, as they called it. Night-watching before the Blessed Sacrament was undertaken by the Juniors for an hour at a time. Strict silence was kept for these last days of Holy Week. On Good Friday they rose early and meditated as usual. Breakfast followed at seven o'clock and the Mass of the Pre-sanctified (as it was then called) took place at eight. Br. Gartlan preached during dinner, and in the afternoon the devotion of the Three Hours was given at St. Joseph's. Fr. Harper preached. Tenebrae was sung at six o'clock and instead of the Litanies of the Saints the *Miserere* was said at nine. The ceremonies of Holy Saturday were held in the morning and lasted from seven until ten. Easter Sunday was celebrated with a High Mass in the domestic chapel, and permission was given to those who wished to attend the eleven o'clock High Mass at St. Joseph's. Some notion of the singing at the services can be gathered from an account of 'Holy Week at Roehampton' of some years later. The author manages to retain and communicate something of the period and atmosphere:

At twenty minutes before eleven on Palm Sunday morning, each one who was to take part in the ceremony put on his surplice and took his place in the stalls. The new sacristy not yet being finished, it was not possible for all to walk in in processional order. Punctually at the time announced the *Hosanna* was begun—the palms blessed. All the community having approached in admirable order and received their palms, the whole congregation came up to the rails and kissing the palm and hand of the celebrant returned with their branches to their places. While this was going on the choir sang in very fine harmony the *Pueri Hebraeorum*, and this was sung by the Juniors to the Gregorian tune alternately till the distribution was over. . . .

The second verse of the *Gloria laus* found Roehampton metamorphosed.

Such unwonted strains stealing on the silent Sabbath breezes to the
Common brought a head out of every window, and not a few, we understand, into the church after the procession. The Passion was really splen-
didly sung, both on Palm Sunday and Good Friday. We doubt if it could
have been excelled in any of the parts. The part of the populace especially
deserved praise. We do not think the *Vah* could have been ever more strikingly sung. A plain Gregorian Mass followed. . . .

We feel incapable of doing justice to the Tenebrae services. They
certainly were carefully and admirably done. They reflected credit on
those to whose management they were entrusted, and ought to have amply
repaid them for their pains. The psalms were sung by the Novices and
Juniors—against each other—the former being in the south, the latter in
the north transepts. Father Divico's[1] [*sic*] inimitable antiphons were
rendered by a carefully chosen choir. The *Miserere* and *Benedictus* were,
as usual, harmonized. The *Laudate*, too, so difficult to be equally harmonized, was perfectly successful. The Novices sang the Lamentations, and
the Juniors, exercising their office of 'lector,' the Lessons. The Juniors
also sang the Prophecies on Holy Saturday, and we overheard the remark
that there were probably few churches that day that had twelve Lectors,
properly so called, to exercise their peculiar office.

On Maundy Thursday the Mass was partly from Mollitor[2] and partly
Gregorian. On Holy Saturday the Mass was one of Gounod's, and was
nobly done—a great contrast with the solemn and stately music of the
three preceding days. And what shall we say of Easter Sunday? Our praise
is poor. The Mass was Gounod's second *Messe des Orphéonistes*, and we
firmly believe that a more spirited and splendid piece of music was never
produced by a body of twenty voices, a harmonium, and a violin. Gounod's
grand *Domine salvam fac*, with its exquisite symphony, was done in such
a manner at the end as to make one wish that her Majesty was just then
passing that she might hear how enthusiastically English Jesuits prayed
for her prosperity.[3]

On Easter Monday the Juniorate's recreation week proper began.
Clearly the main local attraction was the grand military review on
Wimbledon Common.[4] Hopkins went to see it in the morning and
says that had he not been prevented by visitors he would have gone

---

[1] P. Francesco de Vico, S.J.: *Antiphons and Responses of Matins and Lauds for the
last Three Days of Holy Week* (1877).

[2] This might be intended for Johann Baptist Molitor (1834–1900), a fairly prolific
composer of Catholic church music.

[3] Anon, 'Holy Week at Roehampton', *LLNN*, xiv (July 1881), 241–2. After this ful-
some praise the writer lets fly the odd brickbat.

[4] See *The Annual Register, 1874*, pt. ii, pp. 34–6.

again in the afternoon. Something of his enjoyment and excitement is reflected in the description in his Journal:

Went up in the morning to get an impression but it was too soon, however got this—caught that inscape in the horse that you see in the pediment especially and other basreliefs of the Parthenon and even which Sophocles had felt and expresses in two choruses of the *Oedipus Coloneus*, running on the likeness of a horse to a breaker, a wave of the sea curling over. I looked at the groin or the flank and saw how the set of the hair symmetrically flowed outwards from it to all parts of the body, so that, following that one may inscape the whole beast very simply.—They kept firing the furze—brown-ambery flames, waving in grasslines and leaping off in laces and tatters, landscape sweating through gadroons and turbulent liquid vapour as through bullseye glass, burnt twigs flying.[1]

He finished this entry with a glimpse of the march past: 'an unsheathing of swords by some cavalry, which is a stirring naked-steel lightning bit of business, I think'.

The Thursday of Easter week found Hopkins again at the Victoria and Albert Museum in company with a recently arrived foreign scholastic. His diary shows that in addition to the gem collection his attention was held by the exhibition of Japanese craft.[2] The same day John Walford, his 'Angel Guardian' of noviceship days and predecessor at the Oratory School, arrived and stayed for the best part of a week.[3]

The 'Rec' week ended on Saturday, and at 8.30 a.m. on Sunday the Juniors were having a reading lesson from Fr. Harper: Monday saw the usual school day ordo restored. However, the return to work was softened by the month's Blandyke taken on the 16th. The weather seems to have been encouraging, for the Juniors' Journal reads: '16 April. 12 Juniors obtained leave to row on the river but outriggers were forbidden.' And spring finds its way into Hopkins's diary:

April 20—Young elmleaves lash and lip the sprays. This has been a very beautiful day—fields about us deep green lighted underneath with white daisies, yellower fresh green of leaves above which bathes the skirts of the elms, and their tops are touched and worded with leaf too. . . . my eye was struck by such a sense of green in the tufts and pashes of grass, with

---

[1] *Journals and Papers*, pp. 241–2.
[2] Ibid., entry for 9 Apr.
[3] Information from Manresa Minister's Journal. Walford left on 14 Apr.

purple shadow thrown back on the dry black mould behind them, as I do not remember ever to have been exceeded in looking at green grass.[1]

But if there was quickening into life to record there was also death:

April 25, Saturday, eve of the Feast of St. Joseph's Patronage Br. Alexander Byrne died of rapid consumption. He was a novice but had been one of my pupils[2]

Once again the front benches in the Chapel would have been turned inwards and set back to make room for the catafalque and coffin, and probably there was a quick run-through of the Dirge and the 'Dies Irae' by the novices and Juniors before the Solemn Requiem and burial in the cemetery in Manresa's own grounds.

May, June, and July passed quietly, and Hopkins, having noted for 23 May 'the weather has been so wintry: I even got chilblains again',[3] puts down for July, 'Heat has come on now'.[4] The ecclesiastical feasts were fittingly kept, and there was usually some special treat to mark the occasion. The entry which follows besides illustrating this provides an example of the Juniors' presuming permission, only this time they judged erroneously:

24 May. Whit Sunday.
High Mass in Chapel at 9. Dinner at 12.30. $\frac{2}{3}$? glasses Salmon—Lamb—Tart—Dessert—Talking. Novices and Juniors to Churches. (The latter came in at 9.30 p.m. *en Masse*!! two companies only had had leave.) [MMJ]

Probably some small penance was imposed.

At the end of the month the Rector, Fr. Porter, on the doctor's advice left Manresa to take the waters at Carlsbad.

Hopkins went several times to Kew Gardens, which are within easy walking distance of Roehampton. After his visit on the May Blandyke the Old Palace found its way into his Journal, 'a pretty picture—ruddled red brick over a close-shaven green-white lawn'; and he added the further impression 'chestnuts in bloom and a

---

[1] *Journals and Papers*, pp. 242-3.
[2] Ibid. The Province suffered the loss of a second scholastic within a week: Br. William Vincent Marchant (1852–74) had died at Bournemouth on 15 Apr.
[3] Ibid., p. 244.
[4] Ibid., p. 249, entry for 9 July.

beech in a fairy spray of green'.[1] And returning from Kew in June he picked up on the way home 'some fumitory and white bryony, which last kept a long time, the leaves warping and coiling strongly in water'.[2] His bryony lasted over three weeks.

Towards the end of June the Provincial arrived to celebrate the feast of St. Aloysius[3] (21 June) at Manresa: 'After dessert', the Juniors' Beadle wrote, 'Fr. Prov[incial] came and sat with the Juniors at their benches. Afterwards we prepared Tickets for admission to Parliament for Fr Prov. to get signed for us.' After the June Triduum[4] (26th–28th) and vow renovation on the feast of Saints Peter and Paul we read the entry: '10 went to Parliament and took lunch and bottles of wine with them' [JBJ]. And on 2 July:

> Mr. Hopkins with 9 others went to Parl.[5] . . . Yesterday and today Fr McLeod lent us the account in the Times of the Debate on Home Rule, to be read aloud for such as cared to hear, during recreation. [JBJ]

Towards the middle of the month Hopkins again went with a party of Juniors to Westminster, this time to the House of Commons to listen to the debate on the Schools Endowment Bill 'moved by Lord Sandon, who spoke well; so did, not *so* well, Mr. Forster in reply. We heard Newdigate. Gladstone was preparing to speak and writing fast but we could not stay to hear him. Lowe, who sat next him, looked something like an apple in the snow'.[6]

A few days earlier Hopkins had been to Brompton Oratory evidently hoping to see his closest friend of Oxford days, Addis. Unfortunately he missed him, since he was away, but adds in his Journal:

> I met Mr. David Lewis, a great Scotist, and at the same time old Mr. Brande Morris was making a retreat with us: I got to know him, so that oddly I made the acquaintance of two and I suppose the only two Scotists in England in one week[7]

---

[1] Ibid., p. 243, entry for 7 May.
[2] Ibid., p. 248, entry for 25 June.
[3] They had had the 'Six Sundays in honours of St Aloysius', and as we saw earlier in the Noviceship section they practised other devotions, for example, the Ten Fridays in honour of St. Francis Xavier, and the annual novena to the same saint in March.
[4] See also *Journals and Papers*, p. 248.   [5] Ibid.
[6] Ibid., p. 249, entry for 14 July.
[7] Ibid., p. 249, entry for 9 July. Hopkins was in London several times this

Fr. Porter returned from Carlsbad to Manresa on 10 July. Rector's day was celebrated on the 21st and after dinner a seance was given in his honour under the cedar tree.[1] Earlier in the day some of the Juniors had gone by train to London with permission to enter places free of admission: many had tickets for the Zoo.

Two days later the Rector's day at Beaumont was kept, and as is customary an invitation was sent to neighbouring Jesuit Houses for a few Fathers to attend the celebration. Hopkins went from Manresa together with Fr. Porter and Fr. MacLeod. Hopkins remembers:

It was a lovely day: shires-long of pearled cloud under cloud, with a grey stroke underneath marking each row; beautiful blushing yellow in the straw of the uncut ryefields, the wheat looking white and all the ears making a delicate and very true crisping along the top and with just enough air stirring for them to come and go gently; then there were fields reaping. All this I would have looked at again in returning but during dinner I talked too freely and unkindly and had to do penance going home.[2]

By this time the end-of-year's exams. were imminent. Halfway through the month the Juniors' Beadle had noted in his log, 'matter of examen settled', which left the Juniors with a little over a fortnight for revision. The examination in mathematics lasting an hour and a half was held on 25 July. The exam. for which Hopkins was responsible began the following Wednesday.

29 July.
10.20 dictation of questions in Rhetoric in School Room for 1st Class 10.30 Examen in Rhet. for 2 hours. For 2nd Class Exam. 10. 3 Studies[.] 5.50 Latin theme till 7.30.

Thurs. 30th.
Oral Exam before Fr Provincial 9.30 till 11.30[.] 11.30 Recreation till Washing. 3. Exam continued till 5.15. Recreation till 6. For 2nd Class Rhet Exam 9.30 till 11.30. In afternoon 6 of this class went to Parl [iament]. [JBJ]

year: '17 March. Fr. Minister [Fr. Goldie] & Mr. Hopkins to Oratory for Exposition' [MMJ]. 'May 23 . . . I went one day to the Academy and again June 12, when Fr. Johnson . . . kindly sent me to town with Br. Bampton for change.' *Journals and Papers*, p. 244.
[1] For GMH's comments on the cedars at Roehampton see his entries for 9 and 12 July in Ibid., p. 249.
[2] Ibid., entry for 23 July.

A question to which one would like an answer is 'How effective was Hopkins as a teacher?' His own reactions to the work are to be found in hints scattered throughout his letters. During his short spell as a schoolmaster at the Oratory in 1868, he complained: 'Teaching is very burdensome, especially when you have much of it: I have.'[1] The strain is also apparent in his coaching at Stonyhurst for the London Intermediate and B.A. examinations: 'I like my pupils and do not wholly dislike the work, but I fall into or continue in a heavy weary state of body and mind in which my go is gone . . .'[2] A similar ambivalence attaches to his lecturing in classics in later years at University College, Dublin, where one of the forms his acute melancholy took was a 'daily anxiety about work to be done'.[3] His distress rose to the pitch of forcing him to admit that his state was 'much like madness',[4] and in March 1889 in a letter to his brother Lionel he confessed: 'As a tooth ceases aching so will my lectures intermit after tomorrow for Shrovetide.'[5] Hardly an expression of joy.

My own conclusion is that Hopkins was at his happiest and best when coaching the able scholarship candidate. Two instances suggest this. First, at Mount St. Mary's College in 1878, on the occasion of his pupil's winning a Jesuit intercollegiate prize, he wrote with a mixture of modesty and evident satisfaction:

I was more pleased than I should have thought possible, but he is clever and hardworking and I had not much to do with the result. I shall not easily have so good a pupil again. He is eager to take down everything I say and repeats it with minute accuracy long afterwards.[6]

And some years later, writing from Dublin, he referred with similar pleasure to one of his students

a young Scotch Protestant, the best and brightest of all my pupils, who takes a most visible pleasure in learning and being taught and whom therefore to teach is correspondingly a pleasure . . .[7]

This same undergraduate is surely behind Hopkins's comment on

---

[1] *Further Letters*, p. 231.   [2] Ibid., p. 251.   [3] Ibid., p. 256.
[4] Ibid.   [5] Ibid., p. 193.
[6] Ibid., p. 150.   [7] Ibid., p. 178.

the quality he generally looked for in pupils when he wrote to
Patmore within the same week:

> It is well, I believe, to have a kindness for that large class of people
> with plenty of intelligence and plenty of moral teachableness who cannot
> take a hint but yet will follow, study, master, and put in practice a clear
> and patient explanation. It is the class I should like to [be] useful to. It
> has none of the knowing in it but many of the young.[1]

What of other assessments of Hopkins as teacher? I offer two diver-
gent examples and the reader may choose as he pleases. First an Indian
critic:

> He was a success in Dublin, for he had that particular combination of
> profound scholarship and profound sympathy for the young which makes
> for abiding popularity in a teacher.[2]

While nearer home an Irish Jesuit has stated:

> His career as a teacher had not been successful in the English Jesuit
> schools, and those who remembered his lectures in Dublin seem to be
> agreed in their verdict that he was quite unable to impart the knowledge
> which he had gained at Oxford as a pupil of Nettleship and Jowett.[3]

But to return to the Juniorate. Hopkins himself looking back eight
months later from St. Beuno's told Bridges how much he would
have liked an invitation to visit him, 'what a pleasure it would have
been and what a break in the routine of rhetoric, which I taught so
badly and so painfully!'[4] Painfully for whom? Teacher or taught or

---

[1] *Further Letters*, p. 376.

[2] K. R. Srinivasa Iyengar, 'Gerard Manley Hopkins', *The New Review* (Calcutta),
vii (Mar. 1938), 264.

[3] Aubrey Gwynn, 'The Jesuit Fathers and University College' in *Struggle with
Fortune*, ed. Michael Tierney (Dublin [1954]), p. 32. Two other opinions seem useful.
Bridges, in his introduction written only a few years after Hopkins's death, to a selected
group of poems in vol. 8 of *Poets and Poetry of the Century* [1893], ed. A. H. Miles,
wrote: 'He was not considered publicly successful in his profession', p. 162. 'He seems
to have entirely satisfied the Society as classical examiner at Dublin. That drudgery,
however, and the political dishonesty which he was there forced to witness, so tortured
his sensitive spirit that he fell into a melancholy state', p. 163. Irish Jesuit colleagues
commented: 'Some of his pupils appreciated his powers and took advantage of his
scholarly teaching; but on the whole he was not happy either in the College work or in
the drudgery of the examinations for which he was not well fitted.' *A Page of Irish
History: Story of University College, Dublin, 1883–1909*, compiled by Fathers of the
Society of Jesus (Dublin and Cork, 1930), pp. 105–6.

[4] *Letters to Bridges*, p. 30.

both? In recording the depression he felt at this time Hopkins recalls his state of the previous year.[1]

I was very tired and seemed deeply cast down till I had some kind words from the Provincial. Altogether perhaps my heart has never been so burdened and cast down as this year. The tax on my strength has been greater than I have felt before: at least now at Teignmouth I feel myself weak and can do little. But in all this our Lord goes His own way[2]

However, the school year was now over and after a few days in which he marked the Latin proses he went on 4 August to Beaumont College's Speech Day. Perhaps it is to this occasion that the following paragraph refers:

In the summer of 1874 Fr. Peter Gallwey, as Provincial, visited the College, and made a speech in the cricket field to the boys, among whom was Louis Cavendish, the grandson of the Lord Chief Justice, Sir Alexander Cockburn. Sir Alexander was present on the occasion, and it was doubtless by way of paying a compliment to the legal profession, that Fr Gallwey was induced to urge the boys to cherish 'their cricket laws, their College laws, their country's laws and their Stanislaus'.[3]

Hopkins went back to sleep the night at Manresa but returned next day to join the Beaumont Community who were going to Teignmouth for their Villa. Despite the fact that he begins his holiday journal by saying that 'This seems a dull place', his notes fill seven printed pages.[4] After a fortnight on the Devon coast Hopkins returned for a few days to Beaumont which he seems to have liked. He was captured by the charm of Windsor Castle and writes with affection:

I think there can be no place like it—the eye-greeting burl of the Round Tower; all the crownlike medley of lower towers warping round; red and white houses of the town abutting on these, gabled and irregularly jut-jotted against them, making a third stage or storey[5]

He returned to Roehampton on 24 August and two days later was told he was to go to Theology. The Minister's Journal states simply: 'Mr Hopkins left for St Beuno's.'[6]

[1] See the end of Hopkins's diary entry for 16 Aug. in *Journals and Papers*, p. 236.
[2] Ibid., pp. 249–50.
[3] *The History of St. Stanislaus' College, Beaumont* (Old Windsor, 1911), p. 39.
[4] *Journals and Papers*, pp. 250–6.
[5] Ibid., p. 256.
[6] The Journal continues: 'Mr Clarke came to take his place.'

CHAPTER 5

The Theologate 1874–1877

NEXT morning, Friday, 28 August, Hopkins was up half an hour earlier than usual, possibly so that he could make an early start on his journey to the Theologate at St. Beuno's College.[1] He was met at St. Asaph by two fellow Theologians, and his diary entry for this day has a cheerful sound. It begins with the early morning in Roehampton: 'I saw the full moon[2] of brassyish colour and beautifully dappled hanging a little above the clump in the pasture opposite my window', and concludes at St. Beuno's where Mr. Bacon had put scarlet geraniums in his room, and 'everyone was very kind and hospitable'.[3]

The following day he sent his father an account of the house and garden:

The house stands on a steep hillside, it commands the long-drawn valley of the Clwyd to the sea, a vast prospect, and opposite is Snowdon and its range, just now it being bright visible but coming and going with the weather. The air seems to me very fresh and wholesome.[4]

Then he gives more details of the college:

It is built of limestone, decent outside, skimpin within, Gothic, like Lancing College[5] done worse. The staircases, galleries, and bopeeps are

---

[1] For the history and photographs of St. Beuno's, the Rock Chapel, and the Vale of Clwyd, see A. Thomas, 'Hopkins, Welsh and Wales', *Transactions of the Honourable Society of Cymmrodorion*, Session 1965, Part II (1966), 272–85. To the list given there on p. 272, n. 1, should be added J. Roderick O'Flanagan, *Through North Wales with my Wife. An Arcadian Tour* [1884], pp. 132–9.

[2] Full moon was on 27 Aug. at 1.28 p.m.

[3] *Journals and Papers*, p. 257.   [4] *Further Letters*, p. 124.

[5] GMH has been somewhat unkind to Lancing. But he may not have seen the College for a dozen years or more since his younger brother, Arthur, who was educated there, left in 1865. Lancing was designed by R. C. Carpenter and his son R. H. Carpenter. For the history and photographs of the College see Basil Handford, *Lancing College 1848–1948* (Hove [1948]), and *Illustrated London News*, 24 July 1948, pp. 96–9. Evelyn Waugh has written of the chapel of his old school: 'I know no more spectacular post-Reformation ecclesiastical building in the kingdom.' *A Little Learning* (1964), p. 98.

inexpressible: it takes a fortnight to learn them. Pipes of affliction convey lukewarm water of affliction to some of the rooms, others more fortunate have fires. The garden is all heights, terraces, Excelsiors, misty mountain tops, seats up trees called Crows' Nests, flights of steps seemingly up to heaven lined with burning aspiration upon aspiration of scarlet geraniums: it is very pretty and airy but it gives you the impression that if you took a step farther you would find yourself on Plenlimmon, Conway Castle, or Salisbury Craig. With best love to detachments stationed at Hampstead.[1]

Hopkins would certainly have presented himself to his new Rector, Fr. Jones,[2] on the evening of his arrival, nor was this his first meeting with him, since Fr. Jones had given the annual retreat at St. Mary's Hall in 1872 when Hopkins was a second-year Philosopher. Next day, the Beadle of the Theologians recorded in his log: 'Fr. Jones left for Beaumont to give the community retreat.' He did not return until late at night on 9 September, accompanied by Fr. Coleridge who was to give the Theologians their retreat for the year. The purpose of going into detail about the Rector's movements is merely to bring out the point that in his absence Hopkins began to learn Welsh. The problem of conscience this provided for Gerard I have discussed elsewhere.[3]

Before the retreat began on the 10th, Hopkins occupied the interval in getting to know the neighbourhood.[4] His diary covering this period shows that he walked to Cŵm churchyard, to 'Bryn Bella', the house of Mrs. Piozzi, to St. Asaph, and Trefnant. The 10th itself was a Blandyke and he used the holiday to visit the well Ffynnon-Fair and Cefn Caves

[1] *Further Letters*, pp. 124–5.
[2] James Jones (1828–93; see Boase v, Sutcliffe), Jesuit priest, born on 28 Mar. 1828 at Benada Abbey, Co. Sligo. Educated at Clongowes Wood College, Dublin. Entered the S.J. novitiate in Nov. 1850; ordained priest in 1857. Parish work in Demerara for several years acting for a time as Vicar General to Bishop Etheridge. 1869, parish work at Yarmouth. Oct. 1871 became Professor of Moral Theology at St. Beuno's, GMH being among his students; Rector of the College, 1873–6. It was at Fr. Jones's suggestion that GMH wrote 'The Wreck of the Deutschland'. Provincial, 1876–80, and sent by Propaganda to Jamaica as Apostolic Visitor. Afterwards returned as Rector to St. Beuno's from 1880–5, remaining as Professor of Moral Theology until 1892. Autumn 1892 appointed English Assistant to Fr. General. Died from typhoid fever at Loyola, Spain, on 12 Jan. 1893. (*Letters to Bridges*, pp. 42, 43, 44 'our Provincial'; *Correspondence with Dixon*, pp. 14 'my rector', 29 'the Provincial'; *Journals and Papers*, pp. 226, 257, 258 'the Rector'.)
[3] 'Hopkins, Welsh and Wales', pp. 273–9.
[4] A map of St. Beuno's district is given in *Journals and Papers*, p. 548.

from which the view of the deep valley of the Elwy, the meeting of two, which makes three, glens indeed, is most beautiful. The woods, thick and silvered by sunlight and shade, by the flat smooth banking of the tree-tops expressing the slope of the hill, came down to the green bed of the valley. Below at a little timber bridge I looked at some delicate flying shafted ashes—there was one especially of single sonnet-like inscape—between which the sun sent straight bright slenderish panes of silvery sunbeams down the slant towards the eye and standing above an unkept field stagged with yellow heads of ragwort. In the evening I watched a fine sunset from the tower: the place is famous for them[1]

The retreat given by Fr. Coleridge, his 'oldest friend in the Society',[2] was of greater importance than usual since its close was marked for Hopkins by a step forward in the religious life. Afterwards he wrote to his mother:

I have been in an eight days' retreat ending on Friday night. On Friday, Saturday, and today ordinations have been going on here; sixteen priests were ordained this morning. I received the tonsure and the four minor orders yesterday. The tonsure consisted of five little snips but the bishop must have found even that a hard job, for I had cut my hair almost to the scalp, as it happened, just before. The four minor orders are those of Doorkeepers, Readers, Exorcists, and Acolytes: their use is almost obsolete.[3]

Gerard was probably feeling elated and part of the reason for this may be deduced from the entry in the Beadle's log for the day preceding the conferring of minor orders:

17 Tuesday. Fr. Gal[l]wey left at 1.30. Besides seeing the ordinandi, he called at the rooms of all.

And Hopkins, recounting, the Provincial's visit to his mother added: 'It seems he wrote a letter giving me leave to spend a week with you at Lyme on my way or beside my way here, but I had already started. You will be vexed at this; at the same time it shews how thoughtful he is.'[4]

But to go back a little. Almost as soon as he arrived in Wales, he both felt and recorded the impact of the scene about him:

Sept. 6—With Wm. Kerr, who took me up a hill behind ours (ours is Mynefyr), a furze-grown and heathy hill, from which I could look round

[1] *Journals and Papers*, p. 259.   [2] *Further Letters*, p. 138.
[3] Ibid., p. 126.   [4] Ibid., p. 127.

the whole country, up the valley towards Ruthin and down to the sea. The cleave in which Bodfari and Caerwys lie was close below. It was a leaden sky, braided or roped with cloud, and the earth in dead colours, grave but distinct. The heights by Snowdon were hidden by the clouds but not from distance or dimness. The nearer hills, the other side of the valley, shewed a hard and beautifully detached and glimmering brim against the light, which was lifting there. All the length of the valley the skyline of hills was flowingly written all along upon the sky. A blue bloom, a sort of meal, seemed to have spread upon the distant south, enclosed by a basin of hills. Looking all round but most in looking far up the valley I felt an instress and charm of Wales.[1]

For the present the charm of the Welsh landscape is garnered and stored in his 'treasury of explored beauty'[2] to be drawn on later. The accumulation of the notions and images which went to the making of 'Pied Beauty', for example, can be identified and traced with little difficulty.[3]

In North Wales, just as in Lancashire, Hopkins explored his new surroundings not only with eyes but also with ears. Within a day or two of his arrival he is writing to his mother persuasively of the beautiful sound of Welsh: 'It is . . . euphonious and regular. People think it has no vowels but just the contrary is true: it is almost all vowels and they run off the tongue like oil by diphthongs and by triphthongs—there are 20 of the latter and nearly 30 of the former.'[4] Again, apparently after the retreat, he seizes the opportunity to learn something of another language completely new to him. For among those who had received minor orders with him was a Maltese scholastic, and Hopkins notes in a paragraph of his diary:

I talked to this Br. Magri[5] about Maltese. It is mainly Arabic, he said,

[1] *Journals and Papers*, pp. 257–8. Hopkins tells his mother: 'The Welsh landscape has a great charm and when I see Snowdon and the mountains in its neighbourhood, as I can now, with the clouds lifting, it gives me a rise of the heart.' *Further Letters*, p. 127.

[2] Ibid., p. 202.

[3] See 'Hopkins, Welsh and Wales', pp. 281–3.   [4] *Further Letters*, p. 126.

[5] Emmanuel Magri (1851–1907), Jesuit priest, born at Valletta, Malta, on 27 Feb. 1851. Studied law for three years before entering the Society of Jesus in May 1871; ordained priest in 1881. 1883–8, taught at College of St. Julian, and at the philosophate at Naxxar. 1893–8, Prefect of Studies at Gozo seminary. 1906, Superior of S.J. residence at Catania. Died at Sfax near Tunis on 29 Mar. 1907. He spoke Latin, French, English, Spanish, and Italian in addition to Maltese, and had a reading knowledge of Hebrew, Syriac, Arabic, and Greek. Important pioneer work in the collecting of Maltese folklore. (*Journals and Papers*, p. 259 (2).)

with a groundwork of Punic. Newspapers are published in it in European 'script': an Oriental character would have been better, because some sounds cannot be expressed in our letters except by a convention. Rather to my humiliation I found great difficulty in hearing the gutturals (*gh, kh*, and another there is). They are real *gutturals*, that is / uttered deep in the throat. I made him say *ghali* (high, dear) many times: at first it seemed no different from *ali*; then it seemed a difference made on purpose but not in the lettering of the word . . . It is clear how differently quickened the ear must be to meaning and unmeaning sounds: it seemed to me very hard to think one could catch the difference between *ghali* and *ali* in quick conversation, or at a distance.[1]

Further, the final sentence of this paragraph reveals Hopkins's sustained interest in prosody. Maltese verse, he concludes,

is either by quantity or accent (with rhyme) but I found that this quantitative verse is not in use: I think it may be theoretical only. In the word we tried it was plain the accent followed the quantity / above two syllables, just as in the modern accentuation of Latin words

This may be no more than a fragment, but perhaps not without its part in his evolving sprung rhythm.

This encounter with Emmanuel Magri serves to underline a delightful trait in Hopkins's character, for on other occasions also we find him apparently going out of his way to entertain foreigners.[2] Two reasons suggest themselves as explanation. First, it may have been just plain goodness of heart on his part which led him to put himself out to be friendly to strangers. Secondly, it gave him an opportunity to add to his store of phonology and philology. But whatever the reason, he showed tact and discretion in his encounters with foreigners by raising for discussion their own language—a topic which presumably they could speak about with ease and some degree of assurance.

But the summer vacation came to an end at last and on 1 October schools reopened:[3]

Rise 5.30. Veni Creator, Mass of H. Ghost, & Benediction. Latin

---

[1] *Journals and Papers*, p. 259.

[2] Compare the following instances: 'April 9 (1874)—To Kensington museum with Br. Tournade the young Frenchman bound for China', ibid., p. 242, and 'May 17—Took Br. Tournade to Combe Wood . . .', ibid., p. 243; 'May 7—To Kew Gardens with . . . Br. Younan a young Syrian from Calcutta', ibid.

[3] See the entry for the date in Iibid., p. 260.

discourse by Fr. Tosi[1] in recreat[n] room at 8. Brkfast 8.30. [Theologians' Beadle's Journal]

Before he began the theological part of his training, Hopkins's references in his letters to the subject of theology—I prescind from his grasp of doctrine—were confined to a recognition of the vastness of the subject, an awareness of his own ignorance, and a firm conviction that his course in theology was most likely to last four years.[2] This last point is of some importance and will be returned to later.

Some details of the studies had been mentioned in a letter to his father:

Holidays till the 2nd of October. After that hours of study very close— lectures in dogmatic theology, moral ditto, canon law, church history, scripture, Hebrew and what not.[3]

The pattern of the day, the week, and the semester at the theologate was much the same as that followed at St. Mary's Hall, and so the full details of the timetable need not detain us. Fr. Clarke provides a summary of the theologate curriculum:

Here the work is certainly hard, especially during the first two years. On three days in the week, the student who has passed successfully through his philosophical course has to attend two lectures in the morning and three in the afternoon. The morning lectures are on moral and dogmatic theology; and those in the afternoon on canon law or history, dogmatic theology, and Hebrew, the last for half an hour only. Besides this, on each of these afternoons there is held a circle or disputation such as I have described above. In theology these disputations are as a rule fiercer and more searching than in the philosophical course. There often

[1] Luigi Tosi (1835-82), Jesuit priest, born at Rome on 21 June 1835. Entered the S.J. novitiate at St. Andrea, Rome, in Feb. 1855. 1861-4, theology at Rome; ordained priest, 1862. 1868, Prefect of Studies in the German College, Rome. Taught dogmatic theology in England, 1870-5, first at Roehampton, and afterwards at St. Beuno's College, GMH being among his students. 1876, parish work in Tuscany. Failing health caused him to retire to Castel Gandolfo where he died on 21 Apr. 1882. (*Journals and Papers*, p. 260.)

[2] The references are self-explanatory and are given chronologically:
16 Oct. 1866—'Ten years and a lifetime are too little [to decide which is the Church of Christ], when the vastness of the subject of theology is taken into account', *Further Letters*, p. 93; 31 Dec. 1867—'Challis and me, who are not theologians', ibid., p. 49; 4 Jan. 1872—'I have not read a word of theology yet', ibid., p. 236; 22 Mar. 1872—'I shall be ... sent to my theology for three or four years', ibid., p. 56; 2 Aug. 1873— 'I am to go to my theology, which is a four year's business', ibid., p. 122; 4 Aug. 1873— 'Then I am to begin my theology and the course lasts four years', ibid., p. 58; 20 Feb. 1875—'Study theology—for four years from last September', *Letters to Bridges*, p. 30.

[3] *Further Letters*, p. 124.

arises, not the *odium theologicum*, but the eager advocacy with which even Jesuits defend their own opinions. The men are older, and bolder too, and take a delight in searching out any supposed weakness in the arguments proposed to them, so that there is no danger of any latent fallacy or inadequate proof escaping the observation of the more keen-sighted members of the class. In addition to these constant disputations there is held every three months a more solemn assembly of the same kind, at which the whole house is present and the rector presides, in which two of the students are chosen to defend for an hour continuously a number of theses against the attacks of all comers, the professors themselves included.

During the third and fourth years of the course of theology, lectures in Scripture are substituted for those on moral theology and Hebrew. At the end of the third year the young Jesuit (if a man of thirty-four or thirty-five can be accounted young) is ordained priest, and during his last year his lectures are fewer, and he has privately to prepare himself for a general examination in theology, on which depends in great measure whether he has the grade of a professed father in the Society or the lower degree of what is called a 'spiritual coadjutor'.[1]

In this account no mention is made of the 'case of conscience' which was held regularly on Tuesday evenings. The case to be discussed—hand-written or chromographed—was displayed on the notice-board about mid-week, two Theologians were instructed to prepare solutions, and a third would study it, and be ready to give his opinion if asked; all were expected to have studied it in advance. A case of conscience figured in the letter of a later Theologian:

I had, among other things, to decide what course of action should be pursued by a flabbergasted Bishop who had just heard the confession of a dying priest to the effect that he (the priest) had never had the slightest faith in any of the Sacraments which he had administered for thirty years, and was in fact a complete Atheist. Of course the case was purely imaginary.[2]

The first case of conscience this semester was on 27 October.

As to the general state of studies[3] at St. Beuno's some indication

[1] 'Training of a Jesuit', pp. 223–4.
[2] Katharine Kendall, *Father Steuart* (1950), p. 68.
[3] The library at Hopkins's disposal contained not only the classic and standard works in moral and dogmatic theology but also a good selection of more recent work. Ample resources, too, were available for the study of Scripture, canon law, church history, and patristics. The nucleus of the present library at the Pontifical Athenaeum, Heythrop, was formed from the theological and philosophical libraries at St. Beuno's and St. Mary's Hall. It has been constantly added to over the years and now contains approximately 150,000 volumes. Unfortunately, no printed catalogue yet exists.

has been given by Fr. Crehan, who was himself for several years Professor of Fundamental Theology in the theologate of the English Province, and therefore speaks from first-hand knowledge of the Province tradition. Of the study of theology in 1887, that is, only a decade after Hopkins's time, he writes:

That sacred science was at a low ebb among English Catholics. There was of course the one striking figure of Newman at Birmingham, but elsewhere thinkers were as becalmed. Leo XIII's call for a revival of Scholasticism had hardly reached the shores of England. Some constructive thinking on Church and State had been attempted as a result of the outcry over the Vatican Decrees and Gladstone's pamphleteering; at Maynooth Dr. Walter MacDonald was battling fiercely with the hazardous theories of Mivart, but in historical theology English Catholic scholarship was far to seek.[1]

Hopkins's teachers included the Rector, Fr. Jones, who taught moral theology and presided at the 'cases', Fr. Perini,[2] who taught Hebrew and Scripture, Fr. Morris for Canon Law and Church History, and Fr. Tepe[3] for dogma. According to Fr. Crehan, the latter was 'of a solid Suarezian exhaustiveness in speculative matters, but no historian of dogmas'.[4] That Suarezianism was the mainstay of the Province's theological faculty during Hopkins's time I have no reason to doubt, and find little difficulty in accepting Fr. Devlin's assertion 'that Suarez and Suarez only was taught at St Beuno's in his time'.[5]

[1] Joseph Crehan, *Father Thurston*, p. 22.

[2] Emilio Perini (1835–93), Jesuit priest, born at Chioggia in the province of Venice in Sept. 1835. Educated in the local diocesan secondary school. Entered the S.J. novitiate at Verona in Oct. 1853. Philosophy at Rome, 1857–9, theology at Rome, 1863–6; ordained priest in 1866. Theologian to Cardinal Berardi at Vatican Council I. Forced to leave Rome in 1870 because of the uprising. Came to England, first to Roehampton, 1871–2, and later to St. Beuno's, 1872–86, where he taught Scripture and Hebrew, with GMH among his students. Returned to Italy in 1886 and did pastoral work in Modena until his death there on 24 Feb. 1893.

[3] G. Bernhard Tepe (1833–1904; *Lexikon für Theologie und Kirche*, Hurter, *Nomenclator Literarius Theologiae Catholicae*), Jesuit priest, born at Linden, Germany, on 17 Oct. 1833. Entered the S.J. novitiate at Friedrichsburg in Apr. 1861; ordained priest at Maria Laach in 1868. Taught dogmatic theology at St. Beuno's College, 1869–71, 1872–1902, GMH being among his students. Returned to Valkenberg and died there on 24 Dec. 1904.

[4] *Father Thurston*, p. 22. In a letter (10 Dec. 1964) Fr. Crehan gave me as his opinion: 'For Suarez I think that Province tradition is pretty clear. We had after all a continuous teaching tradition unbroken by French revolution or suppression of S.J.'

[5] *Sermons and Devotional Writings*, p. 292. On the other hand, I do not agree with

A glimpse of Fr. Morris's lecture style has come down to us:

He read his lectures [in Canon Law] for half an hour in the evening in English. He would not allow us to take notes during them; so you had simply to give yourself up to listen, and a very pleasant half hour it was, an interval of sunshine in a day otherwise neither stormy nor gloomy, but certainly trying, the school-day, namely, of the theologian.[1]

Hopkins's reaction to the theology course first occurs in a letter to Bridges written four months after it had begun: 'I have had no time to read even the English books about Hegel, much less the original . . . The close pressure of my theological studies leaves me time for hardly anything: the course is very hard, it must be said. Nevertheless I have tried to learn a little Welsh . . .'[2] So much for studies. Other activities too were carefully organized.

Generally speaking the week fell into a regular pattern. On Sunday and Tuesday afternoons there was a walk to be taken in companies chosen for you in advance. These were referred to as 'lotteries' since it depended on the luck of the draw who your companions were. Thursday was the weekly recreation day and you were free to go out for the day with sandwiches, but without money. On Sundays a tone and a dominical were preached, and the custom was that the first tone in the academic year was preached by the most junior scholastic measured by length of time in the Society, and the first dominical by the scholastic 'oldest' in the Society; this year the first tone and dominical were delivered on Sunday, 18 October. On Sundays, too, there was a debate. This took place after Benediction and before supper. A typical entry for a Sunday in the Journal kept by the Beadle reads:

Devlin's statement that 'it was almost certainly through Suarez that [Hopkins] came to know Scotus', *Sermons and Devotional Writings*, p. 292. For according to Hopkins himself it was in Aug. 1872, as a second-year philosopher that he noted: 'At this time I had first begun to get hold of the copy of Scotus on the Sentences . . . and was flush with a new stroke of enthusiasm . . . just then when I took in any inscape of the sky or sea I thought of Scotus', *Journals and Papers*, p. 221. Several years later Hopkins wrote to Dixon: 'Suarez is our most famous theologian: he is a man of vast volume of mind, but without originality or brilliancy; he treats everything satisfactorily, but you never remember a phrase of his, the manner is nothing. Molina is the man who *made* our theology: he was a genius and even in his driest dialectic I have remarked a certain fervour like a poet's.' *Correspondence with Dixon*, p. 95.

[1] J. H. Pollen, *The Life and Letters of Father John Morris* (1896), p. 177.
[2] *Letters to Bridges*, pp. 30–1.

Nov. 1874

8. Sunday. As usual: tone: companies: Ben.: Debate: Dominical.

But it is worthwhile pausing on the subject of debates[1] because of what they tell us about the *ethos* of St. Beuno's in general, and the fresh light they throw on Hopkins in particular. The subjects debated ranged over a varied selection of topics, including religion, politics, education, sociology, and ethics. Among motions debated and carried were: 'That Catholics should support the movement for the disestablishment of the Church of England', 'That it is desirable as far as possible to substitute day-schools for boarding-schools', that 'Women should be withheld from voting in elections for Parliament', 'That it is a subject for congratulation that the Queen has assumed the title of Empress of India', 'That the parochial clergy should interest themselves in the establishment of clubs and clubhouses for the use of the Catholic working classes', and that 'The present movement for closing public houses on Sunday does not deserve our support'. On the other hand they rejected these motions: 'That Catholics should as far as possible abstain from controversy on religious subjects', that 'In the present state of the Church a schoolmaster is more profitable to souls than a preacher', that 'Catholic education has suffered from the connection of our Colleges with the London University', and 'That an "Edinburgh Sabbath" is less objectionable than a "Paris Sunday" '.

The debates averaged thirty-two a year and Hopkins spoke on decreasingly few occasions. In his first year he spoke eighteen times, in the second year fourteen times, and in the third only eight. Of the forty debates in which he took part, on twenty occasions he spoke in favour of the motion, and twenty times in opposition. Without wishing to assert that Hopkins invariably debated in accordance with his personal preference, it seems to me that the position he adopted, as shown in the records, strikingly confirms his views on a number of topics known to us from his letters and diaries. A few examples will show this. He spoke in favour of the motion that 'The practice of keeping a diary is exceedingly useful and worthy the adoption of all' (carried), and that 'A theological student should eschew all literature not bearing on his studies' (carried). His

[1] See Appendix 3. St. Beuno's Debating Club.

opposition to the following motions comes as no surprise: 'Painting is a more powerful aid to religion than music' (defeated), 'To the orator matter is more important than manner' (defeated), and 'That the sooner the Welsh language dies out the better' (carried).

Hopkins himself was the proposer of the following motions: 'Eminence in arms is a better object of national ambition than eminence in commerce' (defeated), 'That it is never lawful to tell a real untruth'[1] (carried), and 'That the state does well in compelling parents to educate their children' (defeated).

His support of this last motion chimes in with the enlightened position he adopted in two other debates on the question of education. He spoke in opposition to the view that 'Education of the lowest class of society should not be made compulsory' (defeated), and favoured the notion that 'Under proper arrangements women may claim to be admitted to degrees in literature and science (medicine included)' (defeated). Again, in view of the fact that he was the eldest in his family, his speaking against the opinion that 'Inheritance by primogeniture is preferable to an equal division of property' (carried), surely contains autobiographical overtones. It is clearly Hopkins the humorist who supported the two motions that 'A little knowledge is not a dangerous thing' (defeated), and that 'There is no harm in making April Fools'[2] (carried). Occasionally his position poses a problem. What are we to make of his opposition to the motion 'Men make circumstances and not circumstances men' (carried)?

What of other recreations? Of games and sports there is little mention, no football nor cricket, though in April 1877 we read that lawn tennis was 'inaugurated'. The Beadle's Journal makes reference to fishing, climbing, and skating, and they went swimming certainly at Villa.

In mid-October the Bishop[3] paid St. Beuno's a visit, since his illness had prevented his performing the ordinations.

---

[1] Compare with this the drill sergeant's opinion of Gerard as a schoolboy at Highgate: 'A lie indeed! *He* tell a lie? Why, he would rather die!' Lahey, *G. M. Hopkins*, p. 6.

[2] On 1 Apr. 1873, it will be recalled, Gerard had read a paper entitled 'Thoughts on Mobs' to the Phil. and Lit. Society at St. Mary's Hall. I suggested earlier that the day may have chosen the subject.

[3] James Brown (1812–81; see *DNB*, Boase i, Gillow), first Bishop of Shrewsbury,

Oct. 12. Monday.

Morning as usual. The Right Rev. Dr. Brown of Shrewsbury with his secretary, Rev. Allen, came at 2.30. Freed till supper in consequence, commun^y assembled at front door to receive his Lordship. [TBJ]

The free half-holiday took Hopkins

by the woods on the Rhuallt and the view was so like Ribblesdale from the fells that you might have thought you were there. The sky was iron grey and the valley, full of Welsh charm and graceful sadness, all in grave colours lay like a painted napkin[1]

The Bishop remained for a fortnight in the house and early in his visit secured a day's holiday for the Theologians. Hopkins on this occasion repeated his last walk to Cŵm and Rhuallt:

Oct. 19—I was there again with Purbrick, at the scaffolding which is left as a mark of the survey at the highest point. We climbed on this and looked round: it was a fresh and delightful sight. The day was rainy and a rolling wind; parts of the landscape, as the Orms' Heads, were blotted out by rain. The clouds westwards were a pied piece—sail-coloured brown and milky blue; a dun yellow tent of rays opened upon the skyline far off. Cobalt blue was poured on the hills bounding the valley of the Clwyd and far in the south spread a bluish damp, but all the nearer valley was showered with tapered diamond flakes of fields in purple and brown and green[1]

Hopkins enjoyed the opportunity afforded for walking the surrounding countryside and the next Blandyke found him hill-climbing

up Moel y Parch, from the top of which we had a noble view, but the wind was very sharp. Snowdon and all the range reminded me of the Alps: they look like a stack of rugged white flint, specked and streaked with black, in many places chiselled and channelled. Home by Caerwys wood, where we saw two beautiful swans, as white as they should be, restlessly

born at Wolverhampton on 11 Jan. 1812. Educated at Sedgley Park School, 1820-6, and at St. Mary's College, Oscott, 1826-37. Ordained priest on 18 Feb. 1837. Professor and Prefect of Studies at Oscott, 1837-44. President of Sedgley Park School, 1844-51. Consecrated Bishop of the newly created see of Shrewsbury on 27 June 1851. His diocese comprised Cheshire, Shropshire, and the six counties of North Wales, and therefore included St. Beuno's College, St. Asaph, where he ordained GMH priest on 23 Sept. 1877. Celebrated the silver jubilee of his episcopate in Shrewsbury Cathedral on 27 July 1876, and also at St. Beuno's on 30 July; GMH wrote 'The Silver Jubilee' (*Poems*, no. 29) for the occasion. Died at St. Mary's Grange, near Shrewsbury, on 14 Oct. 1881. (*Further Letters*, p. 140; *Journals and Papers*, p. 259.)

[1] *Journals and Papers*, p. 261.

steering and 'canting' in the water and following us along the shore: one
of them several times, as if for vexation, caught and gnawed at the stone
quay of the sluice close under me[1]

Winter had already begun, as his diary and letters make clear.

Nov. 11—Bitter north wind, hail and sleet. On the hills snow lying and
the mountains covered from head to foot.[2]

All the valley is under snow. It freezes and there has been skating today—
tempered by catastrophes and wettings to the middle—on a lake called
Ilyn Helyg. Hitherto we had floods of rain.[3]

In this same letter Hopkins draws attention to the sustained uneventfulness of life at St. Beuno's, telling his mother that he has
kept his letter 'in case anything should turn up but nothing has'.[4]
Eventually he fills up his letter with a postscript on the state of his
jerseys and the shortcomings of the College's laundry methods:

On coming here they shrank at the wash to that degree that the pain of
wearing one for a day lasted round the chest for two days after. I got pieces
put in but they were still so uncomfortable that I cast them: besides they
were almost worn out. The laundress here, unlike the admirable and
queenlike Miss Holden at Stonyhurst, does not know her trade and I am
afraid some harm will happen to the new jerseys too.[5]

The same static quality of theologate life is reflected in the Beadle's
Journal[6] as the following entries written during Advent show only
too well:

Dec.

11 Friday. As usual. Penances: Expos & Ben [Exposition and Benediction].
Fast-day Dinner 12.

12 Saturday. Schools i.e. (Lectures). Missioners[7] off to work.

13 Sunday. As usual: tone: walk: Ben: Debate: Dominical.

---

[1] *Journals and Papers*, p. 262.   [2] Ibid., pp. 261-2.
[3] *Further Letters*, p. 129.   [4] Ibid., p. 130.   [5] Ibid.
[6] The sparseness of the entries also indicates that many of the day-to-day occurrences
were taken for granted. The Beadle in theology—less punctilious than his counterparts
in the philosophate and novitiate—does not even bother to note the refectory reading.
We are only made aware that reading took place in the refectory when its absence is
noted, or when it is replaced by, say, a dissertation. In fact, a paragraph in Hopkins's
diary (*Journals and Papers*, p. 262, entry for 15 Dec.) tells us more about what was read
than does the Beadle's Journal for the three years Hopkins remained in the College.
[7] The missions were at St. Asaph and Denbigh. Priests went to these places to say
Mass and administer the sacraments. From time to time we also read of some of the
Fathers going to give retreats and missions, or to preach on special occasions.

14 Monday. As usual: penances: missioners returned.

15 Tuesday. As usual: case: Fr Minister goes into retreat.

16 Wednesday. As usual: fast-day, dinner 12.

17 Thursday. Weekly recreation. No companies, 1° because Minister in retreat, 2 because snow on the ground.

18 Friday. As usual: Penances: Exhort: Expos & Ben. Fast Day.

Christmas and the New Year passed without comment by Hopkins. The Beadle's Journal notes for 25 and 31 December respectively:

The Mass was *Gregorian*, & a great success.

Ben & Te Deum 7.30. The Te Deum was a most lamentable performance showing neglect of preparation. After supper an attempt was made to exhibit the Magic Lantern in the recreation-room:—there was a deficiency of light.

At the beginning of February 1875 Hopkins's own Journal ceases. On 4 February he had spent the month's Blandyke in Denbigh with a fellow-scholastic and found it

a taking picturesque town. Seen from here, as Henry Kerr says, it is always beautiful. The limekiln under a quarried cliff on this side of the town is always sending out a white smoke and this, and the greyer smoke of Denbigh, creeping upon the hill, what with sun and wind give fairy effects which are always changing

The day was bright, the sun sparkling through a frostfog which made the distance dim and the stack of Denbigh hill, as we came near, dead mealy grey against the light: the castle ruins, which crown the hill, were punched out in arches and half arches by bright breaks and eyelets of daylight. We went up to the castle but not in: standing before the gateway I had an instress which only the true old work gives from the strong and noble inscape of the pointedarch. We went to eat our lunch to a corner opening by a stone stile upon a wilderness by which you get down to the town, under the outer wall, overgrown with ivy, bramble, and some graceful herb with glossy lush green sprays, something like celery[1]

The final entry in his Journal not only suggests that he is now receiving regular lessons in Welsh, but provides further evidence of his interest in folklore, and goes some way towards substantiating his own assertion of 'warming to all Celts'. At five o'clock one

[1] *Journals and Papers*, pp. 262-3.

morning in the hay-making season, he tells us, his Welsh teacher had seen

three little boys of about four years old wearing little frock coats and odd little caps running and dancing before her, taking hands and going round, then going further, still dancing and always coming together, she said. She would take no notice of them but went on to the house and there told them what she had seen and wondered that children could be out so early. 'Why she has seen the kipper-nappers' her grandmother said to her son . . .[1]

For the remainder of this academic year there are only three of Hopkins's letters to draw upon. The first of these, written in February, begins with a mild reproach to Bridges for not having invited him to Maddox Street, when Gerard was teaching rhetoric at Roehampton—an invitation which he might easily have accepted at the time. Then he continues, as mentioned earlier, by pointing out that pressure of work leaves him no time for reading Hegel (recommended by Bridges), nor for scarcely anything outside the matter of the theology course.[2] He adds by way of explanation:

I do not afflict myself much about my ignorance here, for I could remove it as far as I should much care to do, whenever it became advisable, hereafter, but it was with sorrow I put back Aristotle's Metaphysics in the library some time ago feeling that I could not read them now and so probably should never. After all I can, at all events a little, read Duns Scotus and I care for him more even than Aristotle and more *pace tua* than a dozen Hegels. However this is me, not you. But it explains why I can do nothing more than say how much I like to hear about you and how glad I am you are as you say, nearer the top than the bottom of Hegel's or anybody else's bottomless pit.[3]

The other two letters, both to his mother, concern family affairs, and in the first of these he attempts to dispel, or diminish her fears and prejudices against the Jesuits, which may have been aroused by recent articles in the *Quarterly Review*:

I am glad you have not such an altogether unfavourable opinion of the Society. If those 'very bad things' done by it in its time are historical actions, such as the iniquitous charges of instigating Gunpowder Plot,

[1] *Journals and Papers*, p. 263.
[2] Only a month earlier (17 Jan.), Hopkins in the Sunday night debate had spoken in favour of the motion that 'A theological student should eschew all literature not bearing on his studies.' The motion was carried.   [3] *Letters to Bridges*, p. 31.

murdering Cardinal I forget who in China, or introducing brandy among the Canadian Indians, incredible and well shewn up as such charges are, I cannot undertake to speak to their falsehood out of my own examination, for I have no time for the history of the Society or any other history. But if they are doctrines and moral teaching set your heart at rest about them: I live in the midst of all that and I know or can easily ascertain what we do and have taught.[1]

Then he touches on the weather and his health:

Such a backward spring I cannot remember. Now things begin to look greener and the cuckoo may be heard but our climate on the hillside is a touch Arctic. I have recovered from a cold I caught lately and am well but for daily indigestion, which makes study much harder and our shadowless glaring walks to my eyes very painful.[2]

He concludes with paragraphs on cures at St. Winifred's Well, and an outbreak of religious persecution in Poland.[3]

He begins his next letter written towards the end of April some two months later, by thanking his mother for a mysterious edible present —'like eating death and cremation'[4]—which she had sent him to help to build up his strength. The suggestion is that his health is not all that it might be. He apologizes for the infrequency of his letters home, and at the same time gives an oblique indication of having resumed an interest in musical composition:

I hope to write to Grace but the pressure of the approaching examinations makes me unwilling to do more correspondence than necessary just now. I will then either enclose my *Tantum Ergo* or say why not, but anyhow I hope you shall see it sooner or later.[5]

In the course of this year the Beadle's Journal noted among a miscellany of items, a variety concert, readings from Shakespeare, a gift of champagne from the Rector of Farm Street, a toast for Pius IX's eighty-third birthday, and a library reorganization project in which all the Theologians seemed to have assisted. Fr. Morris, who had been teaching church history, left in May for Louvain to revise his Canon Law so that he could return and profess the subject at

---

[1] *Further Letters*, p. 131.   [2] Ibid., p. 132.
[3] Cf. 'The Russian Persecution of the Polish Church', in *The Tablet*, 6 Mar. 1875, p. 293; 'The Persecution in Poland', ibid., 27 Mar. 1875, pp. 390–2; 'The Persecution in Poland', ibid., 10 Apr. 1875, pp. 469–70.   [4] *Further Letters*, p. 133.
[5] Ibid., pp. 133–4. Cf. 'At the same time my music seemed to come to an end.' *Journals and Papers*, p. 258.

St. Beuno's. During this year Hopkins's name never occurs in the Beadle's Journal apart from a note of his arrival and reception of minor orders. But in July it appears twice, in each case for examination purposes. On 3 July he was examined in moral theology, and on the 27th in dogma; he passed in both.

Villa for Hopkins was cut short this year and for this there is no reason given. The scholastics went to Villa in two batches, the first group composed of twelve *ordinands* and six first-year Theologians was away from 2 to 16 August, Hopkins being among those left behind. It is not clear when the second set left for Barmouth,[1] but the entry for 23 August reads: 'Fr. Rector off to Barmouth *en route* for London, taking with him Mr. Gerard Hopkins to join the villa party.' [TBJ].

Of Hopkins's second year in theology there is little to relate, though that little is momentous for his poetry; there are also four letters for this period—three to his mother, and one to his father. The Province catalogue for this year records after his name 'Beadle of the Moral Theology School'.

Rather surprisingly, Hopkins makes no mention in his letters of the ordinations that September (1875), which would seem to have constituted a record. For that year as it happened

there were Capuchins from the neighbouring Monastery of Pantasaph, making with the Jesuits a total of twenty-five, the largest number of priests, we were told, ordained at one time in Great Britain since the Reformation.[2]

Soon after the newly ordained had departed, rooms were redistributed, but this year no choice was allowed. You took what you were given. Rooms were allocated by the Minister on the Rector's order, no reason being given for this break with tradition.[3]

---

[1] Probably the 16th, for they returned on the 30th, and the custom was, and is, to spend a fortnight away.   [2] Scott, *H. S. Kerr*, pp. 132–3.

[3] The rules were carefully laid down: 'With the approval of the Rector rooms were redistributed by choice subject to the following conditions,

    1. Priests
    2. Seniority in theology
    3. Seniority in the Society
    4. Age

N.B. One *certificated* invalid was privileged in having first choice before the above conditions were published.' [TBJ, entry for 2 Oct. 1874.]

For 3 December, the feast of St. Francis Xavier, the Beadle's
Journal notes: 'Ad lib sermon at dinner by Mr G. Hopkins. *N.B.
Sermon purely Ab Lib.*'[1]

This year (1875) winter began early, and was both hard and pro-
longed. The Beadle noted stormy weather in his Journal for both
the fourth and fifth of November, while the entry for the ninth
reads 'Snow storm from 3 p.m.' The rest of the month was marked
by heavy rain.[2] December began 'very cold and foggy', and soon
weather conditions are reported as 'freezing hard', and on the sixth
'snowing nearly all day', and for the next three days skating was
possible. It was on 6 December that the German emigrant-ship
Deutschland, sailing from Bremen to New York, was wrecked on the
Kentish Knock sand, near Harwich, and Hopkins would have read
the report of the disaster in *The Times*. Now although Hopkins was,
as he claims in the poem,

> Away in the loveable west,
> On a pastoral forehead of Wales,
> I was under a roof here, I was at rest,
> And they the prey of the gales;
> ('The Wreck of the Deutschland', st. 24, ll. 1-4.)

yet it is clear that he was experiencing at first hand[3] something of
the bitter and fierce weather conditions endured by those drowned
in the wreck. Of the many storm references in the poem one must
suffice to illustrate:

> Into the snows she sweeps,
> Hurling the haven behind,

---

[1] The entry for the feast of All Saints, 1 Nov. 1875, states that one of the Fathers
'preached spontaneously' having asked permission to do so [TBJ]. It may have been at
this time that Hopkins translated into both English and Welsh the Latin hymn 'O Deus,
ego amo te', traditionally, though erroneously, attributed to St. Francis Xavier (see
Poems, nos. 170 and 171). I hope to write on this topic at some later date.

[2] *Whitaker's Almanack* for 1877 states (p. 43): 'In this month rain fell during 20 days.
The total fall this month was 3·36 inches; *above* the average of 1860-65 by 0·95 inch.'

[3] This winter grimly persisted well into the New Year as the Beadle's log shows:
'Jan. 6, 1876. Weather very cold; Jan. 7. Snow and E. Wind; Jan. 8. Snow again; Jan. 9.
Hard frost; Jan. 23. Gale at night; Feb. 23. Tremendous gale all day; March 6. Terrible
weather, rain, snow, hail, wind and sunshine; March 19. Heavy snow all day. Since Ash
Wednesday the weather has been most abominable; April 11. Great fall of snow last
night; April 12. Heavy fall of snow; April 17. Cold East wind.' We can see why Hopkins
could write on 24 Apr. 1875: 'Such a backward spring I cannot remember . . . our
climate on the hillside is a touch Arctic.' *Further Letters*, p. 132.

The Deutschland, on Sunday; and so the sky keeps,
   For the infinite air is unkind,
And the sea flint-flake, black-backed in the regular blow,
   Sitting Eastnortheast, in cursed quarter, the wind;
   Wiry and white-fiery and whirlwind-swivellèd snow
Spins to the widow-making unchilding unfathering deeps.
                         ('The Wreck of the Deutschland', st. 13.)

When Hopkins actually composed his poem is not certain, but
writing on Christmas Eve to thank his mother for sending him
cuttings about the wreck, he tells her, 'I am writing something on
this wreck, which may perhaps appear but it depends on how I am
speeded.'[1]

One would like to know why this particular shipwreck should
have given rise to the poem. After all the *Captain* which sank in
September 1870, and which he noted in his diary,[2] involved a far
heavier loss of life. Or coming nearer in time, on 4 November 1875,
only a month before the *Deutschland* was wrecked, the steamship
Pacific, coming from Vancouver, foundered, 150 being drowned.[3]
And, in fact, on the very day the *Deutschland* ran aground there was
a coal-mining disaster at Swaithe Main Colliery at Barnsley in Yorkshire in which 150 lives were lost.[4]

However, Hopkins himself emphasizes the significance the wreck-
ing of the *Deutschland* had for him: 'It made a deep impression on
me, more than any other wreck or accident I ever read of.'[5] And a
few years later he told Bridges, 'what refers to myself in the poem
is all strictly and literally true and did all occur; nothing is added for
poetical padding'.[6] Perhaps, also, it was only now that Hopkins
was ready to write. For writing to Canon Dixon in October 1878 he
explained how he had burnt his early verse and had given up writing
poetry until his superiors should expressly desire him to do so:

so for seven years I wrote nothing but two or three little presentation
pieces which occasion called for. But when in the winter of '75 the
Deutschland was wrecked in the mouth of the Thames and five Franciscan

---

[1] *Further Letters*, p. 135.
[2] 'Sept. 7—The *Captain* floundered', *Journals and Papers*, p. 203. *Whitaker's Almanack*
for 1871 (p. 222) records: 'Her Majesty's turret-ship *Captain* is capsized in a gale in
the Bay of Biscay; 17 persons only escaped out of about 540 officers and men.' See also
Journals and Papers, p. 411, n. 203. 1.
[3] See the *Annual Register*.   [4] Ibid.
[5] *Further Letters*, p. 135.   [6] *Letters to Bridges*, p. 47.

nuns, exiles from Germany by the Falck Laws, aboard of her were drowned I was affected by the account and happening to say so to my rector he said that he wished someone would write a poem on the subject. On this hint I set to work and, though my hand was out at first, produced one. I had long had haunting my ear the echo of a new rhythm which now I realised on paper.[1]

Ripeness, it would seem, is all.

During the Christmas vacation this year the community at St. Beuno's tried a spelling-bee, the parlour-game recently introduced from America.[2] Fr. Morris acted as quiz-master and the Rector promised a prize. The winner this time was Mr. R. F. Clarke,[3] his nearest rival being beaten by accidentally mistaking the word 'ingenious' for 'ingenuous'. The 'hard' words which did for the rest, according to the Beadle's log, were: foolhardiness, hiccough, chrisom cloth, imperturbable, yolk, weevil, mischief, pronunciation, rosery (bed of roses), ate, allegiance,[4] lackadaisical.

They tried the game again two months later on Shrove Tuesday: 29 Feb. 1876.

Villa day. Rise 5.30. Breakfast 8. No visitors here. Entertainment in recreation room at 7. A spelling Bee at Fr. Rector's special request. He spontaneously offered a prize which Mr. G. Hopkins won,[5] ... The hard words were 'epaulet', 'phlegm', 'catarrh', 'cotemporary', 'supererogatory', 'connoiseur' [sic], 'unparalleled', 'lineament', 'sempstress', 'medlar'.[6] [TBJ]

In the same letter in which he tells his mother of his success he goes on to say, 'We now have entertainments on holidays. This was one and glees and songs are very nicely sung, pieces are read from Dickens, George Eliot etc, scenes from Shakspere, speeches, poems and so on.'[7] Earlier in the day on this same Shrove Tuesday, Hopkins had been out walking with a fellow Theologian, their goal to climb Moel Fammau. His personal delight is reflected in his exquisite description:

As we walked along the hills towards it the valley looked more charming

---

[1] *Correspondence with Dixon*, p. 14.
[2] See the *Annual Register* for 1875, p. 111, and for 1876, p. 16.
[3] *Further Letters*, p. 137.
[4] 'I was disgracefully felled by *allegiance*', ibid.
[5] Ibid., p. 136.
[6] Hopkins states the word was 'meddler', see ibid.   [7] Ibid.

and touching than ever: in its way there can hardly be in the world anything to beat the Vale of Clwyd. The day was then threatening and
clouded, the sea and distant hills brimmed with purple, clouds trailing
low, the landscape clear but sober, the valley though so verdant appeared
of a pale blush-colour from the many red sandstone fresh-ploughed
fields. Clarke and I made one of the only two couples that reached Moel
Fammau. When we had come down into the valley the day became very
beautiful. Looking up along a white churchtower I caught a lovely sight—
a flock of seagulls wheeling and sailing high up in the air, sparkles of white
as bright as snowballs in the vivid blue.[1]

In June, on the 12th to be exact, Hopkins was one of the two
defendants in the theological disputation held that term. The thesis
he defended is not stated, but from the title of the dissertations read
at dinner and supper the same day, on 'The faith and sanctity of the
minister of the sacraments', and 'The sacrament of the Eucharist',
respectively, it is clear that Hopkins's subject was drawn from 'De
Sacramentis'. At the disputation he would have expounded his
matter, defended his thesis, and answered objections in Latin
throughout.

In the course of the next month Hopkins began two poems,
'Moonrise'[2] and 'The Woodlark',[3] but did not finish either. The
first of these begins:

I AWOKE in the Midsummer not-to-call night, ¹ in the white and the walk
    of the morning:
The moon, dwindled and thinned to the fringe ¹ of a fingernail held to
    the candle,
Or paring of paradisaïcal fruit, ¹ lovely in waning but lustreless,
Stepped from the stool, drew back from the barrow, ¹ of dark Maenefa
    the mountain . . .

From the evidence provided in these lines, namely, the relation of
the waning moon and the mountain, it is possible with a knowledge
of the local geography to deduce with some degree of certainty the
room that the poet occupied at this time. It has been claimed that

---

[1] *Further Letters*, p. 137.

[2] *Poems*, no. 137, dated 19 June 1876. The phases of the moon this month were:

Full Moon	7th 12.37 a.m.		New Moon	21st 10.17 p.m.
Last Quarter	15th 3.15 a.m.		First Quarter	28th 3.14 p.m.

[3] *Poems*, no. 138, dated 5 July 1876.

only two rooms in St. Beuno's afford such a view, and these are situated in what the Theologians refer to as 'The Mansions'.

His next three poems in English, Welsh, and Latin,[1] were *vers d'occasion*, specially asked for, and written to commemorate the episcopal silver jubilee of the local diocesan bishop. The celebration of this event was one of the year's highlights for St. Beuno's,[2] and probably enjoyed all the more by Theologians and professors alike now that the annual exams. were out of the way. Hopkins offered to copy out the English poem 'The Silver Jubilee' for his father but suggested that he might wait to see it until it was published together with Fr. Morris's sermon since 'it looks nicer in print'.[3] The Bishop having stayed to celebrate the feast of St. Ignatius Loyola among the Jesuits, departed the following day, and the day after this the first half of the community set out for their annual holiday at Barmouth.[4] Hopkins went to Villa with the second batch on 16 August and sometime during the fortnight there rowed up the Mawddach one morning with some fellow scholastics as far as 'The George', took breakfast there, returning to the mouth of the estuary a few hours later on the ebb tide. The inn, though not named, is immortalized in 'Penmaen Pool'.[5] Even a brief acquaintance with Barmouth suffices to confirm the accuracy of Hopkins's observation as shown in the sixth stanza of the poem:

> The Mawddach, how she trips! though throttled
> If floodtide teeming thrills her full,
> And mazy sands all water-wattled
> Waylay her at ebb, past Penmaen Pool.

Villa over, the community returned to St. Beuno's to hear the announcement read out in the refectory that their Rector, Fr. Jones, had been appointed Provincial, and was to go immediately to Mount Street, the main London house, to be formally installed in his office.

---

[1] *Poems*, nos. 29, 172, and 173 respectively.
[2] See A. Thomas, 'G. M. Hopkins and the Silver Jubilee Album', *The Library*, Fifth Series, vol. xx, no. 2 (June 1965), 148–52.
[3] *Further Letters*, p. 140.   [4] Ibid., p. 139.
[5] *Poems*, no. 30. For some account of what the Theologians did at Villa, and photographs of Penmaen Pool, and 'Aber House', Barmouth, where they stayed, see A. Thomas, 'Hopkins, the Jesuits, and Barmouth', *Journal of the Merioneth Historical and Record Society*, vol. iv, pt. iv (1964), 360–4.

The Beadle adds in his Journal, 'Great regret at losing our Rector'. Just over a week later the ex-Provincial, Fr. Gallwey, arrived as acting Rector, though his appointment as Rector was not officially announced until the beginning of November.

Two important results followed Fr. Gallwey's appointment. The first concerned the Theologians in general, the second Hopkins especially.

First, from the entries in the Journals kept by the Beadle and Minister¹ it is evident that the new Rector made it plain to the house at large that the tail was not to wag the dog. This is not to say that his rule was an iron one—he was much too wise for that—but the firmness of control is everywhere apparent. This tightening up of government, however, in the main is sensed rather than stated, but occasionally became explicit as the following extracts show:

28 January 1877.

Rev. Fr. Rector . . . wished all to consult a Professor or Superior . . . on the advisability of reading this or that author or book, then fortified with the sanction of one of the above Revd Fathers to obtain the minister's leave to take the book out of the Library. His reverence drew attention to the rule of silence and of speaking Latin. It was not necessary to obtain leave to visit another provided the business transacted came under 'obiter et perpaucis' [in passing, and in very few words]. Beyond this leave was necessary. [TBJ]

19 February.

F. Rector called all the priests together and said it was his wish that all masses not assigned by rule or by special orders should be applied to discharge the obligations incurred by the house for money received. [St. Beuno's Minister's Journal]

15 September.

F. Rector objects to the scholastics walking in the garden after dark. [TBJ]

With regard to Hopkins himself, while I have no wish to maintain that but for Fr. Gallwey this would not have been Gerard's *annus*

---

¹ I have not been able to trace any Journal kept by the Minister at St. Beuno's prior to 1877. The Journal I did find is headed 'Minister's book commenced Jan. 1877', and this runs until Apr. 1887. It seems to me quite likely that the fact that a log was kept even from Jan. 1877 may well have been due to the insistence of Fr. Gallwey in the matter. This volume is now at Heythrop College, Oxon.

mirabilis in poetry, still the new Rector's general kindliness and approval—a fact proved by the obviously affectionate references of Hopkins himself—probably helped considerably in encouraging Gerard's poetry to develop and flourish.

Others, too, benefited from the Rector's encouragement. Fr. Gallwey's biographer, at this time also reading his theology, quotes the Rector's reputation for being 'ever eager to start fresh experiments',[1] and that he 'noted and encouraged signs of exceptional ability in younger men, and left nothing undone to develop them'.[2] So it comes as no surprise to find that in November a new Essay Society, or Academy, was established to meet fortnightly on Saturday evenings. At these meetings a paper in English or French lasting about half an hour was read followed by questions and discussion.[3]

So far little has been said of the everyday domestic details at St. Beuno's; this paragraph must make good the deficiency. The community of between fifty and sixty included about eight or nine lay brothers and among these were a cook, a carpenter, and a tailor. One of the brothers brewed the beer and in mid-April he was freed to

---

[1] Gavin, *Memoirs of Fr. Gallwey*, pp. 3–4.   [2] Ibid., p. 162.

[3] At the first meeting of the Essay Society on 2 Nov. 1876, a committee was elected to draw up rules, and one of the upper community was invited to be President. The Academy was to meet on alternate Saturdays at 4.45 p.m. (later from 16 Dec. changed to 6.40 p.m.) from November until the end of April. During Hopkins's final year at St. Beuno's the papers read were as follows:

1876
18 Nov.   'The power of the Church to grant indulgences'
 2 Dec.   'Early history of the Vulgate'
16 Dec.   'Ballerini's view on usury'
30 Dec.   'St. Cyprian on the unity of the Church'
1877
27 Jan.   'St Augustine's *City of God*'
10 Feb.   'Jansenism and the Port Royalists'
24 Feb.   'The nebular theory of creation'
10 March   'The theory of a comparative theology'
24 March   'Galat II in reference to the supremacy of St Peter'
14 April   'The claims of primitive man to an earlier age than Adam', or in other words
           a review of some of the arguments of Sir J. Lubbock in his Pre-historic
           Times
21 April   'Evolution'
28 April   'The composition of place in the Spiritual Exercises'
The last paper of this year's session (28 Apr.) was read by GMH. I refer to it later.

undertake a full-time spring-cleaning campaign which involved a large-scale programme of white- and colour-washing. Although he had now ceased brewing, 'it is not quite certain', says the Minister's Journal, 'that there is enough beer to last until October'. The College had its own farm managed by a bailiff but did not grow all the vegetables it needed, and when, for instance, their own supplies of potatoes were exhausted, they had to buy outside. Buying locally often proved expensive since prices in the neighbouring small towns were somewhat inflated. This applied to other foodstuffs too. For example, meat and butter were dear locally, and from time to time the Minister got his supplies sent by rail from Manchester, and even on one occasion from Cork. One entry in the Minister's Journal states that he had ordered a side of beef and a sheep from Manchester: 'The last side of beef cost 7d [a pound] while here we pay 8½d.' Other household matters are scattered throughout the same Journal—a local craftsman from Holywell supplied two dozen Windsor chairs at 3s. 9d. apiece, and gave an allowance of 2s. on the old chairs. The old mattresses were sent to be remade, fetched in a cart from Holywell, and when returned stacked round the kitchen fire to air. One or other of the lay brothers, sometimes alone, sometimes with the Minister, went to Liverpool or Manchester to buy such items as timber, cloth, bedding, and even a new cloth (at the wholesale price of £4. 15s. 0d.) to recover the billiards table. A man is called in to clean the clocks, another from Liverpool who spends a fortnight repairing the organ,[1] and the sweep takes two days to clean the chimneys.

On rare occasions one of the other Jesuit houses sends some rather sumptuous present—a supply of grapes, turkeys, hares, pheasants, venison, and once even champagne. But these items are extraordinary, and generally the second glass of wine on feast days is matter for comment. The house Journal usually makes dull reading, but a single entry can suddenly make one of the rare red-letter days spring to life: 'Our bailiff shot 11 brace of partridge today', 'Vesta (our watch-dog mastiff) sent to show at Rhyl and got 1st prize', and 'Fr Morris left for York with two fan-tails for the Nuns'.

---

[1] For Hopkins's comments on the 'grunting harmonium' which did duty instead of the organ, see *Further Letters*, pp. 127, 134.

A word is called for on the heating of the house since this has obvious bearings on the health of the community. Hopkins, it will be remembered, almost as soon as he arrived at the college, told his father that 'pipes of affliction convey lukewarm water of affliction to some of the rooms others more fortunate have fires'.[1] But fires did not begin until mid-October and ceased in mid-April. Hopkins's opinion of the central-heating system finds confirmation in an entry in the Beadle's Journal: '29 Nov. 1874. As the pipes did not do their duty in the recreation room, fire was allowed to be lighted there. The leave for fires was extended also to the rooms in the new wing, for the same reason.' The new wing mentioned here recurs several times and seems to have been a constant source of trouble. Towards the end of February 1875, the Beadle writes, 'Three of the newly-built rooms facing the court were pronounced not fit to sleep in in consequence of the snow working its way through the roof.' Two years later the Minister's log from which the next three extracts are taken is still telling the same tale:

21 Jan. 1877.
When the west or N.W. wind blows the rooms in Tower Hamlets new and old get very cold.

27 Feb.
Great and well-founded complaint of cold from the dwellers in New Tower Hamlets . . . The boiler supplying the hot water pipes heated as much as possible could not raise the temperature in the eastern rooms of Tower Hamlets (new) above 46° [Fahrenheit]. Had fires lighted in the Provincial's and strangers' rooms at which some scholastics sat. At consultation all were agreed that something should be done to guard against the danger to which students' health is exposed, but what?

A week earlier one of the scholastics had given cause for alarm when he was attacked

by a rush of blood to the head. Dr says this resulted from excessive cold to which occupying a room in [the] western front in the attic story he is necessarily subject. The pipes were as hot as possible but could not

[1] *Further Letters*, p. 124. In the December before Hopkins arrived at St. Beuno's, the debating society had for its subject 'That fires and not hot water pipes should be used to heat a student's room'. The motion was debated for two sessions and was ultimately carried by an overwhelming majority.

contend against the continual currents of cold air rushing in thro chinks in doors, windows, walls and floors.

There is no certain evidence to show that the community as a whole was directly affected by the chronic damp and cold,[1] but the situation can scarcely have bolstered morale. To the question of Hopkins's health I want to turn presently.

Towards the end of February Gerard wrote 'in a freak' the two sonnets 'God's Grandeur' and 'The Starlight Night', and sent early drafts of them to his mother for her birthday.[2]

Hopkins's health must be taken in conjunction with his studies, for it seems likely that these two concerns may have induced his superiors to decide that he ought not to spend a fourth year in theology. This in turn meant that he could not be professed of the four vows since he had not completed the 'Long' course.

For his first two years at St. Beuno's his health seems to have been satisfactory enough, nothing more that we know of than colds and indigestion.[3] As in his years at St. Mary's Hall, his superiors saw to it that he did not fast during Lent more than once a week.[4] But even indigestion, he told his mother in 1875 during his first-year theology, 'makes study much harder',[5] and we have already heard him tell Bridges of the pressure of theological studies and the difficulties of the course. In June of the same year he gives as his excuse for not writing to his sister Grace 'the pressure of the approaching examinations makes me unwilling to do more correspondence than necessary just now'.[6] But it is in the March of his final year in theology (1877) that he sounds as tired and depressed as he was at the end of his philosophy course,[7] and tells his mother:

I am to be examined in moral theology to see whether I am fit to hear confessions. Going over moral theology over and over again and in a

---

[1] Even within a month of Hopkins's departure from St. Beuno's a solution has not been found as the Minister's Journal makes clear: '26 Sept. 1877 . . . builder at work trying to settle rooms in tower hamlets so that draught may be excluded.'

Poems, nos. 31 and 32, dated 23 Feb. 1877 and 24 Feb. 1877, respectively. A facsimile of the two sonnets appears in *Further Letters*, facing p. 144. The weather entries in the Beadle's Journal about this time read as follows: 'Feb. 20 A wild and stormy day; Feb. 22. Walk ad lib owing to rain; Feb. 25. Wet afternoon; Feb. 28. Frost.'

[3] *Further Letters*, pp. 132, 141.   [4] Ibid., pp. 138, 144.
[5] Ibid., p. 132.   [6] Ibid., pp. 133–4.
[7] *Journals and Papers*, p. 236, end of the entry for 16 Aug.

hurry is the most wearisome work and tonight at all events I am so tired I am good for nothing.[1]

Nevertheless, on 3 March he passed his examination 'ad audiendas confessiones',[2] but this brought little relief, if any, for a month later he confides to Bridges, 'I am very very tired, yes "a thousand times and yet a thousand times" and "scarce can go or creep".'[3]

A week later he preached the Sunday evening Dominical[4] which his fellow Theologians found excruciatingly funny. In this sermon he drew a comparison between the Clwyd Valley and the Sea of Galilee, and the novelty combined with his unusual treatment seems to have convulsed his audience:

People laughed at it prodigiously, I saw some of them roll on their chairs with laughter. This made me lose the thread, so that I did not deliver the last two paragraphs right but mixed things up. The last paragraph, in which *Make the men sit down* is often repeated, far from having a good effect, made them roll more than ever[5]

On the Monday following Palm Sunday (25 March), Hopkins went to Caernarvon to stay with Fr. Jones,[6] the priest in charge of

---

[1] *Further Letters*, p. 143.

[2] '3 March 1877, Saturday. Mr G. Hopkins passed his examen "ad audiendas" ' [TBJ], and see *Letters to Bridges*, pp. 32, 40.

[3] Ibid., p. 33.

[4] *Sermons and Devotional Writings*, pp. 225–33.

[5] Ibid., p. 233.

[6] John Hugh Jones (1843–1910; see *Dict. of Welsh Biog.*), secular priest, born at Bala, North Wales, in May 1843. Educated at Bala Grammar School, and also by private tutor. Entered Jesus College, Oxford, in 1862, intending to prepare for Anglican orders, but was received into the R.C. Church by J. H. Newman in Oct. 1865 before completing his course. Some time after, he entered St. Edmund's College, Ware, and later became a student at St. Beuno's College, St. Asaph. For a period in 1871 he was in deacon's orders at Bangor where he preached in Welsh and English; ordained priest in Mar. 1872. His obituary notice in the *Carnarvon and Denbigh Herald* was later to claim: 'When he was ordained, there was not another Catholic priest in Wales could preach in Welsh.' GMH stayed with him at Caernarvon at the end of Mar. 1877 in order to improve his Welsh (*Further Letters*, p. 146). (The Beadle's Journal states: 'March 26. Mr. G. Hopkins went to Carnarvon to improve his "Welsh" under the tuition of the Rev. Mr. Jones.' The Journal shows that he returned on 29 Mar.) Priest in charge of Caernarvon from 1872 for thirty-six years, also helping to found a church and school at Pwllheli. In 1908 appointed as tutor in Welsh to St. Mary's College, Holywell, by Bishop Mostyn. Died there on 15 Dec. 1910. The Catholic church at Caernarvon is now dedicated to St. Helen. From the *Catholic Directory* it would seem that the dedication was changed 1890-1.

SS. Peter and Paul as the Catholic church there was then called. Unfortunately, as he points out, his visit was cut short:

> During the holidays—it was in Holy Week—I went to Carnarvon and should have been there a fortnight but had to return in a few days on account of a misfortune which overtook my host's servant. It was for my Welsh that I went.[1]

One of the remedies not infrequently mentioned in the house Journals, which was prescribed for those rather run down in health or under the weather, was to send them out in the pony and trap in the hope that the drive would do them good. From the Minister's log we learn that on 7 April, Hopkins, together with two others of his community, 'had an out and returned to dinner at 7.30'.

In his next letter Hopkins sounds somewhat hard pressed: 'And now at present I have a sermon to preach for Monday[2] and paper to read on the next Saturday.[3] I have a cold and cough just now, things I seldom have, but they are going away; and I am thinner, I think, than ever I was before now, but hope to be all right with summer.'[4] He might have added, that is if he knew at the time, that he was producing a presentation poem[5] to honour the famous Dominican, Fr. Thomas Burke, who had come to St. Beuno's half-way through April to make a retreat and for a rest.

Hopkins, too, must have been showing signs of fatigue, for the entry in the Beadle's Journal states: 'Mr. G. Hopkins went to Rhyl for the good of his health.'[6] He returned on the 14th. While there, he

---

[1] *Further Letters*, p. 146.

[2] 'April 26. Mr. G. Hopkins preached during dinner' [TBJ].

[3] 'Saturday, April 28th 1877. The last meeting of the Academy for this session was held this evening under the presidency of Fr Rector, Fr Minister being absent. About 16 were present to hear *Mr. G. Hopkins* read a paper on *The Composition of place in the Spiritual Exercises*. The essayist maintained that 1° the composition was always of a real, never of a fictitious place—2° it is not principally intended to keep the mind from wandering or to assist the imagination—3° Its true object is to make the Exercitant present in spirit at the scenes, persons, etc. so that they may really act on him and he on them.' (*Records of Essay Society*.) This is an important piece of information because of the light it throws not only on Hopkins's attitude to the Spiritual Exercises, but also on his religious writings generally, not to mention his view of the role of the imagination. Detailed discussion of its import falls outside the scope of the present work.

[4] *Further Letters*, pp. 145–6.

[5] 'Ad Reverendum Patrem Fratrem Thomam Burke O.P. Collegium S. Beunonis Invisentem', *Poems*, no. 174, dated 'Apr. 23, 1877'.

[6] The Minister's Journal for the same date reads: 'Mr. G. Hopkins went to Rhyl for

wrote 'The Sea and the Skylark'.[1] Sometime during this month one of his most beautiful sonnets, 'Spring', was written:

NOTHING is so beautiful as Spring—
 When weeds, in wheels, shoot long and lovely and lush;
 Thrush's eggs look little low heavens, and thrush
Through the echoing timber does so rinse and wring
The ear, it strikes like lightnings to hear him sing;
 The glassy peartree leaves and blooms, they brush
 The descending blue; that blue is all in a rush
With richness; the racing lambs too have fair their fling.

What is all this juice and all this joy?
 A strain of the earth's sweet being in the beginning
In Eden garden.—Have, get, before it cloy,

 Before it cloud, Christ, lord, and sour with sinning,
Innocent mind and Mayday in girl and boy,
 Most, O maid's child, thy choice and worthy the winning.

Perhaps like 'In the Valley of the Elwy',[2] this was a product of the Whitsun vacation which began on Saturday afternoon 19 May and lasted until the morning of Wednesday 23 May.

On the following Thursday, the weekly recreation day, the Minister's Journal records a pleasant social occasion involving the College's neighbours:

24 May 1877.

The Fransiscan [sic] novices and Novice master from Pantasaph came by appointment to dine. The Master sat at [the] Rector's table[,] the Novices with six of ours interspersed at the central table. On this table there was wine from the beginning. Then after about five minutes Fr Rector gave Deo Gratias and ordered wine for all the tables[.] A recitation in honour of St Francis[3] then took place after this a few songs then our guests were

health.' *Ex officio* the Minister in a Jesuit house is responsible for the health of the community.
  [1] *Poems*, no. 35, dated, 'Rhyl, May 1877'.
  [2] *Poems*, no. 34. This has now been dated 'May 23, 1877'. See Norman H. MacKenzie, 'Gerard and Grace Hopkins', *The Month*, N.S. 33 (June 1965), 348.
  [3] There is nothing to indicate that Hopkins was present on this occasion, nor who was responsible for the 'recitation'. In 'The Wreck of the Deutschland' Hopkins wrote 'Joy fall to thee, father Francis, / Drawn to the Life that died' (st. 23, ll. 1-2). The not too distant Franciscan monastery at Pantasaph, in the cemetery attached to which Jesuits who died at this time at St. Beuno's were buried, must have been well known to Hopkins. Another Catholic poet, Francis Thompson, was later to find solace at Pantasaph Monastery.

shown thro the house and grounds and departed[.] On their arrival water was provided in chapel gallery rooms that they might wash their feet. A trap was provided to take them home at our expense.

This month, momentous in Hopkins's poetry career, closed with the composition of 'The Windhover', considered by many to be his finest and most successful poem:

> I CAUGHT this morning morning's minion, king-
> dom of daylight's dauphin, dapple-dawn-drawn Falcon, in his riding
> Of the rolling level underneath him steady air, and striding
> High there, how he rung upon the rein of a wimpling wing
> In his ecstasy! then off, off forth on swing,
> As a skate's heel sweeps smooth on a bow-bend: the hurl and gliding
> Rebuffed the big wind. My heart in hiding
> Stirred for a bird,—the achieve of, the mastery of the thing!
>
> Brute beauty and valour and act, oh, air, pride, plume, here
> Buckle! AND the fire that breaks from thee then, a billion
> Times told lovelier, more dangerous, O my chevalier!
>
> No wonder of it: shéer plód makes plough down sillion
> Shine, and blue-bleak embers, ah my dear,
> Fall, gall themselves, and gash gold-vermilion.

This was the poem that Hopkins himself regarded as 'the best thing I ever wrote'.[1]

Hopkins's name occurs three times in the house journal entries for June:

27 June. Mr. G. Hopkins to Rhyl and back. [TBJ]

30 June. Mr. G. Hopkins to Rhyl and back. [TBJ]

On 28 June, the Minister's Journal relates that Hopkins with Fr· Minister and two others started in a trap for Pant y Coed:

At Dodd's [the] shaft suddenly smashed but happily they all escaped unhurt[;] the new horse Bob bought a fortnight ago was in the shafts. Dr. Turnour[2] called.

---

[1] *Letters to Bridges*, p. 85.

[2] Arthur Edward Turnour (1819–94), physician and surgeon. M.D. Edinburgh 1840; M.R.C.S. Eng. 1840. Justice of the Peace for county and borough of Denbigh; senior surgeon Denbighshire infirmary; a leading churchman in diocese of St. Asaph; former Mayor of Denbigh; died on 7 Aug. 1894 at 'Grove House', Denbigh, funeral sermon preached by the Bishop of St. Asaph; buried in family vault at Whitchurch.

On 24 July, having completed three years in theology, Hopkins sat his final examination at St. Beuno's. Was he put out at not being allowed to go on with his companions of the Long course to do a fourth year? If he was, he kept it to himself. Certainly he may have been disappointed if his earlier expectations are anything to judge by. At the end of his philosophy course he had written that after a period of teaching he was to go to theology 'which is a four year's [sic] business'.[1] And even as late as the January of his final year in the theologate he informs Baillie, 'I hope to be ordained priest next September and after that shall be here, I suppose, for another twelvemonth.'[2] It may be that some time after this date and before the middle of June when the list of theses to be defended at the examination was given out, that Hopkins was told that this year was to be his last at St. Beuno's, but it is possible that he was not informed until after his examination. A possible hypothesis is this. Hopkins was showing signs of strain resulting from a combination of deteriorating health and the mental fatigue of studies of a sort (including study methods) not wholly congenial to him. He may have been told, or decided, to relax more, and hence produced the poems we have seen, and indulged in literary criticism. I am not suggesting that he threw his cap over the windmill, for it was not in his nature to do so. Literary criticism was not to be allowed to usurp the place of studies, as he made plain to Bridges in the June of this year:

Having both work here to do and serious letters to write I shrank from the 'distressing subject' of rhythm, on which I knew I must enter. I could not even promise to write often or answer promptly, our correspondence lying upon unprofessional matter.[3]

Nor do I suggest that he had no interest in theology. On the contrary, in referring to his preparation for his last examination in moral theology, he tells Baillie:

You see moral theology covers the whole of life and to know it it is best

1 *Further Letters*, p. 122. Similarly, he told Edward Bond, 'I am to begin my theology and the course lasts four years', ibid., p. 58. And shortly after entering the theologate he told Bridges that he was studying theology 'for four years from last September', *Letters to Bridges*, p. 30.
2 *Further Letters*, p. 242.
3 *Letters to Bridges*, p. 41.

to begin by knowing everything, as medicine, law, history, banking. But law is what I should most like to know.[1]

But the real extent of his theological interest can be seen in his sermons and other devotional writings. A further indication of sustained interest in theology, but also possibly evidence of disappointment at the implied deficiency in himself, is to be found in a letter of the following year in which he tells Bridges, 'I . . . employ myself in making up my theology'.[2] On the question of Hopkins's personal expectations I find myself in disagreement with that able Hopkins scholar, the late Fr. Christopher Devlin, who claimed that Hopkins 'was wounded three times in his expectation of a full and useful life: first as a scholar, secondly as a preacher, and thirdly as a writer'.[3] The assertion is made but the evidence is lacking. On the contrary, I agree with Professor Gardner's view that 'he betrayed no real anxiety about becoming an academic scholar or a popular preacher'.[4] Of Hopkins's hopes as a writer I have written elsewhere.[5]

But in addition to the dubious state of his health his *penchant* for the opinions of Duns Scotus may have served to bar him from a fourth year of study.[6] Fr. Lahey, Hopkins's first biographer, states that his

avocation for Scotism eventually became a passion with him . . . so that he was often embroiled in minor duels of intellect. However, he completed a successful course of theology at St. Beuno's and left there with the reputation of being one of the best moral theologians among his contemporaries.[7]

Again, one would like to see the evidence for the several points

[1] *Further Letters*, p. 241. I recognize that this might also be taken as a further indication of dilettantism.

[2] *Letters to Bridges*, p. 55.

[3] *Sermons and Devotional Writings*, Introduction, p. xiii.

[4] 'Anvil-Ding and Tongue that Told', *The Month*, N.S. 25 (Feb. 1961), 83.

[5] 'Gerard Manley Hopkins—"Doomed to succeed by failure" ', *Dublin Review*, ccxl (Summer 1966), 161–75.

[6] Yet Newman writing of the Society of Jesus in 1858 had observed: 'It is plain that the body is not over-jealous about its theological traditions, or it certainly would not suffer Suarez to controvert with Molina, Viva with Vasquez, Passaglia with Petavius, and Faure with Suarez, de Lugo, and Valentia. In this intellectual freedom its members justly glory.' From 'The Mission of St. Benedict', in *Historical Sketches*, ii, new impression (1899), 369.

[7] *G. M. Hopkins*, p. 132.

asserted. Certainly Hopkins is still reading Scotus during his theology and cares for him, he tells Bridges, 'more even than Aristotle, and more *pace tua* than a dozen Hegels'.[1] His adoption of Scotist views may well have led to a clash of opinion with his examiners, and since he was examined orally any differences between him and his teachers would, as a result, have been more likely magnified than diminished. This opinion is confirmed by those who knew him in Ireland:

as a theologian his undoubted brilliance was dimmed by a somewhat obstinate love of Scotist doctrine, in which he traced the influence of Platonist philosophy. His idiosyncrasy got him into difficulties with his Jesuit preceptors who followed Aquinas and Aristotle. The strain of controversy added to bad health had marred his earlier years . . .[2]

Even after theology Scotus remained for Hopkins 'the greatest of the divines and doctors of the Church'.[3]

Seen in the context outlined, it is perhaps possible to perceive in what was Hopkins's last reference to Scotus a rueful autobiographical hint:

And so I used to feel of Duns Scotus when I used to read him with delight: he saw too far, he knew too much; his subtlety overshot his interests; a kind of feud arose between genius and talent, and the ruck of talent in the Schools finding itself, as his age passed by, less and less able to understand him, voted that there was nothing important to understand . . .[4]

But whatever transpired at his final examination, Hopkins was allowed to set off the following day, 25 July,[5] to spend the best part

[1] *Letters to Bridges*, p. 31.
[2] *A Page of Irish History: Story of University College, Dublin, 1883-1909*, compiled by Fathers of the Society of Jesus (Dublin and Cork, 1930), p. 105. And see a later testament: 'Hopkins was mercilessly chaffed for his Englishness by his colleague, Père Mallac, a French lawyer and freethinker who became Catholic and Jesuit and belonged to the philosophy faculty in the College. These were the days of Anglo-French tension, even before Fashoda, but I imagine that behind the chaffing, more than politics, there lay the eternal feud between Platonist and Aristotelian. Hopkins leaned towards Plato and Duns Scotus, but the black-avised Mallac stood fiercely for the Stagyrite.' C. P. Curran, 'Memories of University College, Dublin: the Jesuit Tenure, 1883-1908', in *Struggle with Fortune: A Miscellany for the centenary of the Catholic University of Ireland 1854-1954*, ed. Michael Tierney (Dublin [1954]), p. 224.
[3] *Sermons and Devotional Writings*, p. 45.
[4] *Further Letters*, p. 349.
[5] *Letters to Bridges*, p. 41. Date also confirmed by Journals of the Minister and the Beadle.

of three weeks with his family. During this time he took the opportunity of calling on Bridges at Bedford Square, dining with him, and
even staying the night.[1] His return to Wales on 13 August, which he
was now soon to leave, was tinged by a mixture of joy and sadness:
'No sooner were we among the Welsh hills than I saw the hawks
flying and other pleasant sights soon to be seen no more.'[2] This
year he had not been to Barmouth, but was back at St. Beuno's to
welcome on their return those who had been to Villa.[3]

The time which remained until the beginning of the retreat prior
to ordination passed comparatively uneventfully—the Rector went
to Ireland, three American seminarians 'dropped in to spend a
few days', and Vesta got his first at Rhyl dog show. The month's
Blandyke fell on the 28th and in the evening there was an extempore
concert after dinner in the open air, probably on the Coffee Walk.

Three poems remain to be mentioned from this period since all
were written at St. Beuno's—'Hurrahing in Harvest', 'The Lantern
out of Doors', and 'The Caged Skylark'.[4] Of the first of these, dated
1 September 1877, Hopkins tells us it 'was the outcome of half an
hour of extreme enthusiasm as I walked home alone one day from
fishing in the Elwy'.[5] Perhaps a word is called for on fishing at St.
Beuno's. First, there are several entries in the Minister's Journal
recording the Minister's attempts, sometimes successful, sometimes
not, to get the local landowners to give permission to fish their
waters. The Beadle's Journal shows that a number of Theologians
were keen anglers. On one occasion the enthusiasts, or 'Dufferhood'
as they are referred to, were out by half-past six in the morning for a
day's sport, and as early in the year as mid-February. Their haul?

19 April 1876.
The fishermen . . . returned for supper with 8¾ lbs of fish.

21 April . . . returned 7.30 p.m. with 8¼ lb of trout.

25 Sept. Fishermen took several good fish, one a four-and-a-quarter
pounder.

[1] *Letters to Bridges*, pp. 42, 43.
[2] *Further Letters*, p. 146, and cf. 'Much against my inclination I shall have to leave
Wales', *Letters to Bridges*, p. 43.
[3] *Further Letters*, p. 147.
[4] *Poems*, nos. 38, 40, and 39 respectively.   [5] *Letters to Bridges*, p. 56.

It is with a sense of temerity that I recount the appalling fishing-story connected with Hopkins which circulates in the English Province, but honesty demands no less. The story goes that the Beuno's fishermen on their return from a day's sport asked each other what they had caught. Back came the stock answers: 'Nothing', 'A two pounder', 'A twelve incher', and so on. Some one turned to Hopkins and asked, 'And what did you catch?' The poet replied, 'I caught this morning morning's minion, kingdom of daylight's dauphin . . .'!

About the other two sonnets mentioned above I have nothing to add.[1]

Eventually, the great day arrived for which Hopkins had now been preparing and waiting nine years. It was preceded by a retreat which began on 15 September. In accordance with the special privilege enjoyed by the Society of Jesus, Hopkins received the major orders of subdeacon, deacon, and priesthood, on successive days, namely, 21, 22, and 23 September. The entry in the Minister's Journal for the last of these three dates reads:

Sunday. Ordinandi sleep until eight[.] Breakfast (meat for all) by special order of the Rector, 7.30. Ordinations 10 (over at 12.5) all those yesterday made deacons . . . were today made priests . . . Three were appointed to conduct people to their seats[,] keep order, &c in the Chapel[,] three to lead them from hall door to Chapel. Lunch laid out in refectory[;] five tables placed crosswise gave fifty places[;] sweets[,] fruit & flowers placed on tables. Six of Schol [scholastics] served. Roast Mutton, Soup, ham & fowls was the lunch provided together with tongues, peas, French beans, &c. After the lunch the guests strolled about the grounds and the community took a meat lunch. Then there was an impromptu concert in the recreation room. . . . After that Solemn Te Deum and Benediction. Then the guests nearly all departed. . . . After dinner according to tradition . . . the senior ordinatus proposed the Bishop's health. He that of the Rector. He that of the ordinati. . . . After this music in the recreation room.[2]

---

[1] Professor Norman MacKenzie has written: 'The autograph of *The Lantern out of Doors* bears only the year, "1877", but it seems to me to belong to the autumn, when evening fogs obscured the Welsh valleys. Moreover, its mood corresponds closely with the sense of impending loss, amounting almost to bereavement, against which Hopkins had to contend that autumn, after learning that he would not be able to spend a fourth year with his friends at St. Beuno's.' 'Gerard and Grace Hopkins', *The Month*, N.S. 33 (June 1965), 348.

[2] I found it necessary to punctuate this paragraph throughout. The Beadle's Journal for the same date supplies the information: 'Great concourse of visitors . . . The weather was threatening.'

Along with Hopkins fifteen others were raised to the priesthood by Bishop James Brown. Scarcely any of the guests are named, and in any case they seem relatively few to the sixteen new priests. None of Hopkins's relatives is mentioned as being present.

Within the same week there was another celebration—Fr. Gallwey's silver jubilee of his ordination. Surely the occasion, you would think, for a presentation piece by Hopkins, but there is no record of one. Before September was out the preparations for the new academic year were under way—rooms changed, books given out, new choirmaster chosen, and so on. But this would scarcely concern Gerard, not only because he had finished his course, but because he had been sick in bed[1] from 29 September. The Minister's Journal records: 'Dr. Turnour [came] with Denbigh house surgeon and performed successfully on Mr. G. Hopkins circumcision.'[2] Dr. Turnour was at the College on 4 October, and the entry in the Minister's Journal for the 8th reads: 'Dr. Turnour visited Fr. Hopkins.' Hopkins was allowed up the next day and tells his mother 'in a few days' time I shall be completely recovered'.[3] In the same letter, he informs her of his appointment to Mount St. Mary's College, Spinkhill, near Sheffield, having but recently heard the news himself.[4] He had some inkling of what to expect and what his new job required:

The work is nondescript—examining, teaching, probably with occasional mission work and preaching or giving retreats attached: I shall know more when I am there. The number of scholars is about 150, the community moderately small and family-like, the country round not very interesting but at a little distance is fine country, Sheffield is the nearest great town.[5]

On the morning of 19 October, he left at nine-thirty for Mount St. Mary's.

[1] On Tuesday, 9 Oct., Hopkins wrote to his mother, 'Since Saturday week [29 Sept.] I have been sick in bed.' *Further Letters*, p. 148.
[2] The relevant corresponding entry in the Beadle's Journal reads: 'Oct. 19, Friday. F. G. Hopkins left at 9.30 for the Mount. (He had for some time previous been confined to his bed in consequence of an operation skilfully performed by Dr. Tourner [*sic*]).'
[3] *Further Letters*, p. 148.
[4] Hopkins had written on 15 Aug.: 'I have heard no appointments yet.' Ibid., p. 147.
[5] Ibid., p. 148.

CHAPTER 6

The Tertianship 1881–1882

DURING his first four years as a priest Hopkins was given a variety of appointments—bursar at Mount St. Mary's, select preacher at Farm Street, London, supply work for a short time at (Bedford) Leigh in Lancashire, and on the parish at St. Francis Xavier's, Liverpool, and St. Joseph's, Glasgow. From this last address he wrote to Canon Dixon in mid September 1881:

> I came here on the 10th of last month, to supply for a fortnight or so, but my stay has been prolonged and now I think will last almost till the time, Oct. 10th, when I am due ... to begin my 'tertianship' or the third year of noviceship we make before taking our last vows.[1]

Hopkins arrived at Roehampton on Saturday, the 8th, and had the week-end to get himself settled in. He and his newly arrived fellow tertians were welcomed with porter, and on Sunday there was a 'postea' with the upper community. Monday, the feast of St. Francis Borgia, third General of the Society, marked the official opening of the tertianship and was celebrated as a double-table day, as well as by a cold-meat breakfast. Three days later the Beadle of the novices is writing, 'The Tertian fathers came to outdoor works today', and notes that one of them read aloud at dinner and supper,[2] while another served at table. The tertianship had begun.

The tertian's day-to-day duties are explained by Fr. Clarke:

> He has to sweep and dust the rooms and corridors, to chop wood, to wash plates and dishes, besides going over again the spiritual work of the novice, the long retreat of thirty days included. He has also during this year to study the institute of the Society, and during Lent to take part in some one of the public missions which are given by the various religious orders in the large towns and centres of population. This final year sometimes follows immediately on his theology, sometimes after an interval of

---

[1] *Correspondence with Dixon*, p. 52, and cf. *Letters to Bridges*, pp. 134–5.
[2] See Appendix 2D, Refectory reading in the Tertianship, 1881–2.

a year or two, during which he is employed in one of the colleges or missions of the Society. When it is over he is generally well on in the thirties . . .[1]

The actual rules for the tertians were these:

1. One of their number to be appointed bidell.
2. They are to have a fixed order of the day, including lesson by heart, manual works, study of the Institute, spiritual reading and evening meditation.
3. On one day in the week one will read in the Refectory, or serve in the Refectory or kitchen.
4. They will tell their faults in the Refectory once a week, asking their penances of the Minister.
5. They will have a conference on the Institute twice a week, and once a week on some spiritual subject, the bidell presiding.
6. They will not read newspapers, periodicals, etc., nor any books but spiritual books during the Tertianship.
7. They are not to go out of the grounds alone without leave.
8. They may speak to the Fathers of the house and to the old laybrothers, but not to the Juniors or Novices, nor to visitors out of recreation time. No one can go to London, or pay a visit, without permission. Tertian fathers have not faculties [for confession] for one another, nor for other fathers: but all non-tertian fathers have faculties for Tertians.

Hopkins's first letter (to Dixon) from the tertianship shows him buckling down to the life: 'We see no newspapers nor read any but spiritual books. In Lent we go out to give retreats and so on; beyond that *in eremo sumus*.'[2] In his reply the Canon, understandably enough, showed that he did not entirely appreciate the purpose of Gerard's third year of probation, and wrote more wistfully than obtusely: 'So you are entering on your last year of novitiate. I suppose you are determined to go on with it: but it must be a severe trial—I will say no more.'[3] This misapprehension on the Canon's part had the fortunate effect of drawing from Hopkins a valuable explanation both of the purpose of the tertianship generally and his personal attitude to his vocation and religious life:

I see you do not understand my position in the Society. This Tertianship

---

[1] 'Training of a Jesuit', p. 224. J. H. Pollen adds that the tertianship is 'intended to help the young priest to renew his spirit of piety and to learn how to utilize to the best of his ability all the learning and experience he has acquired', *Cath. Encycl.* xiv. 84.

[2] *Correspondence with Dixon*, p. 69.   [3] Ibid., p. 70.

or Third Year of Probation or second Noviceship, for it is variously called in the Institute, is not really a noviceship at all in the sense of a time during which a candidate or probationer makes trial of our life and is free to withdraw. At the end of the noviceship proper we take vows which are perpetually binding and renew them every six months (not *for* every six months but for life) till we are professed or take the final degree we are to hold, of which in the Society there are several. It is in preparation for these last vows that we make the tertianship; which is called a *schola affectus* and is meant to enable us to recover that fervour which may have cooled through application to study and contact with the world. Its exercises are however nearly the same as those of the first noviceship. As for myself, I have not only made my vows publicly some two and twenty times but I make them to myself every day, so that I should be black with perjury if I drew back now. And beyond that I can say with St. Peter: To whom shall I go? *Tu verba vitae aeternae habes.* Besides all which, my mind is here more at peace than it has ever been and I would gladly live all my life, if it were so to be, in as great or a greater seclusion from the world and be busied only with God. But in the midst of outward occupations not only the mind is drawn away from God, which may be at the call of duty and be God's will, but unhappily the will too is entangled, worldly interests freshen, and worldly ambitions revive. The man who in the world is as dead to the world as if he were buried in the cloister is already a saint. But this is our ideal.[1]

And later Hopkins told Dixon, 'my vocation puts before me a standard so high that a higher can be found nowhere else'.[2]

The difference in opinion on vocation, or rather of emphasis, between the two priests, reveals itself in the difference in attitude of each towards his poetry, and the Canon had the honesty and humility to admit that his friend was fired on religious grounds by higher motives than himself. He generously conceded to his former pupil at Highgate:

you have a vocation in comparison of which poetry & the fame that might assuredly be yours is nothing. I could say much, for my heart bleeds: but I ought also to feel the same: and do not as I ought, though I thought myself very indifferent as to fame.[3]

But on the question of Hopkins's view of fame—a point of the highest importance to an understanding of the motivation of this

[1] Ibid., pp. 75–6.
[2] Ibid., p. 88.
[3] Ibid., pp. 89–90.

priest-poet—I have written elsewhere.[1] In brief, for Hopkins literary interests had to take second place, even give way entirely, when they clashed with religious duties or seemed to hinder his religious life and ideals.

We have seen already that during his final year in theology, Hopkins had turned to literary criticism in his letters to Bridges. On his appointment to the staff at Stonyhurst, on his own initiative, he had got in touch with Dixon, his former teacher, and between the two there began a detailed discussion of their poetry and literary theories. Dixon expressed his gratitude to Hopkins without stint: '. . . as to your criticisms. I cannot enough thank you for them. They are entirely invaluable & I hope to profit by them.'[2] Hopkins had already pointed out that he must let literary matters drop for 'they are quite out of keeping with my present duties', adding with a touch of graciousness and affection, 'I am very glad my criticisms should be of any service to you: they have involved a labour of love.'[3] The cost of this sacrifice to him must have been considerable, much as any of us might feel at giving up something we know we do well. For Hopkins, despite his diffident disclaimer of being unable to speak with critical authority in literature,[4] was passing judgements as notable for their insight as their trenchancy, and which later critics have willingly endorsed. A few examples written at this time will serve as illustration.

For myself I have been accustomed to think, as many critics do, that Dickens had no true command of pathos, that in his there is something mawkish; but perhaps I have not read the best passages.[5]

He tells Dixon that he finds Kingsley's style, and also, on occasion, Browning's, 'a frigid bluster', adding:

A true humanity of spirit, neither mawkish on the one hand nor

---

[1] 'Gerard Manley Hopkins—"Doomed to succeed by failure" ', *Dublin Review*, ccxl (Summer 1966), 161–75.

[2] *Correspondence with Dixon*, p. 90.

[3] Ibid., p. 87. Some weeks earlier he had written to Bridges: '. . . at Roehampton, I am pretty well resolved, I will altogether give over composition for the ten months, that I may *vacare Deo* as in my noviceship proper.' *Letters to Bridges*, p. 135.

[4] 'I feel ashamed however to talk of English or any literature, of which I was always very ignorant and which I have ceased to read.' *Correspondence with Dixon*, p. 87.

[5] Ibid., p. 73.

blustering on the other, is the most precious of all qualities in style, and this I prize in your poems, as I do in Bridges'. After all it is the breadth of his human nature that we admire in Shakespeare.[1]

In the same letter he complained that he had been unable to finish the *Ring and the Book* because of its moral coarseness, but goes on to say:

So far as I read I was greatly struck with the skill in which he displayed the facts from different points of view: this is masterly, and to do it through three volumes more shews a great body of genius,

and adds in a shrewd foray of comparative criticism:

I remember a good case of 'the impotent collection of particulars' of which you speak in the description of the market place at Florence where he found the book of the trial: it is a pointless photograph of still life, such as I remember in Balzac, minute upholstery description; only that in Balzac, who besides is writing prose, all tells and is given with a reserve and simplicity of style which Browning has not got. Indeed I hold with the oldfashioned criticism that Browning is not really a poet, that he has all the gifts but the one needful and the pearls without the string; rather one should say raw nuggets and rough diamonds. I suppose him to resemble Ben Jonson, only that Ben Jonson has more real poetry.[2]

He agrees with Dixon about Carlyle's 'incapacity of general truths', adding, 'I always thought him morally an impostor, worst of all impostors a false prophet. And his style has imposture or pretence in it. But I find it difficult to think there is imposture in his genius itself.'[3]

Nor did Hopkins's criticism stop short of the most recent contemporary work—always the most acid of tests. He could be perfectly clear-sighted and impartial in evaluating the work of his friends. Writing to Bridges of Dixon's 'Ode on Conflicting Claims' he asserts that of the manuscript pieces this was

the best of all . . . at least the execution is nearly perfect and on a level with the thought and feeling, in which he is always a master and never makes a false note. This poem is one of extreme excellence. But he is unequal and the unequality lies in execution, chiefly in his diction, which varies from rich to meagre. He has not a sure hand like Tennyson and will let fall a weak stanza: this is against his success. His command of pathos is exquisite and he excels in all tragic feeling, and that with an extreme purity, a

[1] Ibid., p. 74.   [2] Ibid., pp. 74–5.   [3] Ibid.

directness of human nature, and absence of affectation which is most rare.
... His other great excellence is pure imagination, ... I hope he will push
on with the epic or romance you saw, for he will be more telling in a long
than in short pieces, as is natural in one who is rich in matter and imperfect in form. I see no reason why he should not write the finest narrative
poem of this age: he will never acquire Tennyson's workmanship and
infallibly telling freedom of stroke, which is indeed half of art, but he
much excels him in other gifts.[1]

However, to resume to the tertianship. The community at Manresa, numbering about a hundred, was the largest Hopkins had yet
been in since joining the Society. To be more accurate there were
at Manresa five carefully segregated communities living under the
same roof, each following its own ordo and set of rules, though com-
bining on certain occasions. These five communities were: (1) the
upper community consisting of seven Fathers headed by the Rector,
Fr. John Morris, who was also novice master, (2) nine tertians and
the tertian master, Fr. Whitty, (3) twenty-four Juniors, (4) eleven
lay brothers, and (5) fifty novices.

Fr. Morris's government according to his biographer

reflected the qualities of the man—vigour, decision, and largeness of mind.
In his idea, a Rector should make himself felt, otherwise he was unfaithful
to his duty, he was put into his office in order to give a unity and personality to the administration, and his powers were granted to him in order
to be used, he was meant not only to reign but to govern. Further, as he
always had very definite views on the points which presented themselves
to his mind, disliking vagueness and uncertainty in any form, he always
knew his own mind and made it up quickly, and he followed definite lines
in his government, so that it was possible to foretell how he would act
under given circumstances.

If he had anything to complain of, he told the person in question without
delay, so that the matter might be settled at once. This directness and
high-mindedness gave a sense of security to those who worked under him.
They felt that they could not lightly forfeit his esteem, while he endeared
himself to them by his generosity and unselfishness.[2]

Looking back, his novices claimed that

his chief characteristics were his precision and exactness (or, as it is called,
'logicality') of mind, and a wonderfully warm heart. He was logical in

---

[1] *Letters to Bridges*, p. 139.
[2] J. H. Pollen, *The Life and Letters of Father John Morris* (1896), pp. 238–9.

carrying out the principles by which he guided himself, and logical almost to a fault in the manner in which he taught them to others. He was precise in seeing that all rules, whether they regarded the ceremonies of the Church or the customs of the community, were carried out to the letter. But the depth and warmth of his affection formed his most remarkable gift. Personal love of our Lord amounted in him almost to a passion. His generosity . . . was most striking. The influence he exercised was due far more to his character than to any speech or action that can be described on paper.[1]

Hopkins told his mother, 'Fr. Morris's novices bear his impress and are staid: we used to roar with laughter if anything happened, his never do.'[2]

The major event of the tertianship is the Long Retreat and this began on Monday 7 November, and was given by the tertian instructor, Fr. Whitty. The order followed much the same pattern as that gone through in the noviceship, but with certain modifications better suited to the more mature spiritual and physical development of the exercitants. For example, some of the meditations were made at midnight.[3]

Hopkins kept fairly full notes of this retreat.[4] I choose one instance which seems especially relevant to Hopkins's own choice of remaining unrecognized. It is too long to be given in full, but the extract is sufficient to indicate something of Fr. Whitty's approach.

The Hidden Life

The Life of Christ Our Lord from the Twelfth to the Thirtieth Year

'De vita'—Nov. 19 1881 (Long Retreat)—Fr. Whitty gave last night the following pregnant thoughts: (1) *Erat subditus illis*: the hidden life at Nazareth is the great help to faith for us who must live more or less an obscure, constrained, and unsuccessful life. What of all possible ways of spending 30 years could have seemed so ineffective as this? What might

---

[1] Ibid., pp. 236–7.   [2] *Further Letters*, p. 161.

[3] Fr. Morris, who did his own tertianship in Tronchiennes, Belgium, in 1876, wrote: 'We have got through the long retreat with very little fatigue. I found the midnight meditations (of which we had sixteen) not at all tiring, and they did not unfit one for the meditations of the day, as I rather expected. Of course I felt tired from time to time, but the day's repose when it came freshened one up again for a new beginning. We had three such repose days.' Pollen, *The Life and Letters of Father John Morris*, p. 180.

[4] Dated notes from this Long Retreat will be found in *Sermons and Devotional Writings*, pp. 135, 161, 176, 177, 179, 180, 181, 183, 184, 187, 191, 195, 200 ff., 205.

not Christ have done at Rome or Athens, Antioch or Alexandria! And
sacrificing, as he did, all to obedience his very obedience was unknown.
Repulsiveness of the place: a traveller told him, who had been twice to
Nazareth, that even now it keeps its fame for rudeness and worthlessness.
But the pleasingness of Christ's life there in God's eyes is recorded in the
words spoken when he had just left it: 'This is my beloved Son' etc.[1]

Here is part of the note which Hopkins made on an ailment common
enough in the religious life of the layman no less than the cleric—
tepidity—a sort of spiritual inertia:

> Spiritual tepidity then is not the being between hot and cold, for in that
> state every soul must be that has neither perfect charity nor mortal sin,
> taking these terms or limits to be what the metaphor means by heat, that
> is / the boiling point of heat, and by cold or the freezing point: but it is
> the passage downwards only from hotter to colder, it is to be cooling or to
> have cooled. And since the water must always be getting hotter, never
> cooler, while the pot is on the fire, it is implied, to keep up the figure, that
> the pot has been taken off, that is to say / that the soul is no longer acted
> on by grace but is left to nature. And this is what Father Whitty says is the
> meaning of tepidity.[2]

Someone who also did his tertianship under Fr. Whitty, afterwards
came to look upon the notes which he had taken at the time as

> a mine of valuable spirituality and suggestive thoughts on the Exercises.
> One consideration was masterly above all, and will, I am sure, be still
> remembered by my fellow Tertians. It was on the subject of tepidity. Like
> all that he said, it was consoling even when severe, and the exceeding
> kindness of his heart appeared in all his exhortations and points of medita-
> tion.[3]

Hopkins, too, was singularly impressed by the tertian master's
simple wisdom and holiness and still recalled his words two years
later:

> I remembered Fr Whitty's teaching how a great part of life to the
> holiest of men consists in the well performance, the performance, one may
> say, of ordinary duties[4]

The repose days which separated the 'weeks' of the Exercises fell on
16 and 24 November, and 1 December. Hopkins used the first of

---

[1] *Sermons and Devotional Writings*, p. 176.
[2] Ibid., pp. 207–8.
[3] 'Father Robert Whitty', *LLNN*, xxiii (Jan. 1896), 352.
[4] *Sermons and Devotional Writings*, p. 253.

these to fit in a second visit to the dentist in London.[1] Over all three repose days he spread the writing of a long letter to Dixon,[2] towards the end of which he allowed himself to wander into an illuminating appraisal of nineteenth-century poets which reveals a gift for analysis and classification.

This modern medieval school [Morris, Rossetti, Burne-Jones, and GMH would include Dixon] is descended from the Romantic school (Romantic is a bad word) of Keats, Leigh Hunt, Hood, indeed of Scott early in the century. That was one school; another was that of the Lake poets and also of Shelley and Landor; the third was the sentimental school, of Byron, Moore, Mrs Hemans, and Haynes Bailey. Schools are very difficult to class: the best guide, I think, are keepings. Keats' school chooses medieval keepings, not pure nor drawn from the middle ages direct but as brought down through that Elizabethan tradition of Shakspere and his contemporaries which died out in such men as Herbert and Herrick. They were also great realists and observers of nature. The Lake poets and all that school represent, as it seems to me, the mean or standard of English style and diction, which culminated in Milton but was never very continuous or vigorously transmitted, and in fact none of these men unless perhaps Landor were great masters of style, though their diction is generally pure, lucid, and unarchaic. They were faithful but not rich observers of nature. Their keepings are their weak point, a sort of colourless classical keepings: when Wordsworth wants to describe a city or a cloudscape which reminds him of a city it is some ordinary rhetorical stage-effect of domes, palaces, and temples. Byron's school had a deep feeling but the most untrustworthy and barbarous eye, for nature; a diction markedly modern; and their keepings any gaud or a lot of Oriental rubbish. I suppose Crabbe to have been in form a descendant of the school of Pope with a strong and modern realistic eye; Rogers something between Pope's school and that of Wordsworth and Landor; and Campbell between this last and Byron's, with a good deal of Popery too, and a perfect master of style. Now since this time Tennyson and his school seem to me to have struck a mean or compromise between Keats and the medievalists on the one hand and Wordsworth and the Lake School on the other (Tennyson has some jarring notes of Byron in *Lady Clare Vere de*

---

[1] Information from Manresa Minister's Journal. Hopkins visited the dentist five times during his tertianship on the following dates: 5 and 16 Nov., and in 1882 on 16 and 19 Jan., and 25 July. He wrote to Bridges in Feb. 1882, 'I am, as you must remember, like a novice, have been to town only to see the dentist, and could not hope to visit you.' *Letters to Bridges*, p. 141.

[2] 'It [Dixon's letter] reached me on the first break or day of repose in our month's retreat; I began answering it on the second, but could not finish; and this [1 Dec.] is the third and last of them.' *Correspondence with Dixon*, pp. 92–3.

Vere, Locksley Hall and elsewhere). The Lake School expires in Keble and Faber and Cardinal Newman. The Brownings may be reckoned to the Romantics. Swinburne is a strange phenomenon: his poetry seems a powerful effort at establishing a new standard of poetical diction, of the rhetoric of poetry; but to waive every other objection it is essentially archaic, biblical a good deal, and so on: now that is a thing that can never last; a perfect style must be of its age. In virtue of this archaism and on other grounds he must rank with the medievalists.[1]

The retreat was now nearing its close, and a week later, on the feast of the Immaculate Conception, the Minister's Journal records: 'Thurs. 8. The Tertian Fathers finished their Long Retreat this morning.[2] They had wine with the other Fathers after dinner. 2 glasses of claret in the Refectory.' The day ended with solemn Benediction. The following Sunday's entry reads: 'Fr. G. Hopkins said the late Mass'; this would have been the eleven o'clock Mass at St. Joseph's.

Christmas was fast approaching, and every day from the 17th until Christmas Eve the entry 'decorations' appearsi n the Journal kept by the Novices' Beadle, and we find Hopkins writing, 'Things have a general topsy-turvy cheerful air, Christmas is being hung everywhere.'[3] On the 20th, his brother Lionel called and stayed to dinner,[4] and Gerard wrote afterwards:

We had a pleasant afternoon together, somewhat clouded however by the inordinate and inexpressible smoking of the chimney of the guest-room. But after he had gone I had a worse misfortune in my own room, where the gale blew the soot all over the place and made things miserable. This only happens when the wind is in that one quarter.[5]

In the same letter he says that he has heard after many years' silence from Henry William Challis, one of his old Oxford friends.

---

[1] *Correspondence with Dixon*, pp. 98–9. I have not quoted what Hopkins wrote on the sonnet and its history (ibid., pp. 85 f.) in October of this year, since his literary criticism is not my primary concern. Nevertheless, I agree with Professor Abbott that Hopkins's remarks are of peculiar importance in view of his own practice.

[2] See also ibid., p. 96.

[3] *Further Letters*, p. 160. The novices would have decorated St. Joseph's church as well as Manresa. Later in the same letter Hopkins tells his mother that he had modernized a recently discovered Middle English hymn and provided the footnotes, presumably at the request of superiors. It appeared in *The Month* for Jan. 1882. See *Further Letters*, pp. 161, 444–5.

[4] Information from Manresa Minister's Journal.

[5] *Further Letters*, p. 160.

Hopkins spent Christmas at Manresa and in all probability went to the concerts put on by the Juniors and novices, and was present when that year's Innocent Porter was chosen. The Minister saw to it that the feast was fittingly kept up in the refectory, and the community seemed to have fared well:

Dec. 25.
Dinner at 1. Bacon and eggs for first dish. 3 glasses of wine (one during dinner) with dessert, apples, oranges & biscuits. Pousse & coffee for Fathers who were joined by the Tertians. [MMJ]

And for the feast of the Holy Innocents (28 December) we read:

Dinner at 3 fowls, turkey, ham, jellies, blancmange. There was fusion of Fathers of the house & strangers with the others. The Tertians came to Fathers' room for coffee. Seance at 5.30.

Not all the Tertians remained in the house for the holiday however. 'Our little community of "Tertians" [Hopkins writes] is much diminished: some have been called off altogether and others have been despatched for Christmas duty here and there.'[1] Hopkins himself, according to the Minister's Journal, went to supply at Brentford[2] on New Year's Eve, but seems to have been expecting to leave earlier since he told Bridges on 18 December: 'I do not expect to be much longer here.'[3] And writing to his mother on New Year's Day he says:

. . . I am hourly expecting orders to return to Liverpool. One of our Fathers, who was for the best part of two years my yokemate on that laborious mission, died there yesterday night after a short sickness, in harness and in his prime. I am saddened by this death, for he was particularly good to me; he used to come up to me and say 'Gerard, you are a good soul' and that I was a comfort to him in his troubles. His place must now be supplied and it must be by one of two, both in this house; I feel little doubt it will be by me and that this is probably the last night I shall spend at Roehampton.[4]

But he was wrong and no replacement was sent to Liverpool from Manresa.

---

[1] Ibid.
[2] St. John the Evangelist, Boston Park Road, Middlesex. Hopkins, it will be recalled, had helped to open a catechism centre there when a novice. See also *Journals and Papers*, p. 197.
[3] *Letters to Bridges*, p. 140.
[4] *Further Letters*, p. 162.

After the holiday the house resumed its customary uneventful routine, and only occasionally from the iceberg-tip glimpses of the Minister's log can we sense anything of the life beneath:

1882

Jan. 4	Pig brought from Beaumont for the farm. Evans brought back the Magic Lantern.
Jan. 6	St. Joseph's school treat—Magic Lantern, Xmas tree, &c. from 4 to 7 p.m. Benediction at 7 sung by the children.
Feb. 7	Agreement signed by Kate Giddings to undertake our washing & mending from March 1. Notice given to Mrs. Nesbit to leave by that day.
March 1	Evans to London for ironing stove.
March 3	Evans fetched washing machine fr. London.
March 6	Began washing again at the laundry.
May 19	Evans to London to sell fruit.
July 13	Work on roof finished at last. Has been much impeded by wet for last ten days. First broad beans from garden today.

Spiritual activities call for little comment here. Since this was the noviceship, the practices and devotions would be the same as those we saw earlier. Vows were renewed on 15 January and 29 June. Hopkins would have eaten his dinner and supper listening to Juniors preaching 'dominicals', and novices delivering themselves of May and 'Vow' sermons, amongst them the Modernist, George Tyrrell, then a second-year novice.

Fr. Christopher Devlin has already pointed out that

the bulk of Hopkins's spiritual writing was done during his year of tertian-ship, especially during the Long Retreat of November–December 1881. There are earlier entries and there are important later entries; but the creative year was 1881–2. All his ideas stem from the making of the Spiritual Exercises; he has several valuable comments on the text of the Exercises; and it seems that parts of his work were meant as raw material for a treatise on the Exercises.[1]

Later Devlin claims:

During his year of tertianship . . . Hopkins had been flooded with light on religious subjects which boded well for his poetry. In several of his letters to Bridges of the following year there are impromptu explanations of Catholic mysteries, both beautiful and profound. He was standing at a focal point from which he could see the origin and progress of many

[1] *Sermons and Devotional Writings*, p. 107.

possible creations. He had, in fact, at least five works in mind: three in prose and two in verse. In prose there were: his commentary on the Exercises already begun;[1] a treatise on the idea of sacrifice in ancient religions; and a work on Greek Lyric Art which would have included a revolutionary principle of criticism, 'the undercurrent of thought governing the use of images'. In verse there were his 'great ode' on Edmund Campion, and the drama of St Winefred; the inspiration of both of these, which went back to autumn of the previous year, had received fresh impetus from his insight into 'the great sacrifice'.[2]

What is stated here is true, but it also needs stressing that Hopkins's spiritual writing had a wider application than his personal creative progress whether literary or religious. The training he was receiving was directed to prepare him for an active ministry and Hopkins recognized this as his letter to Bridges at the beginning of February shows:

I have no time for more than business-like letter writing. At the beginning of Lent I am to take duty at Preston . . . and from the Fourth Sunday in Lent (March 19) to Palm Sunday (April 2) I am to help in mission-services to be given at Maryport on the coast of Cumberland (not so far from Carlisle), I am now therefore closely employed preparing discourses and instructions.[3]

The Minister's Journal shows that he left Manresa on 20 February, and presumably he went straight to Preston. But some change in arrangements ensued for he began his mission a week earlier than he had told Bridges he would. This is made clear from the old church notice-book still kept at the Benedictine church of Our Lady and St. Patrick in Maryport.[4] This contains an announcement given out on the second Sunday of Lent (5 March), to the effect that on

[1] Devlin seems not to have known of the paper 'The Composition of place in the Spiritual Exercises' which Hopkins read to the Essay Society at St. Beuno's in Apr. 1877.

[2] *Sermons and Devotional Writings*, p. 213.

[3] *Letters to Bridges*, pp. 140–1.

[4] 'The mission was commenced in 1838, and the church built 1844–5 at a cost of £1,400. The number of Catholics then was about 300. . . . On Sunday, February 4, 1882, the church was reopened after having undergone an enlargement of some 15 ft. in order to accommodate the increased congregation that had arisen owing to the commencement of the new docks. Fr. J. J. Cummins, O.S.B., the incumbent, acted as architect. . . . In 1889, the Catholic population of Maryport was 1,700.' Kelly, *Historical Notes on English Catholic Missions*, p. 274. I am grateful to Fr. E. R. Croft, O.S.B., the present parish priest (1966), for making the transcript from the notice-book.

the following Sunday, 12 March 1882, the feast of St. Gregory the Great, Apostle of England, 'A mission begins at 10.0 a.m. Frs White[1] and Hopkins S.J. will conduct it.' Then follow details of the times of the Mission services. Admission to all services was free except on Sundays, but a collection was made each evening. It was pointed out that the expenses of the Mission were not light and so it was hoped the congregation would be generous. The entry for the day of the opening of the mission reads:

Sun.: 12th March 1882—3rd Sun. of Lent;—
A notice. Mission begins at 10 o'clock, Sermon, etc. & Mass sung by
    Fr. Hopkins, S.J.

Subsequent entries read:

Sun: 19th March 1882—4th Sun. of Lent:
10 a.m. Sung Mass—Sermon by Fr. Hopkins, S.J.

Sun: 26th March 1882.
Sung Mass. Sermon by Fr. Hopkins, S.J.
Mission closed in the evening.

The local paper commented:

During the past fortnight mission services have been conducted at Our Lady and St. Patrick's Church, Maryport, by the Revs. Fathers Hopkins and Waterton [*sic*], and have been largely attended. On Sunday evening last the inauguration of the 'Children of Mary' took place. The candidates wearing white veils, occupied seats in the lady chapel. The Rev. Father Hopkins preached an appropriate and eloquent sermon. The choir having been strengthened by some professional singers, the Benediction service was exceedingly well sung, especially the 'Tantum Ergo.' Upwards of 750 persons were present at the service. [*The Maryport Advertiser and Weekly News*, 24 March 1882.]

The notice in the *Tablet* helps to fill in the details:

A very successful mission has been preached . . . during the last fortnight by the *Revv. Fathers White* and *Hopkins, S.J.* The services have

---

[1] Alfred White (1829–87), Jesuit priest, born in Dublin on 1 June 1829. Educated at Stonyhurst College. Entered the S.J. novitiate at Hodder in Sept. 1848. Taught in Malta for four years and also at Manchester. Ordained priest in 1859. Worked on the parish at Wakefield from 1864 for twenty-three years. Preached a mission with GMH at Maryport, Cumberland, in spring 1882 (*Letters to Bridges*, pp. 140, 143; *Correspondence with Dixon*, pp. 101, 103). R.C. chaplain to Wakefield Prison from 1882. Died on 22 Dec. 1887.

been very well attended and more than 900 Easter Communions were
made. On the Feast of St. Joseph between forty and fifty aspirants were
consecrated Children of Mary by F. Cummins, O.S.B.; and on Monday
last the Bishop of the diocese administered Confirmation to 200 persons,
amon[g]st whom were some recent converts. [*Tablet*, 1 April 1882.]

Hopkins for his part seems to have thrown himself into the work and
let himself go, for shortly after it ended, writing to Bridges, he
explains that the mission in which he had taken part was

something like a Revival without the hysteria and the heresy, and it had
the effect of bringing me out and making me speak very plainly and
strongly (I enjoyed that, for I dearly like calling a spade a spade): it was
the first thing of the sort I had been employed in.[1]

Hopkins's assignment at Maryport provided him with the opportunity of meeting Dixon, and thereby compensating for his disappointment of the previous year.[2] The two poets met at Carlisle
for a few hours in the afternoon, and after Dixon had given him
dinner and shown him round the cathedral, Hopkins went on to
St. Wilfrid's, Preston. The encounter, as sometimes happens to those
who correspond intimately but without meeting, proved an embar-
rassment and found Dixon tongue-tied. Hopkins, writing to him a few
days later, lays bare a shared personal trait:

I wish our meeting cd. have been longer for several reasons, but to
name one, I fancied you were shy and that time would have been needed
for this to wear off. I think that for myself I have very little shyness left in
me, but I cannot communicate my own feeling to another.[3]

[1] *Letters to Bridges*, p. 143. The last quarter of the nineteenth century saw intensive
revivalist campaigns in this country, notably under the two American evangelists,
Moody and Sankey—a subject debated, as mentioned earlier, when Hopkins was in the
theologate. Again, from its reorganization in 1878, the spiritual operations of the
Salvation Army had expanded rapidly. Fr. Steuart, S.J., in one of his letters described
an incident which took place not far from St. Beuno's during the sweeping Welsh
evangelical revival of 1904–6 under Evans Roberts: 'The Welsh revival is all around us.
Last Sunday five people were baptised in the River Elwy at St. Asaph. Unfortunately I
didn't know of it in time, or I should certainly have gone to see it, as many of our
people did. The "catechumens" were led into the river by the Minister, dressed in their
best clothes, and plunged right under by him. At any rate it shows that there's some faith
left in the people yet.' Kendall, *Father Steuart*, p. 70.

[2] See *Correspondence with Dixon*, p. 65.

[3] Ibid., p. 104. Next day GMH wrote to Bridges: 'Partly through this sightseeing and
more through shyness on his part (not on mine) we did not get much intimate or even
interesting talk. I was amused when his hat blew off in English Street to watch his
behaviour. I wish I could have been with him longer.' *Letters to Bridges*, pp. 143–4.

Face to face, communication was impossible to them both. Dixon in his reply admitted:

I dare say I seemed 'shy': I have an unfortunate manner: & am constantly told that I am too quiet: I have often tried to overcome it: but the effort is always apparent to those with whom I am, & never succeeds. You must therefore forgive it: it is not from want of feeling or affection.[1]

Hopkins was kept at St. Wilfrid's hearing Lenten confessions,[2] and returned to Manresa on 5 April. But no sooner was he back than he was told to go on supply at St. Elizabeth's at Richmond in Surrey, where the parish priest had been taken ill. Hopkins remained there from Maundy Thursday until Easter Monday,[3] and may therefore have carried out for the first time the greater part of the Holy Week liturgy on his own.

The rest of April passed quietly but not entirely uneventfully. Fr. Provincial's day was kept on the 20th, and the Minister carefully noted: 'Meat at breakfast. 83 at first table. Fowls & Curry, Beef & Mutton, Asparagus, Jellies, Blancmange, Coffee & Pousse for Fathers and Tertians in recreation room. Seance at 5.30.' And two days later he records for official purposes the numbers in the house:

Scholastic Nov.	34	Laybrothers	9
Laybrother Nov.	10	Tertians	9
Juniors	26	Fathers of the house	7
			95

Next day, a Sunday, his Journal notes:

The Bishop of Leeds[4] said the Community Mass. Fr. G. Hopkins said the 11 o'clock Mass [at St. Joseph's] . . . Bishop of Leeds dined in the refectory.

In the middle of the ensuing week, Hopkins broke new ground as far as his personal ministry was concerned, by giving a retreat lasting eight days to Mr. Plant, an elderly gentleman[5] who came to

[1] *Correspondence with Dixon*, p. 104.   [2] *Letters to Bridges*, p. 143.
[3] Information from Manresa Minister's Journal.
[4] Robert Cornthwaite (1818–90). See W. Maziere Brady, *Annals of the Catholic Hierarchy in England and Scotland*, A.D. *1585–1876*, iii (Rome, 1877), 398; *Tablet*, 21 and 28 June 1890, pp. 986, 1024.
[5] Information from the Manresa Minister's Journal. I have been unable to find out anything further about Mr. Plant. Hopkins replying to Bridges on the subject of Turkish

Manresa as a private retreatant. When this was over Hopkins took
the opportunity to reply to Baillie who had written when he was
away preaching his Lenten mission. His answer ranges over a
variety of topics—a comparison of the rival squalor of Liverpool
and Glasgow, T. H. Green, the philosopher, whom he discusses with
a touch of patronage but also with pity, the previous century's wide
knowledge of antiquity, a point on which he is in agreement with
Baillie, and some details of a few of their common acquaintances.
Hopkins ends this letter on what sounds like a note of envy: 'Ah!
you will have heard the Nibelungs' Ring.[1] You must tell me your
impressions.'[2] Wagner's genius in joining text and music together,
in the light of Hopkins's own attempts and achievements in com-
bining matter and manner—both in poetry and music—is sufficient
to account for his special interest.

The middle of May saw Hopkins writing to Bridges to arrange a
day convenient to them both, so that Bridges might see Manresa's
grounds to advantage. In the same letter, as also in the next, Hopkins again shows intense absorption in natural surroundings:

... the great gale of the 30th [April] felled three of our trees and blighted
the foliage in a way I never saw before.[3] The lime tops are almost bare: the
young leaves being withered have been falling in the East winds of late
and on the ground look like tealeaves after boiling dried.

But we have a remarkable show of buttercups. I suppose you would not
see the like in Italy.[4]

June 5 ... I have been studying the cuckoo's song. I find it to vary much.

baths wrote: '. . . by the by too many Turkish baths are not good. An old gentleman
(commercial) that I gave a retreat to here nearly died in one.' *Letters to Bridges*, p. 147,
letter dated 7 June 1882.
    [1] The *Annual Register* for 1882 in the section 'Art, Drama, and Music' states: 'One
of the leading features of the year has been the striking advance of German, and
especially of German dramatic music . . . two great schemes for the production of German Opera were launched during the season. The one which had for its specific object
to introduce to an English audience Wagner's great Trilogy, "The Niebelung's Ring,"
. . . opened its career at Her Majesty's on May 5.'
    [2] *Further Letters*, p. 250.
    [3] Cf. 'A very remarkable and serious gale visited London and the southern counties of
England, blowing with great force, and for some hours bringing the thermometer below
freezing point. The damage done to the foliage of the chestnuts and limes was irrepar-
able, and in the London parks and gardens the number of trees of all descriptions which
were uprooted was greater than in any gale of previous years.' *Annual Register, 1882*,
p. 19.
    [4] *Letters to Bridges*, p. 144.

In the first place cuckoos do not always sing (or the same cuckoo does not always sing) at the same pitch or in the same key . . .[1]

Bridges came to Manresa on the feast of the Ascension (18th) and brought with him a young nephew whose presence Hopkins suggests had a dampening effect on their conversation. However, writing later, Hopkins begins politely enough:

My heart warmed towards that little Bertie Molesworth (I do not mean by this that he is so very small), so that if you were to bring him again I shd. be glad to see him. (But I am afraid he felt dull. He is shy I dare say.) However I expect he is no longer with you. It cannot be denied nevertheless that the presence of a third person is a restraint upon confidential talk.[2]

In the course of his visit to Manresa, Bridges having toured the grounds and seen the laden greenhouses wanted to purchase some of the fruit. But Hopkins prevented his doing so and wrote later: 'Davis the gardener was discontented that I would not let you buy his peaches: he wd. have let you have them on reasonable terms, he said.'[3] A friendly altercation must have resulted, for Hopkins writing from Stonyhurst in September rallied Bridges: 'you could not make me wretched now by either stealing or buying fruit'.[4] Bridges was to recall the incident half a century later:

> And so,
> when the young poet my companion in study
> and friend of my heart refused a peach at my hands,
> he being then a housecarl in Loyola's menie,
> 'twas that he fear'd the savor of it, and when he waived
> his scruple to my banter, 'twas to avoid offence.[5]

Nor was this the only occasion on which Bridges overrode his friend's conscience. Hopkins, as we saw, had made it clear that poetry was to be put aside during the time of tertianship, and although Bridges had sent him the manuscript of *Prometheus the Firegiver*, he reaffirmed his decision: 'About the book I will not write.'[6] Bridges in

---

[1] *Letters to Bridges*, pp. 145–6.   [2] Ibid., p. 145.   [3] Ibid.   [4] Ibid., p. 152.

[5] *The Testament of Beauty*, Book IV, *Ethick*, ll. 433–8. But the quotation should be read in the light of its context, ll. 406–58.

[6] *Letters to Bridges*, p. 146. In February GMH had told Dixon that Bridges's account of *Mano* made him 'eager to see it', adding however, 'but that cannot be yet'. *Correspondence with Dixon*, p. 103.

his reply seems to have suggested that his refusal to comment sprang from his low opinion of the piece,[1] wringing from Hopkins the retort, 'You might surely have guessed that I had some reason for my silence. It was not want of admiration.'[2] And at the end of the letter he praises *Prometheus* generously: 'how beautiful and masterly it is, what a sense of style . . . how vigorous the thought . . . how Greek, . . . and yet so fresh'. Nevertheless, he was reluctant to be forced in the matter.

Bridges's self-acknowledged indelicacy in failing to respect Gerard's feelings seems to have clouded their friendship and appears to even greater disadvantage in his reluctance or inability to understand the Society of Jesus and all that it stood for in Hopkins's life. When Hopkins has to mention the Society to him he treads so warily that he might be walking on eggshells or quicksands: '. . . the right to secrecy in correspondence which, as you know, we Jesuits surrender . . . the sentence would be tedious to finish'.[3] Hopkins's unwillingness to pursue the issue recalls his remark to Bridges some years earlier, 'You say you don't like Jesuits. Did you ever see one?'[4]

But Hopkins was led to protest more strongly after Bridges had attended the Corpus Christi procession. Gerard had tried to dissuade him from attending since duties would prevent his giving his full attention to his friend. It is possible that Bridges may not have received the letter in time. The spectacle he witnessed is related in the novice Porter's diary:

3.30 Procession started from sacristy to the sanctuary cross-bearer leading the way followed by twelve novices. Choir of Juniors & Novices 22 all in cottas. 4 Juniors in copes & 4 in dalmatics & six priests in chasubles. D. & S.D. [Deacon and Subdeacon] in dalmatics. Father Whitty in cope. All vestments white. 4 Juniors carrying canopy.

After the O Salutaris procession started from sanctuary thro door nearest the chapel along the walk under the cedars singing the Pange Lingua and the litany of Our Lady & passed without stopping through the door near the shoeplace singing the Lauda Sion and then into St George's Hall where the B. St was elevated and the 'Adoro te devote' was sung kneeling. Benediction was then given after the Tantum Ergo and the

---

[1] This is only one of many occasions when one regrets Bridges's having destroyed his side of the correspondence.
[2] *Letters to Bridges*, p. 146.   [3] Ibid., p. 141.
[4] Ibid., p. 40.

Procession left for the Chapel singing the Lauda Sion where the Tantum
Ergo was again sung and Benediction given. The visitors etc. occupying
the back benches in the chapel.

Hopkins commented to Bridges:

I wish our procession, since you were to see it, had been better: I find
it is agreed it was heavy and dead. Now a Corpus Christi procession shd.
be stately indeed, but it shd. be brisk and joyous. But I grieve more, I am
vexed, that you had not a book to follow the words sung: the Office is by
St. Thomas and contains all his hymns, I think. These hymns, though they
have the imperfect rhetoric and weakness in idiom of all medieval Latin
verse (except, say, the Dies Irae: I do not mean weakness in classical
idiom—that does not matter—but want of feeling for or command of *any*
idiom), are nevertheless remarkable works of genius and would have
given meaning to the whole, even to the music, much more to the rite.
It is long since such things had any significance for you.[1]

The strain in which Hopkins continues scarcely conceals the extent
of his wounded feelings:

But what is strange and unpleasant is that you sometimes speak as if they
had in reality none for me and you were only waiting with a certain dis-
gust till I should be disgusted with myself enough to throw off the mask.
You said something of the sort walking on the Cowley Road when we were
last at Oxford together—in '79 it must have been. Yet I can hardly think
you do not think I am in earnest. And let me say, to take no higher
ground, that without earnestness there is nothing sound or beautiful in
character and that a cynical vein much indulged coarsens everything in us.
Not that you do overindulge this vein in other matters: why then does it
bulk out in that diseased and varicose way in this?

The significance of the festival for Hopkins is explained in his
next letter.

Corpus Xti differs from all other feasts in this, that its reason and occasion
is present. The first Christmas Day, the first Palm Sunday, Holy Thursday 'in Caena Domini', Easter, Whitsunday, and so on were to those who
took part in them festivities *de praesenti*, but now, to us, they are anniver-
saries and commemorations only. But Corpus Christi is the feast of the
Real Presence; therefore it is the most purely joyous of solemnities.
Naturally the Blessed Sacrament is carried in procession at it, as you saw.
But the procession has more meaning and mystery than this: it represents
the process of the Incarnation and the world's redemption. As Christ went
forth from the bosom of the Father as the Lamb of God and eucharistic

[1] *Letters to Bridges*, p. 148.

victim to die upon the altar of the cross for the world's ransom; then rising returned leading the procession of the flock redeemed / so in this ceremony his body *in statu victimali* is carried to the Altar of Repose as it is called and back to the tabernacle at the high altar, which will represent the bosom of the godhead. The procession out may represent the co-operation of the angels, or of the patriarchs and prophets, the return the Church Catholic from Christ's death to the end of time. If these things are mismanaged, as they mostly are, it is not for want of significance in the ceremony.[1]

In spite of such important differences their friendship survived.

The letters of this period also help to fill in more details of Hopkins's priestly work at this time, and additional confirmation is supplied by the Minister's Journal:

Sat. 27 May
F. G. Hopkins to Brentford[2] to hear Confessions.

Sat. 17 June
Fr G. Hopkins to Westminster[3] to supply for the Sunday haymaking.

On 16 July, the Journal shows that he was operating on home ground again, and the local congregation at St. Joseph's heard him sing the eleven o'clock Mass. From the same source we learn that on 22 July he spent the day at Hampstead, presumably with his family, 'returning at 10.15 p.m.'

By now Hopkins was already in the last month of his tertianship. Unfortunately, we have no letter of his for August to point to what he was feeling or doing, but there are a few earlier indications. Despite the novice-like way of life—'one day is pretty much as another'[4]—he seems to have been happy enough at Manresa, at least to judge from scattered comments. Early on in the tertianship he had told Dixon, 'In this retirement the mind becomes both fresh and keen',[5] and commending the beauty of Manresa's surroundings to Bridges, he wrote, 'This spot . . . is still beautiful. It is besides a

---

[1] Ibid., p. 149.

[2] St. John's, see *Letters to Bridges*, p. 148. The entry in the Minister's Journal for 11 June reads: 'Fr. G. Hopkins said the 11 o'clock Mass . . . went to Brentford.'

[3] St. Mary's, see p. 55, n. 3. Hopkins returned to Manresa on 19 June. He was there again 1–3 July. On 16 June he told Bridges, 'Do not come on Sunday, for I shall be away taking duty at Westminster.' *Letters to Bridges*, p. 149.

[4] *Further Letters*, p. 249.

[5] *Correspondence with Dixon*, p. 69.

great rest to be here and I am in a very contented frame of mind.'[1]
Again, half-way through the year he told him, 'I find the life trying—
weakening, I mean. But the calm of mind is delightful: I am afraid
I shall leave it behind.'[2]

What Hopkins means by 'weakening' is not clear, for on the whole
he appears to have enjoyed good health throughout this year and his
one important reference to the subject is perhaps even more significant for the glimpse it gives us of horseplay among the tertians.
They are, after all, human.

You remember my consulting you [he writes to Bridges] about a fall
in which I broke a ligament of my right arm: you told me it might not
heal for eighteen months. I felt it at all events for twelve and even now I
am not sure that if I were to throw my arm far enough and hard enough
back I might not feel it still; only, as Abernethy said, 'why the devil should
I do *so*?' Now the other day I did what I had no business to do; I tried
my strength with another man by clasping my hands, cross-fingered, with
his and each thrusting forward. Now I had the best of him if only he had
played fair, but he brought my left arm down, which is not allowed, and
twisted it so hard that something is wrong at the wrist and within these
three days, weeks after the event, it has become more painful. This is
when I bend it forward, hunch, or κυρτῶ (is the Greek for it) the wrist.
Now is this too, do you think, a broken ligament? and will it take a year
and more to mend? and will it at last be as strong as before? But I should
say that at the time, unlike my fall down stairs, there was no pain but that
of straining, no feeling of a snap.[3]

The wrong must have righted itself for we hear no more about it.

With the beginning of the retreat, before the taking of final vows,
the end of the tertianship was truly in sight. The retreat began under
Fr. Whitty, but he was taken ill and the Rector took over.[4] Hopkins
employed his time to good purpose:

I did in my last week at Roehampton write 16 pages of a rough draft
of a commentary on St. Ignatius' Spiritual Exercises. This work would
interest none but a Jesuit, but to me it is interesting enough and, as you
see, it is very professional.[5]

[1] *Letters to Bridges*, p. 138.   [2] Ibid., p. 141.
[3] Ibid., p. 138.
[4] Information from Manresa Minister's Journal.
[5] *Letters to Bridges*, p. 150. The retreat lasted from 7 to 14 Aug. For some of Hopkins's
notes at this time see *Sermons and Devotional Writings*, pp. 129, 184, 185.

His note on God's 'Power or Operation' written on the last day of the retreat serves to illustrate his professionalism:

God's Power or Operation, which is attributed especially to the Third Person, is put in the second instead of the third place (the 3rd instead of the 4th Point) because St Ignatius is dwelling on the thought of communication, and the Holy Ghost is the communication or the communion of the Father and the Son. It is by communication of his power that God operates the likeness of himself in things, so that this exertion or operation comes between his presence and his essence (or nature)—Aug. 14 1882[1]

Finally, on 15 August, the feast of the Assumption, the day on which St. Ignatius and his first companions had pledged themselves to perpetual poverty, chastity, and obedience at Montmartre, Paris, some 350 years earlier, Hopkins repeated the same promises himself. The ceremony took place during the nine o'clock Mass which was celebrated by the Provincial, Fr. Purbrick, at St. Joseph's. Eight Fathers pronounced their last vows. First, three of the eight repeated the four vows of the Professed, followed by the remaining five, among them Hopkins, who took those of Spiritual Coadjutors.[2] From the house records we learn:

There was singing during the Mass, the whole service ending about 9.45. The Accolade [i.e. fraternal embrace] was given to all in the Sacristy after the taking of the lesser vows. Breakfast for Fathers in exercitants' dining-room at 10.15. Dinner 3. Salmon, Chickens, Chops, Beef, Mutton. . . . About 90 [including visitors] sat down.[3] . . . Coffee and pousse for the Fathers in the Recreation Room. Séance at 5.30 in the Novices' Hall.[4]

In the evening the Rector gave solemn Benediction at St. Joseph's.

---

[1] *Sermons and Devotional Writings*, p. 195.

[2] Final vows are taken either as professed or spiritual coadjutors, the criterion of the division being largely academic achievement. Externally all who are priests have the same life and work, but only the professed are eligible for the major offices of the Society. The professed constitute the Society in its fullest sense. They may hold any office. They alone participate in general congregations. They make solemn religious vows and, in addition, a special vow of obedience to the pope. They also promise neither to desire nor to seek any dignity in or out of the order. Others are admitted among the spiritual coadjutors. Except for their exclusion from the very highest offices, these engage in all the activities of the Society. They bind themselves only by simple vows. Occasionally, because of special talents, some of these are raised to the profession.

[3] The Novices' Beadle's Journal states: 'Dinner today was in the Refectory for the first time since it was painted & whitewashed.'

[4] From Manresa Minister's Journal. The entry for a week later, Tues. 22 Aug., states: 'F. G. Hopkins left for Stonyhurst.'

Fourteen years had passed since Hopkins in his mid twenties had entered the Society's noviceship. Now at the age of thirty-eight his training was over and his life's work apparently stretched ahead. Fourteen years in the Society and only half that number left to him of life. But at the time he was not to know that, and death, like the 'terrible' sonnets, lay in the future. Had he entered the Society as poet or versifier? Clearly a debatable question. One thing is certain, it was during these years that his genius, power, and originality waxed, ripened, and came to flower within the grey and sombre walls of St. Beuno's, set on the side of the valley of the Clwyd.

In the Jesuit who finally emerged, the priest blended with the poet; the one no less than the other the product of the years of training.

APPENDIX 1

Manley Hopkins and the Roman Catholic Priesthood

MANLEY HOPKINS, the poet's father, became Consul-General for Hawaii in London in 1856 and retained the position for over forty years. In 1862 he published a history of Hawaii to which the Bishop of Oxford, Samuel Wilberforce, contributed the preface. A second edition appeared four years later in 1866 'revised and continued'. Some of the revisions are of considerable importance and suggest that the earlier edition was too Roman Catholic by half.

Both Manley Hopkins and his wife were deeply religious high-Anglicans and they saw to it that their children were well-grounded in religious instruction and practice. Manley himself was for a time churchwarden of St. John's, Hampstead, and helped to manage its funds as well as teach in its Sunday schools. When his father's history of Hawaii was published Gerard was eighteen, an age at which many young men are thinking about their future career. Hopkins went up to Oxford the following year, and the ideas imbibed at the family fireside may well have continued to ferment.

We have no proof that Gerard read his father's history of Hawaii, but it seems not unlikely that the religious views expressed there were occasionally a common household topic. If the extracts given below reflect Manley Hopkins's view of the Roman Catholic church and its priesthood, then it seems to me that unwittingly he could have been responsible for turning his son's mind in the direction of his future vocation. It is possible, too, that Gerard may have read Sir James Stephen's essay 'The Founders of Jesuitism' which first appeared in the *Edinburgh Review* in July 1842, and which was later republished in the first volume of his *Essays in Ecclesiastical Biography* (1849), from which Manley Hopkins quoted. Perhaps of even greater significance is the fact that Manley Hopkins chose to single out for quotation from Sir James what he said on Jesuit obedience. The self-sacrifice demanded by obedience is the key to the understanding of Gerard Manley Hopkins's vocation.

Extracts from *Hawaii: The Past, Present, and the Future of its Island-Kingdom* (1862).

They [American Protestant Missionaries] have made, indeed, an essential mistake in their conception of a religion,—producing it in a cold didactic form, with nothing to allure the heart and understanding through the medium of the senses and aesthetic tastes. They have not chosen to see that all religions worthy of the name of systems, combine moral sanctions with an outward worship. At the commencement of the Scriptures we read of sacrifices and altars; and in the Apocalyptic wonders which conclude the inspired canon, we read of elders and living beings worshipping before God's throne, and the infinite choir of harpers sending forth their everlasting melody.

It must not be supposed that these accusations are gratuitous and unfounded. They are all based on facts contained in many documents, and from the mouths of many witnesses. They lead to the conclusion that religion still waits to be seen in the Hawaiian islands in its true colours,—winning, persuasive, holy, and altogether lovely. [pp. 385–6]

Manley Hopkins goes on to quote from R. H. Dana's impressions which were recorded in a letter to the *New York Tribune*. Dana pointed out the superiority of Roman Catholic methods in teaching religion over that of the Protestant missionaries, and criticized the latter for failing to capture the natives' attention and interest and also for excluding them from any active participation.

It is not difficult [says Dana] to see the Roman Catholic Church, with its open doors, free sittings, daily mass and vespers, its corps of teaching and visiting nuns, its sacramental system, its worship addressed to the mind and heart through the eye and ear, as well as by the word to the understanding; with its service, which gives a part to all, and especially its system of commemorations, and, in the modern sense, its 'spiritualism' of angels and departed saints, has strongly enlisted the almost vacant native faculties. [p. 387]

Manley Hopkins continues with a further quotation which shows the Roman Catholic missionaries to have better 'internal and external personal qualifications' (p. 388). He then goes on to quote from Dr. Rae's series of articles 'Thoughts on the System of Legislation' published in the *Polynesian*, 1861, in which the following footnote occurred:

I do not recollect having been in any mixed company in these islands where the subject of the Protestant mission was introduced, without hearing either a sneer, a sarcasm, or a reproach against it. On the other hand, wherever I have been, and with whomsoever I have met, I have never encountered one, except in controversy, who did not speak in terms of respect of the Catholic Priesthood. Some have expressed surprise, that men could be found at this time of day thus to sacrifice their lives: some have spoken of their *culte* as savouring of superstition; but all have granted them the praise of sincere self-devotion—all have expressed a desire that their labours might benefit the natives. I simply note a fact—it is for the reader to draw the conclusion. [p. 388]

Manley Hopkins accuses the American [Protestant] missionaries of not having

truly Christianised or regenerated the nation. Their proceedings have been attended with grave and obvious faults. They have been wrong in their present-ment of Christianity to the native mind. They have presented Christianity as a severe, legal, Jewish religion, deprived of its dignity, beauty, tenderness, and amiability. They have not made the people love religion. [p. 384]

Later Manley Hopkins suggests that the American missionaries made a mistake by concentrating excessively on teaching transcendental doctrine (e.g., the Trinity, Justification, Original sin, and free-will), whereas a 'more simple and parental education was required' (p. 392). He continues:

Men will not be driven into Christianity like sheep into a pen; and the human heart refuses to be transformed by enactments, penalties, and imprisonments. Of means within our own power for religious advancement, the contemplation of examples is the most certain and the most powerful—to gaze on holiness in fellow-men, and, most of all, to gaze upon the Prince of Purities, until He becomes in our eyes 'fairest among ten thousand, and altogether lovely.' 'It is the burthen of Xavier's letters,' writes Sir James Stephen, 'that the living exhibition of the Christian character is the first great instrument of Christian conquests over idolatry; and that the inculcation of elementary truth is the second.' [pp. 392-3]

Considering the religious climate of the eighteen-sixties—a decade marked by heated controversy concerning 'ritualism' in the Church of England, and altogether at a far-distant remove from current ecumenism —the preface with which Manley Hopkins found himself obliged to introduce the second edition of his history in 1866, hardly surprises.

On the appearance of my book [he writes] a few angry comments were made on it, chiefly by or on account of the American missionaries. What I wrote, I strove to write impartially, without malice and without fear. [p. viii]

In the spirit of conciliation I have in this edition withdrawn the sketch of a person who played a considerable part in the earlier history of the country. [p. ix]

In my chapter on the English Church Mission, I have endeavoured to correct several misconceptions about it which have obtained currency in England, America, and elsewhere. [p. ix f.]

I am not claiming that Manley Hopkins was writing *pro* Roman Catholic of set purpose, but merely that he presented the Roman Catholic church in a very favourable light, and one which at times commended the priesthood of that church in a highly attractive and impressive way. A temperament such as that of his son, Gerard, could scarcely have escaped the attraction of such an appeal.

APPENDIX 2

Refectory reading 1868–1874, 1881–1882

Note

THE purpose of this appendix is to present so far as possible an accurate list of what was read in the refectory during Hopkins's time of training as a Jesuit. The information has been taken from the Journals kept by successive beadles and since these varied in diligence and accuracy the records are far from uniform. Occasionally there are awkward omissions. But since my aim is to provide a body of information on matter read which may have contributed something to the poet's consciousness I have had to attempt to reduce the sources to workable order. In doing so I have sometimes found it necessary to expand abbreviations, provide fuller titles, and supply authors' names. My approach was empiric and I simply searched the libraries of the various houses concerned and noted the edition(s) I found. In the few instances where I was unable to find a copy of any book or pamphlet in a Jesuit house, I traced and checked the work in the British Museum or Bodleian libraries.

A typical day's reading would have been:

At dinner:
1. A passage of Scripture.
2. An extract from Rodriguez, *Practice of Perfection*.
3. A booke specially selected for current reading (e.g. a saint's life, church history, etc.).
4. *Martyrologium Romanum*.

At supper:
1. *Ménologe*.
2. Book (No. 3) continued from dinner.

Where no other indication is given it may be presumed that the book selected for current reading once begun was continued even for many weeks. Periodicals have not been listed in Appendix 2E. At the head of the individual sections I have indicated the particular source of the information, and who was responsible for the choice of the books to be read.

A. *Refectory reading in the Novitiate*
(*Manresa House, Roehampton*)
September 1868–September 1870

(The information given below is taken from the Journal kept by the beadle of the novices. The Rector and novice master, Fr. Christopher Fitzsimon, would have decided the books to be read.)

1868

7 Sept. (Monday)
Nieremberg, *Temporal and Eternal*, bk. 5, cc. 7, 9 f; Arnold, *Imitation of the Sacred Heart*, bk. 3, c. 26.

8 Sept.
Ribadeneira, 'Nativity of the Blessed Virgin' in *Lives of the Saints*; Fleuriau, *Life of Blessed Peter Claver* (Oratorian edition).

16 Sept.
[Long Retreat begun tonight.]

17 Sept.
Gen 1; Parsons, *Christian Directory*, c. 3; La Colombière, *Spiritual Retreat*, from preface to page 4.

18 Sept.
Gen 2; Parsons, c. 3; Ponte, Fundamental meditation in *Meditations*.

19 Sept.
Gen 3; La Colombière, pp. 4–5; Parsons, c. 8.

20 Sept. (Sunday)
Mk 9; Parsons, c. 10, 11 sect. 3; La Colombière, pp. 6–13.

21 Sept.
Deut 32: 15–29; Parsons, c. 10; Arnold, bk. 1, cc. 23–4; Parsons, began 2nd book.

22 Sept.
Matt 25: 31–46; Parsons, pt. 2, c. 1; Arnold, bk. 1, cc. 10–12.

23 Sept.
Lk 7: 36–50, 15; Arnold, bk. 1, cc. 12–15; Parsons, pt. 2, c. 1.

24 Sept.
Is 52; Arnold, bk. 2, c. 1; Parsons, pt. 2, c. 1; Ponte, II, introduction and first

two parts. 1st Consideration on St Francis Xavier, in *An Instruction to performe with fruit the Devotion of Ten Fridays in Honour of S. Francis Xavier.*[1]

25 Sept.

Lk 1; Ponte, 2nd and 3rd meditations of 2nd week; Thomas à Kempis, *Imitation of Christ*, bk. 2, c. 6.

26 Sept.

Lk 2: 1–20; Ponte, II, med. 18–19, 24–5; Arnold, bk. 2, c. 6.

27 Sept. (Sunday)

Lk 2: 22–40, Matt 2: 13–23; Ponte, II, med. 25–6, 31; La Colombière, pp. 18–22.

28 Sept.

Lk 2: 41–52; La Colombière, pp. 22–5; Ponte, II, med. 29–30; Arnold, bk. 2, c. 12.

29 Sept.

Matt 16: 13–28; Ponte, III, med. 7–8; Arnold, bk. 2, cc. 13–14.

30 Sept.

Matt 3; La Colombière, pp. 25–7; Ponte, III, med. 3–4; Arnold, bk. 2, c. 15.

1 Oct.

Matt 4: 1–11; La Colombière, pp. 27–8; Ponte, III, med. 4–5; Arnold, bk. 2, c. 16.

2 Oct.

Matt 4: 12–25; La Colombière, pp. 28–36; Rules of the Society (English); Thomas à Kempis, bk. 3, c. 7 (English).

3 Oct.

Jn 11: 1–46; Pastoral of Bishop Grant; Dechamps, *The Second Eve*, c. 31.

4 Oct.

Rules of the Society; Jn 12: 1–20; La Colombière, pp. 36–50.

5 Oct.

Jn 12: 20–50; La Colombière, pp. 50–60; St Ignatius, Letter on Obedience; Arnold, bk. 2, c. 7.

6 Oct.

Mk 14: 32–50; Arnold, bk. 2, c. 12, bk. 3, c. 6; Ponte, IV, med. 21; La Colombière, pp. 61–5.

7 Oct.

Mk 14: 53–72; Ponte, IV, med. 23, 28, 30.

---

[1] Subsequent entries for this religious devotion omitted.

8 Oct.

Lk 23: 1–25; Ponte, IV, med. 32, 33, 35.

9 Oct.

Jn 19: 1–12; La Colombière, pp. 65–7; Ponte, IV, med. 37–8; Thomas a Kempis, bk. 2, c. 11 (English).

10 Oct.

Jn 19; 13–25; La Colombière, pp. 69–71; Ponte, IV, med. 40–2; Arnold, bk. 3, c. 7.

11 Oct.

Jn 19: 38–42; Matt 27: 57–66; Ponte, IV, med. 54–5, 43; La Colombière, pp. 71–3; Arnold, bk. 3, cc. 26–7.

12 Oct.

Jn 19: 23–8; Ponte, IV, Fundamental meditation on the Passion, 56–7.

13 Oct.

Is 53; Ponte, IV, med. 1 contd., V introd. and med. 1; Arnold, bk. 3, c. 21.

14 Oct.

Matt 28: 1–16; Ponte, V, med. 3–6; La Colombière, pp. 73–6.

15 Oct.

Mk 16: 1–11; La Colombière, pp. 82–101; Ponte, V, med. 2, 7.

16 Oct.

Lk 24: 13–53; La Colombière, pp. 101–9; Thomas à Kempis, bk. 3, c. 5 (English).

17 Oct.

Jn 20: 19–31; La Colombière, pp. 109–18; Ponte, V, med. 11–12; Arnold, bk. 2, c. 8.

18 Oct. (Sunday)

Acts 1: 1–11, 2: 1–11; La Colombière, pp. 118–31; Ponte, V, med. 18.

[*Te Deum* sung at Benediction in thanksgiving for all graces received during the Spiritual Exercises.]

19 Oct.

Apoc 21; La Colombière, pp. 132–59; Ponte, Introduction to the unitive way; Parsons, *Christian Directory*, bk. 12, pt. 1.

20 Oct.

Apoc 22; La Colombière contd.; Parsons, bk. 12, pt. 1. contd.

21 Oct.

'Messenger of the Sacred Heart' read.

29 Oct.
The Life of Blessed Alphonsus Rodriguez.

31 Oct.
Languet, *The Life of the Venerable Mother Margaret Mary Alacoque* (extracts).

1 Nov. (Sunday)
'All Souls' from Butler's *Lives of the Saints.*

3 Nov.
Rules of the Society; St Ignatius, Letter on Obedience.

4 Nov.
'Annals of the Propagation of the Faith'.

7 Nov.
Began the *Month.*

15 Nov. (Sunday)
'The Victorious Novices'.

19 Nov.
Reading from *Dublin Review.*

24 Nov.
[Drane], *Biographical Memoir of Henry Dormer.*

1 Dec.
Rules of the Society.

2 Dec.
Rules finished; Ribadeneira, 'Life of St. Francis Xavier'.

8 Dec.
Ribadeneira, 'The Immaculate Conception'.

12 Dec.
Morris, *Life of St. Thomas à Becket,* begun.

25 Dec.
Ribadeneira, 'Life of St. Stephen'.

26 Dec.
Ribadeneira, 'Life of St. John Apostle, and Evangelist'.

31 Dec.
Ménologe of the Society begun at supper for Jan. 1st.

1869
1 Jan.
Rules of the Society.

2 Jan.
Rules finished; St Ignatius, Letter on Obedience.

5 Jan.
Ribadeneira, 'The Feast of the Epiphany'.

6 Jan.
Ribadeneira on 'The Feast of the Epiphany' finished, as also Life of St. Thomas of Canterbury by Canon Morris. At supper began 'Messenger of the Sacred Heart'.

10 Jan. (Sunday)
Triduum reading.

12 Jan.
Gaudier, *The Love of Our Lord Jesus Christ, God and Man.*

14 Jan.
'Annals of the Propagation of the Faith'.

18 Jan.
Dublin Review.

21 Jan.
L'Abbé de T., *The History of the Church of Japan.*

22 Jan.
Gallwey, 'Funeral sermon of Hon. Charles Langdale, S.J.'

24 Jan.
'The Nineteenth General Council; or, The First Council of the Vatican'— supplement to *The Tablet.*

25 Jan.
Broeckaert, *Life of the Blessed Charles Spinola, S.J.*

1 Feb.
Rules of the Society (English); Ribadeneira, 'The Purification of the Blessed Virgin Mary'.

4 Feb.
Butler, 'The Martyrs of Japan'.

6 Feb.
Pastoral of Bishop Grant for Quinquagesima Sunday.

12 Feb.
Dupanloup, 'The Future Oecumenical Council'.

19 Feb.
'Annals of the Propagation of the Faith' for January.

24 Feb.
'Messenger of the Sacred Heart'.

1 Mar.
Rules of the Society (English).

2 Mar.
Harper, 'Tell no man of the vision' (sermon).

6 Mar.
Coleridge, 'Religion judged by the world' (sermon).

7 Mar.
'Messenger of the Sacred Heart' for February.

11 Mar.
Ribadeneira, 'The Life of St. Gregory the Great, Pope, and Doctor of the Church'.

14 Mar. (Sunday)
Matt 26: 1–35.

15 Mar.
Gospel of St. Matthew continued.

16 Mar.
Faber, *The Foot of the Cross*, the section on the Fourth Dolour.

25 Mar.
Jn 13–17.

27 Mar.
Fr. Faber's *Foot of the Cross* read for the last time finishing with the Seventh Dolour page 406. Only part of the 5th and 6th Dolours had been read.

28 Mar. (Easter Sunday)
'The Resurrection' from Sister Emmerich's *The Dolorous Passion of Our Lord Jesus Christ*.

29 Mar.
Pastoral Letter of Bishop Grant; *Tablet* supplement on Vatican Council; Sister Emmerich continued.

30 Mar.
Gallwey, *Convent Life and England in the 19th Century*.

1 Apr.
Rules of the Society (Latin).

3 Apr.
Two articles from the *Month* read at dinner and supper. At supper the Consideration and Practical Sayings of St Aloysius appointed for the first of the six Sundays in his honour were read.[1]

4 Apr. (Sunday)
Dublin Review.

10 Apr.
'Messenger of the Sacred Heart' for March.

15 Apr.
'Annals of the Propagation of the Faith' for March.

17 Apr.
Patrignani, *Manual of St. Joseph.*

26 Apr.
Tablet supplement on Vatican Council.

27 Apr.
'Messenger of the Sacred Heart' for April.

30 Apr.
Ménologe read at dinner after Rodriguez.

3 May
Rules of the Society.

6 May
Ribadeneira, 'Of the Admirable Ascension of our Lord'.

7 May
St Ignatius, Letter on Obedience.

8 May
Tablet supplement on Vatican Council.

10 May
Life of St. Francis Jerome commenced at dinner.

16 May (Whit Sunday)
Ribadeneira, 'The Coming of the Holy Ghost'.

18 May
The *Month* for May (an article only—a review).

21 May
Coleridge, 'The Latter Days' (four sermons).

[1] Subsequent entries for this religious devotion have been omitted.

27 May
Prologue to Faber, *The Blessed Sacrament*.

29 May
Pastoral of Bishop Grant.

31 May
Triduum reading.

1 June
Rules of the Society.

5 June
Pastoral of Bishop Grant; Hathaway, 'The Temptations of Our Lord' (four sermons).

7 June
Pastoral from Archbishop Manning.

12 June
'Messenger of the Sacred Heart' for May.

17 June
Shortland, *The Corean Martyrs*.

20 June (Sunday)
The Life of St. Aloysius.

26 June
'Annals of the Propagation of the Faith' for May.

30 June
The principal intention for the month of July read out from the 'Messenger of the Sacred Heart' for July.

1 July
Rules of the Society.

3 July
'Messenger of the Sacred Heart' for June.

5 July
'Messenger of the Sacred Heart' for July.

8 July
'Japanese Sketches' and another article from the *Month*.

11 July
An article in the *Dublin Review*.

14 July
'Father Azevedo and his Companions, or, the Forty Jesuits', in *Pictures of Christian Heroism*.

16 July
Dublin Review resumed.

17 July
Christie, *Union with Rome* (five lectures).

23 July
Wilberforce, *A Sketch of the Lives of the Dominican Missionaries in Japan*.

31 July
Ribadeneira, 'The Life of St. Ignatius Loyola'.

1 Aug. (Sunday)
Rules of the Society.

5 Aug.
'Messenger of the Sacred Heart' for July.

9 Aug.
Two articles from the *Month* for August.

10 Aug.
Gallwey, *The Angelus Bell* (five lectures).

13 Aug.
Sermons by Fathers of the Society of Jesus, vol. I.

15 Aug. (Sunday)
Ribadeneira, 'The Feast of the Assumption of our Blessed Lady'.

18 Aug.
Pye, *Why do we believe?*

20 Aug.
'Annals of the Propagation of the Faith' for August.

24 Aug.
Caddell, *A History of the Missions of Paraguay*.

31 Aug. [First day of the Community of Retreat]
Holy Scripture: Rodriguez, *Practice of Perfection*, pp. 375–82; *Ménologe*; Nieremberg, *Temporal and Eternal*, pp. 467–70.

1 Sept.
Rules of the Society; Nieremberg, pp. 478–81, 104–7; *Ménologe*.

2 Sept.

Nieremberg, pp. 109–15.

3 Sept.

Ménologe; Parsons, *Christian Directory*, pt. 2, c. 1, pp. 378–81.

5 Sept. (Sunday)

Intention for the month read from the 'Messenger of the Sacred Heart'; Parsons, pp. 381–   .

8 Sept.

'Japanese Sketches' from the *Month*; *Tablet* supplement on Vatican Council.

[12 Sept. Fr. Fitzsimon left, ceasing to be master of novices. 13 Sept. Fr. Gallwey, the new novice master, arrived. He would now choose the reading.]

17 Sept.

Eccles 1; *Ménologe*; Parsons—'End of Man'—forward.

18 Sept.

Wisdom 17; Parsons 'On Sin'.

19 Sept. (Sunday)

Jer 2: 4–13, 19–22; Parsons 'On Hell'; *Ménologe*.

20 Sept.

Jon 3, 4; Parsons 'On Death'.

21 Sept.

2 Mac 6: 17–31; Parsons 'Rare examples of true resolution'.

22 Sept.

Charlevoix, *The History of the Church of Japan.*

2 Oct.

Rules of the Society (English).

1 Nov.

Ribadeneira, 'The Feast of all Saints'.

26 Nov.

Gen 1; *Ménologe*; Faber, *The Creator and the Creature*, pp. 69–70; Thomas à Kempis, *Imitation of Christ*, bk. 3, c. 10.

27 Nov.

Genesis contd.; Faber.

28 Nov. (Sunday)

Genesis contd.; Faber.

29 Nov.

Genesis contd.; Faber.

1 Dec.
Matt 7: 7–29; Faber.

2 Dec.
Book of Jonas; Faber.

4 Dec.
Gen 37; Faber.

5 Dec. (Sunday)
Gen 40; St. Bonaventure, *Life of Christ*.

6 Dec.
Gen 43; Bonaventure.

7 Dec.
Gen 44; Bonaventure.

8 Dec.
Ribadeneira, 'The Feast of the Immaculate Conception of the Virgin Mary, our Lady'.

9 Dec.
Gen 45; Bonaventure.

10 Dec.
Tobias 1; Bonaventure.

11 Dec. [G. M. Hopkins appointed Beadle, or Porter.]
Tobias 2; Bonaventure.

12 Dec. (Sunday)
Matt 5–7; Jn 2; Mk 2, 3: 1–19; Rules of the Society.

13 Dec.
Jn 6: 1–15; Faber, *The Blessed Sacrament*, bk. 3, para. 7.

14 Dec.
Jn 9; Faber; Emmerich, *Dolorous Passion of our Lord*.

15 Dec.
Rules; Emmerich, med. 2–6 about.

16 Dec.
Rules; Emmerich.

17 Dec.
Rules; Emmerich—'The Passion' c. 1 forward.

18 Dec.
Rules; Emmerich.

19 Dec.
Rules; Emmerich, cc. 38, 44.

20 Dec.
Rules; Emmerich, c. 50 forward to page 304.

21 Dec.
Rules; Faber, *Creator and Creature*, bk. 3, c. 4 (*our own God*) at page 412.

22 Dec.
Rules; Faber.

23 Dec.
St. Austin's *Confessions*, bk. 9, para. 17; Jn 14: 1–20.

24 Dec.
Apoc 21 omitting 12–20; Charlevoix' *History of Japan*: life of Fr. Francis Mastrilli begun.

[The Porter's Journals have no further references to refectory reading until 14 April 1870. Hopkins ceased to be Porter on 19 February and was replaced by Brother McMullin.]

1870
14 Apr.
Emmerich, *Dolorous Passion of our Lord*, meditation about the 'Last Pasch'.

15 Apr. (Good Friday)
Emmerich.

17 Apr. (Easter Sunday)
Rutter, *The Life of Christ*.

31 Aug. (1st day of the Community Retreat)
Ecclus 2; Nieremberg, *Of Adoration in Spirit and Truth*.

1 Sept.
Jer 35; Nieremberg.

2 Sept.
Matt 18; Nieremberg; Thomas à Kempis, *Imitation of Christ*, bk. 1, c. 21.

3 Sept.
Matt 6; Nieremberg.

4 Sept.
Acts 9; Nieremberg.

5 Sept.
Is 53; Nieremberg.

6 Sept.

Jn 17; Nieremberg.

7 Sept.

Chapter of faults; Nieremberg.

B. *Refectory reading in the Philosophate* (*St. Mary's Hall, Stonyhurst*)

October 1870—June 1873

(The information given below is taken from the Journal kept by the beadle of the Philosophers. The books to be read during each of these three years were decided by Fr. Weld, Fr. McCann, and G. M. Hopkins respectively.)

1870

2 Oct. (Sunday)

Rules of the Society.[1]

10 Oct.

Letters and Notices for September; *Life of Mary Queen of Scots.*

12 Oct.

Manning, 'The Archbishop of Westminster on the invasion of Rome'.

13 Oct.

The *Month* for September begun. An article on 'The Educational Crisis'.

16 Oct. (Sunday)

Letters from *Letters and Notices* for September read.

17 Oct.

Articles from the *Month* for October.

18 Oct.

'Annals of the Propagation of the Faith' for July.

23 Oct. (Sunday)

Dublin Review for October.

2 Nov.

Sermon of Mgr. Dupanloup.

4 Nov.

Article from the *Month* for September.

---

[1] The Rules of the Society were read at the beginning of most months.

5 Nov.
Coleridge, 'The Christian Kingdom' (sermon).

6 Nov. (Sunday)
Manning, *The Temporal Power of the Vicar of Christ.*

27 Nov.
Lingard, *The History and Antiquities of the Anglo-Saxon Church.*

3 Dec. (Sunday)
Ullathorne, Sermon on the Council.

5 Dec.
Article from the *Month.*

7 Dec.
'Sympathy with the Pope' an account of a meeting in Dublin reported in 'The Freeman's Journal' of 1 Dec. 1870.

14 Dec.
Article from the *Month*, 'Unknown works of Sir Thomas More'.

16 Dec.
Dublin Review for October.

27 Dec.
Manning, 'The Vatican Council' (Pastoral Letter).

1871
5 Jan.
Month for Jan.–Feb., begun at supper; Shea, *History of the Catholic Missions among the Indian Tribes of the United States 1529–1854.*

12 Jan.
Triduum reading.

21 Jan.
Dublin Review for January.

31 Jan.
Vaughan, *The Life and Labours of S. Thomas of Aquin.*

2 Feb.
Rose, *Ignatius Loyola and the early Jesuits.*

18 Feb.
Dr Turner's Lenten Pastoral.

27 Mar.
Life of S. Thomas finished; Morrison, *Discovery of Jerusalem.* [MS. reads *Recovery of Jerusalem*, cf. entry for 6 May below.]

3 Apr.
Is 53; St Bernard, Sermon II in Dominica Palmarum.

4 Apr.
First half of the Passion according to St Matthew; St Bernard, (III in Dom. Palm.); Guéranger, *The Liturgical Year* for Holy Week.

5 Apr.
The Passion according to St Matthew finished; St Bernard, (Feria iv Heb. Penos.) [sic; probably 'feria iv hebdomadae sanctae' intended, since 5 April was the Wednesday in Holy Week.]; *Liturgical Year*, etc.

6 Apr.
Half of St Mark's Passion (Latin); *Liturgical Year*, 'Morning of Maundy Thursday'; St Bernard, 'In Coena Domini'.

7 Apr.
Passio S. Marc. finished; St Bernard, 'De Passione Domini'.

8 Apr.
Mk 15: 42–6; St Bernard, 'De Lamentatione Virginis'.

10 Apr.
Ordinary reading.

6 May
Book on Jerusalem (Morrison) finished; *Month* for May–June commenced.

15 May
Dublin Review.

17 June
Triduum reading.

9 July
Lacordaire, *Conférences.*

6 Aug. (Sunday)
[Chesney], *Battle of Dorking*, [cf. *Journals and Papers*, p. 213].

31 Aug. (Community Retreat)
Gen 1; Ponte 'On the end of man'; Parsons, *Christian Directory*, c. 3 'On the end of man'.

1 Sept.
Gen 3; Ponte, I, med. 2 f. 'On sin', p. 89.

2 Sept.
Lk 21; Ponte, I, p. 139—'Particular Judgement'.

3 Sept. (Sunday)
Lk 1: 26–80, 2: 1–20; Ponte, 'The Incarnation and the Nativity'.

4 Sept.
Lk 2: 41–52; Ponte, 'On our Lord's life at Nazareth, and of our Lord's being lost in the Temple'.

5 Sept.
Matt 26: 1–35; Ponte, 'On the Last Supper and on the Agony in the Garden'.

6 Sept.
Matt 26: 57–75; Ponte, 'Of our Lord in the house of Caiphas'.

7 Sept.
Matt 28; Ponte, VI, med. 5, p. 54.

9 Sept.
Month for Sept.–Oct.; 2nd series of Lacordaire's *Conférences*.

18 Sept.
Oakeley, *The Priest on the Mission*.

7 Oct.
Manning, *The Fourfold Sovereignty of God*.

17 Oct.
Montalembert, *The Monks of the West*.

1 Nov.
Oakeley, 'The Sanctity of the Christian Vocation' (sermon).

3 Nov.
Mumford, *A Remembrance for the Living to pray for the Dead*.

5 Nov. (Sunday)
Tablet supplement—'Pastoral of the Bishops of Ireland on Education'.

9 Nov.
The *Month*.

22 Nov.
Père Ponlevoy, *Acts of the Captivity and Death of the Fathers Pierre Olivaint, Leon Ducoudray, Jean Caubert, Alexis Clerc, and Anatole de Bengy. Priests of the Society of Jesus*.

14 Dec.
Ramsay, *Monseigneur Darboy*.

1872
10 Jan.
Triduum Reading.

20 Jan.
Tablet supplement—Cardinal Cullen's speech on 'Irish Education'.

27 Jan.
Letters and Notices.

11 Feb.
Bishop Turner's Pastoral Letter.

16 Feb.
Woodstock Letters, 1st number.

[13 Mar. According to GMH an account of the religious conversion of de Rancé was read which brought him to tears (*Journals and Papers*, p. 218). The Porter's Journal does not record this reading.]

15 Mar.
Two pages from the 'Messenger of the Sacred Heart'.

18 Mar.
A chapter on Devotion to St. Joseph.

20 Mar.
The Passion (Latin); [Faber], *Foot of the Cross.*

24 Mar. (Palm Sunday)
Passio Domini nostri Jesu Christi; *Foot of the Cross.*

5 Apr.
'Syria. Revival of Christianity'; Lefebvre, *Louise Lateau.*

18 Apr.
Lasserre, *Our Lady of Lourdes.*

24 Apr.
Dublin Review.

9 May (The Ascension)
Two sermons of St Leo in Latin on the feast.

17 June
Triduum reading.

27 Aug.
Burke, *The Men and Women of the English Reformation*, vol. 2.

31 Aug. (Community Retreat)
Reading at table exactly the same as last year with one exception (see Sunday).

1 Sept. (Sunday)
Rules of the Society begun at supper and are to be continued at supper until finished.

4 Sept.
Nieremberg, *Of Adoration in Spirit and Truth.*

6 Sept.
The ordinary amount out of Thomas à Kempis.

27 Oct. (Sunday)
Allies, *The Formation of Christendom.*

1873
2 Jan.
Triduum reading.

23 Feb. (Sunday)
Bishop Vaughan's Pastoral Letter.

9 Apr.
Passio Domini nostri; Newman, 'Mental Sufferings of our Lord in his Passion' (sermon).

11 Apr.
The Passion according to St. John; Segneri, 'The Incomparable Passion of Christ' (sermon).

12 Apr.
Newman, 'The Glories of Mary for the sake of her Son' (sermon).

16 June
Triduum reading, etc; Thomas à Kempis.

C. *Refectory reading in the Novitiate and Juniorate*
(*Manresa House, Roehampton*)
September 1873—June 1874

(The information given below is taken from the Journal kept by the beadle of the novices. The Rector and novice master, Fr. George Porter, would have decided the books to be read.)

10 Sept.
Fairplay, *Notes of the Wandering Jew, on the Jesuits and their Opponents.*

15 Sept.
Luis de Granada, *The Sinner's Guide.*

19 Sept.
Coleridge, 'Giving Glory to God' (sermon).

20 Sept.
Genelli, *The Life of St. Ignatius of Loyola.*

3 Oct.
Rules of the Society.[1]

6 Nov.
An extract from Ribadeneira's *Lives of the Saints.*

7 Nov.
[Foley], *The Life of Blessed Alphonsus Rodriguez.*

26 Nov. (First day of the novices' Long Retreat)
Wisdom 1; Faber, *The Creator and the Creature,* c. 1.

27 Nov.
Ps 103; Faber.

28 Nov.
First lamentation of Jeremias; Parsons, *Christian Directory*—'Nature of Sin'.

29 Nov.
Second lamentation of Jeremias; Salazar, *The Sinner's Conversion*—'On Hell'.

30 Nov. (Sunday)
Second lamentation of Jeremias; Salazar, 'On Death'.

1 Dec.
Ecclus 16–17; Salazar, 'The Particular Judgment'.

2 Dec.
Jer 35; Rules of the Society; Salazar, 'General Judgment'.

3 Dec.
Rules; Parsons.

4 Dec.
Tob 1; Rules; Gaudier, *The Love of Our Lord Jesus Christ, God and Man.*

---

[1] The Rules of the Society were read at the beginning of most months. References to religious devotions have been omitted.

5 Dec.
Tob 2; Rules; Gaudier.

6 Dec.
Tob. 3; Rules; Gaudier.

7 Dec. (Sunday)
Tob 5; Rules; Gaudier.

8 Dec.
[Sermon preached at dinner]; Gaudier.

9 Dec.
Tob 14; Rules; Gaudier.

10 Dec.
2 Mac 6; Rules; Gaudier.

11 Dec.
Common Rules; Dan 3; Gaudier.

12 Dec.
Common Rules; Jn 9; Gaudier.

13 Dec.
Matt 10, 19; Gaudier finished; Grou, *The School of Christ.*

14 Dec. (Sunday)
Lk 7; Grou.

15 Dec.
Raising of Lazarus; Common Rules; Grou.

16 Dec.
Jn 13 first half; Common Rules; Pinamonti, *The Cross in its True Light.*

17 Dec.
Jn 14; Common Rules; Pinamonti.

18 Dec.
Jn 15–17; Common Rules; Pinamonti.

19 Dec.
Jn 17; Rules of Modesty; Pinamonti.

20 Dec.
Jn 18; Rules of Modesty; Pinamonti.

21 Dec. (Sunday)
Matt 28: 1–10; St Ignatius, Letter on Obedience; Parsons, *Christian Directory*
pt. 1, c. 12.

22 Dec.
Matt 28: 11–20; Letter on Obedience; Parsons.

23 Dec.
[no reading given]

24 Dec.
Jn 21; Faber, *Bethlehem*—'The Midnight Cave'.

25 Dec.
Faber.

26 Dec.
Fullerton, *The Life of Luisa de Carvajal*.

1874
15 Jan.
Triduum reading.

26 Jan.
Life of Luisa de Carvajal finished today; Encyclical letter of the Pope read at supper.

28 Jan.
Goldie, *The Life of Blessed John Berchmans*.

14 Mar.
Boero, *The Life of the Blessed Peter Favre*.

2 Apr.
First half of the Passion according to St John; Palma, *The History of the Sacred Passion*—Sixth Word on the Cross.

4 Apr.
Palma.

26 June
Triduum reading.

27 June
Orleans, *The Life of Saint Stanislaus Kostka*.

D. *Refectory reading in the Tertianship*
(*Manresa House, Roehampton*)
November 1881—July 1882

(The information given below is taken from the Journal kept by the beadle of the novices. The Rector and novice master, Fr. John Morris, would have decided the books to be read.)

1881

2 Oct.
Rules of the Society.[1]

7 Nov.
Faber, *The Creator and the Creature.*

[26 Nov. Novices' Long Retreat began]

3 Dec.
La Colombière, *Spiritual Retreat.*

8 Dec.
La Colombière; Faber.

17 Dec.
'The Canonisation' (Blessed John Baptist De Rossi, Laurence of Brindisi, Benedict Joseph Labre, confessors, and Blessed Clare of the Cross, virgin), from *The Tablet*, 17 Dec. 1881.

24 Dec.
Faber's *The Creator and the Creature* finished; 'The Nativity of Christ' from Butler's *Lives of the Saints.*

1882

3 Jan.
Edersheim, *The Temple.*

11 Jan.
Triduum reading.

5 Feb.
The Temple finished; Faber, *Spiritual Conferences.*

6 Mar.
Faber's *Spiritual Conferences* left off; Coleridge, *Life of Our Lord.*

---

[1] The Rules of the Society were read at the beginning of most months. References to religious devotions have been omitted.

26 Mar. (Sunday)
Palma, *The History of the Sacred Passion.*

28 May (Whit Sunday)
'On Whitsuntide' from Butler's, *The Moveable Feasts, Fasts* . . .

24 June
First Pastoral Letter of Bishop Coffin.

26 June
Special book on St. Peter.

18 July
Darras, *A General History of the Catholic Church* begun; Drane, *Life of Mother Margaret Mary Hallahan* finished [commencement not recorded].

E. *List of Books read in the Refectory 1868–1874, 1881–1882*

Anonymous works appear under the first significant word. Anonymous lives of saints, etc., will be found under the saint's Christian name (e.g. Alphonsus, Aloysius, etc.). The place of publication is London unless stated otherwise.

Allies, Thomas William, *The Formation of Christendom,* 3 vols. 1865–75.

Aloysius Gonzaga, St.: Anon., *The Life of St. Aloysius Gonzaga: of the Society of Jesus.* Dublin, n.d.; Anon., *The Life of St. Aloysius Gonzaga, of the Company of Jesus,* 1867 (No. 1. Library of Religious Biography, edited by Edward Healy Thompson); Anon., *S. Aloysius Gonzaga Proposed as a Model of a Holy Life by particular Practices of Devotion calculated for Keeping Six Sundays successively in Honour of the same saint.* From the Latin edition. Saint Omer, 1751.

Alphonsus Rodriguez, St.: Anon., *Life of the Blessed Alphonsus Rodriguez.* Translated from French. n.d.; two anonymous manuscript 'Lives' translations, dated 1825.

Arnold, Fr. [Pierre Joseph Arnoudt, S.J.], *The Imitation of the Sacred Heart of Jesus.* In four books. Translated from the Latin by a Father of the same Society [J. A. M. Fastré, S.J.] [1866].

Augustine, St., *Confessions.* Too many translations to list.

Austin, St., see St. Augustine.

Bernard, St.: The library at St. Mary's Hall, Stonyhurst, contained: Sancti Bernardi, *Opera Omnia,* ed. Joannis Mabillon, O.S.B. Editio quarta emendata et aucta. 2 tom. Paris, 1839; S. Bernardi, *Sermones de tempore,* ed. J. M. Mandernach, Cologne and Bonn, 1863. I have been unable to identify the sermon 'De Lamentatione Virginis'.

Boero, Giuseppe, S.J., *The Life of the Blessed Peter Favre* [translated by Henry James Coleridge, S.J.], 1873.

Bonaventure, St., *The Life of our Lord and Saviour Jesus Christ.* . . . with the life of the author, taken from the Rev. Alban Butler's *Lives of the Saints.* Dublin, 1840.

Broeckaert, Joseph, S.J., *Life of the Blessed Charles Spinola, of the Society of Jesus*: with a sketch of the other Japanese martyrs, beatified on the 7th July, 1867. New York, 1868.

Burke, S. Hubert, *The Men and Women of the English Reformation.* 2 vols. 1871.

Butler, Alban, *The Moveable Feasts, Fasts, and other annual observances of the Catholic Church.* Dublin, 1839.

—— *The Lives of the Fathers, Martyrs, and other principal saints*; compiled from original monuments, and other authentic records; illustrated with the remarks of judicious modern critics and historians. . . . In twelve volumes. Dublin, 1845.

Caddell, Cecilia Mary, *A History of the Missions in Japan and Paraguay*, 2 pts., London and New York, 1856.

Charlevoix, Pierre François Xavier de, S.J., *The History of the Church of Japan.* (See L'abbé de T. The copy of *The History of the Church of Japan* in the novitiate has 'Charlevoix' on the spine but 'L'Abbé de T.' on the title-page. On this confusion of attribution see Joannes Laures, *Kirishitan Bunko*, Sophia University, Tokyo, 1940, pp. 172–3.)

[Chesney, George Tomkyns], *The Battle of Dorking. Reminiscences of a volunteer.* From *Blackwood's Magazine*, May 1871. (Cf. *Journals and Papers*, p. 213.)

Christie, Albany James, S.J., *Union with Rome.* Five afternoon lectures preached in the church of the Immaculate Conception, Farm Street. 1869.

Coffin, Robert Aston, C.SS.R., 'First Pastoral Letter of the Bishop of Southwark. 11 June 1882.' (In general it contains an exhortation to holiness in the clergy, and to love of Christ our Lord in the laity. It was to be read throughout the diocese on Sunday 25 June. See *The Tablet*, 1 July 1882.)

Coleridge, Henry James, S.J., 'Religion Judged by the World.' A sermon preached on the third Sunday of Lent, Feb. 28, 1869, in the church of the Immaculate Conception, Farm Street. 1869. [Printed at Roehampton.]

—— 'The Latter Days.' Four sermons in *Sermons by Fathers of the Society of Jesus*, i, 1869.

—— 'The Christian Kingdom.' A sermon preached on Rosary Sunday (Oct. 2, 1870), 1870.

—— 'Giving Glory to God.' A sermon . . . in preparation for the departure of the English pilgrims to Paray-le-Monial, 1873.

—— *Life of Our Lord*, probably *The Works and Words of Our Saviour*, 1882. (An introductory note states: 'The present work is mainly a republication of the greater part of the work published by the writer some years ago under the title "The Life of our Life" '.)

Cullen, Paul, 'Irish Education'. Speech of the Cardinal-Archbishop of Dublin at the great meeting held in the pro-Cathedral, Dublin, on the 17th January, 1872. (Supplement to *The Tablet*, 20 Jan. 1872.)

Darras, Joseph Epiphane, *A General History of the Catholic Church from the commencement of the Christian era until the present time*. Translated from the French, with an introduction and notes by M. J. Spalding, Archbishop of Baltimore. 4 vols. New York, 1866.

Dechamps, Victor Augustine Isidore, *Cardinal, The Second Eve; or, The Mother of Life*. Recollections and prayers for every day in the month of Mary, and for other days consecrated to the Mother of God [1866].

[Drane, Augusta Theodosia], *Biographical Memoir of the Hon. Henry Edward Dormer*, late of the 60th Rifles, R.I.P. 1867.

Drane, Augusta Theodosia, *Life of Mother Margaret Mary Hallahan*. 1870.

Dupanloup, Félix Antoine Philibert, *The Future Oecumenical Council*. A letter by the Bishop of Orleans to the clergy of his diocese. Translated by Henry S. Butterfield and E. Robillard, 1869.

—— 'Sermon of Mgr. Dupanloup'—possibly 'Joan of Arc' by Monseigneur Félix, Bishop of Orleans. A discourse delivered on May 8, 1869, in the cathedral of Holy Cross, Orleans. Translated by Emily Bowles, 1869. This sermon was printed at Roehampton.

Edersheim, Alfred, *The Temple, its Ministry and Services*. [1874.]

Emmerich, Anna Catherina, *The Dolorous Passion of Our Lord Jesus Christ . . .* with a preface by the Abbé de Cazalés, 1862.

Faber, Frederick William, Cong. Orat., *The Blessed Sacrament; or, The Works and Ways of God*, 1855.

—— *The Creator and the Creature; or, The Wonders of Divine Love*, 1858.

—— *The Foot of the Cross; or, the Sorrows of Mary*, 1858.

—— *Bethlehem*, 1860.

—— *Spiritual Conferences*, 3rd ed., 1870.

Fairplay, John, *pseud., Notes of the Wandering Jew, on the Jesuits and their Opponents*, Dublin, 1873.

'Father Azevedo and his Companions; or, the Forty Jesuits', in *Pictures of Christian Heroism*. With preface by the Rev. Henry Edward Manning, D.D., 1855.

Fleuriau, Bertrand Gabriel, S.J., *The Life of the Venerable Father Claver, S.J.* Translated from the French, 1849.

[Foley, Henry, S.J.], *The Life of Blessed Alphonsus Rodriguez, Lay-Brother of the Society of Jesus*, 1873.

Francis Jerome, St.: *Lives of St. Alphonsus Liguori, St. Francis de Girolamo, St. John Joseph of the Cross, St. Pacificus of San Severino, and St. Veronica Giuliani*: whose Canonization took place on Trinity Sunday, May 26th, 1839. (A note states that the life has been extracted from *Vita del B. Francesco di Girolamo, scritta dal Padre Longaro degli Oddi, S.J.* Rome, 1806.)

Francis Xavier, St., *An Instruction to performe with fruit the Devotion of Ten Fridays in honour of S. Francis Xaverius Apostle of the Indies. Much practised in Rome and augmented particularly of late by some most authentick miracles wrought by the intercession of this glorious Saint. Upon which score he is taken as particular Patrone of allmost all Italy.* [St. Omers, 1670?]. (The dedication runs: 'To the Honourable the Lady Mary Caryll Abbesse of the English Benedictin Dames at Dunkerque.' and is signed 'N.N.'.)

Frogier de Ponlevoy, Armand, *Acts of the Captivity and Death of the Fathers Pierre Olivaint, Leon Ducoudray, Jean Caubert, Alexis Clerc, and Anatole de Bengy. Priests of the Society of Jesus.* Translated from the French, 1871.

Fullerton, Lady Georgiana Charlotte, *The Life of Luisa de Carvajal*, 1873.

Gallwey, Peter, S.J., 'A discourse preached in the chapel of Houghton at the funeral of the Hon. Charles Langdale, S.J. December 9th, 1868.' [1868]. (Reprinted in *Salvage from the Wreck* [1890].)

—— *The Angelus Bell.* Lectures on the remedies against desolation, in *Sermons by Fathers of the Society of Jesus,* vol. i, pt. 2, 1869.

—— 'Convent Life and England in the Nineteenth Century.' Two sermons preached in the church of the Immaculate Conception, Farm Street, March 7, 1869, on occasion of an appeal on behalf of the Little Sisters of the Poor [1869].

—— 'St. Joseph and the Vatican Council.' The substance of a sermon preached at the opening of St. Joseph's Chapel, Roehampton, March 19, 1870. 1870.

Gaudier, Antonius, S.J., *The Love of Our Lord Jesus Christ, God and Man, its source, practice and fruit. . . .* Translated by the Rev. George Tickell, S.J., 1864.

Genelli, Christoph, S.J., *The Life of St. Ignatius of Loyola.* Translated from the German by M. Charles Sainte Foi and rendered from the French by Thomas Meyrick, S.J., 1871.

Goldie, Francis, S.J., *The Life of the Blessed John Berchmans*, 1873.

Grant, Thomas, 'Pastoral Letters' of the Bishop of Southwark. *Rosary Sunday* [4 Oct.] *1868* (progress and needs of the diocese); *Quinquagesima Sunday* [7 Feb.] *1869* (A Lenten exhortation and an appeal for diocesan orphanages); *Low Sunday* [4 Apr.] *1869* (publishes and explains what is meant by declaration of a Year of Jubilee by Pius IX); *First Sunday of June 1869* (on subject of Catholic Schools).

Grou, Jean Nicolas, S.J., *The School of Christ . . .*, Translated by the Rev. A. Clinton, Dublin, 1874.

Guéranger, Prosper Louis Paschal, O.S.B., *The Liturgical Year.* Translated from the French by the Rev. Dom. Laurence Shepherd. 13 vols. Dublin, 1867–1901. (The volumes covering Advent to Paschal time were published 1867–71; the volumes for the time after Pentecost, 1879–1901.)

Harper, Thomas Norton, S.J., 'The Silence of Christian Transfigurations.' A sermon preached on the second Sunday of Lent (Feb. 21, 1869) in the church of the Immaculate Conception, Farm Street [1869].

Hathaway, Frederick, S.J., 'The Temptations of Our Lord.' Four sermons in *Sermons by Fathers of the Society of Jesus*, vol. i, 1869.

Ignatius Loyola, St., 'Letter on Obedience'—*Epistola S.P.N. Ignatii ad Patres et Fratres Societatis Jesu qui sunt in Lusitania*—'De Obedientiae Virtute', 26 Martii 1553. *Epistolae Praepositorum Generalium*, vol. i, Ghent, 1847. (Novices and scholastics had an English translation of this letter in their copy of the rules.)

La Colombière, Claude, *The Spiritual Retreat of the Rev. Father Colombière of the Society of Jesus*. Translated from the French. With a preface by the Right Rev. Dr. Manning, Dublin, 1863.

Lacordaire, Jean Baptiste Henri Dominique, *Conférences de Notre-Dame de Paris*, 4 tom., Paris, 1847–51.

[Languet, de la Villeneuve de Gergy.] *The Life of the Venerable Mother Margaret Alacoque, Religious of the Order of the Visitation*. Translated from the French, 2 vols., 1850.

Lasserre, Henri, *Our Lady of Lourdes*. Translated from the French by the Rev. F. Ignatius Sisk, O.C., 1872.

Lefebvre, Ferdinand J. M., *Louise Lateau, the Ecstatica of Bois d'Haine; her life, stigmata and ecstasies*. Translated from the French by J. S. Shepard, 1872.

Leo, Pope St.: The sermons on the Ascension will be found in any collected edition of his works, and in Migne, *Patrologiae Latinae*, liv.

Letters and Notices (LLNN) is a private domestic quarterly of the English Province of the Society of Jesus.

Lingard, John, *The History and Antiquities of the Anglo-Saxon Church* [3rd ed.], 2 vols., 1845.

Luis, de Granada, O.P., *The Sinner's Guide*. In two books. . . . Translated from the Spanish, Dublin, 1825.

Manning, Henry Edward. *The Temporal Power of the Vicar of Christ*, 2nd ed., 1862.

—— 'Denominational Education': a pastoral letter to the clergy and laity of the diocese of Westminster, 1869. (Dated third Sunday [6 June] after Pentecost.)

—— 'The Vatican Council and its definitions': a pastoral letter to the clergy, 1870.

—— 'The Archbishop of Westminster on the invasion of Rome.' (Supplement to *The Tablet*, 8 Oct. 1870.)

—— *The Fourfold Sovereignty of God*, 1871.

Mary, Queen of Scots, *Life of Mary Queen of Scots*. The library contains the following: James Freebairn, *The Life of Mary Stewart, Queen of Scotland and France*, Edinburgh, 1725; Anon., *Mary, Queen of Scots*, Glasgow, 1826; Henry Glasford Bell, *Life of Mary Queen of Scots*, 3rd ed., 1840; John Hosack, *Mary Queen of Scots and her Accusers*, 2nd ed., 1870–4.

Ménologe: a collection of edifying biographies of former members of the Society of Jesus. The library contains the following: Anon., *Ménologe de la Compagnie de Jésus*, Paris, 1844 (lithographed production); Elesban de Guilhermy, *Ménologe de la Compagnie de Jésus, Assistance de Portugal*, 2 vols., Poitiers, 1867–8; Anon., *Menology of the Society of Jesus*, Roehampton, 1874.

Montalembert, Charles Forbes René de, *The Monks of the West*, vols. iii–v. Edinburgh and London, 1867; also *Les Moines D'Occident*, 7 tom., Paris, 1860–77.

Morris, John, S.J., *The Life and Martyrdom of Saint Thomas Becket*, 1859.

Morrison, Walter (ed.), *The Recovery of Jerusalem*. . . . By Capt. Wilson, R.E., Capt. Warren, R.E., with an introduction by Arthur Penrhyn Stanley, 1871.

Mumford, James, S.J., *A Remembrance for the Living to pray for the Dead*. Reprinted from the edition of 1661. With an appendix on the heroic act by John Morris, priest of the same Society, 1871.

Newman, John Henry, Cong. Orat., 'Mental Sufferings of our Lord in his Passion', Discourse XVI in *Discourses Addressed to Mixed Congregations*, 1849; 'The Glories of Mary for the sake of her Son', ibid., Discourse XVII.

Nieremberg, Juan Eusebio, S.J., *A Treatise of the Difference betwixt the Temporal and Eternal*. . . . Translated into English by Sir Vivian Mullineaux, Knight. And since Reviewed according to the tenth and last Spanish Edition. 1672; also Dublin, 1793; 10th ed., Dublin, 1849; 12th ed., Dublin, 1872.

—— *Of Adoration in Spirit and Truth*. . . . Translated into English by R. S. S. I. [Richard Strange, S.J.] [St. Omers], 1673; also, with a preface by the Rev. Peter Gallwey, S.J., 1871 (No. 1 of St. Joseph's Ascetical Library, Roehampton printed).

Oakeley, Frederick, 'The Sanctity of the Christian Vocation.' A sermon preached in St. Edmund's College Chapel, on the feast of All Saints, 1847; reprinted in Oakeley, *Practical Sermons preached in 1847–8*. 1848.

——*The Priest on the Mission*, 1871.

Orléans, Pierre Joseph d', S.J., *The Life of Saint Stanislaus Kostka, Novice of the Society of Jesus* [translated by John Laurenson, S.J.], Richmond, 1816.

Palma, Luis de la, *The History of the Sacred Passion*. From the Spanish . . . the translation revised and edited by Henry James Coleridge of the same Society, 1872.

Parsons, Robert, S.J., *Christian Directory*. The library contains many editions of this work: [St. Omers], 1622; London, 1650, 1687, 1700, 1716, 1739; Dublin, 1852, 1861.

'Pastoral Letter of the Bishops of Ireland.' Supplement to *The Tablet*, 4 Nov. 1871.

Patrignani, Giuseppe Antonio, S.J., *A Manual of Practical Devotion to the glorious Patriarch Saint Joseph*. . . . Translated from the Italian . . . revised by a member of the Society of Jesus, Dublin, 1849.

Peter, St.: 'Special book on' read 29 June 1882. I have not been able to identify this.

Pictures of Christian Heroism. With Preface by the Rev. Henry Edward Manning, D.D., 1855.

Pinamonti, Giovanni Pietro, S.J., *The Cross in its True Light; or, the weight of tribulation lessened*, 1775; another edition, Dublin, 1851.

Pius IX, Pope (Giovanni Maria Mastai-Ferretti), Encyclical Letter dated from Rome, 21 Nov. 1873. A translation appeared as a supplement to *The Tablet* for 6 Dec. 1873. The Latin text is to be found in *Acta Sanctae Sedis*, vii. 465–79.

Ponte, Louis de [Luis de la Puente, S.J.], *Meditations on the Mysteries of our Holy Faith; together with a treatise on Mental Prayer.* Translated from the Spanish by John Heigham, 6 vols., 1852–4.

Pye, Henry John, *Why do we believe? A consideration of the claims of the Roman Catholic Church . . .* [1869].

Ramsay, Grace [Kathleen O'Meara], *Monseigneur Darboy*, 1871.

Ribadeneira, Pedro de, S.J., *The Lives of Saints, with other feasts of the year, according to the Roman Calendar. . . .* Translated into English by W. P. Esq.; the second edition corrected and amended. 2 parts, 1730.

Rodriguez, Alonso, S.J., *The Practice of Christian and Religious Perfection.* Written in Spanish . . . translated from the French copy of M. l'abbé Régnier des Marais. 3 vols., Dublin, 1840; other three-volume editions, Dublin, printed in 1846, 1861, 1870; copies of two French editions: *Pratique de la Perfection Chrétienne* traduit de l'espagnol par M. l'abbé Régnier des Marais, 4 tom., Toulouse, 1699, and 6 tom., Lyons–Paris, 1831.

Rose, Stewart, *Ignatius Loyola and the early Jesuits*, 1870.

Rules of the Society of Jesus in *Institutum Societatis Iesu*. 3 vols. Florence, 1892–3. Copies of the Rules in English were printed at Manresa Press, Roehampton, in 1863, 1875, 1884, etc.; and in Latin in 1874, etc. Prior to these editions copies were obtained from abroad.

Rutter, Henry, the Rev., *The Life, Doctrine, and Sufferings of Our Blessed Lord and Saviour Jesus Christ, as recorded by the Four Evangelists.* With moral reflections, critical illustrations, and explanatory notes . . . with an introduction by the Very Rev. F. C. Husenbeth, D.D., V.G., Provost of Northampton. n.d.

Salazar, Francisco de, *The Sinner's Conversion reduced to Principles.* Written originally in Spanish. . . . Translated from the French by T. R. [T. Richmond], 1823.

Segneri, Paolo, S.J., 'The Incomparable Passion of Christ', in *The Quaresimale*, translated from the original Italian by James Ford. Third series, 1860.

Sermons by Fathers of the Society of Jesus, vol. i, pt. 1, 1869, pt. 2, 1870. (In addition to the sermons of Frs. Coleridge, Gallwey, and Hathaway already listed, this volume contains three sermons by Fr. T. B. Parkinson, an additional sermon by Fr. Coleridge, and two by Fr. Harper.)

Shea, John Dawson Gilmary, *History of the Catholic missions among the Indian tribes of the United States 1529–1854*. New York, 1855.

Shortland, Canon John R., *The Corean Martyrs: a narrative* [1869].

'Syria. Revival of Christianity. Its Miracles and its Martyrdoms, related by P.' *The Tablet*, 16 and 23 Sept. 1871.

T., L'Abbé de [Jean Crasset, S.J.], *The History of the Church of Japan*. Written originally in French . . . and now translated into English by *N.N.*, 2 vols., 1705–7.

Thomas à Kempis, *Imitation of Christ*. Too many editions of this work to list.

Triduum Reading:
At supper on the day before: A letter (29 Jan. 1647) of our Very Rev. Father Vincent Caraffa, on the religious employment of the three days of recollection preceding the renewal of vows. On the first and second day: a letter (9 Feb. 1669) of our Very Rev. Father John Paul Oliva, concerning the observance of secrecy in manifestation of conscience and the freedom of subjects in writing to the General. General admonitions; decrees of General Congregation; subjects of which Ours may speak; rules of Scholastics; rules of modesty; a letter (17 Nov. 1706) of our Very Rev. Father Michael Angelo Tamburini to the Fathers and Brothers of the Society of Jesus, on promoting the desire and love of spiritual things. On the third day: at dinner, the Chapters of Faults of renovants; at supper, *Imitation of Christ*.

Turner, William, 'Pastoral Letters' of the Bishop of Salford. On the Italian invasion of Rome, the consequent imprisonment of the Holy Father, and the Franco-German War, see *The Tablet*, 25 Feb. 1871, p. 244. I have not been able to trace a copy of the Lenten Pastoral read in the refectory on 11 Feb. 1872.

Ullathorne, William Bernard, O.S.B., 'The decree of the Vatican Council' (a letter dated 19 Oct. 1870); 'The accord of the infallible Church with the infallible Pontiff', Dec. 1870. (This is No. 10 of the Doctrinal Papers issued by the Catholic Truth Society.)

Vatican Council: 'The Nineteenth General Council; or, the First Council of the Vatican.' Supplements to *The Tablet*, Jan. 1869–Nov. 1869. Much of the matter was reprinted in book form, *The Year of Preparation for the Vatican Council*. Including the original and English of the Encyclical and Syllabus, and of the Papal Documents connected with the Convocation, 1869.

Vaughan, Herbert Alfred, 'Pastoral Letter' of the Bishop of Salford: 'The charge of disloyalty brought against Catholics', *The Tablet*, 1 Mar. 1873, pp. 277–8.

Vaughan, Roger Bede, O.S.B., Archbishop of Sydney, *The Life and Labours of S. Thomas of Aquin*, 2 vols., 1871–2.

'The victorious Novices or Account of trials and sufferings undergone by some novices of Spain and America for fidelity to their vocation in the Society of Jesus on the occasion of the banishment of the Society from the Spanish states in the year 1767.' (This is a manuscript in several hands. It contains the following note: The account which regards the Novices of Spain has been taken and arranged from some documents edited by F. Carayon, in his work entitled Documents inédits: and that which regards the American Novices has been taken from the life of Brother Clement Baigorri, and another document entitled: 'L'anno di patimenti', both in the 'Menologio' of Patrignani with the continuation of F. Boero for the months of January and February.)

Wilberforce, Bertrand A., O.P. [Arthur Henry Wilberforce], *A sketch of the lives of the Dominican Missionaries in Japan*; including those of the martyrs beatified by Pius IX. . . . With a preface by his Grace the Archbishop of Westminster [1869].

Woodstock Letters, vol. i, no. 1, Jan. 1872. This is a private domestic publication of the American Assistancy of the Society of Jesus.

Examen et Bullae: Examen generale et Bullarum delectus in usum novitiorum Societatis Jesu. Roehampton, 1864. The work is in three parts: I—'Primum ac generale examen iis omnibus qui in Societatem Jesu admitti petunt, proponendum', followed by the following papal Bulls: Julius III, 'Exposcit debitum', St. Pius V, 'Aequum reputamus', Gregory XIII, 'Ascendente Domino', Gregory XIV, 'Ecclesiae Catholicae', Pius VII, 'Sollicitudo omnium'; II—Decretal letters concerned with the canonization of the following Jesuit saints: Ignatius Loyola, Francis Xavier, Francis Borgia, Aloysius Gonzaga, Stanislaus Kostka, John Francis Regis, Francis Jerome, and the three Japanese martyrs; III—Paul III, 'Regimini', 'Injunctum nobis', 'Cum inter', 'Exponi nobis', 'Licet debitum', Benedict XIII, 'Redemptoris nostri', Benedict XIV, 'Gloriosae Dominae', Clement XIII, 'Apostolicum'.

APPENDIX 3

St. Beuno's Debating Club

Standing Rules are:

(1) That any one who has secured a seconder may stand up to make a proposal of change in the constitution of the club; notice of the motion having thus been given, it will take precedence of the subject fixed for discussion on the next day of meeting.

(2) The President has the privilege of speaking as a member.

(3) The debate is open to all comers to speak or to attend.

The following resolutions were carried:

I. That the subjects for discussion be presented in a polemical form.

II. That no more than five minutes be allowed to any speaker.

III. That the meetings be held once a week on Sundays immediately after Benediction.

IV. That the members be not seated round a table but speak from their places on opposite sides of the room.

1874–1875

Second Session of the St. Beuno's Debating Club

4 Oct. 1874.

The adoption of cremation is to be deprecated.

Motion adjourned

11 Oct.

Resumed debate.

Carried

18 Oct.

Inheritance by primogeniture is preferable to an equal division of property.

GMH spoke against   Carried

25 Oct.

The immediate suppression of Ritualism would not aid the advance of Catholicism in England.

Carried

1 Nov. 1874.
Catholic education has suffered from the connection of our Colleges with the London University.

Defeated

8 Nov.
A prefect's life is preferable to a master's.

Defeated

15 Nov.
Bazaars are an undesirable method of collecting money for religious purposes.

Defeated

22 Nov.
Philosophy is more useful against the errors of the day than either science or theology.
GMH spoke against   Carried

29 Nov.
Education of the lowest class of society should not be made compulsory.
GMH spoke against   Defeated

6 Dec.
The following formula 'The position of Catholics has been in no wise changed by the decrees of the Vatican Council' being liable to misrepresentation cannot safely be adopted in the present contest between Gladstone and Rome.
GMH spoke for   Carried

13 Dec.
In passing through foreign countries it is rather the spirit of the Society to visit than pass by the interesting objects that lie within easy reach.

Defeated

20 Dec.
The practice of keeping a diary is exceedingly useful and worthy the adoption of all.
GMH spoke for   Carried

27 Dec.
Eminence in arms is a better object of national ambition than eminence in commerce.
GMH moved the motion   Defeated

31 Dec.
A college (such as Stonyhurst or Beaumont) on board a sea-going ship is a good suggestion.
GMH spoke for   Carried

3 Jan. 1875.
A religious ought not to allow himself to be photographed.

Carried

10 Jan.
It is desirable that the clergy (secular and regular) should mix in the society of their flocks.
GMH spoke against

Drawn

17 Jan.
A theological student should eschew all literature not bearing on his studies.
GMH spoke for

Carried

24 Jan.
A little knowledge is not a dangerous thing.
GMH spoke for

Defeated

31 Jan.
The Society in the British Isles should not farm its lands.
GMH spoke for

Defeated

7 Feb.
Painting is a more powerful aid to religion than music.
GMH spoke against

Defeated

14 Feb.
Women should be withheld from voting in elections for Parliament.

Carried

21 Feb.
In our colleges there should be public games (out-door) compulsory on all boys.

Carried

28 Feb.
In the present state of the Church a schoolmaster is more profitable to souls than a preacher.
GMH spoke against

Defeated

7 March
The boys in the lower schools should be taught singing.

Carried

14 March
To the orator manner is more important than matter.
GMH spoke against

Defeated

21 March
The presence of a body of secular divines at St Beuno's is desirable.
GMH spoke against

Result not given

4 April 1875.

Religious instruction is not sufficiently attended to in our colleges.

                                                                    Carried

11 April

It is desirable to form a league for the adoption of a uniform system of Latin pronunciation on the basis of Italian.

N.B. By the phrase 'on the basis of Italian' it is meant to oblige only to such sounds as are common to English and Italian.

GMH spoke for   Drawn

18 April

There is no patriotism without some prospect of a fight or a competition, a struggle with the foreigner.

GMH spoke against   Defeated

25 April

Classics should not be obligatory in day-schools of the middle-classes.

                                                                   Defeated

2 May

Men make circumstances and not circumstances men.

GMH spoke against   Carried

9 May

Priests ought never to enter a Ritualistic church.

                                                                    Carried

23 May

Every room without exception should have in addition to the fire-place, some direct and uninterrupted communication with the outer air.

                                                                    Carried

30 May

Boating, sea bathing, and easy access to splendid scenery make a good villa.

                                                                   Defeated

1875–1876

Third Session of the St. Beuno's Debating Club

10 Oct. 1875.

That we ought not to admit the term *Roman* Catholic.

GMH spoke for   Defeated

17 Oct.

That the Accolade [*amplexus*, brotherly embrace] should be introduced into the English Province.

                                                                   Defeated

24 Oct. 1875.

That the practice of anonymous criticism of the writings and doings of others should not be tolerated.

GMH spoke against   Defeated

31 Oct.

That the advancement of material civilization is injurious to true progress.

GMH spoke against.   Carried

7 Nov.

That it is not desirable as yet to make the wearing of the tonsure obligatory on the English clergy.

                                                      Defeated

14 Nov.

What we want in England is the conscription.

                                                      Carried

21. Nov.

That the unanimous verdict according to the English system of trial by jury is preferable to the verdict of the majority according to the Scotch system.

                                                      Carried

28 Nov.

That an 'Edinburgh Sabbath' is less objectionable than a 'Paris Sunday'.

                                                      Defeated

5 Dec.

That Moody and Sankey's visit did more good than harm.

GMH spoke for   Defeated

12 Dec.

That the state does well in compelling parents to educate their children.

GMH moved the motion   Defeated

19 Dec.

That the existing law against street-begging ought to be repealed.

                                                      Defeated

26 Dec.

That to stimulate study by appeals to the stomach is a false principle of education.

                                                      Defeated

29 Dec.

That a boy ought not to be admitted into a higher school until he has gained half marks in the final examinations of the school beneath.

GMH spoke against   Carried

9 Jan. 1876.
That the present state of society calls for the introduction of sumptuary laws.
Defeated

16 Jan.
That it is unreasonable to censure cock-fighting.

Carried

23 Jan.
That it is desirable as far as possible to substitute day-schools for boarding-schools.
GMH spoke for   Carried

30 Jan.
That it is inexpedient for a priest to meddle in politics.

Carried

6 Feb.
That some corporal punishment should always be added to imprisonment in the case of crimes of violence committed by men.

Carried

13 Feb.
That as a general principle, it is better that masters should go up with their boys.
GMH spoke against   Carried

20 Feb.
Under proper arrangements women may claim to be admitted to degrees in literature and science (medicine included).
GMH spoke for   Defeated

27 Feb.
Our colleges will do well to avail themselves of the London University scheme for school examinations.

Drawn

5 March
The present movement for closing public houses on Sunday does not deserve our support.

Carried

12 March
There is no harm in making April Fools.
GMH spoke for   Carried

19 March
Even in printed treatises on the extent of the Pope's power it is better to maximize than to minimize.

Carried

26 March 1876.

The boys in our colleges should attend a late Mass with sermon on Sundays.

Carried

2 April

That novels should not be allowed in a school library.

Drawn

9 April

That the sooner the Welsh language dies out the better.

GMH spoke against   Carried

23 April

An author cannot reasonably complain of a foreign government not protecting his copyright.

Defeated

30 April

That a system of itinerant preaching would conduce greatly to the spread of the faith in England.

GMH spoke for   Carried

7 May

That the establishment of a Catholic College at a non-Catholic University would under any circumstances be injurious to religion.

GMH spoke for   Carried

14 May

That the 'Month' cannot command that influence which is worthy of the Society unless our scholastics practise theological writing.

GMH spoke against   Carried

21 May

That it is a subject for congratulation that the Queen has assumed the title Empress of India.

Carried

28 May

That Catholics should support the movement for the dis-establishment of the 'Church of England'.

Carried

1876–1877

Fourth Session of the St. Beuno's Debating Club

23 Oct. 1876.

That a subordinate part in maintaining the discipline of our colleges should be entrusted to the elder boys.

Carried

30 Oct. 1876.
That it would be an advantage if Ours had all their studies before being sent to teach in the colleges.

Defeated

5 Nov.
That the University boat race as a public spectacle ought to be prohibited by the academic authorities.

Drawn

12 Nov.
That this community shall agree to speak French for half an hour daily during time of recreation.

GMH spoke against   Carried

19 Nov.
That it is advisable that a hand-ball court be erected at St Beuno's.

Carried

26 Nov.
That craniotomy is under no circumstances whatever a lawful practice.

GMH spoke against   Adjourned

3 Dec.
Resume debate—motion amended: That craniotomy, though never to be formally encouraged, may be tolerated as a last resource.

GMH spoke for   Amendment carried and there-
                                                      fore the original motion lost.

10 Dec.
That the parochial clergy should throw themselves into the movement in favour of total abstinence.

Drawn

17 Dec.
That it is lawful and expedient to baptize an heretic at the point of death even though he has expressed no desire to be received into the Church.

Carried

24 Dec.
That a second class passenger travelling first class without necessity is bound to restitution.

GMH spoke against   Defeated

27 Dec.
That the parochial clergy should interest themselves in the establishment of clubs and clubhouses for the use of the Catholic working classes.

Carried

31 Dec. 1876.

That priests in the confessional should dissuade their penitents from frequenting public theatres.

Defeated

7 Jan. 1877.

That it is never lawful to tell a real untruth.

GMH moved the motion   Carried

14 Jan.

That the establishment of religious conferences is a crying want in our large cities. (Qu'il est urgent dans les grands centres d'établir les conférences religeuses.)

GMH spoke against   Carried

21 Jan.

That it is easy to defend the Inquisition against the attacks of heretics.

Carried

28 Jan.

That it would be an advantage to our colleges to have a yearly examination in classics and mathematics to be conducted by examiners external to the college.

Defeated

4 Feb.

That Mr Tooth[1] deserves the sympathies of Catholics.

Drawn

11 Feb.

That it would be of advantage to the theological studies to have one common textbook adopted throughout the whole Society.

Carried

18 Feb.

That every scholastic of the Society should have assigned to him from the end of his noviceship some branch of study in which he could labour to excel.

GMH spoke for   Carried

25 Feb.

That the present extensive system of magazines is injurious to the highest kind of literature.

Carried

4 March

That Catholics should as far as possible abstain from controversy on religious subjects.

Defeated

---

[1] The Rev. Arthur Tooth (1839–1931), the well-known 'Ritualist.' See Charles E. Lee, *Father Tooth: a biographical memoir* (1931).

11 March 1877.
That priests on the mission should not give more than an inappreciable time to the reading of newspapers.

Carried

18 March
That the study of natural science in our colleges should be introduced in the lower schools.

Carried

25 March
That it would be an advantage to our theologate if it were in a large town.

Defeated

15 April
That in spite of the iniquities of the Turks it is not desirable that they should be expelled from Europe.

Carried

22 April
That the education of youth in the present day is not sufficiently Spartan and that a return should be made to the system of 50 years ago.

Carried

29 April
That the privileges granted to the Society before the suppression still remain intact.

Carried

6 May
That the modern system of education is not suited to promote the highest mental development.

GMH spoke for   Carried

13 May
That in the ordinary providence of God, a nation as such is only converted at a comparatively early stage of its civilization.

Carried

27 May
That the suggestion of founding in perpetuum a seminary for the education of 500 ecclesiastical students deserves the enthusiastic support of all the clergy, secular and regular, and the laity of England.

Carried

1877–1878

Fifth Session of the St. Beuno's Debating Club

14 Oct. 1877.

That our preaching suffers from the neglect of the art of rhetoric and declamation.

Carried

(Hopkins left St. Beuno's for Mount St. Mary's College, Spinkhill, near Sheffield, on 19 October.)

BIBLIOGRAPHY

PRIMARY SOURCES

Manuscript

Novices' Beadle's Journal. (NBJ)
Juniors' Beadle's Journal. (JBJ)
Philosophers' Beadle's Journal. (PBJ)
Theologians' Beadle's Journal. (TBJ)
Manresa Minister's Journal. (MMJ)
Stonyhurst Minister's Journal.
St. Beuno's Minister's Journal.

Unpublished undergraduate essays and notebooks of GMH at Campion Hall, Oxford.

Printed

(The books listed below are published in London except where stated otherwise. The chief abbreviations adopted in the text follow each entry.)

The Letters of Gerard Manley Hopkins to Robert Bridges, edited by Claude Colleer Abbott, 1935. (*Letters to Bridges*.)

The Correspondence of Gerard Manley Hopkins and Richard Watson Dixon, edited by Claude Colleer Abbott, 1935. (*Correspondence with Dixon*.)

Further Letters of Gerard Manley Hopkins including his Correspondence with Coventry Patmore, edited by Claude Colleer Abbott, 2nd edn. 1956. (*Further Letters*.)

The Journals and Papers of Gerard Manley Hopkins, edited by Humphry House, completed by Graham Storey, 1959. (*Journals and Papers*.)

The Sermons and Devotional Writings of Gerard Manley Hopkins, edited by Christopher Devlin, S.J., 1959. (*Sermons and Devotional Writings*.)

Poems of Gerard Manley Hopkins, 4th edn. based on the 1st edn. of 1918, edited with additional notes by W. H. Gardner and N. H. MacKenzie, 1967. (*Poems*.)

SECONDARY SOURCES AND REFERENCES

Basset, Bernard, *The English Jesuits: from Campion to Martindale*, 1967.

'C.B.' [Clement William Barraud], 'Reminiscences of Father Gerard Hopkins', *The Month*, cxxxiv (Aug. 1919), 158–9.

Beaumont College, Old Windsor: *The History of St. Stanislaus' College. A record of fifty years, 1861–1911*. [By Francis Charles Devas, in collaboration with others], Old Windsor, 1911; see also *Jesuit Directory 1921*, pp. 46–7.

Bremond, André, 'La poésie naïve et savante de Gerard Hopkins', *Etudes*, ccxxi (Oct. 1934), 23–49.

Bridges, Robert Seymour, 'Memoir' in *The Poems of Digby Mackworth Dolben*, Oxford, 1911; reprinted in *Three Friends*, 1932.

Carroll, Martin C. 'Gerard Manley Hopkins and the Society of Jesus', in *Immortal Diamond*: studies in Gerard Manley Hopkins, edited by Norman Weyand, 1949.

Chadwick, Hubert, *St. Omers to Stonyhurst*, 1962.

Champneys, Basil, *Memoirs and Correspondence of Coventry Patmore*, 2 vols., 1900.

Clarke, Richard Frederick, 'The Training of a Jesuit', *Nineteenth Century*, xl (Aug. 1896), 211–25.

Collins, James, 'Philosophical Themes in G. M. Hopkins', *Thought*, xxii (Mar. 1947), 67–106.

Copleston, Frederick Charles John Paul, *A History of Philosophy*, 1946– .

Cox, John George Snead, *The Life of Cardinal Vaughan*, 2 vols., 1910.

Crehan, Joseph Hugh, *Father Thurston*. A memoir with a bibliography of his writings, 1952.

—— 'More light on Gerard Hopkins', *The Month*, N.S. 10 (Oct. 1953), 205–14.

Cruise, Edward, 'Development of the Religious Orders', in *The English Catholics 1850–1950*, edited by George Andrew Beck, 1950.

Culkin, Gerard, 'The English Seminaries', *Clergy Review*, N.S. 35 (Feb. 1951), 73–88.

Curran, C. P. 'Memories of University College, Dublin: the Jesuit tenure, 1883–1908', in *Struggle with Fortune*, edited by Michael Tierney, Dublin [1954].

Davis, Henry, 'Seminary Standards', *Clergy Review*, N.S. 18 (Mar. 1940), 224–32.

Devlin, Christopher, 'Hopkins and Duns Scotus', *New Verse*, no. 14 (Apr. 1935), 12–17.

—— 'Time's Eunuch', *The Month*, N.S. 1 (May 1949), 303–12.

—— 'The Image and the Word—I and II', ibid., N.S. 3 (Feb. and Mar. 1950), 114–27, 191–202.

Dezza, Paolo, *Alle origini del neotomismo*, Milan, 1940.

Downes, David Anthony, 'The Hopkins Enigma', *Thought*, xxxvi (Winter 1961), 573–94.

Dublin—University College: see under Curran, Gwynn, *A Page of Irish History*; Tierney.

Dwyer, J. J., 'The Catholic Press, 1850–1950', in *The English Catholics 1850–1950*, edited by George Andrew Beck, 1950.

Emmaus, Bishop of (James Laird Patterson), 'Recollections of Henry James Coleridge', *The Month*, lxxviii (June 1893), 153–67.

'An Evening with the Stonyhurst Philosophers', in *The Tablet*, 8 Dec. 1888, p. 894.

[Fitzgerald, Percy Hetherington], *School Days at Saxonhurst*, by 'One of the Boys', Edinburgh, 1867.

Fitzgerald, Percy Hetherington, *Stonyhurst Memories; or, Six Years at School*, 1895.

—— *Father Gallwey: a sketch.* With some early letters, 1906.

Foley, Henry, *Records of the English Province of the Society of Jesus*, 7 vols., 1877–83.

Foucher, Louis, *La philosophie catholique en France au XIXe siècle avant la renaissance thomiste et dans son rapport avec elle 1800–1880*, Paris, 1955.

Gardner, William Henry, 'A Note on Hopkins and Duns Scotus', *Scrutiny*, v (June 1936), 61–70.

—— *Gerard Manley Hopkins, 1844–1889.* A study of poetic idiosyncrasy in relation to poetic tradition. . . . A centenary commemoration, 2 vols., 1944–9.

Garraghan, Gilbert J., 'The project of a common scholasticate for the Society of Jesus in North America', *Archivum Historicum Societatis Jesu*, ii (1933), 1–10.

Gavin, Michael, *Memoirs of Father P. Gallwey, S.J.* [With portrait], 1913.

Gerard, John, *Stonyhurst College, Its life beyond the seas, 1592–1794, and on English soil, 1794–1894* (Centenary Record), Belfast, 1894.

Glenn, Paul Joseph, *The History of Philosophy.* A text-book, etc. St. Louis and London, 1929.

Gorman, William James Gordon, *Converts to Rome*, 1884.

Grigson, Geoffrey Edward Harvey, *Gerard Manley Hopkins.* [With a portrait], 1955. [Bibliographical series of Supplements to 'British Book News'.]

Gruggen, George and Keating (Joseph), *Stonyhurst. Its Past History and Life in the Present*, 1901.

Gwynn, Aubrey, 'The Jesuit Fathers and University College', in *Struggle with Fortune*, edited by Michael Tierney, Dublin [1954].

'Halieutes' [Fr. John Gerard, S.J.], 'The Stonyhurst Fisheries', *Stonyhurst Magazine*, i (May 1883), 177–81, with two sketch-maps.

Hewitson, Anthony, *Stonyhurst College, its Past and Present*, Preston, 1870; 2nd edn. . . . enlarged, etc. Preston, 1878.

Hickie, Charles V., 'In the early seventies', *Stonyhurst Magazine*, xviii (Feb. 1926), 317–22.

Hoban, Brendan, 'The Philosophical Tradition of Douay', *Ushaw Magazine*, lxiii (Dec. 1953), 145–59.

Hocedez, Edgar, *Histoire de la théologie au XIXe siècle.* 3 tom. Brussels and Paris, 1948–52.

[Holt, Geoffrey], 'The Phils', *Stonyhurst Magazine*, xxxiii (Oct. 1960), 508–13.

'Holy Week at Roehampton', *Letters and Notices*, xiv (July 1881), 236–43.[1]

---

[1] *Letters and Notices* is a private domestic quarterly of the English Province of the Society of Jesus. Abbreviated *LLNN*.

Hughes, Thomas Aloysius, *Loyola and the Educational System of the Jesuits*, 1892.

Ignatius, St., of Loyola [Iñigo Lopez de Recalde], *The Spiritual Exercises of Saint Ignatius*. A new translation by T. Corbishley, S.J. [1963].

Institutum Societatis Iesu, 3 vols., Florence, 1892–3.

Jesuit Directory and Calendar for 1921 [etc.], edited by David H. Thompson 1921, etc.

Keating, Joseph, *Stonyhurst*, Letchworth, 1909.

Kendall, Katherine, *Father Steuart, Priest of the Society Jesus*. A study of his life and teaching, etc., 1950.

Kleutgen, Joseph, *Ars dicendi priscorum potissimum praeceptis et exemplis illustrata*, edn. 4a's, Hertogenbosch, 1865.

Lahey, G. F., *Gerard Manley Hopkins*. [With a portrait], 1930.

Leflon, Jean, 'Les grands séminaires de France au XIXᵉ siècle', *Etudes*, cccxix (Nov. 1963), 175–86.

Lester, Edmund, 'Edmund Lester' contributed to *Conversions to the Catholic Church*. A symposium, edited by Maurice Leahy, 1933.

MacKenzie, Norman H., 'Gerard and Grace Hopkins', *The Month*, N.S. 33 (June 1965), 347–50.

Maher, Michael, and Bolland (Joseph), 'Stonyhurst College', in *The Teacher's Encyclopaedia of the theory, method, practice, history and development of Education at home and abroad* . . . edited by A. P. Laurie, v (1912), 171–82.

Manning, Henry Edward, 'The Work and the Wants of the Catholic Church in England', *Dublin Review*, N.S. 1 (July 1863), 139–66; reprinted in *Miscellanies*, i (1877), 25–71.

Manresa House, Roehampton: 'Manresa House, Roehampton', *LLNN*, xxx (Jan.–Oct. 1910), 313–21, 386–91, 468–76, 521–7; ibid., xxxi (Jan.–Apr. 1911), 36–41, 91–6; see also under 'Holy Week at Roehampton', *Jesuit Directory 1921*, pp. 100–1; 'Reminiscences of Novice-Days', Thurston.

Mathew, David, 'Old Catholics and Converts', in *The English Catholics 1850–1950*, edited by George Andrew Beck, 1950.

Meadows, Denis [George Denis Meadows], *Obedient Men*, New York, 1954.

Milburn, David, *A History of Ushaw College*. A study of the origin, foundation, and development of an English Catholic seminary. With an epilogue, 1908–62. Durham, 1964.

Newman, John Henry, 'The Mission of St. Benedict', *Historical Sketches*, ii, new impression, 1899.

—— *The Letters and Diaries of John Henry Newman*, edited by Charles Stephen Dessain, xi, 1961.

Örsy, Ladislas, 'University Training in the Church', *The Month*, N.S. 32 (Sept. 1964), 120–8.

Pachtler, G. Michael, *Ratio Studiorum et Institutiones Scholasticae Societatis Jesu*, iv, Berlin, 1894. [This is Band XVI of *Monumenta Germaniae Paedagogica*, herausgegeben von Karl Kehrbach.]

A Page of Irish History: Story of University College Dublin 1883–1909. Compiled by Fathers of the Society of Jesus, Dublin and Cork, 1930.

Paget, Stephen, *Henry Scott Holland*. . . . Memoir and letters. 1921.

Pelzer, A., 'Les initiateurs Italiens du néo-thomisme contemporain', *Revue Néo-Scholastique de Philosophie*, xviii (1911), 230–54.

Perrier, Joseph Louis, *The Revival of Scholastic Philosophy in the Nineteenth Century*, New York, 1909.

Petre, Maude Dominica Mary, *Autobiography and Life of George Tyrrell*, 2 vols., 1912.

Pick, John Barclay, *Gerard Manley Hopkins, Priest and Poet* [With portraits], 1942; 2nd edn., 1966.

Pollen, John Hungerford, the Younger, *The Life and Letters of Father John Morris, of the Society of Jesus, 1826–1893*, 1896.

—— 'An Unobserved Centenary', *The Month*, cxv (May 1910), 449–61.

—— 'The Restoration of the English Jesuits, 1803–17', ibid., cxv (June 1910), 585–97.

—— 'The Recognition of the Jesuits in England', ibid., cxvi (July 1910), 23–36.

—— 'The Centenary of the Restoration of the Society of Jesus', ibid., cxxiii (Jan. 1914), 56–71.

—— 'Society of Jesus' contributed to the *Catholic Encyclopedia*, xiv. 81–110.

Purcell, Edmund Sheridan, *Life of Cardinal Manning*, 2 vols., 1895.

'Reminiscences of Novice-Days, 1865', *LLNN*, xxx (Apr. 1910), 386–91.

Rickaby, Joseph, 'In Memoriam, Richard Frederick Clarke', *The Month*, xcvi (Oct. 1900), 337–44.

Riet, Georges van, *L'Epistémologie thomiste*. Recherches sur le problème de la connaissance dans l'école thomiste contemporaine, Louvain, 1946; English translation from 3rd revised and augmented edition by Gabriel Franks, i, St. Louis and London, 1963.

Roehampton: see under 'Manresa House, Roehampton'.

St. Beuno's College, St. Asaph: 'St. Beuno's College', *LLNN*, xxxi (Apr.–Oct. 1911), 73–82, 168–79, 241–8; *Jesuit Directory 1921*, pp. 104–5; Thomas Roberts, 'Seventy-five years at St. Beuno's: a farewell retrospect', *LLNN*, xxxix (Jan. 1924), 19–33; H. Keane, 'St. Beuno's 1848–1948', ibid., lvi (Sept. 1948), 189–202.

St. Mary's Hall, Stonyhurst: 'St. Mary's Hall, Stonyhurst, 1828–1926', *Stonyhurst Magazine*, xviii (June–July 1926), 469–71; D. Whyte, 'St. Mary's Hall', *LLNN*, lvi (Jan. 1948), 15–17.

'St. Mary's Pond', by 'A.E.I.', in *Stonyhurst Magazine*, ii (Apr. 1887), 407–8.

Schreiber, Ellis, *The Life of Augustus Henry Law, Priest of the Society of Jesus*, 1893.

Scott, Mary Monica Constable Maxwell, *Henry Schomberg, Kerr, sailor and Jesuit*, 1901.

Srinivasa Iyengar, Kodaganallur Ranaswami, 'Gerard Manley Hopkins', *The New Review* (Calcutta), vii (Jan.–Mar. 1938), 1–11, 113–25, 264–73.

Stapleton, Hon. Mrs. Mary Helen Alicia Bryan, *A History of the Post-Reformation Catholic Missions in Oxfordshire*, with an account of the families connected with them, 1906.

Steinmetz, Andrew, *The Novitiate; or, a year among the English Jesuits: a personal narrative*, 1846.

Stonyhurst College, Lancashire. See under the following: Chadwick; 'An Evening with the Stonyhurst Philosophers'; Fitzgerald; Gerard; Gruggen and Keating; 'Halieutes'; Hewitson; Hickie; [Holt]; *Jesuit Directory 1921*, pp. 107–8; Keating; Maher and Bolland; 'St. Mary's Hall'; St. Mary's Pond'; Walton.

Sutcliffe, Edmund Felix, *Bibliography of the English Province of the Society of Jesus, 1773–1953*, Roehampton, 1957.

Synopsis historiae Societatis Jesu [By Ludwig Schmitt. Revised by Alphonsus Kleiser and J. B. Goetstouwers], Louvain, 1950.

'T' [of *Punch*] (i.e., Joseph Peter Thorp), *Friends and Adventures*, 1931.

Thomas, Alfred, 'Hopkins, the Jesuits, and Barmouth', *Journal of the Merioneth Historical and Record Society*, vol. iv, pt. iv (1964), 360–4.

—— 'G. M. Hopkins and the Silver Jubilee Album', *The Library*, Fifth series, vol. xx (June 1965), 148–52.

—— 'A Note on Gerard Manley Hopkins and his Superiors 1868–77', *Irish Ecclesiastical Record*, civ (Oct.–Nov. 1965), 286–91.

—— 'G. M. Hopkins and "Tones" ', *Notes and Queries*, N.S. 12 (Nov. 1965), 429–30.

—— 'An Uncollected Letter of Gerard Manley Hopkins', *Dublin Review*, ccxxxix (Autumn 1965), 289–92.

—— 'A Hopkins fragment replaced' (a letter), *TLS*, 20 Jan. 1966, p. 48.

—— 'G. M. Hopkins: an unpublished triolet', *Modern Language Review*, lxi (Apr. 1966), 183–7.

—— 'Hopkins, Welsh and Wales', *Transactions of the Honourable Society of Cymmrodorion*, Session 1965, Part II (1966), 272–85.

—— 'Gerard Manley Hopkins—"Doomed to succeed by failure" ', *Dublin Review*, ccxl (Summer 1966), 161–75.

—— 'Father Gerard Manley Hopkins: the Centenary of his entrance into the Society of Jesus', *The Jesuits: Year Book of the Society of Jesus 1967–1968* (Rome, 1967), pp. 54–7.

—— 'Was Hopkins a Scotist before he read Scotus?', *Studia Scholastico-Scholastica 4. De doctrina Ioannis Duns Scoti*, vol. iv. Scotismus decursu saeculorum (Romae, 1968), 617–29, two plates.

—— 'Hopkins and the Rejection of "The Wreck of the Deutschland" ', *English Studies*, xlix, no. 6 (Dec. 1968), 542–6.

Thurston, Herbert Henry Charles, 'The Romance of a Religious House [Manresa House, Roehampton]', *The Month*, cxxviii (Nov. 1916), 424–36.

Tierney, Michael, *Struggle with Fortune*. A miscellany for the centenary of the

Catholic University of Ireland, 1854–1954. General editor: Dr. M. Tierney. Dublin [1954].

Treneer, Anne, 'The Criticism of Gerard Manley Hopkins', *Penguin New Writing*, no. 40, edited by John Lehmann, Harmondsworth, Middlesex, 1950, pp. 98–115.

Trevor, Meriol, *Newman. Light in Winter*, 1962.

Ueberweg–Heinze, *Grundriss der Geschicte der Philosophie*, v, Basel, 1953.

University College, Dublin. See under Curran; Gwynn, *A Page of Irish History*; Tierney.

Walton, Joseph, 'Stonyhurst Life', *The Month*, xx (Mar. 1874), 325–36.

Ward, Maisie, *The English Way. Studies in English sanctity from St. Bede to Newman* by M. C. D'Arcy . . . Hilaire Belloc [and others] . . ., edited by Maisie Ward, 1933.

Ward, Wilfrid Philip, *The Life and Times of Cardinal Wiseman*, 2 vols., 1897.

—— *The Life of John Henry Cardinal Newman*, based on his private journals and correspondence, 2 vols., 1912.

Waugh, Evelyn, 'Come Inside' contributed to *The Road to Damascus*, i, edited by John Anthony O'Brien [1949].

For full bibliographies of editions and work on Hopkins, reference may be made to the following: W. H. Gardner, *Gerard Manley Hopkins, 1844–1889*, i (1944); W. A. M. Peters, *Gerard Manley Hopkins*. A critical essay towards the understanding of his poetry (1948); *Immortal Diamond*, edited by Norman Weyand (1949); Jean Georges Ritz, *La poète Gérard Manley Hopkins. L'homme et l'oeuvre*, 2 vols., Paris, 1959; *Cambridge Bibliography of English Literature*. For later and more recent work see *Abstracts of English Studies*; *Annual Bibliography of English Language and Literature*; *Archivum Historicum Societatis Iesu*; *Index Bibliographicus Societatis Iesu*; *PMLA* Annual bibliographies; *Year's Work in English Studies*; *Victorian Studies*.

BIBLIOGRAPHY

INDEX

A' Beckett, Gilbert Abbott, *The Siamese Twins*, 116 n. 2.
Abbott, Claude Colleer, 56 n. 4, 196 n. 1.
Aber House, Barmouth, 171 n. 5.
Addis, William Edward, 2, 3 & n. 1, 13, 145.
Aeschines, 130.
Aeterni Patris, Encyclical of Leo XIII, 96 n. 1.
Allen, Rt. Revd. Samuel Webster, Bp. of Shrewsbury, 161.
Allen, Most Revd. William, Cardinal, 15.
Allies, Thomas William, 8 n. 1.
Aloysius, St., 36, 73 n. 4, 107, 118, 123, 145.
Alps, 23, 161.
Anderdon, Fr. William Henry, S.J., 17 n. 4.
Andrea, Most Revd. Girolamo d', Cardinal, death, 13.
Angers, 64.
Anglican orders, 3, 11.
Aristotle, 93, 94, 99, 100 n. 2, 183 & n. 2; *Metaphysics*, 164.
Arnold, Matthew, 134 n. 3; *Empedocles on Etna*, 123, 133.
Arrochar, 110.
Arundel prints, 88, 120.
Augustine, St., 20.

Bacon, Fr. Francis Edward, S.J., *69*, 72, 150.
Baillie, Alexander William Mowbray, 7 n. 3, 9, 10, 12, 19, 44, 58 n. 2, 98, 113, 132, 133, 140 nn. 1, 7, 203; GMH expecting to take Orders, 9, 12; visits GMH at Manresa, 66; GMH on the philosophy course, 98; GMH's admiration of Aristotle, 99; GMH on fishing, 108 n. 2; GMH calls but AWMB out of town, 110 n. 2; GMH on *Macbeth* at Stonyhurst, 116; GMH on the countryside around Stonyhurst, 124–5; GMH expecting to do a fourth year of theology, 181; GMH on moral theology and law, 181–2.

Balliol College, Oxford, 11; GMH 'the Star of Balliol', 42 n. 1.
Balloch, 110.
Balzac, Honoré de, 191.
Bampton, Fr. Joseph Maurice, S.J., 131 n. 2, 140 n. 2, 146 n.
Barker, Fr. Thomas Aloysius, S.J., *79*, 81.
Barmouth, 166, 171, 184.
Barnes, 24, 54, 60.
Barnes, William, 80 n. 2.
Barnsley, 168.
Baron, Fr. John, S.J., *80*, 81.
Barraud, Fr. Clement William, S.J., 106, 127 n. 6.
Battle of Dorking, The, 108 n. 3.
Bayly ('Bailey'), Nathaniel Thomas Haynes, 195.
Beaumont College, Old Windsor, 16, 30, 115, 129, 151, 198; visit by D. M. Dolben, 14; GMH attends the Academy, 138; GMH visits, 140, 149; GMH attends Rector's day, talks too freely, and does penance going home, 146; GMH goes on holiday with the Community to Teignmouth, 149.
Beckx, Very Revd. Pierre Jean, General of the Society of Jesus, 95, 101, 129 n. 2.
Bedford Leigh, 187.
Bedminster, St. Raphael's Chapel, 12 n. 4.
Bellasis, Fr. Richard Garnett, Cong. Orat., 140–1.
Belmont Priory (now Abbey), 3, 8, 13.
Benedict, St., 9, 13.
Benedictines, 8 & n. 6, 9, 13, 17 n. 1.
Bessborough, 2nd Earl of, William (Ponsonby), 57.
Billington, 92 n. 1, 104 n. 1.
Birmingham Oratory, 8, 9, 27, 157.
Bison, The, 109.
Blackburn, 110, 119, 126.
Blount, Fr. Charles, S.J., 37, 56 n. 1, 59, 73 n. 2, 138.
Blunt House, Croydon, 9.
Bob, 180.

100–1, 104, 114, 115, 119–20, 127; dress, 106, 108–9; English Academy, 102–3, 115, 121–2; entertainments: readings from Shakespeare, 103, plays and farces, 105, 107, 116–17, operetta, 106–7, concerts, 105, 107, concert got up by GMH, 127, Amateur Christy's Minstrels, 117 n. 2; examinations, 107; exhortations, 123; farces, *see* entertainments; funerals, 106; fusion, 107, 108; games and sports: 101–2, new cricket ground, 118, Stonyhurst cricket, 107, bandy, 102, skating, 105, 106, 115, swimming, 107, 118, billiards, 108, boating, 108, salmon fishing, 108, hockey, 115, rackets, 115; German, 104; health: 124, community suffering from languor, 119, vaccinated, 126 n. 2; heating: coal fires, 89, 114, 119–20; Latin: lectures, 97, panegyric, 118; examinations conducted in, 122; library, 156 n. 3; music, 92, 101, 105, 106–7, 116, 127; path (to Stonyhurst), 118; permissions, 98, 105, 108, 116; Phil. and Lit. Society, 102, 160 n. 2 (*see also* English Academy); pictures: Arundel prints, 120; plays and farces, *see* entertainments; the Pond, 118; *postea*, 91; the *Quamquam*, 92 n. 3; reading in refectory, 101, 103, 108, 127, 139 n. 2, Appendix 2B, 227 ff.; recreation: 91, 105, 108, 120, Thursday the recreation day, 98, *see also* Blandyke, entertainments, games; religious life, 101, 104–5, 106, 108, 115, 117, 118, 120, 123–4; retreat, annual, 119, 123, 151; room: a scholastic's, 89, room change, 114; schools, opening of, 92; sermons and 'tones': 103, 105, 123, 124, Latin panegyric, 118; Spiritual Father: Fr. Gosford, S.J., 91, Fr. Parkinson, S.J., 115; studies, 88 n. 3, 91 n. 3, 92 ff., 104, 106, 114, 116, 118, 122, 123, 137 n. 5; Superior: Fr. Weld, S.J., 91, Fr. Fitzsimon, S.J., 115, Fr. McCann, S.J., 119–20; time-table, 90–1, 101, 106, 115; *tridua*, 117, 118, 121, 123; villa: Innellan, 108–10, Douglas, 118–19, 123, 126–7; visit of Bp. Vaughan, 120; visitation, Provincial's, 107, 117; vows, renovation of, 117, 118, 123; weather, 89, 104, 105, 106, 124, 125–6.

Piozzi, Mrs. (Mrs. Thrale), 151.

Pius IX, Pope, 67; 'Holy Father', 71.
Pius X, Pope St., 68 n. 1.
Plant, Mr., 202–3.
Plato, 183 n. 2; Platonist philosophy, 183.
Plays and farces, *see* Drama.
Plenlimmon, 151.
Pocock, Isaac, *The Omnibus*, 117 n. 2.
Polish Church, Russian persecution of, 165 & n. 2.
Pollen, Fr. John Hungerford, S.J., 15 n. 3, 16, 17, 18, 19 n. 1, 30, 188 n. 1.
Polynesian, The, 212.
Ponsonby, William, 2nd Earl of Bessborough, 57.
Ponte, P. Louis de, S.J. [Luis de la Puente], 72 n. 6.
Pope, Alexander, 134, 195.
Popes: Pius IX, 67, 71, 165; Leo XIII, 157; St. Pius X, 68 n. 1.
Porter, Rt. Revd. George, S.J. (later Archbp. of Bombay), *129*, 144, 146, 232; 'Fr. Rector', 138, 139 n. 1.
Preston, 110, 117 n. 2, 129, 199; St. Wilfrid's, 201, 202; R.C. procession, 117.
Pro-cathedral, Our Lady of Victories, Kensington, 71.
Prometheus the Firegiver, 204–5.
Punch, 114.
Purbrick, Fr. Edward Ignatius, S.J., 12 n. 2, 17, 209; 'Fr. Rector', *90*, 91, 92, 100, 103, 104, 105, 106, 107, 119, 122 n., 126.
Purbrick, Fr. James, S.J., 161.
Purcell, Edmund Sheridan, 17 n. 5.
Pusey, Revd. Dr. Edward Bouverie, 2, 7, 18, 42 n. 1; Puseyites, 14.
Putney, 24 n. 1, 54, 60; Church of Our Lady of Pity and St. Simon Stock, 77.

Quarante 'Ore, 61 n. 3.
Quarterly Review, 164.
Quarterly Series, 18.

Rae, Dr., 212.
Rancé, A. J. Bouthillier de, 127, 231.
Raphael Santi, 130.
Ratcliff, Walter, 27 n. 3, 78, 80, 81.
Rawes' Church, Fr. (St. Francis of Assisi), Notting Hill, 71.
Raynal, Rt. Revd. Dom Paul Wilfrid O.S.B., Abbot, *3*, 13.

PRINTED IN GREAT BRITAIN
AT THE UNIVERSITY PRESS, OXFORD
BY VIVIAN RIDLER
PRINTER TO THE UNIVERSITY